Cross-Cultural
Approaches to
Leadership Development

CROSS-CULTURAL APPROACHES TO LEADERSHIP DEVELOPMENT

Edited by
C. Brooklyn Derr,
Sylvie Roussillon,
and Frank Bournois

QUORUM BOOKS
Westport, Connecticut • London

Library of Congress Cataloging-in-Publication Data

Cross-cultural approaches to leadership development / edited by C. Brooklyn Derr,
Sylvie Roussillon, and Frank Bournois.
    p. cm.
   Includes bibliographical references and index.
   ISBN 1–56720–466–X (alk. paper)
    1. Leadership—Cross-cultural studies. I. Derr, C. Brooklyn (Clyde Brooklyn).
 II. Roussillon, Sylvie. III. Bournois, Frank.
 HD57.7.C765 2002
 658.4'07124—dc21   2001019587

British Library Cataloguing in Publication Data is available.

Library of Congress Catalog Card Number: 2001019587
ISBN: 1–56720–466–X

First published in 2002

Quorum Books, 88 Post Road West, Westport, CT 06881
An imprint of Greenwood Publishing Group, Inc.
www.quorumbooks.com

Printed in the United States of America

The paper used in this book complies with the
Permanent Paper Standard issued by the National
Information Standards Organization (Z39.48–1984).

10 9 8 7 6 5 4 3 2

Contents

Tables and Figures

TABLES

FIGURES

Introduction

C. Brooklyn Derr, Sylvie Roussillon, and Frank Bournois

THE TIMELESSNESS OF LEADERSHIP DEVELOPMENT

As Professors Dai and Zheng point out in this book, the Confucian ethic of ancient China dictated a system of leadership development. Roussillon alludes to the fact that the ancient Greeks also had their own leadership development practice. Selecting, training, and developing future leaders are timeless and classic issues that extend beyond our current transition from the industrial to the information economy—issues that have evolved with the changing economies of the world. However, in the post–World War II era of large-scale and stable hierarchies, leadership development became a well-honed process. Frequently referred to as "high-potential (HIPO) management," "managing strategic human resources," or "succession planning," a carefully designed system emerged for selecting future leaders, training and developing them, and fine-tuning their knowledge and skills for top-level positions.

Even in the new post-1990 information economy, leadership development continues to be an important subject, and many of these same terms and concepts are being used. Since 1995, 3,947 books with the word *leadership* in the title have been published in English (Amazon.com May 2001). Modern Internet search engines bring up over eight thousand English-language entries that pertain to the subject of leadership. During this moment of transition to what some term "a new world of work," we nevertheless find companies also using more classical methods of leadership development alongside those focused on a very different, modern organizational imperative.

DEVELOPING FUTURE LEADERS IN THE 1970–1990 INDUSTRIAL ORGANIZATION

Derr and his colleagues (1987, 1988, 1989, 1989) and Roussillon and Bournois (1992, 1997, 1998) have researched and described some of the systematic high-potential or future leadership practices most prevalent during the twenty years prior to the 1990s and still in practice today. Following is an overview of these kinds of leadership development approaches.

Patterns and trends exist in the way companies viewed (and still view in some cases) future leadership development at the peak of the industrial economy, in which large, stable, hierarchical organizations prevailed. When asked, "Does your company designate some employees as high-potential?" all of the thirty-three U.S. and sixty European companies surveyed (Derr 1987, Derr, Jones, and Toomey, 1988) affirmed that they had HIPO leadership development programs of one form or another, even if not explicitly labeled as such. This research is summarized in the chapter by Derr, Briscoe, and Buckner that follows.

A common element in all the respondents' definitions of leadership development was that an employee with ultimate potential would move up the hierarchy into increasingly important management positions and eventually reach a position close to the top. Indeed, *potential* was operationally defined as the ability to move up into valued senior leadership positions.

LEADERSHIP DEVELOPMENT IN THE POST-1995 WORLD OF WORK (INFORMATION ECONOMY)

The problem with a strictly HIPO leadership development perspective at the turn of the twenty-first century is that we are now in transition as we shift from an industrial to an information economy. As the chapters by Hesterly and Derr and Bournois point out, numerous phenomena characterize this transition. In addition to a changing business situation, Bournois argues, nation-states have fewer civil servants and preestablished careers.

To begin with, the economy is a global one where a small group of people can make decisions that affect the whole world. Modern communication and transportation, cheap labor abroad, and economic interdependence are globalizing the economy and causing employers to require international skills and awareness in their leaders. Second, the need to compete at a fast pace in terms of innovation, production, and implementation means flattening traditional hierarchical structures to simplify and eliminate useless layers of management insulation, resulting in fewer leadership positions. Third, current technology that can transmit information instantly and simultaneously makes middle managers and traditional face-to-face means of communication more obsolete. Fourth, shareholder influence, a factor rising in significance since the 1970s, creates built-in conflicts of interest between leaders and workers, because key professionals and executives are both employees and stockholders. Workers want stability, job security, and high salaries; managers want stock prices to rise so that they can make retirement-level fortunes by selling off businesses. Finally, a lack of loyalty between employer and employee creates new management development systems. Mutual loyalty is being exchanged for mutual reciprocity: the employer agrees to provide employment as long as the employee is valuable to the company; the employee agrees to stay as long as the company provides the best economic opportunity available. Employers look increasingly outside their companies to the labor market for competent and cutting-edge workers while providing state-of-the-art training and career development to valuable internal employees. Aspiring leaders also rely on marketability and mobility to provide employment and stability.

Another overall factor that will influence leadership development in the new information economy is demography: in the United States, at least, jobs will increase and workers will decrease over the next decade, making young educated and skilled employees more valuable. So even while companies are ruthlessly outsourcing, downsizing, and discarding second-class workers, they will also have to focus on recruiting, retaining, and valuing the best employees. Companies of the future will have to utilize fully and value HIPOs developed from within and external leaders from the marketplace. Both factors must be considered in developing future leaders.

NATIONAL CULTURE AS AN INTERVENING VARIABLE IN LEADERSHIP DEVELOPMENT

Future leadership development in this new global economy must also consider the national culture and background of potential leaders as significant variables in training techniques, methods, and philosophies. Nationality affects one's cognitive maps, values, demeanor, and language. It also affects leadership development and selection by determining basic assumptions about what leaders look like, how they behave, what their style is, how they work, whether they are men or women, whether they are black or white, and so on. Schcin (1985) developed a model that represents three different levels of culture that define and shape career patterns and HIPO training and development. Fifteen of the chapters of this book provide wonderful examples of cultural diversity and its influence in leadership development.

Schein (1985, 8) defines culture as the "basic assumptions and beliefs that are shared by members of an organization" and discusses three levels of culture. He labels the first *artifacts*, referring to the visible manifestations of a culture such as behavioral patterns, dress codes, and the most obvious configurations of time and space. Artifact culture is observed easily but deciphered with difficulty.

The second level in Schein's cultural model is labeled *values and norms*, guiding beliefs, preferences, or norms—the manifest or espoused values of a culture—for instance, its emphasis on achievement or affiliation, on competition or collaboration, and on confrontation or avoidance of conflict. This level is more difficult to assess but can be partly inferred from the analysis of artifacts.

The third level, or deep culture, is termed *basic assumptions*. These are the invisible, preconscious or unconscious, nondebatable, taken-for-granted, underlying cognitive structures that determine how group members perceive, think, and feel. Basic assumptions confer meaning to manifest values and overt behavior and can be considered the fundamental assumptions about humankind, nature, and activity that are patterned into cultural paradigms. Examples of such underlying assumptions are ideas like time is limited, nature is to be mastered and shaped by human beings, and people can change their behavior at will. Such infrastructure is very difficult to uncover but, once unearthed, is highly meaningful in interpreting social reality. Although artifacts may easily illustrate differences across cultures, the interpretations of such differences will require some understanding of these fundamental assumptions.

The Schein culture model indicates that basic assumptions are at the foundation of culture; artifacts, though important, are the more superficial layer. Espousing and subscribing to values and norms and speaking and behaving in certain ways are significant manifestations of culture, but they are not as profound a representation of the culture as are basic assumptions. In multinational corporations employees from all nations act out the part of the organizational culture, even changing some of their beliefs and values to correspond to those of the organization. But at the deepest level, they do not alter their fundamental assumptions about life and work. Derr and Laurent (1989) have arranged Schein's ideas as a triangle (see Figure I.1) to illustrate these concepts.

Basic assumptions are mostly rooted in broad cultural settings such as nations. Common early childhood practices, language, religion and philosophy, geography, early education and educational systems, and attitudes about work and life in the family and society are formative in determining the basic assumptions of a given culture. Artifacts, values, and norms—although important, influential, and key manifestations of basic cultural assumptions—emerge as differentiated translations and representations through different organizational histories. They are less deep or culturally embedded than basic assumptions, more likely to change over time, and more symbolic of social reality. Organizational culture usually operates at this artifact, values, and norms level of the cultural edifice.

It is possible that the concept of national culture is most salient in countries with normative and common early childhood patterns that play formative roles in all citizens' lives. In more heterogeneous countries, where formative experience is less pronounced and more diverse, one's religious or ethnic subculture may play an important function somewhat analogous to that of a more homogenous national culture. Nevertheless, research supports the proposition that nationality alone is a significant parameter in determining a person's internal approach to career and leadership (Hofstede 1996; Laurent 1986).

Figure I.2 represents a second part of this theoretical formulation, namely, the factors that influence the role of culture in leadership dynamics. According to

Figure I.1
Derr-Laurent Triangle

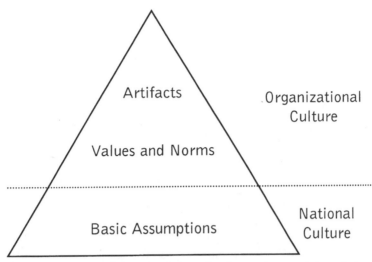

Source: C. B. Derr and A. Laurent. 1989. The internal and external career: A theoretical and cross-cultural perspective. In *Handbook of Career Theory*, edited by M. B. Arthur, B. S. Laurence, and D. T. Hall. New York: Cambridge University Press, 465. Reprinted with the permission of Cambridge University Press.

this model, national culture is the most determinant factor in influencing a person's cognitive map through the shaping of basic assumptions. Hambrick (1991) concludes that one's culturally embedded assumptions may be altered via strong corporate culture and the impact of strong cross-national experiences. So a French expatriate who has lived extensively in the United States and Sweden may, in fact, have formed some constructs different from those formed by someone who had never left France.

National culture also impacts the culture of organizations by selecting and framing particular sets of organizational values, norms, and artifacts that are consistent with its basic assumptions. Such perceived values, norms, and artifacts related to the world of work in organizations and occupations constitute the leadership context. Thus leadership selection and development are directly influenced by organizational cultures that themselves mediate and differentiate the broader contextual effect of national cultures.

In summary, the model is meant to suggest that broad and deep ecological contexts—like national cultures—have a significant impact on leadership and its development in two major ways. First, national culture shapes an individual's self-definition of a leader through fundamental ideas about self and work acquired from early experience in families and schools—the primary carriers and reproducers of culture. Second, national culture shapes the cultural filters of individuals so that they perceive the world of work and leadership development

Figure I.2
Cultural Model of Leadership Dynamics

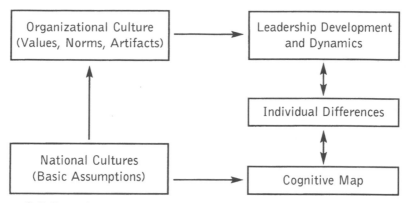

Source: C. B. Derr and A. Laurent. 1989. The internal and external career: A theoretical and cross-cultural perspective. In *Handbook of Career Theory*, edited by M. B. Arthur, B. S. Laurence, and D. T. Hall. New York: Cambridge University Press, 466. Reprinted with the permission of Cambridge University Press.

through the norms, values, and assumptions they have already learned in the culture.

The model is meant to be neither mechanistic nor deterministic. Broad cultural environments are differentiated into subcultures that provide the ground for the emergence of substantial variability among institutions and across individuals. There is also evidence that individuals socialized in a particular culture may adjust quite successfully to the requirements of other cultures. Thus French engineers, for example, whose ideas about leadership may have been strongly shaped by their national culture, can nevertheless operate successfully within the context of an American organization's culture and conform to the requirements of a U.S.-oriented firm. Alternatively, when multinational organizations seek to impose criteria, policies, and practices on their foreign subsidiaries that run counter to local values, local cultures find their own inventive ways of reinterpreting such requirements.

An important contextual variable in this model is "individual differences." Although the concept of national culture as we are using it here is powerful in formulating leadership constructs, people are noted for their ability to make personal choices and deviate from family and cultural values. There are diverse personal experiences within any common context. Hence, it is important to recognize that cultural/ethnic orientation is also influenced by individual differences.

Part I of this book, "Cross-Cultural Approaches to Leadership Development," demonstrates how national culture creates different systems of leadership selection and development based on the different assumptions of specific national cultures. The cultural variable will become increasingly significant in future methods of training leaders, as business and specific companies become more multinational. Different national influences may cause challenges and obstacles to corporate unity and integration. For example, an American woman educated and trained among bright, talented, and qualified female professionals may find her assumptions about work and gender challenged if she works for a French corporation. Although not a "radical feminist," she will carry her American perspective on gender issues to her work and may find it in conflict with basic French assumptions (see Oddou and Derr 1999, Chapter 16). The modern American perspective on gender in the work place is characterized by assumptions such as the belief that there should be equality of opportunity (e.g., between men and women); the belief that women can have both a career and a personal life, which must be accommodated at home; the belief that sexuality (including flirtation) should be separate from the office; the belief that what one does outside work also impacts the workplace (work is paramount); the belief that getting a job depends on merit and market forces (market orientation). French assumptions on the same issues may include different, often conflicting, beliefs such as the belief that individuals differ as a result of social class and educational background; the belief that women can have both a career and a personal life but that motherhood is paramount and should be accommodated at work; the belief that at work women must use all their resources (including their attractiveness) to have influence; the belief that women should be women, wherever they are, including at the office, but that what one does outside the workplace is nobody's business (personal life is paramount); and the belief that one should be guaranteed a job and enough income to live (socialist orientation).

It is exactly these kinds of differences and possible conflicts that create the model of diversity versus collaboration (DC) discussed later. Different national cultures introduce different assumptions and values about business and corporate relationships into systems of leadership development. National culture also influences perceptions of the collaboration and integration required for business success.

THE DIVERSITY-COLLABORATION (DC) MODEL

Buying leadership from the labor market and requiring skill sets and intellectual capital that change according to market conditions are leadership requirements of the new world of work and demand flexibility, quick learning, change management, and an ability to work across diverse boundaries (national boundaries, functions, genders, age, companies). Add to this the fact that many talented professionals now work at home or away from the central workplace one to two days per week and some are very time/space flexible, working wherever they reside. Self-managed teams join and disband on demand, and loyalty is often to the team or project, not the company (Malone and Laubacher 1998, 146). All of this leads to flexible but diverse work organizations as talent from around

Figure I.3
Diversity-Collaboration (DC) Model

the globe comes and goes fluidly. One of the key roles of a leader is somehow to hold them all together.

This is the "diversity" part of the model and, carried too far, presents several risks: (1) no unity of effort; (2) difficulty in collaboration due to diverse personalities, values, and orientations with little relationship or corporate cultural "glue" to offer unification; and (3) lack of loyalty and commitment by talented employees to an organization. All of these factors often result in high turnover, low retention, loss of intellectual capital, lack of personal investment, and a failure to prioritize the needs of the organization.

On the other hand, the industrial economy model of leadership development described previously is perhaps overly integrated. Future leaders or HIPOs used to be internally socialized over time, cloning the perspectives of current top management. Future leaders were mostly male, because to drop off the upward position/experience escalator in order to give birth or care for children was to be permanently derailed onto the "mommy track." Many of the best and most creative future leaders left the carefully orchestrated "tournament model" (Rosenbaum 1979) since success depended as much on conformity and blind obedience as it did on results. More and more HIPO systems of large multinational corporations were similar, and, indeed, as Wilkins (1989) and Schein (1985) point out, they were controlled by corporate culture and common visions as much as by reporting systems and standard operating procedures.

As Laurence and Lorsch (1967) described in their classic study, the best companies organize to match the demands of their external environments and their key stakeholders: customers, suppliers, employees, shareholders. Every industry has a different market or business setting in which it must compete. In many fast-moving situations similar to ones in the new information economy, success requires a company to be both highly diverse and somewhat integrated.

Therefore, the Diversity-Collaboration (DC) Model of developing future leadership is important, and in the conclusion it provides the content in which the contents of this book are considered (see Figure I.3). In this model, a company adjusts the dynamic tension between diversity and collaboration to meet its future leadership (talent pool) requirements. The new information economy fa-

vors individual technostars and entrepreneurs. Many of these operate autonomously as "free agents" going to the highest bidder. Add to this mix global
talent from India, Brazil, and China, plus working parents who want to telecom-
mute as much as possible, and you have diversity in the extreme.

Few companies can succeed without unity of effort, common goals, some
interdependence among key employees (e.g., teams, task forces, committees),
and basic commitment to the values, stakeholders, and requirements of the business. Few organizations are willing to risk reliance upon only "free agent" leaders (those from the outside). Most feel more comfortable mixing talented
outsiders with highly acculturated, loyal, dedicated insiders—similar to the
HIPOs of the old industrial economy. Thus, integrative leaders, common vision
and goals, corporate culture, and required interdependence counterbalance this
propensity toward diversity.

But the extent to which leadership tilts to one side ("diversity") or the other
("collaboration") depends on the business situation. The key moderating influences are *national culture* (it may be done differently, probably just as effectively, in one culture versus another); *industry* (information technology is
different from retailing or natural resources); the *importance of various stakeholders* (in the United States and the United Kingdom it is critical to please
shareholders and their financial analysts; customers in Japan may require higher
quality than in the United States, which is more price-sensitive); and *globality*
(for a global company, it is likely that leadership development practices may
mirror those of its key global competitors, a trend that will counterbalance the
influence of national culture).

The various chapters on leadership development from diverse countries provide us insight into the utility of the DC Model. They describe their context and
diverse situations and in so doing outline the side to which they lean in developing future leadership.

DEFINITIONS

Whereas Roussillon's Chapter 18 devotes considerable space to the psychological concept of potential to lead, the word *leader* has ancient origins but may
be defined differently in diverse fields and cultures. We have elected to define
these people as persons who

1. may eventually be part of the leadership team of their company, at least one of the
   top fifty in a large corporation or in the management group of a smaller enterprise
2. have the authority and responsibility for helping establish the strategic direction of
   the firm
3. have wide-ranging autonomy in their decision-making powers or, in collective leadership groups, are part of the key decision-making group
4. enjoy higher status, more monetary rewards, and greater wide-ranging organizational
   power than all but a few of their peers (depending on the size of the organization)

High-potential employees (HIPOs) are often the ones identified by the company as those with the potential to become leaders.

We also recognize that not all top-level leaders are managers (Dalton and Thompson 1986; Sandholtz 1998). Indeed, in technology-based and professional organizations, some of the most valued and influential leaders may be technical gurus, senior partners, product champions, and internal entrepreneurs. They still perform key leadership functions, such as articulating the company strategy, using their power in responsible ways to advance company goals, representing the organization successfully both outside and inside the enterprise, and helping to choose and develop future company leaders. Ulrich, Zenger, and Smallwood (1999) assert the idea that effective leadership is more than desirable attributes. It consists of attributes *and* results; they articulate fourteen results effective leaders should attain.

CONTENT OF THE BOOK

Part I is at the heart of this book. It consists of fifteen chapters that present diverse aspects of leadership development that all have one characteristic in common: they reflect the cultural dispositions of their countries and their basic national culture assumptions about leaders, leadership, and leadership development. All regions of the world are represented. The developing world viewpoint (in Latin America, Poland, Africa, and Vietnam) is contrasted with that in the more economically developed countries such as the United States, France, and Japan. Even countries where highly developed and competitive global corporations reside, however, have definite cultural differences (e.g., contrasting the United States with France, Japan, and Germany). Although leaders are important to all and vary in degrees of their organizational effectiveness, each company and each nation have cultural differences and cultural assumptions that influence leadership development. The two chapters on China are fascinating because one speaks of historically imbedded cultural assumptions and the other of modern-day influences. They demonstrate how the past influences the present.

Part II articulates a theory of leadership development. Chapter 16 by Hesterly and Derr outlines new business imperatives in the information economy and their implications for organizations and future leadership. Bournois's Chapter 17 focuses on current human resource strategies and management issues associated with developing future leaders. Roussillon's Chapter 18 delineates leadership bedrock: the psychological dimensions of a leader and leadership that don't change much situationally or over time and that pose ongoing challenges to companies.

In the conclusion, we discuss our perceptions of the need for different kinds of future leaders and, for allowances for cultural diversity in the leadership development formula. We relate the contents of the book to the DC Model.

ACKNOWLEDGMENTS

We would like to thank those who helped with editing this book—especially compensating for awkward language translations and cultural styles: Allison (Sunny) Stimmler, Spencer Rogers, Tara Robinson, Linda Wilkens and Robert Spencer. Sunny Grames Stimmler was a very effective and active editorial assistant and was instrumental in helping overcome some of the problems mentioned in the "Conclusion." We would also like to thank Melissa Wood for helping us manage the project.

REFERENCES

Amazon.com. May 2, 2001.

Bournois, F., and S. Roussillon, eds. 1998. *Préparer les dirigents de demain*. Paris: Éditions d'Organisation.

Bournois, F., and S. Roussillon. 1992. The management of high-flyer executives in France. *Human Resource Management* 3(1):37–56.

Dalton, G. W., and P. H. Thompson. 1986. *Novations: Strategies for career management*. Glenview, Ill.: Scott-Foresman Publishers.

Demb, A., and C. B. Derr. 1989. Managing strategic human resources: Leadership for the 21st century. *European Management Journal* 7(2):148–158.

Derr, C. B. 1987. Managing high potentials in Europe: Some cross-cultural findings. *European Management Journal* 5(2):72–80.

Derr, C. B., and A. Laurent. 1989. The internal and external career: A theoretical and cross-cultural perspective. In *Handbook of Career Theory*. Edited by M. B. Arthur, B. Laurence, and D. T. Hall. New York: Cambridge University Press, 454–471.

Derr, C. B., C. Jones, and E. L. Toomey. 1988. Managing high-potential employees: Current practices in thirty-three U.S. corporations. *Human Resource Management* 27(3):273–290.

Hambrick, D. C. 1991. The impact of culture on leadership. Unpublished presentation to the Academy of Management. August. Miami.

Hofstede, G. 1996. *Cultures and organizations: Software of the mind*. New York: McGraw-Hill.

Laurence, P. R., and J. W. Lorsch. 1967. *Organization and environment*. Boston: Harvard Business School Press.

Laurent, A. 1986. The cross-cultural puzzle of international human resource management. *Human Resource Management* 25(1):91–102.

Malone, T. W., and R. J. Laubacher. 1998. The dawn of the e-lance economy. *Harvard Business Review* September/October: 145–152.

Oddou, G., and C. B. Derr. 1999. *Managing internationally: A personal journey*. Ft. Worth, Tex.: Dryden Press.

Oddou, G., C. B. Derr, and J. S. Black. 1995. Internationalizing managers: Expatriation and other strategies. In *Expatriate Management: New Ideas for International Business*. Edited by J. Selmer. Westport, Conn.: Quorum Books, 3–16.

Rosenbaum, J. E. 1979. Tournament mobility: Career patterns in a corporation. *Administrative Science Quarterly* 24:220–241.

Roussillon, S., and F. Bournois. 1997. Identification and development of potential for management and executive positions in France. *Career Development International* 2(7):341–346.

Sandholtz, K. 1998. The four stages of career growth: How to achieve greater impact and influence on the job. Unpublished research report, the Novations Group, 5314 North 250 West, Suite 302, Provo, Utah.

Schein, E. H. 1985. *Organizational culture and leadership*. San Francisco: Jossey-Bass.

Ulrich, D., J. Zenger, and N. Smallwood. 1999. *Results based leadership*. Boston: Harvard University Press.

Wilkins, A. L. 1989. *Developing corporate character*. San Francisco: Jossey-Bass.

PART I

Cross-Cultural Approaches to Leadership Development

1

Managing Leadership in the United States

C. Brooklyn Derr, Jon P. Briscoe, and Kathy Buckner

As companies prepare future leaders, bolster succession planning, and develop "talent pools" from which to fill key leadership positions, HIPOs (as high-potential employees are typically called) remain important to corporate management development strategies. This chapter provides models for understanding the course of high-potential management and for predicting the changes likely to occur in response to a fast-paced business environment.

THE RESEARCH

The first section of the chapter reviews traditional HIPO practices and is based on research already published in *Human Resource Management* by Derr and his colleagues (Derr et al. 1988). This research included interviews and a survey of thirty-three major U.S. corporations, whose average size was fifty-two thousand employees and average yearly financial turnover was $4.2 billion. Questions for the research were designed to uncover the structure and process of high-potential management within large U.S. companies. The study complements a similar one on the management practices of major European corporations undertaken earlier (Derr 1987).

The second section assesses challenges to traditional HIPO management practices, challenges that arise from the fast-changing global economy, and thus by definition require untraditional responses. The interview schedule and survey developed for the 1988 study were used again in 1995, when we interviewed ten Fortune 200 multinational corporations known for cutting-edge management practices. In the 1995 research a greater emphasis was placed on understanding emerging strategic challenges and identifying the impact these challenges were likely to have on HIPO management practices. (Interview questions for both studies can be found in Appendix 1.)

The third section of the paper offers a model designed to depict current changes in HIPO management practices. After identification of what we believed were the major challenges, it became clear that the original HIPO model developed in 1988 required modifications. To this end we met with approximately twenty knowledgeable human resource (HR) professionals whose corporations were known to have a significant executive development function. Having discussed our 1995 research findings, we collaboratively outlined new assumptions and concepts that would capture the emerging trends. (A description of the collaborations and the participating companies is given in Appendix 2.) A model based on the team's identification of the changes occurring in HIPO management is offered in the chapter. We have also included a case study of an organization that has modified its leadership development process to adapt to changing conditions.

TRADITIONAL CONCEPTS IN THE MANAGEMENT OF HIGH POTENTIALS

How have companies traditionally viewed the high-potential (HIPO) concept? The results from the earlier (Derr, Jones, and Toomey 1988) research suggest common responses to this question. When asked, "Does your company designate some employees as high-potential?" all of the companies surveyed affirmed that they had HIPO programs of one form or another, even if not explicitly labeled as such. Most of the respondents stated that their company had several levels of HIPOs (between two and four), and that the definition depended on the particular stage of development. The three most clearly identified phases of HIPO management consisted of identifying candidates and sorting them out from their peers (Phase I), developing them (Phase II), and then actually going through the leadership succession process (Phase III). Usually, an employee at the first phase was identified as "new" and capable of handling a position two, three, or four levels above his or her current position. A high-potential employee at the second phase was most often a manager viewed as important to the corporation—one seen as a corporatewide resource. A HIPO at the highest phase had the potential to become an important general manager (e.g., the head of a strategic business unit or geographical region) or the director of a major function such as marketing. For most companies, a HIPO at this third stage had the ultimate potential of attaining the most senior positions in the company, even that of chief executive officer.

The 1988 research further showed that the work of Phase I is to generate a pool of newly selected HIPOs, which includes those with three to eight years experience who, formally or informally, are identified as high performers and targeted for future development. At Phase II, HIPOs who perform well in their

Figure 1.1
Inverted Funnel Model

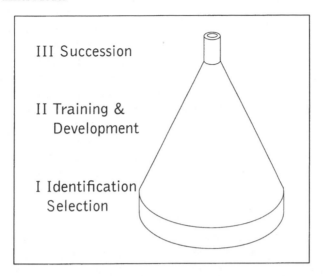

first few assignments are considered solid prospects for future leadership and are provided a variety of training and development experiences. Often known as "comers," they are groomed over a ten- to fifteen-year period for important positions in the firm. However, the organizational pyramid gets very narrow at the top; therefore, many of those who do well in their midcareer do not achieve top management positions. Some voluntarily plateau because of the stress of long hours or corporate politics or, quite often, because such a pattern is incongruent with their life-style. HIPOs in Phase III are, therefore, those heirs apparent who have been developed by the company, who are unambivalent about wanting a significant position of leadership despite the sacrifices this requires, and who are clearly qualified to be high-level leaders. They are the group poised to succeed to the half-hundred positions at the top of the hierarchy.

Figure 1.1 illustrates this three-phase HIPO development system. HIPO development in most large corporations, as illustrated in Figure 1.1, resembled an inverted funnel in which a larger pool of qualified candidates is selected and then filtered to the top. In this model, Phase II was the most lengthy developmental period in the cycle of selecting, training, and fine-grooming future leadership. Many management developers contend that HIPOs have to be ready to assume lower-level Phase III leadership positions by their midforties. If this is the case, it is possible to estimate that among companies adhering to this traditional HIPO model, Phase I selection and culling typically occur at ages twenty-two to twenty-seven and Phase II development usually takes place between ages twenty-eight and forty, or over a twelve-year period.

Typically, local or divisional managers selected the Phase I candidates, who were then "tested" in demanding assignments designed to narrow the field. For example, some employees were given important projects based on their technical expertise, and others were tested as first-line supervisors or junior members of project teams. The HIPOs who met the expectations of more senior managers in these various tests entered into what is often called a *tournament model* of advancement (Rosenbaum 1979). This means that they were given an opportunity to be part of the next series of events or the next "game" rather than be eliminated from the contest. Thus, whereas many were initially considered in the HIPO pool, only a select number of proven candidates advanced to Phases II and III.

Some traditional HIPOs voluntarily dropped out during Phase I. They perceived what it would require to achieve top management status and chose not to make the necessary personal sacrifices, such as relocating every two to four years, working long hours, traveling extensively away from home, and experiencing unrelenting stress.

By the latter stages of Phase II, according to the 1988 study, the candidates had all become "corporate resources" (Schein 1986) and their careers were closely monitored by the corporate staff—most commonly a corporate management review committee (MRC), often chaired by the CEO or another very senior executive, and on which sat influential line managers as well as the director of corporate human resources.

To remain on the traditional HIPO list at Phase II, the individual must not only perform well in a variety of areas but convey an image of competence, devotion to the company, and an executive style that "fits" the executive image. One of the ways in which the high-potential employee showed devotion to the company was through a willingness to change assignments or relocate upon request. Our respondents in the 1988 study stated that HIPOs who refused to change jobs or move to a new location would be perceived as removing themselves from the list. Research at the Center for Creative Leadership (McCall et al. 1988) found that about half of the senior managers they investigated respected a good personal/professional life balance, and half saw such balance as problematic for remaining on the HIPO list.

A common element in all the respondents' definitions was that an employee with ultimate potential would move up the hierarchy into increasingly important management positions and eventually reach a position close to the top. Indeed, "potential" was operationally defined as the ability to move up into valued senior management positions.

Some additional elements of most respondents' definitions of HIPOs were (1) that they advance and change roles faster than their peers; (2) that their careers are carefully monitored and managed (especially during the later stages of development) by senior line executives, human resource professionals, and management review committees; (3) that they are an elite group because of such close scrutiny and career management; (4) that they are on a confidential list, which can be altered according to the list keepers' judgment; and (5) that they are healthy and the company can count on their stamina and their willingness to make the necessary personal sacrifices to continue in their fast-paced career paths. In the European study (1987), Derr found that experience in meaningful international assignment was also important, in Europe, for advancing up the hierarchy.

CURRENT CHALLENGES TO TRADITIONAL HIPO MANAGEMENT

A survey completed in 1995 suggested that some core features of these traditional HIPO management programs remain. High-potential managers are still identified and explicitly developed when circumstances allow. Access to top positions is still carefully managed. Company executives still worry about developing a small group of future leaders and view this as a strategic concern. Nevertheless, several important changes are appearing in HIPO management practices. Here we discuss the challenges companies face as they seek to maintain and improve their programs.

Like their counterparts in other functional areas, human resource (HR) professionals managing HIPO programs face a dizzying array of new and complex organizational changes. The competition offered by an increasingly global economy requires more productivity with fewer resources, while the ever-present technological changes occur so frequently that corresponding functional shifts cannot possibly keep pace. Greater proportions of older American workers meet unpredictable sociocultural and political shifts, making mandatory an emphasis on knowledge and flexibility in the workplace. Customer satisfaction is the only constant in a society moving from being a producer of goods largely consumed internally to being a producer of services for the world (Barney 1995; Pfeffer 1995; Drucker 1992; Senge 1990).

Changes in how organizations are structured and managed also present challenges, such as dispersed work forces (Handy 1990), shrunken and plateaued middle management, lack of loyalty in the work force, and the changing "psychological contract" between managers and their employers, which is particularly important for high-potential management (Mirvis and Hall 1994; Baird et al. 1994; Hall 1993; De Meuse and Tornow 1990). In the years since 1995, the so-called war for talent has meant high turnover among those who have the most career alternatives—often the HIPO group. A survey of 700 companies by the New York–based search firm Thorndike Deland Associates in 1998 found that 70 percent were recruiting managers from the outside (Fisher 1998). This means increased competition in attracting and retaining the best candidates for senior jobs.

Consequently, the human resource professionals we interviewed in 1995 discussed five challenges specifically related to managing today's HIPOs: (1) predicting what kind of managers and leaders will be needed in the future, (2) determining new criteria for competency profiles, (3) maintaining a pool of talent versus a stream of successors, (4) developing "overloaded" managers, and (5) reconciling traditional expectations of high-potential systems with the changing psychological contract.

Predicting Future High-Potential Needs in an Ambiguous Environment

The following are comments by HR executives:

Time lines and stability are history . . . it's very difficult to predict what people will need; we'll never see this stability again.

Our major challenge around this process is forecasting.

Time is moving too fast. People are so stretched and don't have a lot of time. Assumptions are changing so fast that it's hard to keep up.

The problem most threatening to traditional assumptions about managing high potentials is the difficulty in forecasting what kind of managers will be needed in the future, given the pace and complexity of changes currently impacting organizations. HR professionals are faced with the trying task of attempting to position people who can sway the company's structure, culture, and strategy in the direction most likely to maximize a future that none of them can envision.

Perhaps the best solution to this problem was suggested by a communications company representative who said his firm had designed their HIPO system to "reinvent itself every year," instead of waiting for grand redesigns that come about every several years.

Determining New Criteria for Competency Profiles

This area [competency profiling] is sort of a crap shoot. The constraints are that we can't be overly comprehensive with competencies; we must consider the future more, and "process competencies," such as learning, may be more important than more measurable skills [emphasis added].

Traditional competencies are not adequate, high performance is not adequate—we are leaning toward identifying and fostering "learning skills."

As a guide for predicting and selecting which future managers will be successful, many of those with whom we spoke relied on competency profiles. A *competency* usually is a skill or knowledge that distinguishes outstanding performers from merely good or average performers. A competency profile is a set of knowledge, skills, behavior patterns, characteristics, and abilities important for excellence at various levels of leadership. Competencies grew in popularity as the basis for HR systems and processes in the 1990s as human resource leaders searched for ways of defining high performance that were tied to individuals rather than jobs (Briscoe and Hall 1999).

Competency modeling was originally seen as a very scientific process whereby original research was conducted within an organization to determine the cultural and strategy-specific elements that would create employee high performance. A great deal of time and money was invested by many organizations in developing precise competency descriptions. Competencies are intended to establish and align a number of new-style HR processes, including selection, development, performance management, and succession planning.

As competency-based HR processes became more widespread, a number of challenges became obvious. One dilemma was that the original research approach to competency development was expensive and often took months to complete. Moreover, most HR leaders quickly recognized that most competency models were more similar than they were different—most competency lists were 80 percent the same. This raised questions about the wisdom of investing in original research. In an increasingly fast-paced environment, the research-based models are often out of date before they are implemented. With the increase in cost consciousness most organizations are now choosing to invest their HR dollars in applying competencies rather than in creating the models themselves. This means that they either opt for off-the-shelf or generic models or create the models without doing extensive research.

Some organizations have found ways to create distinctive and robust competency models, usually by linking the descriptions of high performance to the business strategy or to a future vision of the capabilities needed in the organization. For example, the drilling organization of a global oil company knew that its survival depended on maintaining its value to its customers, the company's business units. Threatened by the lower prices offered by outside drilling services companies, the group adopted a customer service strategy in order to maintain its competitive advantage. One outcome of the strategy choice was to create a competency model that emphasized relationship building, influence skills, and customer service. The implementation of the competency model allowed a significant perspective change in an organization where technical competencies had traditionally dominated.

Additional challenges have developed from competency application. Some competency models list general competencies that are designed to apply to a broad range of individuals and jobs—often all of the managers in an organization, or even the organization as a whole. An example of this type of general competency is as follows:

Competency: Communication. Keeps others informed about the factors that affect their work; speaks and writes effectively; communicates an effective strategy or direction for the organization.

Although such competencies are short and concise, they offer little direction for employee development or assessment. Some of the elements, such as communicating strategy, do not apply to most jobs. As a result, many general competencies have seen limited use.

A second approach to competency definition is to define each competency very specifically and in a great deal of detail. These competencies usually apply to a specific job or job family, and a different model is required for each job or job family. An example of a senior manager competency is the following:

Competency: Communication. Keeps executive committee informed of events and developments in his/her organization. Effectively articulates the organization's strategy and direction to his/her direct reports and the rest of the organization. Makes effective presentations to analysts and other stakeholders. Guides the investment of the organization's resources in effective communication tools and media. Removes communication barriers between teams or groups in the organization.

Although this type of competency provides much more direction and clarity than the more general type, it also presents a number of challenges. The more specific the competency, the more quickly it will be outdated. Developing competencies for individual jobs is a much more extensive and complex endeavor than identifying one set of competencies for the entire organization.

At a theoretical level, competencies hold obvious appeal as a succession planning and leadership development tool because they describe in behavioral terms a standard of performance. They provide a road map for high potentials and a gauge against which to assess them. However, many HR leaders have struggled with the effective development and application of competencies. Another competency trend is to simplify profiles to reflect fewer, but more reliable and proven, management abilities. After some discussion, one division of a high-tech company decided to give its managers only two guidelines for identifying high-potential candidates: the ability and willingness of the manager to learn from experience and the manager's history as it relates to future potential.

Strategy differences play out in other ways as well. Firms whose competitive advantage depends on thriving in an atmosphere of complexity are trying to assess the ability to work across boundaries (cultures, functions, companies, genders) as a predictor of future success. Other companies we researched are in the midst of trying to identify and develop more general and basic management skills, particularly where success in the past relied too heavily on sheer technical competence or where emerging leaders tended to have a narrow focus. Most competency models identify key types of behavior in three categories: relationship skills (teamwork, influence skills, interpersonal skills); business skills (project management, systems thinking, business focus, customer focus); and technical/functional skills. As business leaders become more clear about what differentiates their businesses, they are moving toward greater precision in identifying their future leadership needs and priorities.

Maintaining a Pool of Talent Versus a Stream of Successors

The following statements illustrate the kind of thinking and solutions that companies shared in their delayered and downsized organizations of the 1990s:

> The term *high-potential* is meaningless—high potential for what? Why focus on key positions? The issue is who comprises the potential management pool for key positions?
> Our last major review of succession planning said that there was nothing really new with HIPOs in the last 20 years, except the move away from individuals to pools, which continues unabated for the most part.

One of the most common strategic problems reported by the HR professionals is the inability to plan for position rotations. Organizations have faced such radical changes in business environments, customers, and products that severe downsizing and restructuring have made it difficult to predict which positions will remain. It has become impractical to plan far ahead for successors in all but a few positions. This reaction by HR professionals to the problem of un-predictable position planning is a move away from the identification, develop-ment, and monitoring of individuals for certain positions. Instead the companies with whom we spoke are focusing on making sure there exists a "pool" of candidates for diverse leadership positions. One executive suggested an emerg-ing role for HR professionals as "internal headhunters" to track down already developed talent.

Hall recommended (1986) that managers be developed *first*, then selected, much like those who prefer to develop a pool of candidates and then select each into a specific job. Whichever method is used, it seems likely that creative efforts such as these are needed for what everyone acknowledges as an unpre-dictable future. The old, rigid succession planning approaches no longer seem viable.

Developing "Overloaded" High-Potential Managers

> Managers are in an untenable position—they are expected to coordinate and communi-cate, but they are also running so hard and are expected to be individual contributors. . . . When you have an organization that is that strapped, where do people find time to be developed? . . . We will try to build development into their job.

Beyond the challenges involved in strategically coping with future uncer-tainty, HR professionals must also deal with HIPO managers' reactions to chal-lenges in their own careers. Managers reportedly have less and less time for training and development.

In fact, many of the companies we queried had lists of high potentials but found that these HIPOs had little time for formal development activities. The common reaction in such situations was to emphasize on-the-job training (OJT). But although OJT is critical for development, some HR managers were hard-pressed to document planned and designed "on-the-job-development" activities or methods to maximize and utilize for development unplanned OJT. Although experience is acknowledged by many as the superior teacher (McCall 1988), learning from unplanned and unsystematic OJT may never take place, despite the rhetoric. OJT for HIPOs needs to be more planned and developmental, with an eye toward methodically facilitating, capturing, and applying learning from developmentally rich job experiences.

Although self-development is becoming the standard in most large organizations, high potentials also face constraints in terms of the amount of time their managers can spend coaching them. In some organizations, managers are turning to outside executive coaches, whom *Fortune* magazine (Morris 2000) calls "part boss, part consultant, part therapist." In most coaching relationships, the coach helps an individual manager with advice and counseling that used to be provided by managers who are now too strapped for time to focus on the growth of their direct reports. In some companies, outside executive coaches are preferred to old-style managers for young HIPOs because they can help challenge undesirable cultures. Coaches help their clients with everything from making personal career decisions to improving business results.

Most of our respondents saw future managers as independently pursuing their own development, with the company providing the necessary tools and resources. "Managing your own career" will most likely become the dictum for future HIPOs, as well as for other managers, but will HIPOs still be carefully selected and developed for future leadership pool positions? Some other comments indicate both problems and potential solutions currently being considered:

> A powerful leverage or "cutting edge" practice might be simply using self-management methods more methodically, with greater coordination with HR.
> The onus is upon the individuals in this environment to take care of their development—learning skills become paramount—knowing the learning skills and how to use them.
> We had 100 percent retention in one group where career planning was done and people got new assignments based on that planning. The old systems really worked.
> There isn't a strategic, systematic design for HIPO development. There is no good link to the job, and we need one.

Reconciling Traditional Expectations of High-Potential Systems with the Changing Psychological Contract

All of the challenges mentioned have contributed greatly to the changing psychological contract between employees and their companies. Many managers are now willing to seek more varied rewards in pursuit of their own career and life satisfaction (Hall and Mirvis 1995). Thus, some managers are refusing risky or undesirable assignments when other personal values and goals prevail. One professional interviewed said:

There is a sea shift in what people are willing to do to "get ahead." People simply say "no" more often. People see risks with failed assignments. There is now more of a weeding out process [by HR, via assignments] and less security. It makes it hard to plan developmental assignments when those who are supposed to be developed aren't willing.

In the face of fears surrounding job security, many HIPOs are reportedly more interested in personal goals not related to pursuing higher positions in the organizational hierarchy. After all, expensive high-level executives are often targets of downsizing, and a person may be more mobile as a specialist than as a manager. Derr (1986) found in his research that talented HIPOs have a variety of ways of defining career success, only a few of them congruent with climbing the corporate career ladder. This is especially true today, and it makes planning for future leadership development difficult. But there are positive aspects as well.

A few of the companies researched are instituting high-potential processes for employees with "unique abilities" (not necessarily future top-level general managers), as well as moving managers laterally in a developmental and even promotional framework. Vertical promotion is no longer seen as the only avenue for HIPO satisfaction or leadership development.

With the turbulent environment, one HR manager interviewed sees high-potential programs as a recruiting advantage. Her view is that it is possible to attract those talented managers who seek professional development and are in a business situation in which stagnation, instability, and lack of developmental opportunities exist.

Whatever their adaptation, companies seem to be changing their assumptions about how traditional high-potential rewards sustain the success of high-potential management systems. Many managers now define their satisfaction differently, and a company has fewer traditional "kudos" to offer.

AN EMERGING MODEL OF HIGH-POTENTIAL MANAGEMENT

In this third section we sketch a model of the emerging shape of HIPO leadership development. Our new metaphor for the identification, selection, development, and positioning of HIPOs is based not only on the survey research done in 1988 and 1995, but on our collaboration with approximately twenty practitioners in the field of human resource management, each representing companies known to have a significant executive development function. A data feedback session at a major university gave the HR professionals, some of whom had participated in the earlier surveys, the opportunity to add perspective to the study results.

Although some of the functions of the traditional HIPO model remain—identification, selection, development—many of the forms and processes of HIPO systems are changing. Challenging the old model (see Figure 1.1), the participating company representatives offered images of what a new model might look like. According to them, the major changes in the old model are a shorter development time for HIPOs, more flexible employee entry and reentry into HIPO development processes, greater numbers of nontraditional HIPOs, and increased attention to external human resources.

Shorter Development Plans

The problem is the time line—you don't always have ten years anymore to train someone. We don't know how much time we have to get someone ready, and the model expands and contracts depending upon the situation. The first thing I see in the model is that the funnel should be flattened.

For the past 20 years we've been working on a time-line assumption that says every high potential needs to touch all these bases and at that point she becomes comprehensively educated and experienced and is worthy of consideration for running a company. During the last twelve months we've realized this assumption is absolutely absurd. . . . We are really confused about what are the competencies for the next five years because what got us here isn't showing us any light in the next five years.

We wouldn't dream of having an individual succession plan at "TECHCO"—because we reorganize every couple of months. Positions don't exist four or five months down the road.

One of the stronger reactions that emerged from our research collaboration was the perception that lengthy development time given to HIPOs, prevalent only a few years ago and implied by the elongated part of the upside down funnel in Figure 1.1, was no longer realistic.

The increasing difficulty of anticipating the direction the organization will take in the future, hence the organization's management needs, precludes long-term management development. Instead, managers are selected and trained for specific slots or are drawn from a talent pool that already has the needed competencies. HR professionals make decisions premised on having only short periods in which to develop managers for key slots.

HIPOs Enter and Leave the Development Process Regularly and at Many Different Levels

The practitioners involved with us in redefining the traditional HIPO model saw the process as changing from one in which younger employees were given early HIPO status and then moved upward, as in Figure 1.1, to one in which people at various levels of the organization become first-time HIPOs, and people at all levels can move on and off the list. The statements that follow illustrate this point:

> We transfer people in and out of the "funnel."
>
> Probably most of the leaders in our company at a rational level hold a model like this [Figure 1.1] as to the way they think it should work. I think in practice we have situations where people get appointed who were not on lists and people who are on lists don't get appointed. . . . Because some people come flying in from left field, they've been in somebody's development chute along the way, probably informally. Then because of opportunity or political influence they've just been moved into a position. Somebody's been thinking about them and growing them, even though they may not have been in the regular "main chimney."

The most striking contrasts to the old model suggested by the research participants are the permeability of the previous HIPO "walls" and the fluidity with which people enter and leave the HIPO "lists." One person, referring to Figure 1.1, put it this way: "I don't think you can use those straight lines. We have people moving in and out all the time; it is more like a sieve, with holes in it— instead of a funnel."

Unique Employees Increasingly Joining Traditional HIPOs

In addition to reports of executives from all levels moving on and off HIPO lists and in and out of "pools," many companies are using HIPO designations and processes to help identify and develop unique employees and prepare them for unique assignments. Our 1995 survey documented instances of companies' creating HIPO paths for knowledge workers and other specialist contributors who did not fit the traditional mold of general managers targeted for top positions. In our research collaboration, an HR professional shared how his company developed certain HIPOs eligible for one-time exotic assignments, usually overseas, where current candidates were in short supply. And beyond the assignment, there was no expectation for further development or designation for certain management roles. In fact, many of the high potentials designated for unique assignments were executives nearing retirement who wanted "one last adventure," a far cry from the traditional use of such assignments to winnow the grain from the chaff. As one collaborator indicated, attention is due "the unique manager," the one with important and needed skills who may not necessarily be on a traditional vertical HIPO track.

This example reveals another difference in current high-potential systems as described by one of our research participants—"to the extent that there is a funnel at all, it is one where there is one valve controlled by the company and one controlled by the individual." Individuals have a much greater say in their HIPO development plans than they did only a few years ago.

What all of these findings combine to illustrate is an approach to using high-potential systems that are more adaptive to diverse managers and employees, at different levels and with different needs. And to be adaptive to people is to be adaptive to changing business environments as well. What are resulting are much more fluid and adaptive but less predictable HIPO systems.

Greater Reliance on Management Resources Outside the Organization

There was a realization among those participating in the research meeting that companies are becoming increasingly reliant upon talent recruited from outside the organization. And, as these outside "resources" enter the organization, they often enter the "talent pools" and become candidates for succession.

One of the interesting implications of this trend recorded at the research meeting was that organizations, perhaps more than ever before, recognize that they will possibly "share" management resources. There was a lot of conversation around this idea:

> We develop a pool of people available for positions as they come up knowing that some of them will be hired at other companies too.
>
> I was thinking about this notion that we're developing for a nation—we're benefiting from each other's development efforts. But as long as that company develops a person then they contribute to the total leadership pool.
>
> When we in-hire, we hire people who come from other companies; we hire them from companies with phenomenal development processes themselves.
>
> This parallels the kind of strategic partnerships that are developed with competitors.

The preceding comments demonstrate a dramatic shift in executive development—the idea that developing executives may be a responsibility and process shared by companies. As one of our research partners said:

> The way it [managing HIPO development] is done now is a closed systems model but, in fact, it is an open system . . . where we are developing for and benefiting from the development of other folks [emphasis added].

So at the same time HIPO processes and models are being developed and improved within a company, they also have cross-boundary implications. Whereas companies have for years combined their managers in university-based training programs, this whole idea has now gone much further. One of the HR professionals with whom we collaborated is contemplating using mentors and "role models" from other companies as coaches to HIPOs in his company, especially when it is impossible to find adequate role models from within. Such an idea symbolizes the scope of the changes under way.

Figure 1.2
Rotary Model

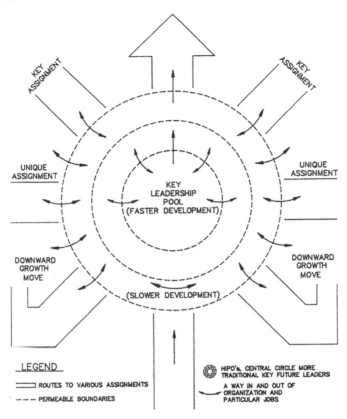

KEY
ASSIGNMENT

KEY
ASSIGNMENT

UNIQUE
ASSIGNMENT

UNIQUE
ASSIGNMENT

KEY
LEADERSHIP
POOL
(FASTER DEVELOPMENT)

DOWNWARD
GROWTH
MOVE

DOWNWARD
GROWTH
MOVE

(SLOWER DEVELOPMENT)

LEGEND

ROUTES TO VARIOUS ASSIGNMENTS

– – – PERMEABLE BOUNDARIES

HIPO's, CENTRAL CIRCLE MORE
TRADITIONAL KEY FUTURE LEADERS

A WAY IN AND OUT OF
ORGANIZATION AND
PARTICULAR JOBS

Creating a New Model of HIPO Management and Development

On the basis of our survey and our data feedback action research, we propose a modified model of HIPO management and development. Instead of an inverted funnel, the new model might be referred to as a *rotary model* (see Figure 1.2). In some parts of the United States and other countries, "rotaries" exist as a form of a circular intersection. Various routes enter the intersection with two-way traffic on each route, and vehicles circle the rotary without stop signs or lights until they make their connection on another route. Although not a perfect analogy, the idea of a rotary intersection serves to a large extent as a useful way to symbolize many of the modifications suggested by our recent research and in contrast to the more classic linear model.

As with the classic HIPO model (Figure 1.1), Phase I and II managers are seen to be recruited into development pools (represented by the circular middle of the new model) and are depicted in the new model in the lower chute or "lane" entering the development pool. Also, as depicted in Figure 1.1, the emergent model includes a pool of candidates who are being explicitly developed for the top positions in the company, as illustrated with the upward straight arrows.

Yet many characteristics differ in the new rotary model. Most notably, HIPOs are now seen as entering (and leaving) development pools from various levels within the organization hierarchy, not just from lower entry levels as in the 1988 model. In addition, HIPOs entering the development arena may do so *directly* from other companies, so the organization boundary of the new model is depicted as being porous or permeable.

Another major difference is that all HIPOs entering the center of the model, those within the development pools, are not necessarily designated as candidates for the top positions in the company or even necessarily for traditional leadership posts. They may be in the HIPO pool to be developed for a particular assignment or for a new position that did not exist before.

Finally, the amount of time spent in the developmental process varies. Some HIPOs, as in the past, may be on a long-term development plan labeled as having potential early in their careers. Other HIPOs might now be knowledge workers who are being developed on a more short-term basis as part of a pool of potential candidates for upcoming horizontal or special moves. There are various possibilities.

Like drivers in vehicles, individuals themselves have more control of their own development and HIPO status—more than they have had before. Once given access to the rotary, employees are in more control of the time they spend inside, taking any particular route that spirals off or deciding whether to exit the rotary altogether.

Within the development pools or rotaries themselves, the model is meant to convey that there are both shorter and longer routes around the rotary. Shorter developmental cycles are symbolized as being closer to the middle of the development pools, and longer development periods are symbolized as being at the outer edge of the circle, much like a wheel. Thus, the leadership pool generally moves faster than its peer group. Managers, professionals, and other employees might enter the development area from any point in the hierarchical level of their organization, and as they become designated as HIPOs for whatever position, they might ultimately "get off" at the same level but in a new assignment. Or perhaps they get off at a higher level, or even at a horizontal level, which is nonetheless a different route. Some may even opt for a downward but high-learning assignment that promises experiences and skills that might help them be more marketable and add more value in the future. The idea is to learn, grow, stretch, and not get stuck.

This model implies an active negotiation or "brokering" role for HR professionals, who can no longer neatly "guide traffic" in one direction toward a single destination. But they still guide the complex plethora of routes that are available to managers, and the management review committee (MRC) still coordinates "traffic flow," making sure there are both enough routes and enough trained managers to make it all work. In addition, the MRC helps strategically by opening up new routes, closing old ones, and redrawing the map when necessary.

In addition to being "traffic cops" and highway engineers, the HR professionals become "internal headhunters," as one of our research participants put it, searching the company for the right self-developed HIPOs to fill positions long established or just emerging. They also join with external headhunters to look outside the company. HR professionals negotiate opportunities and try to find and attempt to influence candidates to take certain positions.

This model is not meant to be comprehensive; nor does it strive to be an intricate representation of all HIPO processes. Rather, it is an emergent image, based upon recent research that better represents the new organizational reality HR professionals and high-potential candidates find themselves grappling with.

A CASE STUDY

Some organizations are actively taking steps to make the new style of succession planning possible by broadening the definition and management of high potentials and by equipping individual employees with more tools for managing their own development. This often occurs in Phase II of HIPO development, in which most of the development of high potentials occurs. For example, a major global chemical company reviewed its succession planning process in the early 1990s and discovered that the current process was inadequate in terms of preparing future leaders. In addition to the economic and business changes described earlier by participants in our study, the leaders of this organization came to the following conclusions about their definition and management of high potentials:

- Position-based leadership development was too often seen as "ticket punching"; HIPOs would move through a prescribed series of developmental jobs without necessarily learning key lessons from the assignment. The HR professionals managing the process had no objective measures or criteria to measure development, except by the jobs the leadership candidate had moved through. This too often led to high potential derailment, and a dearth of capable candidates for top leadership jobs.

- In this organization, no formal competencies had been identified. The company's CEO commissioned a study of what behaviors had been common to the high performers who had been promoted in the past. "Gets Results" was the most prominent behavior on the list, and that was seen as a positive. However, the other behaviors that emerged from the study were "Pleases the Boss" or "Doesn't Rock the Boat." There was a strong desire in the CEO to clarify and prioritize more positive behaviors.

- The organization was in a constant state of change, which meant that targeted positions were often not available when the candidate was ready.

- Those who were identified early in their careers as high potential were sometimes derailed when faced with new and unique challenges; other "late bloomers" sometimes emerged in midcareer or later as significant contributors.

• The high number of key nonmanager, technical contributors in the organization meant that many critical individuals were excluded from the leadership development process, which focused only on managers.

After identifying the key future competencies, the company's leadership partnered with HR professionals to create a research-based development planning process. The creators of the process conducted both internal and external benchmarking to address the problems identified in the existing process, as well as to respond to changes inside and outside the company. Basing the process on research not only led to a more robust system, but also made it more credible to the intended audience, many of whom had started out in the company as research scientists or engineers.

The research conducted in establishing the new process included internal and external sources. For example, in the same study that identified the behaviors that had been required for leadership success in the past (pleasing the boss, getting results, etc.) the researchers explored the behaviors that would be appropriate for the future. "Gets Results" came out on top of the list again but was followed by behaviors such as "Active Learning" and "Straightforward and Consistent." These behaviors were integrated into a competency model that was used to articulate the desired leadership behaviors.

External research included data gathering from outside organizations on the development process itself. For example, research from the Center for Creative Leadership was used to identify potential career derailers and challenges that resulted in key learning. Dalton and Thompson's Four Stages model (Dalton and Thompson 1986; Sandholtz 2000) (see Figure 1.3) was also used as a way of tracking and guiding high-potential growth. The model, summarized in the following, outlines how performance expectations change over time.

Although this model describes development over time, it is somewhat different from the HIPO Phases Model introduced in the first section of this chapter. Whereas the Phases Model describes the traditional plan of most organizations for moving HIPOs through a leadership development processes, the Dalton-Thompson Model identifies changes that knowledge workers and managers make over time as they change the way they contribute to the organization. Thus, the Phases describe the organization's plan for HIPO development; the Four Stages Model describes how individuals should contribute in order to ensure that they remain highly valued by the organization, regardless of their perceived potential or inclusion on a HIPO list. The Four Stages Model provides some flexibility in articulating leadership development needs as most organizations move from the Inverted Funnel Model to the less predictable Rotary Model. It fits well with the trend toward increased self-management of one's career in that it provides a road map for growth over time that is independent of the succession planning process and of the organization chart.

Figure 1.3
Four Stages Model

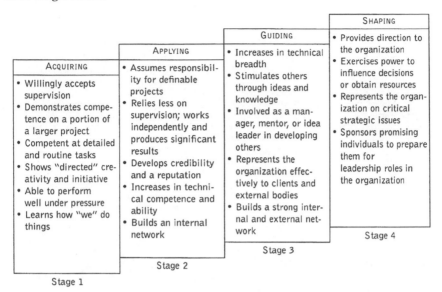

Source: The Four Stages Model © BT. Novations Group, Inc.; used by permission of Kathy Buckner of the B.T. Novations Group.

In addition to sharing the model with management development candidates, those who were designing the succession planning process integrated it with the competency model. This provided a road map for growing in the competencies over the course of a career. It also provided a framework for assessing a person's development over time, and readiness for a key position. A third advantage was that it made a single set of relatively simple competencies applicable across the entire organization. An example of a competency described by stage is provided in Table 1.1.

The Guiding stage in this model clearly reflects the demands of most supervisory-to-midlevel manager jobs; the Shaping stage articulates what executives or senior managers should be doing. These stages were used to articulate role expectations for key jobs. For example, a job might require that a candidate be in the Guiding stage in half of the competencies and in the Shaping stage in the other half. Comparing individual candidate profiles against the job requirements allowed the pool of eligible prospects to be more easily defined.

In the research that led to the creation of the Four Stages Model, Dalton and Thompson also found a large number of nonmanagers who were performing in the Guiding and Shaping stages; thus, the model also allowed for the development of key technical contributors who were not on a management track. This provided a common developmental framework for all key assignments in the organization. Eventually, key elements of the development process were shared

Table 1.1
Four Stages Competencies

Acquiring Stage 1	Applying Stage 2	Guiding Stage 3	Shaping Stage 4
Does the job. Accepts any task and finishes work on time. Accomplishes much in the time available. Picks up loose ends and solves problems. In difficult situations, doesn't make excuses or blame others, tries to make things work anyway; accepts responsibility when work is done wrong in the work group.	Consistent contributor. Shows a sense of responsibility and urgency toward goal accomplishment. Is results versus activity oriented. Has a reputation with the immediate organization and major clients as someone who gets things done well and on time.	Concentrates on value-adding opportunities. Sets ambitious goals and high standards of performance for self and others. Has an excellent reputation and a strong track record in a broad set of activities; exercises leadership in making things happen. Anticipates problems and opportunities before need is apparent to others.	Has a demonstrated ability to lead the organization to operate in a decisive, urgent, and committed way to deliver superior business results that are sustainable and measurable. Helps organization deal appropriately with forces outside the firm and overcome obstacles. Balances long- and short-term priorities.

Source: Used by permission of Kathy Buckner of the BT. Novations Group.

with all professionals and managers in the organization in an attempt to expand the pool of candidates for key positions significantly.

In addition to basing the process on internal and external research, the company's leadership integrated the following features.

Individually Driven

Tools were created to help those designated as HIPOs understand the development process. These tools included training on the development process, a development guide with development-in-place or on-the-job development suggestions for each of the competencies, and instruction and practice in leading a discussion about one's own development plan. The development planning training and the development guide were both designed to structure an individual's on-the-job learning by suggesting projects or assignments that would lead to the mastery of each competency. Individuals also received feedback from their managers (and later multirater feedback) about their performance in the competencies. Putting the development process in the hands of individual employees shifted the focus from managing a clear stream of successors to building widespread bench strength. It also allowed for more individual input on the future of one's career.

Tied to the Competencies

In the development plan, all individuals identified three competencies as strengths and three as development gaps. They then created on-the-job development plans that would help close the gaps.

As the process moved beyond the high-potential candidates, it enabled individuals outside the specifically designated pool to move in and out of key development tracks. Although the organization maintains a high-potential development process, the broader application of the development tools has created a much broader pool of candidates and increased the ability to contribute of those not included on the high-potential list.

CONCLUSION

The emerging model of HIPO development is meant to be descriptive of the hectic, changing arena in which HR professionals and high-level managers find themselves as they try to cope with rapid changes and plan the future leadership needs of their companies. Our research is exploratory and needs further refinement and data-based analysis. Nevertheless, we have observed several fundamental challenges that HR practitioners and academics studying these processes should consider. The case study highlights how some of those changes play out in reality.

The pervasive changes reported by companies about new strategic directions and organizational paradigms bring into question the durability of more traditional managerial approaches. At the very least, current high-potential management systems will have to become more flexible in using competencies to predict, assess, and develop the abilities and skills needed by employees for a radically different and fast-changing organizational world. Also important is a way to recruit and retain already disaffected talent, to manage HIPO processes in a way that demonstrates becoming a HIPO may be beneficial to an employee's career and life. Finally, some provision must be made for providing training and development to high potentials who are already overloaded and perceive themselves as having no time for developmental moves, training, or coaching others. And this must be done in a context in which managers will be directing their own development.

Human resource departments will, in the future, need to be good at continuously redefining competency criteria and competency-based applications so that they readily change to reflect new global business paradigms. The selection of HIPOs will continue to be critical to the competitive advantage a company enjoys, but this selection must be needs-based and drawn from a larger pool than the one offered within company walls.

To accommodate smaller and more decentralized companies speedily, HIPOs will probably continue to be overworked, and chances are good that they will be placed for a significant part of their career with local and regional offices rather than working at headquarters. The weakened structure likely to be found at headquarters will be challenged by the task of turning overworked HIPOs accustomed to local business practices into corporate leaders. Corporate HR will have to find ways to partner with local leadership in order to oversee on-the-job training and talent development, including both positional and geographical developmental moves.

It is important to rethink the definition of a "high potential" as a general manager with the potential to get to a certain level in the hierarchy. The competitive environment of business demands fewer managers, less hierarchy, more knowledge workers, more entrepreneurship, more team leaders, less hierarchical cloning and more diversity, more talent working close to customers and across cultural and functional boundaries, more flexibility, and less company loyalty. Thus, future HIPOs are as likely to be entrepreneurs, technical gurus, product champions, and opinion leaders as managers. They are as likely to emerge from critical cross-national teams, key customer linkages, local organizations, and various skunkwork projects as from key positions at headquarters. They may well be from India, Hungary, or Malaysia and be female and part of a complicated dual-career marriage. What's important is to open up the opportunity structure, cast the net wide, and be clear about what basic competencies and experiences are most valuable for future leaders.

We believe the Four Stages Model is a way to define key competencies for high potentials and a way of guiding their development. It enables HIPOs to be judged on the basis of their contribution to the organization and their continued value over time. As one of our respondents succinctly put it, "The whole issue of HIPO management is more about process, leadership criteria, and conversation than it is about content."

REFERENCES

Baird, L., J. P. Briscoe, L. S. Tuden, and L.M.H Rosansky. 1994. World class executive development. *Human Resource Planning* 17(1):1–15.

Barney, J. B. 1995. Looking inside for competitive advantage. *Academy of Management Executive* 9(4):49–61.

Briscoe, J. P., and D. T. Hall. 1999. Grooming and picking leaders using competency frameworks: Do they work? *Organizational Dynamics* Autumn: 37–52.

Dalton, G., and P. Thompson. 1986. *Novations: Strategies for career management.* Glenview, IL: Scott Foresman.

DeMeuse, K., and W. W. Tornow. 1990. The tie that binds—has become very, very frayed. *Human Resource Planning* 13(3):203–213.

Derr, C. B. 1987. Managing high potentials in Europe: Some cross-cultural findings. *European Management Journal* 5(2):72–80.

Derr, C. B. 1986. *Managing the new careerists.* San Francisco: Jossey-Bass Publishers.

Derr, C. B., C. Jones, and E. L. Toomey. 1988. Managing high-potential employees: Current practices in thirty-three U.S. corporations. *Human Resource Management* 27(3):273–290.

Drucker, P. F. 1992. The new society of organizations. *Harvard Business Review* September–October: 95–109.

Fisher, A. 1998. Don't blow your new job. *Fortune* June 22:159–170.

Hall, D. T. 1993. *The "new career contract": Alternative career paths*. Paper presented at the Fourth German Business Congress: Human Resources. University of Cologne, Germany.

Hall, D. T. 1986. Dilemmas in linking succession planning to individual learning. *Human Resource Management* 25(2):235–265.

Hall, D. T., and P. H. Mirvis. 1995. *The new career contract: Development of the whole person at midlife and beyond* (Technical Report). Boston: Boston University, Executive Development Roundtable.

Hall, D. T., and J. Richter. 1990. Career gridlock: Baby boomers hit the wall. *Academy of Management Executive* 4(3):7–22.

Handy, C. 1990. *The age of unreason*. Boston: Harvard Business School Press.

McCall, Jr., M. W. 1988. Developing executives through work experiences. *Human Resource Planning* 11(1):1–11.

McCall, Jr., M. W., M. Lombardo, and A. M. Morrison. 1988. *The lessons of experience: How successful executives develop on the job*. Lexington, MA: Lexington Books.

Mirvis, P. H., and D. Hall. 1994. Psychological success and the boundaryless career. *Journal of Organizational Behavior* 15: 365–380.

Morris, B. 2000. So you're a player, do you need a coach? *Fortune* February 21: 144–150.

Pfeffer, J. 1995. Producing sustainable competitive advantage through the effective management of people. *The Academy of Management Executive* 9(1):55–69.

Rosenbaum, J. E. 1979. Tournament mobility: Career patterns in a corporation. *Administrative Science Quarterly* 24:220–241.

Sandholtz, K. 2000. The four stages of career growth. BT. Novations Group, Inc., Provo, Utah.

Schein, E. 1986. International human resource management: New directions, perpetual issues, and missing themes. *Human Resource Management* 25(1):169–176.

Senge, P. M. 1990. The leader's new work: Building learning organizations. *Sloan Management Review* Fall:7–23.

APPENDIX 1

Key Interview Questions used in 1987, 1988, and 1995 research

1. Does your company designate some employees as "high potential"? If so, what does your company mean by that term?

2. If your company does not designate some in your organization as high potential, do you have any similar or equivalent formal or informal processes in place? If not, why?

3. Has your concept of high potential changed over the last several years? How?

4. How do you identify and select this group of high-potential employees? What criteria separate these groups?

5. How were these selection criteria developed? Have they been or are they being revised? If so what is the process for such revision?

6. When an employee is identified as "high potential" is he or she told of this status? Why or why not?

7. How do you train and develop your high potentials?

8. What do you consider to be major successes in your efforts to develop "high potentials"; what do you consider to be your major obstacles and challenges?

9. What are the major strategic and other concerns impacting high-potential identification, selection, and development processes in your organization?

10. What kind of changes in your organization's high-potential process do you think will need to occur for it to remain successful? Please explain.

APPENDIX 2

The 1996 research involved the reporting of the 1995 research on emerging HIPO trends and challenges to company members and guests of the Executive Development Roundtable at Boston University's School of Management in December 1995, some of whom had participated in the earlier research. The Executive Development Roundtable's members are typically the highest-level company representative with direct responsibility for executive development efforts. These company representatives meet at regularly scheduled research meetings to discuss and sponsor research related to executive development strategy and applications. After presenting the initial research findings, we divided the company representatives into groups and asked them to discuss generally the implications of the research for their HIPO systems and processes, and specifically to suggest how the HIPO model generated in 1988 would need to be modified to capture current and emerging changes. The following is a list of companies with representatives in attendance who collaborated with us in discussing the emerging model of HIPO management:

Amway Corporation

Avon Products

CSX Corporation

Eli Lilly and Company

Florida Power & Light Company

J. P. Morgan & Co., Inc.

KPMG Peat Marwick

Polaroid Corporation

Reader's Digest Corporation

U.S. Army War College

Xerox Corporation

Apple Computer

Blue Cross/Blue Shield of Massachusetts

Digital Equipment Corporation

Fidelity Investments

Hallmark Cards, Inc.

Knight-Ridder, Inc.

Northern Telecom Ltd.

Price Waterhouse (PricewaterhouseCoopers)

Sun Microsystems, Inc.

Union Carbide Corporation

2

New Wine in Old Bottles: The Challenges of Developing Leaders in Latin America

Joseph C. Bentley

> Neither do men put new wine in old bottles: else the bottles break, and the wine runneth out, and the bottles perish: but they put new wine into new bottles, and both are preserved.
>
> —Matthew 9:17

> The major advances in civilization are processes which all but wreck the society in which they occur.
>
> —Alfred North Whitehead

Although there are numerous attempts to define what leadership is, and many scenarios describing what leaders do, there is little disagreement over the importance of leadership. Few will argue in favor of doing away with leaders or with diminishing the value of effective leadership. All arguments defend the opposite view: given the challenges of increasing complexity and the rise of turbulence in all areas of human experience, effective leadership is an asset of increasing importance for organizations, one that will be even more important in the future. Effective leaders exercising successful leadership will continue to be critical for success in business as well as for societies everywhere.

Important questions remain, however: (1) Who will be fit to lead in a future that promises to be very different from the past? (2) How should these future leaders be selected? How can they be identified? And once selected, how should they be educated and trained? (3) What kinds of organizations, structures, and processes must be created in order to support effective leadership in business organizations so that they will become and remain competitive? (4) What will the leaders of the future be required to do in order to stay alive in an environment that will offer little sanctuary for those who prefer to rest on their oars? In this chapter, these questions are considered as they apply to Latin America.

The framework for the chapter emerges from the words of one of the greatest American presidents, Abraham Lincoln. Facing an uncertain future (the Civil War of 1861–1864), which, if not addressed successfully, could have destroyed the American experiment in democracy, Lincoln described his and our challenge: "As our case is new, so we must think anew and act anew. We must disenthrall ourselves." As we consider the challenges for leaders in the future, our case is also new and therefore we must think and act in new ways; we must find new models, new strategies, new directions. In order to be successful, we must "disenthrall" ourselves.

According to *Webster's Unabridged Dictionary, to disenthrall* is "to become free from bondage; liberate." Becoming free from the bondage of past ideas and beliefs may be the most important requirement for increasing leadership effectiveness in business organization in Latin America as well as the rest of the world. Relinquishing obsolete practices as well as cultural attitudes and values and discovering and developing more appropriate models of leadership emerge as the new challenge for organizations everywhere to remain competitive.

CULTURAL VALUES IN LATIN AMERICA

The average Mexican manager, according to Trompenaars's *Riding the Waves of Culture* (1994), considers the organization where he works (and it is almost always a "he" rather than a "she," at least in the private sector) to be like a family. He "experiences the organization as paternalistic and hierarchical, and, as in many Latin cultures, the father decides how [things] should be done" (p. 9). Are such observations useful? Are they true? And equally important, if they are true, does acting as if an organization were similar to a family make sense?

Although it is difficult to separate out stereotypes from cultural characteristics, there are important differences between cultures that have exerted strong influence upon how things are defined and how actions are taken. And these differences, to the extent that cultures create, support, and maintain strong values and reinforce certain behavior over other types, will undoubtedly continue to make important differences in the future.

Trompenaars (1994) identifies three critical cultural themes: leadership, authority, and power. The ways these themes are expressed in a culture are among the most important of all, since all organizations face a common reality: how to exercise power, enact authority, and therefore offer leadership. What follow are three examples from my own experience of how power and authority are often exercised in Latin America (Bentley 1992).

Team Building in Mexico

Several years ago, in my role as consultant, I was facilitating a team-building session with a senior level executive team. I gave them the assignment to develop a list of characteristics that would define an effective work group. Once the list was developed, my plan was to use it as a standard, then ask them to describe the gaps between their idealized statements and the present level of team functioning. For example, if one of the attributes had been "An effective work team is one that can analyze its own work processes and change them for the better," then the next step would have been to ask members of the team to state how successful the team was in doing just that. The largest gaps between the ideal and the actual would become our working agenda, with the goal of reducing the gaps.

Among the first of the characteristics identified by the team—and placed in the position of highest importance—was "An effective team shows respect for the leader." I was surprised. I had never read nor heard (nor believed) that respect for formal leadership was the most important requirement of an effective team. The group was not only adamant in support of its choice but pleased that they had come up with such an important element. The next thirty minutes was spent reporting to the leader how important respect was and how complete the respect was for him among the members. He was very pleased and showed it.

Slack Time in Panama

During a consulting project with the Panamanian government a number of years ago, I was asked to work with an agency of the government assigned to train and support rural community development specialists. After a week or so of reporting each morning at the office, I began to notice a strange pattern: each morning around 11:00 or 11:30, all work gradually slowed, then stopped altogether. Usually, people did nothing for the rest of the day. When I asked about this pattern, I was told that Ing. Lopez, the director of the agency, generally left specific instructions as to what was to be accomplished during the day with the office manager, then left for the rest of the day (as it turned out, he was moonlighting with another full-time job elsewhere). The work left behind was never enough to keep people busy throughout the day so when the assigned tasks were completed, all work for that day ceased. The unwritten rules soon became clear: do only what has been authorized; do not undertake any work on your own; if you have nothing to do, then the time is essentially yours to do as you wish; but you cannot leave until the day is over.

Once I understood the rules of the game, I spent an interesting, but fruitless hour with Ing. Lopez. Nothing I could suggest, recommend, or advise made any difference. Ing. Lopez was not interested in structuring the work environment so people could be busy all day. Rather he was committed to keeping absolute control of every action and assigning all tasks regardless of the effectiveness or productivity of the office.

Disaster in Colombia

The occasion was a strategic planning presentation to stockholders and employees of a large manufacturing company. I had been working with them for a number of months in the strategic planning process, and all had gathered at a plush hotel to view the presentation. An elaborate (and very expensive) multimedia presentation had been prepared by a public relations firm. The presentation itself was dazzling, combining music, slides, film clips, as well as narration. The trick was coordination. Someone had to be present to push the right buttons and move the correct switches in order for everything to mesh correctly.

The integration and coordination were the responsibility of a young man, perhaps thirty, a staff member of the company. He had been given the assignment precisely because he had been seen as a person of great promise and ability.

At a crucial moment in the presentation, he accidentally activated the wrong slide projector. Realizing his error instantly, he made a lightninglike adjustment and the sequence returned to normal. Two slides had been seen out of order. I noticed it because I had been present for the numerous rehearsals. The chief executive officer (CEO) did not pick up the error but did notice the young man moving quickly as he made adjustments. Turning to the vice president of public relations—the person in charge of the stockholder meeting—the CEO asked what had happened and was given a brief explanation. I was sitting next to the CEO and heard him ask, "So, he made a mistake?" When the answer was "Yes, but no one noticed," the response was quick in coming: "Entonces corralo!" (Then fire him!) And the next day the young man was fired.

Cultural Values

These stories, selected from many others gathered during years of teaching and consulting in Latin America, stand out in my memory because I find them to be dramatic examples of underlying cultural values. No one present during any of these incidents seemed surprised, or even offended, as I was when the young man was fired. We were viewing the events through different sets of lenses. At the rational level, I understood the culture and could make sense of what was happening: the "acting-out" of deeply held values and assumptions:

"Respect for our leaders is required for effective teamwork."

"I and only I should control all that goes on in this office."

"I can fire whom I wish, when I wish, for whatever reason."

"Mistakes in public will not be tolerated."

Table 2.1
Power Distance: Latin America

Mexico	81 (tied for second highest)
Venezuela	81 (tied with Mexico)
Brazil	69 (5th highest)
Colombia	67 (8th highest)
Peru	64 (11th highest)
Chile	63 (12th highest)

These are examples, in Latin America, of deeply held beliefs about the way things are, and the way things should be done: what Schein has called the "Basic Underlying Assumptions" level of culture (1992).

THE HOFSTEDE DIMENSIONS

The Hofstede studies (1980) of a large multinational company identified as HERMES in the study (it was IBM) is a classic in the field of cross-cultural research. Although subsequent review research has identified several important weaknesses in the study, for sheer scope and comprehensiveness as well as introduction of new directions for theory and research, it remains a major contribution.

Data were gathered from employees in HERMES in forty countries, once in 1968 and then again in 1972. Over 116,000 questionnaires were analyzed. In addition, data were also collected from other sources. As has been noted previously, four dimensions of culture were identified: Power Distance, Uncertainty Avoidance, Individualism, and Masculinity. Each of the forty countries received a score on each dimension.

As reported in the research, *power* was defined as the potential for determining or directing the behavior of another person or other persons. The concept of *distance* referred to the degree of perceived inequality between a less powerful and a more powerful person. The range of scores for all forty countries was 11–94, with an average of 51. The higher the score, the more psychological distance was reported between the more powerful and the less powerful. Scores from Latin American countries are reported in Table 2.1.

When describing the implications of a high Power Distance (PDI) score, Hofstede (pp. 119–122) reported the characteristics listed in Table 2.1 as attributes of high PDI organizations.

- Managers are more satisfied with directive or persuasive superiors.
- Managers like seeing themselves as benevolent decision makers.

Table 2.2
Uncertainty Avoidance: Latin America

Peru	87 (5th highest)
Chile	86 (6th highest)
Argentina	86 (tied for 6th)
Mexico	82 (8th highest)
Colombia	80 (10th highest)
Venezuela	76 (11th highest)
Brazil	75 (12th highest)

• Employees fear to disagree with the boss.

• Subordinates consider superiors as being of a different kind.

• Power holders are entitled to privileges.

• Powerful people should look as powerful as possible.

• Coercive and referent power are stressed.

• Other people are a potential threat to one's power and can rarely be trusted.

• Cooperation among the powerless is difficult to bring about because of a low faith in people norm.

Uncertainty avoidance as a dimension of culture is defined by Hofstede as the ease with which novelty and innovation are handled. In cultures marked with high Uncertainty Avoidance scores (such as Japan and Greece) people feel the need for clarity and order so as not to feel threatened by uncertain situations and rapid change. The range of scores for all countries in the study on this dimension was 8–112, with an average score of 64. The Latin American countries were ranked as indicated in Table 2.2.

Cultures ranked high in uncertainty avoidance were described by Hofstede as exhibiting more emotional resistance to change; the view that loyalty to employers is a virtue; a belief that managers should be selected on the basis of seniority; less expectation of risk-taking behavior; a view of conflict in organizations as undesirable; the belief that initiatives by subordinates should be kept under control; a high fear of failure (pp. 176–177).

The third dimension of national culture, as identified by Hofstede, is Individualism. This dimension clarified the extent to which the culture encourages personal initiative and achievement, the importance of private life, and personal separation, as contrasted with a sense of community or collective characterized by a tight social framework, in which the emphasis is upon belonging, fitting in, and giving attention to being a good group member.

The range of scores in Individualism for thirty-nine countries is 91 (United

Table 2.3
Individualism: Latin America

Venezuela	12 (lowest)
Colombia	13 (second lowest)
Chile	23 (7th lowest)
Mexico	30 (10th highest)
Brazil	38 (14th lowest)
Argentina	46 (16th lowest)

States) to 12 (Venezuela) with an average of 51. The lower the score, the less personal achievement and initiative are acceptable. The Latin American countries recorded the scores indicated in Table 2.3. As can be noted, all of the Latin American countries in the sample scored below average on Individualism (higher toward Collectivist values), and although scores did not cluster as tightly as on the previous dimensions, there is a discernible pattern (Hofstede 1980, 230–231).

Behavioral and attitudinal characteristics of cultures low on the Individualism scale are high emotional dependence on companies; managers who aspire to conformity and orderliness; managers who rate security as important; managers who endorse a "traditional" point of view, not supporting employee initiatives and group activities; disapproval of individual initiatives; employees who expect the organization to look after them as in a family, who can become very alienated if the organization disappoints them; and employees who expect the organization to defend them.

The fourth dimension along which national culture can be shown to vary systematically is called Masculinity, with an opposite pole of Femininity. This dimension is best described by McGregor (1967, 23): "The model of the successful manager is a masculine one. The good manager is aggressive, competitive, firm, just. He is not feminine, he is not soft or yielding or dependent on intuition."

Scores on the Masculinity dimension in the HERMES study ranged from 95 (Japan) to 5 (Sweden) and the average was 51. The scores for the Latin American cluster are listed in Table 2.4. Brazil, Peru, and Chile all scored below the mean of 51, toward the Feminine end of the scale.

Phrases that describe cultures with high Masculinity scores include the following: Men should behave assertively and women should care; men should dominate in all settings; traditions are important and can be identified as going back through several generations.

Table 2.4
Masculinity: Latin America

Venezuela	73 (3rd highest)
Mexico	69 (5th highest)
Colombia	64 (9th highest)
Argentina	56 (15th highest)

CULTURAL VALUES

Some tentative conclusions about cultural values in Latin America are in order; they are based on the findings of the Hofstede research and are offered here to clarify what may be the important truths of leadership and organization in Latin America:

1. A large gap exists between those who hold power and those who are expected to respond to power. As a result, authority is important and generally is accepted and respected. Employees are slow to disagree with their bosses, awarding them the rights—even the responsibilities—to make decisions as they see fit.
2. Uncertainty and ambiguity create discomfort, resulting in resistance to change, low levels of risk taking, the smoothing over of conflict, and a reluctance by employees to initiate actions.
3. Belonging and fitting in are important, as are traditional ways of dealing with problems. Employees expect that organizations will take care of them and protect their well-being.
4. Effective leadership is aggressive and decisive; the masculine values of taking charge and dominating are expected.

Some Implications of Present (Cultural) Values in Latin American Business Organizations

> Mexicans will never tell you they don't know. They will never tell you they made a mistake. They will never tell you bad news. (American executive working in Mexico)

Over the years, while teaching, consulting, and leading seminars in Latin America, I have heard the following story, repeated over and over in many different settings. There is a crab merchant who specializes in the freshest and most succulent crabs available. He stores his crabs in two containers, one with no cover and the other fitted with a tight cover. One day a customer asks him why one of the two water-filled containers is covered and the other remains open. "Well, you see," replies the crab seller, "the container without the cover is full of Mexican crabs [or Venezuelan, or Colombian crabs, depending upon the country] and the covered one is full of American crabs."

"And why are the American crabs covered?" asks the customer.

"Well, the crabs are always trying to climb out. In the container with the American crabs, when one starts to escape, the others make a platform and help him up, then he turns back and helps the others. If I don't have the tub covered they will all escape, helping each other."

"And the Mexican crabs? What do they do?"

"I don't have to worry about them at all, so I leave them uncovered. When one starts to climb out, the others reach up and pull him back. They never even come close!"

This story, recited by Mexican (or Colombian) executives for their colleagues, although always told with unfailing good humor and without embarrassment, usually appears as part of the discussion of "What do we have to learn in order to be more successful?" I have never seen anyone offended nor insulted by the story. People inevitably laugh and enjoy the joke. It carries, however, an important truth, one that is central to this chapter: there are cultural values and attitudes (leading to behavior) in the cultures of Mexico, Colombia, Venezuela (as well as in the United States and all other countries in the world that aspire to business success in the global arena) that often are not supportive of effective organizational behavior. In cultures where people "pull each other back, are reluctant to provide support, do not like to see others succeed," as expressed in this story, it is much more difficult to compete successfully with cultures that provide support and help each other to succeed.

CULTURAL DISADVANTAGES

There exist in Latin American cultures, values, beliefs, and attitudes that may not be helpful in a future of competition with world class companies. Consider the cultural values outlined in Table 2.5 and the areas of business that they may affect (Bartlett and Ghosal 1992; Centero 1994; Chesanow 1985; Foster 1992; Joynt and Warner 1996; Kras 1989; Moran and Harris 1982; Riding 1985; Schule et al. 1996; Stephen and Greer 1995; Quezado and Boyer 1988).

This review of Latin American cultural values that may affect business practices is not intended to portray a negative picture of societies that embrace and sustain such values. A similar analysis could be presented for any society or culture. The important point here is the focus upon the degree of support available within a culture for those attitudes and values—leading to behavior, supported and defended by traditions—essential to success in the information age. The basic premise, then, is that there must exist a congruence between cultural values and attitudes and actions that are required for successful competition in the global economy. To the extent that cultural values oppose those required values and behavior patterns, any single business organization may be less successful in competition with organizations that can benefit from that congruence.

Table 2.5
Cultural Values and Beliefs: Latin America

CULTURAL VALUE AND BELIEFS	POSSIBLE IMPACT
Decisions are made by those in authority; others need not be consulted.	Problem solving, Troubleshooting, Strategic implementation
Tradition is revered; Hierarchy provides stability.	Planning, Change management
Evaluations are conducted in ways so that no one "loses face."	Rewards, Recognition, Advancement, Climate
Deference is given to those with power and authority; to offer judgment not in support of the ideas of one's superiors is rare if not impossible.	Decision making, Planning, Problem solving
Schedules are important, but only in relation to other priorities.	Meetings, Coordination, Collaboration, Planning
Removing a person from a position results in loss of status and prestige.	Executive development, Advancement, Motivation
Decisions are often defined as expressions of wisdom by those in authority. Any questioning would imply lack of confidence in his judgment.	Organizational success, Problem finding, Change
Strong beginnings are valued; systematic follow-up is difficult and often not recognized.	Strategic planning, Change management
Life follows a pre-ordained course, and human action is largely determined by the will of God ("Si Dios quiere!")	Change management, Continuous improvement, Organizational adaptability
People are expected to adjust to their environment rather than alter it.	Change management, Strategic planning
A commitment may be superceded by a conflicting request, or an agreement may only signify intention and not be seen as necessarily binding.	Teamwork, Collaboration, Organizational climate, Coordination
Effective leadership is aggressive and decisive; masculine values predominate.	Leadership style, Executive development
Certainty is preferable to uncertainty and ambiguity.	Conflict management, Planning, Leadership style
Education or family ties are the primary vehicles for upward mobility.	Promotions, Motivation, Organizational effectiveness
Withholding information to gain or maintain power is acceptable.	Communications, Decision making
An individual employee has a primary obligation to his family and friends.	Loyalty, Promotions, Motivation

For example, one of the "required" competencies for future organizational success is *rapid cycle time*, the "ongoing ability to identify, satisfy and be paid for meeting customer needs faster than anyone else" (Meyer 1993, 7). As has been noted, this liability is spelled out as Rule 1: "The competitor who consistently, reliably, and profitably provides the greatest value to the customer first, wins"

(Meyer 1993, 9). A business organization seeking to be competitive in the global economy into the next decade because of traditional values related to the definition and management of time, may well see a competitive advantage pass to a competitor that can utilize speed as an advantage.

The Corning-Vitro Story

The failure of a $130 million joint venture between Corning, the giant U.S. manufacturer of ceramic cookware, and Vitro, the largest and most successful glass manufacturer in Latin America, is an example of the problem of the lack of alignment and congruence of cultural values (*New York Times* 1994, 22).

"Vitro and Corning share a customer-oriented philosophy and corporate culture," exclaimed Julio Escamez, a Vitro executive, in an enthusiastic toast offered at the beginning of the alliance. Two years later, however, Corning handed back Vitro's $130 million dowry and called off the marriage. "The cultures didn't match," observed Francisco Chavez, an analyst with Smith Barney Shearson in New York. "It was a marriage made in hell."

Made in hell? And after such an auspicious and favorable beginning? What happened? According to the *New York Times*:

- The Mexicans saw the Americans as too direct while the Vitro managers, in their dogged pursuit of politeness, seemed to the Americans as unwilling to acknowledge problems and faults.
- The Mexicans became convinced that the Americans were moving too fast while the Americans felt that Vitro was too slow.
- The decision-making process was, for the Americans, too embedded in hierarchy: "Loyalty to father and patron" seemed to guide the decisions rather than a focus upon sound business principles. "As a matter of either loyalty or tradition, decisions [were] often left to a member of the controlling family while middle-level managers were not asked their opinions," complained the Americans.
- The way both sides responded to the collapse and failure helps illuminate the cultural differences: "The Americans were willing to discuss what went wrong and attempt to learn from it while the Mexicans were reluctant to criticize anyone, especially a partner."

As if to make the last point, Ernesto Martens, president of Vitro, insisted that it was never a failure of corporate cultures. However, Martens was quoted as saying, "Business in Mexico is done on a consensus basis, very genteel and sometimes slow by U.S. standards" (*New York Times* 1994, 22).

No conclusion can or should be drawn from this account that the business approach supported by one culture or the other is superior. What is important is that the culture of any society, as reflected in the business values and practices of the companies that society, be supportive of the newly emerging demands of doing business successfully in the global economy within the context of the new information era.

Cultural Prisons in Latin America?

First of all, a case can be made that most citizens in most societies—including leaders in business and government—are in danger of becoming trapped in the prisons of the values and patterns of their own culture. Therefore, those leaders in Latin America—the present ones as well as the high-potential leaders of the future—are at risk. The beliefs, assumptions, and values that are absorbed so effortlessly in childhood eventually become a filter through which the world is experienced and events are interpreted. That filter can act as a cataract, narrowing the vision and shutting out the light. That which starts as "is" becomes synonymous with "what should be." This process of defining what is ours as not only the best way but perhaps the only way seems to be most pronounced in those societies with strong religious or moral values that serve to define specifically what is right and what is wrong.

HIPO LEADERS IN JAIL?

It goes without saying that future leaders of business organizations in Latin America—those high-potential (HIPO) individuals who will be expected to lead their companies in the information age and the global marketplace—will face numerous challenges, as will leaders everywhere. Potential for success in this leadership endeavor should serve as the defining ability for HIPO leaders in Latin American and elsewhere.

Among the most serious and complicated of these challenges will be to lead their companies and themselves "out of jail": to plan a jailbreak of sorts from a culture that, although making perfect sense within the cultural context, may not serve well the larger purpose of competing with companies throughout the world (Rosenau 1990). Why will this be such a serious but important challenge? Because some of the traditional values, beliefs, and practices that are prominent in Latin American cultures are in conflict with the new values required by the information age. Unless that conflict can be resolved successfully, there is a danger that companies in Latin America (and elsewhere for that matter) will remain behind, locked up in a cultural prison, captured by the past, unsuited for success in a "new ball game."

EGBC Revisited

If there is a new and emerging global business culture (EGBC), as I believe, then understanding what it is demanding is crucial for success in the future. This EGBC consists of these as well as other important characteristics:

- New approaches of exercising power and authority
- Successful processes of empowerment at all levels
- Faster cycle time: strong demands for faster decision making and faster and more successful follow-up
- Strong commitment to customer satisfaction
- High levels of organization flexibility and adaptability
- Willingness to embrace change
- Successful development and utilization of diverse talents and abilities

If these values of a newly emerging global business culture become dominant, then any discrepancies or gaps between the business values of a particular company (in a specific cultural environment) and those required by a new business world will diminish the probabilities of successful competition in that new marketplace.

LATIN AMERICAN CULTURE REVISITED

Among the prominent cultural values of Latin America that have been reviewed up to now are these:

- Decision making by those in authority
- Reverence for tradition
- Deference toward those in authority
- Strong beginnings; less attention to follow-up
- Si Dios quiere: sense of fatalism
- Certainty preferable to uncertainty or ambiguity
- Traditions of masculine values, including "machismo"
    - Order and stability achieved through hierarchy
    - Evaluations conducted in ways that prevent "loss of face"
    - Expectation that people adjust to their environment, not change it

Now What?
This is a world in which one wanders within and between multiple borders and spaces marked by excess, otherness, and difference. This is a world in which old certainties are ruptured and meaning becomes more contingent, less indebted to the dictates of reverence and established truth.
—Henry Giroux, *Fugitive Cultures*

William Saroyan, the American playwright, when confronted with the reality of his impending death, was reported to have said, "I always knew that we would all have to die sometime. I always thought, however, that I would be an exception. Now what?" In this chapter, with reference to leadership in Latin

America, and especially for those designated as high potential, I have attempted to convince you of the following conclusion: There are large and important gaps between some traditional cultural values, attitudes, beliefs, and practices in Latin America (and most specifically, in business organizations in Latin America) and those newly emerging cultural values required for success in the global marketplace of the information age of the future. I have named this set of values and attitudes the *emerging global business culture* (EGBC). There is, I believe, substantial support for the emergence of a new, worldwide set of beliefs and values that will govern the "best practices" of successful businesses into the foreseeable future.

If the arguments presented are sound, then the question becomes Now what? There are others raising these and similar questions. In *The Americano Dream: How Latinos Can Achieve Success in Business and in Life* (1998), the businessman Lionel Sosa is even more emphatic. Sosa argues that those raised in the cultural traditions of Latin America are not suited for success in the high-powered and rapidly changing world or modern business. It is not the lack of knowledge that holds Latinos back, he argues, but psychological and cultural barriers that "keep us falling further behind." History is at play, here, Sosa believes. The Spanish conquest of native populations in the Americas led to the creation of "an oppressed underclass whose collective psyche became rooted in passivity and underachievement." Sosa identifies what he calls "cultural shackles" imposed upon Latinos to keep them "happy" in their slavery, reinforced by the teaching of the Catholic church over the centuries and still functioning in the modern-day cultures of Latin America.

Sosa identifies those values and attitudes associated with success in the business world in the United States—ambition, pursuit of wealth, individualism, self-reliance, assertiveness—and argues that these and others are regarded with suspicion in the traditions of the Latinos. These "cultural shackles" must be replaced, argues Sosa, with attitudes more congruent with those required for success in a free-market environment. He refers to a "culture of subservience" ingrained in the Latino mind, and argues that what is required is an explicit, conscious effort to get rid of the unproductive baggage. Sosa exhorts Latinos to admit that this "culture of subservience exists, recognize that it must be changed, and then get about the business of changing." Sosa realizes that he is on controversial ground here. He calls what he is preaching "heavy wood." Yet Sosa's arguments are similar to those presented in this chapter, they are directed specifically to Latinos who are the present and future leaders of business organizations that propose competing in the global economy. The traditional Latin culture does in fact carry excess baggage that needs to be examined, understood, and changed. The important question before us is, Now what?

NEW MAPS—OR ELSE!

"We cannot understand, and certainly cannot function within, the new global economy using the old maps of reality that were appropriate" in the past. "The old maps are by now so seriously out of touch with reality that they threaten economic ruin for those who persist in following them" (Mitroff 1988, 5–6). These words, strong and threatening, were published in the 1980's in the book *Break-Away Thinking*. The old maps of reality, entrusted to us by the preceding generation, are no longer accurate for making our way in an entirely new and uncertain world, argues Mitroff. This premise encapsulates neatly the dilemmas faced by future leaders in Latin America and elsewhere. The old versions of "This is the path to success" have become obsolete and must be changed. Here we have the first and greatest challenge for high-potential leaders of the future in Latin America: breaking away from traditional patterns of belief and action!

Mitroff supports his argument with several important observations:

• The problems facing leaders today and into the future cannot be properly defined let alone solved by relying upon old models and traditional solutions.
• The old solutions, "maps," are the product of old ways of thinking.
• Bold, radically new ways of thinking are required if newer and better alternatives are to emerge.
• These new ways of thinking will not see daylight unless the deeper, more hidden patterns, or "road maps of reality," that lie beneath the old ways of thinking surface and are examined (and, of course, changed).

Recommendation 1: Culture Shock

High-potential leaders of the future in Latin America will need to experience what has been called culture shock: a disorienting, frustrating, even frightening experience of learning that one's own culture is not necessarily the correct, appropriate one for achieving certain outcomes or goals. This insight—crucial as an "unfreezing" experience—can be learned in several ways, including living and working in other cultures, working within other companies different from one's own, traveling to other parts of the world, participating in designed and directed simulations. Ways must be found, however, for the high potentials to understand both rationally and emotionally that there is not just one way of making organizations successful and that there are often better, more appropriate ways to be acquired from other cultures.

Recommendation 2: Honest Appraisal

Octavio Paz, Nobel Prize–winning poet and author from Mexico, observed over twenty years ago that the Mexican world (and by inference, much of Latin America) is medieval rather than modern, hierarchical and dogmatic rather than pragmatic and open, and ceremonial, formal, and ritualized rather than sponta-neous or purposeful. These are hard words—not unlike Sosa's "hard wood" referred to earlier—but important. If the business culture of an organization in

Latin America with intentions to become a significant player in the emerging global marketplace supports the medieval over the modern, the hierarchical and dogmatic over the pragmatic and open, the formal and ceremonial over the purposeful, to that extent that organization will be carrying extra baggage into global competition.

High-potential leaders of the future in Latin America must be ready to make honest and rigorous appraisals of the organization culture that must carry them into the future and be able to make careful and useful identification of the gaps between the what is and what will be required. Another way to describe this challenge is to refer to an insight first offered by Bartlett and Ghoshal (1996) when they identified the struggle between the "third-generation strategies" and the "second-generation organizations." Many companies, they observed, have crafted clear and relevant strategic visions for globalization. They then must rely upon organizational structures and cultures incapable of implementing such ambitious and sophisticated initiatives so carefully developed, often with the assistance of high-powered (and high-priced) consulting firms. They further compound the problem; chances of success may be further diluted by "first-generation leaders" who attempt to implement "third-generation strategies" within the limitations of "second-generation organizations." In other words, the existence of a persuasive and elegant strategic plan in and of itself is no guarantee of success without appropriate leadership supported by an organizational culture prepared to implement the planning.

Recommendation 3: Cultural Change Agents

Most organizations do not enjoy the kind of organizational culture required to be successful in the newly emerging global marketplace. All will be required to undergo massive and disruptive change. As Schein (1992) has observed, "The only thing of real importance that leaders do is to create and manage culture and the unique talent of leaders is their ability to understand and work with culture" (5). Once again, strong words with a critical focus, echoed and emphasized by Tushman and O'Reilly (1997): "Managing culture is the most neglected and highest leveraged tool for promotion, innovation, and change" (220). Given the clarity of these statements, what high-potential leaders must learn is relatively simple to state (and extremely difficult to make happen): high-potential leaders of the future in Latin America must become experts in understanding and changing the organization culture. No one makes this argument quite as clearly as Jack Welch (1990), CEO of General Electric, arguably the most successful company ever to compete in the global marketplace, who is reputed to have said something like this: In the nineties the heros will be entire companies that have developed cultures that instead of fearing the pace of change, relish it. Such cultures will not evolve by themselves. In fact, if left alone, most companies will continue to do what has yielded success in the past, even in the face of evidence that there will be little success in the future. Creating and

managing new and different ways of accomplishing goals and objectives will
be high up on the list of required skills and values for the future.

Recommendation 4: Stand in the Gaps

Much has been made in this chapter of the importance of the gaps between
the status quo and the future. High-potential leaders in Latin America, in addition to their operational and strategic responsibilities, must also be experts in
finding and closing those critical gaps that exist between the present state of the
company and the emerging global values culture (EGVC). They must be ready,
in the biblical tradition, to "stand in the gaps."

Recommendation 5: Lifelong Learners

"In a time of change, it is the learners who inherit the future. The learned
find themselves equipped to live in a world that no longer exists." The words
are those of the philosopher longshoreman Eric Hoffer. The message is central
to the argument presented here. In times of rapid change the only remedy for
survival is continuous learning. It is no accident that more and more of the
literature extolls the importance of the "learning organization." High-potential
leaders must transform themselves into continuous learners, not only learning
continuously, but also transforming their organizations into learning organizations. The luxury of separate times for education and learning and for practicing
what one has learned has gone the way of the authoritarian leader. What one
introduces into the competitive organization from formal education quickly becomes obsolete and consequently dangerous. Attempting to lead in the future
relying solely upon what one learned formally is a formula for failure! What
must be learned can only be seen a few years down the road. So here is the
challenge for the high-potential leader: he or she must become expert at continuous learning and at learning about what has not even been imagined
as yet!

Recommendation 6: (More) Power to the People

In a world of ever increasing complexity and change, those who occupy the
upper levels of organizational hierarchies often become increasingly unable to
understand what is really happening within the organization. Overwhelmed with
attempting to understand the competitive environment, the evolution of technology, the emergence of newer and hungrier competitors, senior executives,
apart from the problems of understanding what is happening, have neither the
time nor the means to know enough to make important internal decisions. If
they insist on clinging to outmoded models of "command and control" decision
making, they will soon be solving the wrong problems as well as making bad
decisions. Those "who know" must be encouraged to participate actively in the

decisions leading to taking action in the implementation of plans and strategies. Although the "what" of strategy must necessarily remain with senior executives, the "how" of implementation is best left to those who are closest to the customers and to the experiences of implementation. As Kanter (1983) has observed, "The issue is to create the conditions that enable companies to take advantage . . . of the talents of their people . . . by building an environment where people feel included, involved and empowered" (363).

Of all of these recommendations, this one may be the most difficult for high-potential leaders in Latin America to accept and implement. Immersed as they are—and will be—in cultures that honor hierarchy, finding ways to empower and support people lower down in the organization and learning to listen for their answers will be a formidable challenge indeed. "Organizations will need to give more freedom to individuals that they may be uncomfortable giving," argues Charles Handy (1996), "if employees are to retain their commitment and creativity. . . . They must find the beneficial compromises between corporate need for control and the individual pressure for autonomy" (11–12).

Recommendation 7: Faster and Better

Among the current ongoing redefinition of business processes are constant searches for high-quality products and methods, ever-higher levels of customer satisfaction, and faster and faster delivery of these products. Future leaders in Latin America will no longer have the luxury of "easy time," defined here as a neglect of the importance of being sensitive to the expectations of others in the delivery of goods and services. In a variation on the old conundrum of the three (of these three—faster, lower in cost, and higher in quality—you can only have two), the future is going to require high quality at low cost and "faster and faster." Making it happen is the challenge of the high-potential leader of the future.

NEW WINE AND NEW BOTTLES

> Without leaders, we're just a band of raiders. Leaders are what make us an army.
>
> —Marcos, a Nicaraguan Contra, 1988

For the business organizations of the world, as well as for individuals and institutions everywhere, there is no turning back the clock to more comfortable and tranquil times. The transition from the agricultural era to the industrial era and to the information technology age is irreversible (Handy 1996; Hope and Hope 1997; Lawler 1996; Nolan and Croson 1995; Wind and Main 1998).

Those organizations that plan to compete in the global arena are faced with several central and daunting questions: Where will they find the leaders (the "New Wine") up to the challenge of guiding those companies through the "white water" of the transition and beyond? And what kind of skill, values, talents, and experience will be needed? And, if those leaders can be found and prepared, what kinds of organizations must be created in order to take advantage of that leadership in the world markets?

For Latin American companies and leaders, these questions are not only important but urgent. Arguments presented in this chapter defend the proposition that in addition to all of the challenges of the future, future leaders for Latin American companies must address the reality that many traditional cultural values may represent additional barriers to success in the future. An "extra burden" of cultural baggage must be identified and lifted from the backs of those companies that are serious about world class competition. And, just as important, new and different values, beliefs, and attitudes must be identified and institutionalized.

UNDERSTANDING THE SUCCESSES OF THE INDUSTRIAL AGE

"Why are some countries rich and others poor?" is the question that David Landes addresses in his magisterial *The Wealth and Poverty of Nations* (1998). His answers to this question may cast light upon a similar question that is the central focus of this chapter: Why are some companies successful and others not?

The puzzle of wealthy countries and poor countries has been at the heart of the discipline of economics ever since it emerged as a separate field of inquiry from the earlier traditions of political philosophy. In a letter to David Ricardo, Robert Malthus observed, "The causes of the wealth and poverty of nations [are] the grand object of all enquires in Political Economy" (Skidelsky 1992). Over one hundred and fifty years later, little help with the answers seemed available: "No new light has been thrown on the reasons why poor countries are poor and rich countries are rich" (Samuelson 1973).

Landes (1998) is more optimistic. The answer to the question has emerged: "If we learn anything from the history of economic development, it is that the culture makes all the difference." His argument is straightforward. The Industrial Revolution began in England and was successful because of the presence of cultural values and attitudes that supported directly what the Industrial Revolution required. Among the necessary components, argues Landes, were the following:

- A sense of national cohesion and identity
- The willingness and the capacity to compete and be competitive
- A respect for empirical and technical knowledge and an educational system that made the sharing of that knowledge possible
- Strong support for advancement by merit and ability over family connections

- Belief in the importance of honesty and integrity
- Institutions that provided support for property and private ownership
- Support for the concept that individuals could expect to benefit from and enjoy the rewards of hard work and sacrifice
- The discipline to forgo present consumption for future possibilities
- A climate that encouraged saving and investments

These values, according to Landes, made the Industrial Revolution possible and, as a result, made England a wealthy country. To the extent that other countries shared these as well as other important cultural values, they were able to share in the wealth that flowed from the Industrial Revolution.

SUCCESS IN THE INFORMATION AGE

By changing the focus of the question to, Why are some organizations successful and others not?, and moving into the future, it seems clear that the answer that Landes offers serves us here: "If we have learned anything from a study of organizational behavior, it is that the culture of the organization makes all of the difference."

In this chapter, I have proposed that a new organizational culture is emerging. This new culture—global in scope, defining new and different ways of doing business—will be as essential to the information age as the previous industrial age culture as described by Landes was to the industrial age. Here I am calling it the *emerging global values culture*. It will consist of those attitudes and values needed in the future in order to compete successfully with companies from many different nations and societies. Leaving behind those traditional values that diminish a company's chance for success in the global marketplace and embracing those that will enhance that chance become the most important leadership responsibility for high-potential leaders in the future. This is particularly true for national cultures and traditions that—like some in Latin America—revere and support certain behavior and attitudes that are logically counterproductive for business success in the information age.

"ONLY SUCCESSFUL ONES"

A recent headline in the *Wall Street Journal* (1998) helps make the point: "There Are No German or U.S. Companies; Only Successful Ones." The headline quotes Thomas Middelhoff, newly appointed chairman of Germany's Bertelsmann AG. A subheading continues the argument: "Business Forces Open Borders as Nationalism Yields to Shared Ambitions. Big Egos Remain a Big Issue."

The article reviews the merger between the German automobile company Daimler-Benz AG and Chrysler Corporation of the United States. It continues:

The idea of a merger between . . . Daimler-Benz AG and Chrysler Corp . . . is stunning only in its size and scope, not because one player is based in Stuttgart and the other near Detroit. In the culture that leaders of global business inhabit, *where shared values of open markets, hard money, and standardized technology increasingly take precedence over old-fashioned nationalism, such transnational combinations are logical, and they are becoming more common every day* [emphasis added].

Some important conclusions can be drawn from this point: (1) future leaders of global businesses will inhabit a new, emerging culture with values and expected behavior very different from those of traditional national business cultures; (2) managing this culture successfully will be the key to success in the global marketplace; and (3) in the future, increasingly dominated by the information age, there will be no German or American (or Mexican or Argentine) companies—only successful and unsuccessful ones.

BECOMING DISENTHRALLED

In the opening pages of this chapter, the words of Abraham Lincoln served as a way of signaling that, even as great changes are occurring in the world of business, equally great changes will be required of those who lead into the future. "As our case is new," said Lincoln, "so we must think anew and act anew. We must disenthrall ourselves." To disenthrall means "to become free from bondage." Becoming disenthralled becomes the great challenge for high-potential leaders in Latin America; becoming free of those traditional values and practices that will limit the possibilities of leading successful companies in the coming age.

REFERENCES

Bartlett, C., and S. Ghoshal. 1992. *Transnational management*, 2nd ed. Chicago: Irwin.
Bartlett C., and S. Ghoshal. 1996. Beyond strategy, structure and system to purpose, process, people. In P. Duffy, ed. *The Relevance of a Decade*. Cambridge, MA: Harvard Business School Press.
Bentley, J. 1992. Facing a future of "permanent white water." The challenge of training and development in high-technology organizations. In L. Gomez-Mejia and M. Lawless, eds., *Human Resource Strategy in High Technology*, Vol. 1, Greenwich, CT: JAI Press.
Centero, M. 1994. *Democracy Within Reason: Technocratic Revolution in Mexico*, 2nd ed. University Park; Penn State University Press.
Chesanow, N. 1985. *The World-Class executive*. New York: Rawson Associates.
Coleman, T. 1990. Managing diversity at work? The new American dilemma. *Public Management* 72:9.
de Forest, M. 1994. Thinking about a plant in Mexico? *Academy of Management Executive* 8(1):33–39.
De Lillo, D. 1985. *White Noise*. New York: Viking Press.

Dertonzoset, M., et al. 1989. *Made in America*. Cambridge, MA: The MIT Press.

Foster, D. 1992. *Bargaining Across Borders: How to Negotiate Business Successfully anywhere in the World*. New York: McGraw-Hill.

Geertz, C. 1970. The impact of the concept of culture in man. In E. Hammel, and W. Simmons, eds., *Man Makes Sense*. Boston: Little, Brown.

Geertz, C. 1973. *The Interpretation of culture*. New York: Basic Books.

Geertz, C. 1988. *New York Times*, May 11: 36.

Ghoshal, S., and Bartlett, C. 1995. *Transnational management*. Chicago: Irwin.

Ghoshal, S., and Bartlett, C. 1998. Changing the role of top management: Beyond structure to process. *Harvard Business Review* January/February: 87–98.

Giroux, H. 1996. *Fugitive culture: Race, violence and youth*. New York: Routledge.

Grave, A. 1996. *Only the Paranoid Survive*. New York: Doubleday.

Handy, C. 1994. *The age of paradox*. Cambridge, MA: Harvard Business School Press.

Handy, C. 1996. Beyond certainty. In P. Duffy, ed., *The Relevance of the Decade*. Cambridge, MA: Harvard Business School.

Haven, T. 1993. The change-dazed manager. *Harvard Business Review* September/October: 22–37.

Hofstede, G. 1980. *Culture's Consequences*. Beverly Hills, CA: Sage Publications.

Hofstede, G. 1991. *Culture and Organization: Software of the Mind*. New York: McGraw-Hill.

Hope, J., and K. Hope. 1997. *Competing in the third wave*. Boston, MA: Harvard Business School Press.

Jick, T. 1995. Accelerated change for competitive advantage. *Organizational Dynamics* Summer: 77–82.

Joynt, P., and M. Warner. 1996. *Managing across borders*. London: International Thomson Business Press.

Kanter, R. 1983. *The Changemasters*. New York: Simon & Schuster.

Kegan, R. 1994. *In over our heads*. Cambridge, MA: Harvard University Press.

Kluckhohn, C. 1942. Myths and rituals: A general theory. *Harvard Theological Review* 35: 45–79.

Kluckhohn, C., and F. Strodbeck. 1961. *Variations in value orientations*. Westport, CT: Greenwood Press.

Kras, E. 1989. *Management in two cultures: Bridging the gap between U.S. and Mexican managers*. Yarmouth, ME: Intercultural Press.

Landes, D. 1998. *The Wealth and poverty of nations*. New York: W. W. Norton.

Lawler, E. 1996. *From the ground up: Six principles for building the new logic corporation*. San Francisco; Jossey-Bass.

Meyer, C. 1993. *Fast Cycle Time: How to Align Purpose, strategy, and structure for speed*. New York: Free Press.

McGregor, D. 1967. *The professional manager*. New York: McGraw-Hill.

Mitroff, I. 1988. *Break-away thinking*. New York: John Wiley and Sons.

Moran, R., and P. Harris. 1982. *Managing cultural synergy*. Houston: Gulf Publishing.

New York Times. 1994. Culture does matter, Sept. 11, p. 22.

Nolan, R., and R. Croson. 1995. *Creative destruction*. Boston, MA: Harvard Business School Press.

Pugh, D., and D. Hickman. 1997. *Writers on organizations*, 5th ed. Thousand Oaks, CA: Sage Publications.

Przeworski, A. 1983. *Methods of Cross-national research, 1970–1983: An overview.* West Berlin: Wissenobraftzentrum.

Quezado, F., and J. Boyce. 1998. Latin America. In R. Nath, ed., *Comparative Management.* Cambridge, MA: Ballinger Publishing.

Riding, A. 1985. *Distant neighbors: A portrait of the Mexican.* New York: Knopf.

Rosenau, J. 1990. *Turbulence in World politics: A Theory of Change and Continuity.* Princeton, NJ: Princeton University Press.

Samuelson, P. 1973. *Economics,* 9th ed. New York: McGraw-Hill.

Schein, E. 1992. *Organizational culture and leadership,* 2nd ed. San Francisco: Jossey-Bass.

Schule, et al. 1996. Managing human resources in Mexico: A cultural understanding. *Business Horizons* May/June: 55–61.

Shapiro, B. 1996. Tectonic change in the world of marketing. In P. Duffy, ed., *The Relevance of a Decade.* Cambridge, MA: Harvard Business School Press.

Skidelsky, R. 1992. *John Maynard Keynes: The Economist as Savior, 1920–1937.* New York: Penguin Books.

Smelser, N. 1990. *External and Internal Factors in Theories of Social Change.* Cited in J. Rosenau, *Turbulence in World Politics.* Princeton, NJ: Princeton University Press.

Sosa, L. 1998. *The American Dream: How Latin Americans Can triumph in the United States.* New York: Plume.

Stephen, G., and C. Greer. 1995. Doing business in Mexico: Understanding cultural differences. *Organizational Dynamics* Summer: 39–55.

Trice, H., and J. Beyer. 1993. *The Cultures of work organizations.* Englewood Cliffs, NJ: Prentice-Hall.

Trompenaars, F. 1994. *Riding the Waves of Culture.* Chicago: Irwin.

Tushman, M., and C. O'Reilly. 1997. *Winning through innovation.* Cambridge, MA: Harvard Business School Press.

Wall Street Journal. 1998. There are no German or U.S. Companies: Only successful ones. May 11, pp. 1, 11.

Wind, J., and J. Main. 1998. *Driving change.* New York: The Free Press.

3

Identifying and Developing Future Leaders in France

Sylvie Roussillon and Frank Bournois

THE SITUATION IN FRANCE

When looking into French highflier identification and development, it must be remembered that in France highly significant peculiarities are involved in producing business leaders. Similar to those in other countries where social stratification is particularly strong, France's methods reflect the important influence of authority and elitism to the extent that foreign partners are often surprised.

Whereas many countries use the traditional assessment centers, French firms seem rather reticent about them and doubtful of their value. Many may ask how French people understand the concept of *potential* and how it is linked to performance in present jobs. It seems that the French concentrate more on the development of "highfliers"; they trust the powers of hierarchy observation more than the results provided by sophisticated means of detection and identification.

After reviewing certain French particularities, we discuss the main points of interest revealed by recent studies performed with the help of top business leaders; afterward we discuss the different methods of gaining access to management functions that we have discovered in our studies.

We attempt as well to assess the impact of change on management during the nineties and on the spread of identification methods and highflier career management. There has been a movement away from considering the individual's capacity for adaptation toward an analysis of his or her development of managerial practices. An emphasis has been added regarding the specifics of internal resources, the inevitable ambiguity about the qualities expected of tomorrow's managers, and the importance given to training and its function as a stimulus for change within management as a whole. We are convinced that the question of identifying and developing highfliers, even if it occurs at the top level of the Human Resources Management (HRM) Department, cannot be considered simply a function of HRM. It is becoming an essential element linking the strategic, the organizational, the cultural, and the human resources levels of the firm.

Our research has also enabled us to define the practices and methods that are specifically French. Since 1990 we have been studying the leading French companies and are therefore in a position to describe their policies and methods for identifying and developing highfliers. On the basis of the survey we made in 1991 in seventy large firms and the detailed monitoring we did of some of them, we emphasize certain significant developments, which correspond in many ways to new departures that must be explained.

THE MAIN FEATURES OF FRENCH CULTURE, AS SEEN BY THE NON-FRENCH

Certain features of French management quite astonish the outside observer.

Executive personnel represent a very specific category in French terms. This concept of cadre, or executive (Boltanski 1982), is almost untranslatable into the other European languages and has a pied piper effect on all those who do not belong to this category. The notions of senior executive and top executive, who represent a total of about 180,000 people[1] in the private sector according to our calculations, are defined in essentially legal terms. The senior executive is defined in terms of ceiling contributions to social security (more than four times higher). The French social system is characterized by the importance that it attaches to its elite and their precise definition,[2] whether high-level civil servants in the government, in the army, or in business: the importance accorded by Ph. D'Iribarne (1989) to belonging to a "state" with the attendant rights and duties. He maintains that the French function according to an "honor system" that is different from the "contract system" and the "consensus system" typical in the United States and the Netherlands.

It is important for us to define our use of the term *manager* in relation to the term *executive*. For us, the term *manager* refers to an executive whose function is to coordinate, to direct, and to lead teams. The terms *executive, senior executive*, and *top executive* express status and hierarchical relationship. Even though a well-known expert (a university researcher, even a presidential adviser) may be a senior executive, he or she cannot for all that be a manager. It should be noted that in French we have terms such as *responsible, chief*, and *director* to signify the act of managing, but the word *manager* has become the most used. In the following discussion, the term *highflier* is always used to refer to a high-potential manager.

THE FRENCH CONCEPT OF THE ELITE

Administrators have not been the first to attempt to elucidate the fundamental characteristics and mechanisms of this elitism phenomenon in France. For a long time now, the elite has interested sociologists and historians. At the end of World War II, R. Aron, whose works were reedited in 1985, posed the question of what constitutes the elite and defines it as the minority that fulfill the functions of leadership within the society. According to him, it is composed of five groups: the political leaders, the administrators of the state, those in charge of the economy, the leaders of the people, and the military chiefs. He maintains that in a democracy, the elite must be composed of a number of groups to ensure the balance of power.

Certain historians reject this notion of an elite because they find it impossible to establish criteria for defining it. Vovelle (1974) finds no common element in the behavior of nobles and "bourgeois" in eighteenth-century Marseille and considers that "when forced to face the reality of the facts, the notion of an elite is no more than a popular prejudice and a commonplace." In spite of this definition problem, many authors have tried to define the mechanisms by which the elite is constituted, reproduced, and even dissolved or replaced. Thus Bourdieu (1979), for whom an individual's chance of success depends above all on the way the social system works, has studied the laws of reproduction that enable the ruling classes to ensure their success: the role of networks and the importance of social roots for future social success.

Barbier (1989) in his study of the ruling classes in the north of France under the Second Empire (1848–1871) illustrates the mechanism by which an elite absorbs new members and continues to develop or else is partially replaced by another elite. Barbier clearly shows how the unity of this group grows out of its inbreeding and its belief in common values that simultaneously represent a strength and a weakness: the values of work and thrift, and yet little attention to technological innovation. He shows how the sons lack their fathers' qualities and prefer the charms of a social life; this is what prevents continuity. New men, more open to technological innovation, come to form a different ruling class.

This research, like most studies of this kind that focus on the forming and renewing of a ruling social group, shows that one elite is replaced by another without actually being able to define the mechanisms that are used to carry out the process. All these studies manage to do is show that certain elements of former elites live on in the new one and guarantee adaptation to the new issues of society.

Scott (1995) who compared sixty important studies carried out in the English-speaking world dealing with political and economic elites also considers that the latter are the most difficult to conceptualize. But for all that, we attempt to analyze those mechanisms at work in a firm ensuring the renewal of managers, without forgetting that the methods employed by a firm are an integral part of its socio-economic context and of its mechanisms of selection and reproduction.

THE SOCIAL BASIS UPON WHICH THE MANAGERIAL ELITE IS BUILT IN FRANCE

Foreign authors Jenkins (1988) and Burns et al. (1995), who write about French management, emphasize certain outstanding features that are often more evident to those who are observing from the outside than to those who are from the inside. Among these features, the following are the most frequently mentioned.

Excessive importance is given to certain elitist training systems that guarantee important posts with considerable responsibility for all young graduates. Barsoux and Lawrence (1991), in the work they have done on business management in France, quote a certain disillusioned executive, a self-made man, who asks: "How much longer are we going to stand ineffectually aside and allow people with great talent and potential to be held back and refused development?" The number of autodidactic executives among highfliers and leaders of large firms is particularly low. The notion of a hierarchy of diplomas is firmly established and reinforced by the media that assess the "grandes écoles," emphasizing those that are particularly sought after and ranking their graduates, who are offered special conditions of recruitment and professional advancement within the state and business hierarchy. All this indicates that these graduates embark on a preconceived career pattern without their individual qualities being taken into account. It could even be claimed that the managerial elite in France is selected at the age of fifteen by the educational system, which by means of a successive selection process enables certain students to go to prestigious schools that give access to the most brilliant careers. Foreigners are also amazed by the great importance this system of selection gives to mathematics, to theoretical debate, and to intellectual precocity.

The same emphasis is given to precocity when the young executive is given his first post. In the public service, important responsibilities are frequently given straight away to young graduates from prestigious schools; for example, a young graduate from the famous engineering school Ponts et Chaussées may be appointed directly to the post of Area Construction Engineer. This is unjustified preferential treatment in the eyes of those who come from schools considered less prestigious, even if they have proved their skill and competence through a great deal of experience.

The theoretical aspects *of organization* are esteemed much more than the practical aspect of *application and implementation*, which is a caricature of fayolism.[3] Thus, the young executive may well begin a consultant career with conceptual responsibilities, rather than in a more operational capacity. In fact he or she will often spend only a brief period in this latter role merely to get to know people and pick up information.

Career management in the private sector, particularly highflier career management, has been influenced by the public service standards, particularly in those firms that work in close contact with the state—public companies or those that have been recently privatized and the large industrial firms that work with the state. It is interesting to note that certain firms, for example, le Crédit Agricole (a major financial institution), have set up competitive examinations, similar to those of the public sector, to select their top executives. The public sector in France is typically powerful and homogeneous with a great deal of economic weight, even if at the moment it is being criticized. Marked by its centralized, bureaucratic past, it has considerably influenced the private sector in France.

The ease with which people who have spent the first part of their career in government administration are appointed to important posts in private enterprise is quite astonishing to non-French. This practice, *pantouflage* allows top managers to return to their former positions in public administration if they wish.

Finally, the efficiency and the discretion of the old-boy network, which plays a very active part in the French business world, seem incredible to outsiders. It is said that the general management of British Telecom accuses these networks of having prevented them for a considerable time from setting up in France, whereas the French were able to establish themselves quite easily in Britain. These networks can draw together executives from different fields—political, administrative, managerial, and military—in certain rather exclusive associations, such as business clubs.

Those concerned with highflier career management must be well aware of all these characteristics. The waste of the unused potential of those who have not studied in the "right places" is often deplored. There are others who seem relatively pleased with the present education system since it does cream off efficiently and precociously the executives with the potential the nation needs. Thus, B. Gentil of Entreprise et Personnel[4] (1988) considered that the lack of high-level executives that French companies were complaining of at that time was not really due to the inefficiency of the education system but rather to the absence of a link organized by the firms themselves: "It is not the universities and 'grandes écoles' that are to blame, but the organization of the firms themselves. No firm produces its best executives spontaneously, automatically prepared for facing difficult and demanding careers, even if it recruits the young elite graduates. Only 'high quality' professional learning experience can reveal and prepare the leaders of the future." In France, management is seen as a job requiring many skills, not linked to any one function nor to any specific economic sector.

The most prestigious of our "Grandes Écoles" were created by the state to train competent executives for its service: L'ENA (l'École Nationale d'Agriculture, the National School of Administration) was to train senior civil servants; the École Polytechnic, the armed services, and the École Normale Supérieure lecturers and professors. After they pass an entrance examination, which always attracts the most brilliant members of any age group, the state

Table 3.1
Educational Background of French Leaders

Polytechnic or ENA	50%
"Grande Ecole" (B.S. Degree)	73%
Bac+4 (B.S. Degree)	83%
Bac+5 (M.S. or MBA)	4%
Foreign University	6%
Self-Taught	17%

Source: Bauer and Mourot (1987).

pays for all their studies and pays them a salary while they are at the school. Afterward it helps the best candidates to learn to deal with power within the most important government departments by giving them suitable posts, by introducing them to people who can explain the implicit significance of situations and the subtle ways of dealing with practical realities, and by giving them access to the relevant networks. Throughout their career, colleagues see to it that each group maintains its status and power in the large French industrial firms. Because of their customer-supplier relationships with the state, many may choose high-quality executives from among the senior civil servants.

The French Observatoire des Dirigeants, whose research focuses on the top executives of the two hundred biggest French companies (Bauer and Bertin Mourst 1987), has compiled the information presented in Table 3.1. We do not focus our attention exclusively on the preparation of the "top managers" of the most important firms drawn from the superelite and selected by a very small number of schools. Nor do we concentrate exclusively on the individual careers of certain persons, even if they clearly illustrate the mechanisms and events that most often lead to acquiring the highest posts. We are concerned with analyzing the problem *at the level of the firm*, where the policies and practices for developing executive potential are decided upon and applied.

THE MOST COMMON CHARACTERISTICS IN HIGHFLIER MANAGEMENT

From our studies (Bournois and Roussillon 1997) we may conclude the following:

1. The French approach to the notion of highflier is particularly limited because the concept of potential is seen above all as the ability to rise up within the hierarchy.
2. Performance in previous and present posts is always an indication of the existence of a certain distinctive potential; this performance factor is indispensable, but not in itself sufficient. Corporate commitment, personal ambition, ability to cope with complex

situations, and ability to be identified by the small circle of top team members contribute to the label *high-potential manager*.

3. In France, one of the main functions of the director responsible for executive management consists of organizing the ongoing process for assessing potential rather than setting up scientific potential identification techniques, such as assessment centers, which are commonly used in other countries but are underestimated in France.

4. It must also be noted that the most significant actors in the affair are rarely consulted. In fact, the system suits the executives themselves very well (Livian, Dany, and Sarnin 1992) because they realize that their careers are not very thoroughly managed but consider it normal to have to enact and show initiative as far as advancing their careers are concerned.

THE HISTORICAL PERSPECTIVE

As well as the conclusions resulting from our study, it is important to consider at the historical level, similarly to the method adopted by Chandler (1988), the main means of access to managerial functions.

A condensed analysis of the practices adopted by the large French firms highlights four main periods during which different ways of gaining access to a managerial post appeared. By the term *methods of gaining access* we are referring to the seven methods of access.

These different methods still exist in the firms we have studied; in fact, there are often several methods in the same firm. Table 3.2 shows the period during which a particular method appeared. A bureaucratic period existed before the 1960s; the *competitive exam* and *seniority* were by far the principal means of access in France. Then appeared other methods we have called *stronghold*, the *chosen few, professional, adaptable diversity*, and *searching*. This historical analysis illustrates how important it is to be able to decipher the different methods of reaching top management positions before introducing changes in management development systems.

Technocratic systems are overemphasized in the literature. A new trend is to try to overcome their limitations with more pragmatic and flexible approaches with regard to the new environmental issues.

THE MAIN NEW DEPARTURES

In a general context of open borders and deregulation, the tendencies toward refocusing on the basic functions, development of synergy, and external growth make it necessary for large firms to increase the degree of homogeneity in the different cultures they are concerned with at the various levels—the functional, national, subsidiary, and sectorial. They must all be taken into account.

We must also comment on the main new departures that we have perceived compared with the observations we made at the end of the 1980s and show their relevance to the wider development tendencies manifested by French firms:

Table 3.2
Methods of Gaining Access

	BEFORE THE 1960'S: BUREAUCRATIC PERIOD	1960-1975: SMALL AND MEDIUM-SIZED COMPANY PERIOD	1975-1990: TECHNOCRATIC PERIOD	SINCE 1990: MULTI-FOCUS PERIOD
THE METHOD OF ACCESS	Competitive Exam ("concours")	Stronghold	Chosen Few (selection)	Diversity
PRINCIPAL ACTORS	1 The individual selection mechanisms are derived from the influence of the public sector	1 The "boss" 2 Business pragmatism and informality influence selection	1 The HRD 2 Technocratic tools are used in large multinationals	1 Combination of actors: HRD, top management, the manager himself/herself 2 Greater respect for cultural variety
TOOLS OR MANAGEMENT PROCESSES USED	1 Competitive examinations based on knowledge 2 Career is influenced by rank obtained during examinations	1 No methodology 2 Free choice of people by the boss 3 Revocability	1 Selection tests 2 Succession plans 3 Career reviews 4 Performance centered	1 Meta rules and decentralization 2 Contingent use of tools

Note: A more detailed analysis of these mechanisms appears in Bournois and Roussillon (1997).

1. The difficulties that firms encountered when trying to have a medium-term strategic vision prevents them now from forecasting *predetermined career prospects*.

2. For managers, the barrier executive/nonexecutive is tending to give way to a new barrier, *executive/senior executive, top executive*, and firms are concentrating their effort on preparing senior and top executives.

3. Another barrier is tending to disappear—the one that traditionally separated *leading experts* and *managers*.

4. We are now moving from one precise definition of the criteria used for identifying potential to accepting a *variety of criteria depending on the different situations*—countries, functions, subsidiaries, categories of executives, and others.

5. Instead of the typical career plans organized by the Human Resources Department that all executives were used to, there is now much more weight given to the wishes and characteristics of the executive themselves when building their career path, so executives are now also responsible for their career development, and this assumes *personal and professional projects of their own* (Potel 1997).

6. A fluent command of English as a working language is becoming essential for the great majority of highfliers. It is impossible for their potential to be considered if they do not have a command of this language. This obligation implies, of course, the ability to work in a multicultural team.

And so the systems we see developing tend to maintain the different operating practices and specific methods typical of the countries where the firm is operating. Attempts are being made to add to this diversity by identifying and incorporating the best local practices. Surely this implies that international firms are attempting to strike a balance between respect for local specifications and a sufficient degree of homogeneity in their business practices and concepts, and this at a time when more than half of French firms declare that their outlets are beyond the national borders (Bournois and Roussillon 1996).

NOTES

1. A total of 58,000 salaried CEOs of small to medium-sized firms are included in our figures, whereas official statistics do not include them.

2. For a comprehensive account of the size of the executive population of France, see J-P Ferre (1996), "Qui sont les cadres?" (Who are the executives?) *Bulletin de l'Observatoire des Cadres*, supplement to *Cadres CFDT* 1 (July).

3. The French version of Taylorism; Fayol was an engineer at the beginning of the twentieth century who promoted scientific organization in France.

4. A leading research and consulting institute.

REFERENCES

Aron, R. 1985. *Études sociologiques*, Paris: Presse Universitaire de France.

Barbier, F. 1989. *Le Patronat du nord sous le second empire*. Paris: Eyrolles.

Barsoux, J. L., and Lawrence, P. 1991. *Management in France*. London: Cassell Education.

Bauer, M. 1993. *Les patrons de PME enter le pouvoir, l'entreprise et la famille*. Paris: InterEdition.

Bauer, M., and Bertin Mourot, B. 1987. *Les 200—Comment devient-on un grand patron?* Paris: Seuil.

Boltanski, L. 1982. *Les cadres, la formation d'un groupe social:* Paris: Les éditions de minuit.

Bourdieu, P. 1979. *La distinction, critique sociale du jugement*. Paris: Les éditions de minuit.

Bournois, F. 1991. Gestion des RH en Europe: Données comparées. *Revue Francaise de Gestion* 83: 68–83.

Bournois, F., and Metcalfe, P. 1991. Human resource management of executives in Europe: Structures, policies and techniques. In C. Brewster and S. Tyson, eds. *International Comparisons in Human Resource Management*. London: Pitman.

Bournois, F., and Roussillon, S. 1996. Quid novi pour la gestion et le management des cadres en Europe. *Revue Personnel* March/April:57–62.

Bournois, F., and Roussillon, S. 1997. *Détecter et développer les cadres a haut potentiel*. Paris: Editions d'Organisation.

Burns, P., Myers, A., and Kakabadse, A. 1995. Are national stereotypes discriminating? *European Management Journal* 13(2):212–217.

Chandler, A. 1988. *La main invisible du manager: Une analyse historique*. Paris: Editions Economica.

Gentil, B. 1988. La gestion des resources potentielles en cadres de haut niveau. In *Les enjeux de l'entreprise*. Paris: CEPP:403–406.

Iribarne (d'), Ph. 1989. *La Logique de l'honneur: Gestion des entreprises et traditions nationales*. Paris: Seuil.

Iribarne (d'), Ph. 1991. Review of *Management in France* [Barsoux and Lawrence, 1991]. *Organization Studies* 12(4):610–611.

Jenkins, A. 1988. The French search for a new model of the firm. *Journal of General Management* 14(1):17–29.

Livian, Y.-F., Dany, F., and Sarnin, Ph. 1995. Gestion des carrieres des cadres cue par les cadres en France. Paris: Proceedings of the Association de Gestion de Resources Humaines.

Potel, A. 1997. Le project professionnel au service de l'employabilité. *Gestion 2000* 1 (January/February): 27–43.

Roussillon, S. 1991. Développer les competences de ses collaborateurs. *Revue Personnel* 321 (February): 26–30.

Scott, J. 1995. Les élites dans la sociologie anglo-saxon. In E. Suleiman and H. Mendras, *Be recrutement des elites en Europe* Paris: La Decouverte.

Vovelle, M. 1974. *L'élite ou le mensonge des mots*. Paris: Messidot.

4

Attaining Leadership Positions in France

Sylvie Roussillon

Over the last few years many studies have been conducted in order to analyze the characteristics of economic elites in European countries (Bauer and Mourot 1987; Suleiman and Mendras 1995). They have attempted to create a model of maximum-responsibility jobs by considering factors such as training, capital, and family origin. These questions, which are essentially cultural and sociological, however, fail to consider the mechanisms that determine which individuals rise to high positions in a company.

This chapter examines five models of access to power as observed from the field. Some companies combine several approaches more or less voluntarily and vary according to the country in question. However, this single variable does not explain the preference for one model over another. The psychosocial system used to open the door to promotion is strongly influenced by the sector of activity, the organization of capital (more of a factor in medium-sized companies than in large firms), the links with public office, size, geographical location, and the age of the company; therefore, doubtlessly the management concepts are those of the managers and reflect their beliefs.

We begin by looking at the model of "the chosen few," which is one classically analyzed in literature about human resources, especially the management of high-potential executives. Indeed it is a strategic approach, which has developed tools and methods that can be passed on, whereas the other models are based more on "natural" phenomena that are observed after the fact. Thus we see an approach that acknowledges the impossibility of deliberately controlling all phenomena and considers the choice not to act as itself a choice that allows regulatory mechanisms to develop—mechanisms that are unconscious but active all the same. This choice is only confirmed and maintained insofar as no other pertinent alternative appears.

Each system observed demonstrates strong internal coherence, and so the executives under the system all show a set of qualities and know-how that must be clearly highlighted. In an internal document, "Enterprise et Personnel" (Company and personnel), in 1991, B. Gentil started characterizing three models of career management: administrative, baronial, and technocratic. In all three, he deplored the inability to propose a more egalitarian view of roles in the management of networks that would reveal the informal side.

If we take it literally, the individual chooses to stay and succeed in the firms where he or she is comfortable with the internal dynamism; intrinsic motivation; values of liberty, autonomy, justice, and equality; spirit of criticism and freedom of thought; power; creativity (the list is endless). Then we also admit that each system, by its internal logic, "chooses" the personalities that correspond to its mobilizing values. Furthermore, its way of working reinforces these specific characteristics through the employees' experiences.

A dual process exists for selecting and reinforcing, which we now describe according to the different means of access to managerial posts, concentrating on the skills and values favored through action and regulations. Beyond the justification and ideological techniques of each means we also pay particular attention to the adverse effects of each.

THE CLASSIC MODEL OF "THE CHOSEN FEW"

This model is the most prevalent in American international companies, and Derr et al. describe it accurately in Chapter 1. In this model, the company chooses the best of each segment of the population (junior executives, experienced executives, senior executives, maybe even specialists and executive managers); that means individuals whose results are not only excellent but superior to those of other members are expected to rise through the ranks of the company according to their potential.

This segmentation of the population entails specific treatment (career opportunities, training possibilities, and salary) for those with "potential" in comparison to the other members of the group. The Human Resources Department has a multiple role to play in this procedure as designer of the system, motivator and coordinator of the selection criteria, main player in the selection process, and guarantor of quality, as well as instigator in training and developing the individuals chosen. Often the human resource team plays an important part in planning transfers to coincide with career plans. They often follow up on the high-potential executives individually and influence their career paths more or less directly according to a number of opportunities that lead to diverse experiences: learning to be professional in one activity can lead to a new job; operational positions and positions of responsibility, transfers abroad, responsibility for projects and management all become inevitable steps in the training of the future manager. The strategy to be followed, the selection criteria, the choice of methods, and the career paths chosen are all decided in strict association with general management and department managers. But the impetus behind the system and the follow-up of the individuals are nearly always left to the Human Resources Department, which gives the department a strategic role to play.

As far as the individuals themselves are concerned, their place in this elite is always presented as unstable and dependent on their dedication and quality of results. Companies always insist on this point. In the environment of permanent internal competition they have to keep their distance from other competitors or else be excluded from the list of high potentials. The price to pay is generally seen in assuming a demanding work load, bowing to company demands and accepting its culture, being geographically mobile, and choosing professional life over private life.

In return the individual does not need to concentrate on midterm developments to build a career plan. The personal risk is not about the individual's future, but about the way he or she reacts in the various difficult situations he or she is put in by the company, knowing that there is no room for error. This method is characterized by permanent instability and tension, absence of personal choice, constant evaluation, regular traveling, a desire for power, promotion, and competition. These elements involuntarily give rise to personalities that may display narcissistic tendencies and a forced identification with the firm, which may make the system one likely to choose problematic leaders.

EXAMINATION (TYPICALLY FRENCH MODELS)

The examination system, which is used particularly in France, is a "rite of passage," which clearly differentiates groups of the population by status, right, and duties. Becoming an executive or senior executive is a real competition for which many candidates prepare, although few are successful. Mostly these candidates make an enormous personal effort in their education before they are even presented with the system of differentiation.

This system has been particularly developed in the public services; thus, only the aggregate competitive examination reserved for professors who already have a doctoral degree gives access to jobs of responsibility in medicine, law, or management teaching. The links between top jobs in the government and those in large companies are so powerful that the characteristics of the governmental system are carried over into state-owned companies and strongly influence the private sector as well. It is no surprise then that one of the major banks has a competitive exam for applicants as branch manager that sets the level high. One public organization flooded with applications (four thousand for two hundred jobs, of which 50 percent are filled through internal promotion every year) recently created a competitive exam for the applicants.

These rites of passage often happen at a fixed time and place. The criteria tend to be as clear as possible in order to give an equal chance to all candidates.

Even the unsuccessful candidate benefits from the effort made even if unsuccessful. The candidate is then faced with the difference between his or her self-image, which led to attempting the exam, and the jury's evaluation, which resulted in rejection. For all successful candidates the benefit of the competition is permanent. It allows them to change "castes" or social class and to feel that the competition was the same for everyone (d'Iribarne 1989).

The evaluation criteria in these examinations concern situations outside the domain of work and focus strongly on cognitive elements, which are not necessarily connected to the daily reality of future responsibilities. This means that the aggregate exams in universities and medical schools prepare the individuals for research and teaching through the sheer breadth of knowledge acquired, but certainly not for the management, organization, and political negotiations that will be their daily reality in the managerial positions awaiting them. This procedure highlights intellectual qualities, the capacity to fulfill precise criteria of evaluation, the will for personal progress, individualism, and personal effort. It does not encourage practical qualities, the capacity to manage complex and uncertain situations, nor the team-leading abilities that are nonetheless indispensable at this level of responsibility.

The rules of this system are organized so that the competition is as fair as possible. This presupposes that the individual takes the risk of applying for the exam before proving himself or herself, as with the "chosen few" model. This model corresponds to a society that values stability, a layered representation of hierarchy, and rewarding of individual efforts. The individual belongs to what Ph. d'Iribarne (1989) terms a "condition" with rights and duties that are precisely coded. Belonging to this group is irrefutable and appears justified to the individual and others by success in the exam.

It might seem that the relationship with safety, independence, and freedom is not the same for people who accept and succeed in such a system as for people living in a system of permanent evaluation and insecurity. In the same way, the relationship with challenges and competition is no doubt different.

THE TRADITIONAL MODEL OF SENIORITY

In the seniority method an accident of birth and no account of personal characteristics determines management. In this way it totally eliminates competition and struggle for power—or makes that struggle a fight to the death, as history has often shown. This system puts its trust in the whole social system to train future leaders gradually and to regulate any deficiencies. It means accepting both that the job makes the person and that it is possible to shape a leader, whatever his initial aptitudes, if the training begins very young. Current concepts of social heredity and studies on social reproduction (Bourdieu 1979) tend to bear this out!

Such a model obviously favors patience, respect of the acquired job and tradition, a certain passivity or routine rather than a spirit of initiative and speed. The presentation of the Japanese system shows how it is possible to combine the model of obligation with knowledge of how to create a consensus, knowledge of the company, and recognition by senior managers in order to reach the highest jobs.

This model is increasingly rare in Western companies, but it was commonplace in traditional firms and is still regularly used in promotions. This criterion can indeed be used for a specific category, family, sex, and so on, which is perceived as socially suited for particular functions. It is a model that is easy to set up and indisputable when the company's culture accepts it, and it is one that gives the individual who benefits from it "absolute legitimacy" because it goes beyond the person and his or her acts. Sometimes, the army still functions according to this principle: in the case of a vacancy in the chain of command, the oldest, most highly ranked officer is in charge. Likewise, birthrights existed in France up to the Revolution in 1879, making chance master over individual actions.

Currently in Europe the values of seniority and traditional wisdom linked to age have largely been replaced in companies by those of youth, efficiency, innovation, and change: managers themselves are "old" earlier and earlier, and the age limits for being a manager is regularly lowered in companies, whereas this age limit does not apply in politics, to "owner-employers," members of boards of directors, or the hierarchy within the Catholic church (at least in France). Chapter 10 illustrates how a culture can benefit from this method and its managers, as it does in Japan.

THE PICK-OF-THE-CROP MODEL

The characteristic of the pick-of-the-crop model is the refusal of firms to take responsibility for the preparation of their future managers, whether it be in a purposeful fashion or by default, letting natural forces take their course: they prefer to look for competent people only when they need them, both inside and outside the firm.

It would seem that faced with the limits of high-potential management or the forecasting of future jobs and skills, some companies are falling back on this solution, particularly in the United States: their human resource directors become internal and external "headhunters" (see Chapter 1). Obviously in this model a large number of the firm's managers have pursued a career outside the company in question.

In many French companies an "adviser to the president" exists; the title may vary, but the job is basically to provide an informal memory for the company. The job carries a high level of responsibility in a quasi-managerial position for someone who has been with the company for a long time and knows most of the executives. The adviser is capable of naming the right person for a job from memory, giving an informal but well argued account of the person's skills. The role of the middleman is based on personal influence and not status!

When such an approach is in force, career development is completely up to each individual executive and the only governing factor is the supply and demand of the labor market. The executive has to evaluate the most educational and promising paths to take in order to further his or her career and receives no institutional support in this. This model closely resembles a tournament in which contestants are eliminated in each round.

At first glance this system seems to favor individuals who are capable of acting autonomously, anticipating trends, getting results, and choosing the right projects, and those who know how to demonstrate their capabilities: they can prove these skills in each successive job. Moreover, changing firms frequently develops a capacity to take stock of an organization, integrate its dynamics, work out what the people are like and where the opportunities for development lie, all of which are qualities often required in the modern manager.

However, this process does not develop a feeling of belonging to the firm, nor familiarity with its players, products, markets, or history. The necessity to accumulate positive results and the danger of any counterperformance carry the risk of selecting individualists who do not value their own self-interests above those of their team and who especially focus on the short term to the detriment of a more prospective view. The price to pay for this ephemeral immediacy can be heavy for the firm.

The risks in this model are that the individual may make mistakes and the company may not find the skills it requires at the right time. It is a system that is becoming more widespread, however, particularly in companies that wish to concentrate on their main skills while subcontracting related services. The multiplication of cooperative projects managed by the market rather than by work contracts may even bring into question the necessity for a methodical approach to the preparation of future mangers.

Considering the characteristics of the labor market—unequal, segmented between the structure and protected "in" markets and the secondary and unprotected "out" markets (Bourg 1989), strong mobility and function barriers (Bourg 1989) derived from power struggles designed to maintain the inherent imbalance—this "pick-of-the-crop" model is dependent on mechanisms that favor certain psychological characteristics and competencies of the applicants, which do not necessarily correspond to the requirements of the firm. Good presentational and networking skills are necessary to be successful in this environment, potentially to the disadvantage of some women who may be discriminated against in some networks outside the company (Ibarra 1993).

On the other hand, this type of process leaves room for curiosity and originality, enhancing the extraprofessional values and interest of people wishing personal growth and not simply career development. New family, cultural, and social values can be sought after rather than just professional progress. This model allows for the development of different structures within the company such as associations and worker cooperatives that introduce changes to relations, cooperation, and power sharing that can be rich in innovation (Brunstein 1996).

THE BARONIAL MODEL

The baronial model of preparing future managers is at work in many organizations: managers gather a certain number of junior executives (often those who uncannily resemble them!) who help them in their personal ascension in return for validation of their own career progress. This group evolves together and sometimes breeds feelings of belonging and unity among members. This process emphasizes a middle- to long-term perspective.

The individuals are by no means just numbers whose qualities are incessantly reevaluated by ad hoc committees or who are labeled once and for all by a selection exam. They are known personally by the "boss," who evaluates them over the long haul in a variety of concrete situations, as well as being informally judged by their peers. Loyalty to the boss, submission to his dictates, and allegiance to the group's culture and values are generally guarantees of personal success.

Homogenous beliefs, values, and behavior are necessary to the unity of such a group, and S. Freud's analyses (1913) concerning the role of the boss as spokesperson and medium of identification in a group of peers seem pertinent here. The individuals actually have little freedom and run the risk of becoming courtesans in constant danger of stepping on toes. The dynamics of this approach are organized on a network of interpersonal relations with strong undercurrents and no effort to establish the rules of the game as everyone already knows them! The main player is undoubtedly the superior, who, with the team, controls a field of activity.

Today many companies are trying to limit the power of such baronial methods in order to grant human resource programs a wider view of executive skills, training, and posting to improve control and influence over obscure sectors of the company. This desire for unity is often in the name of a "global optimization" of resources or the necessary development of synergy and cross sections, but the barons and their vassals do not give up without a fight.

This system presents two major risks for the executive: (1) displeasing and being excluded from the group and (2) choosing the wrong leader and stagnating or even regressing. For the firm the system provides a "rich context" (Hall 1979) with many implicit codes, which allow considerable autonomy and power. Unless the boss chooses a new vassal, integration of individuals from other sectors of the company can prove difficult. These baronies nominate individuals for promotion on the basis of services rendered and rewards for loyalty rather than competence and still less on the basis of future requirements. The risk of reproducing clones of the manager, who are psychologically and objectively incapable of opposing him or her, even when it is indispensable, cannot be ignored.

These baronies are often viewed as obstructive by human resource managers, who try to limit their power so that the development of high potentials and transfers may go ahead unhindered.

THE PROFESSIONAL: A GERMAN MODEL

In Germany we come across the professional model. This model is rare in France and it encourages a career within a single company, often in the same job. Individuals' results are constantly evaluated by direct superiors and their chiefs in collaboration with the human resource department. Extensive knowledge of a professional sector and job, the capacity to find a compromise, the progressive development of skills, and a legitimacy that develops gradually lead the individual to the highest positions of responsibility.

International experience would seem to have little influence in this context. This model is closer to the attitude of companies who favor developing their executives' potential rather than selecting executives with potential.

This model gives everyone the time and means to progress and contributes to knowledge of the firm but limits opportunities to learn about other practices and jobs in the company and hinders the rapid ascension of the most brilliant. In fact this system does not seek to set apart an elite but to progress as a whole. It focuses on developing collective skills, creating technical competence, and seeking consensus more than on developing the personal skills of individuals.

In this way several systems for developing future managers can be observed in companies without the use of specific management tools, even if they do happen to use such a traditional method. Each model corresponds to a contract, a set of rules, a promise, possibilities, and specific values that contribute to training and selecting the managers of these different systems.

THE META-MODEL OF DIVERSITY, OR THE MODEL OF DIV-HARMONIZATION

The next model to be examined is that encountered in the large French company Alcatel-Alsthom, which exists in other firms too. This model is mostly found in international companies that have been formed from expansion in the recent past and need to integrate subsidiaries and units from different cultures without losing dynamism.

It is a model that builds on the past (Watzlawick 1978) as it integrates and completes other models already discussed (and that may already wholly or partially exist in a group) without replacing them.

This process is not a system in the sense of the other systems as it focuses on representing the processes that will best complement the practices present in the firm, the firm's strategies, and the necessary development. This meta-model is organized around an understanding of the models already in play and a respect for the variety of approaches, and although it uses certain methods from the "chosen few" concepts, it does not have its universal nature nor the desire for uniformity.

Respect and integration of the different cultural practices in the constitutive subsidiaries of the company are essential in the creation of synergy as a complement to the differences retained. A strong desire for decentralization, respect for autonomy, and local initiative work hand in hand with this model. Pragmatism dictates that there is a minimum that the central power should know, but other than that, decisions remain in the hands of local managers.

This Div-Harmonization model leaves the question of a managerial profile open and rests on the diversity of selection techniques used by different subsidiaries and units. Training, geographical mobility, and networking are used to develop harmony and unity among the managers.

Beyond the specific characteristics of each company that we have mentioned, it is also possible to pinpoint characteristics of this meta-model in several key areas.

- The parent company differentiates between "local" executives in subsidiaries whose careers will remain within that entity and "group" executives, who include directors and future directors as well as international executives and specialists in charge of contributing to the change within the company by sharing their skills.
- The parent company lets the subsidiaries designate "group" executives according to their own specific criteria but ensures that all subsidiaries supply them and discreetly checks the aptitude of the choices from the subsidiary's viewpoint to prevent offloading of undesirables.
- The parent company uses short centralized training courses to inform young executives of the possibilities open to them within the group, thus encouraging initiative among the most audacious.
- On a group level the emphasis is on training rather than identification.
- Group training courses mainly display the following characteristics:
  - Complementary group training programs and subsidiary training programs
  - Intense training and a global vision of the stakes
  - Promotion of executives from a wide spectrum of origins in large numbers so as to provide diversification in the group and better communication between jobs
  - Proposal of a real strategic project in which the trainees are used as internal consultants in working groups, where they will make important recommendations to management or analyze the working practices of different branches performing the same task to encourage the diffusion of the best questions (this project opens up new perspectives and broadens their horizons and networks)
  - An important opportunity for the directors to meet participants, while the latter network and present themselves in order to receive and accept flattering career opportunities

The human resource department tries to influence the qualities developed by certain executives as well as the way they represent the firm's expectations through the choice of training programs, the obligation to work in groups, and the subjects given to participants. The hope is that the executives will extend these messages in their close professional environment through their working

Table 4.1
Five Power Access Models

CORRESPONDING ACCESS ROUTE	CHOSEN FEW	EXAMS	SENIORITY	PICK OF THE CROP	BARONS
MAIN PLAYERS	• The human resource manager or expert • Influence from large American firms	• Born of public administration • Executive chooses to apply	• Players obey rules • Age important	• The executive • The recruiter	• The "boss" • Practical influence of small/mid-sized companies
TOOLS OR MANAGEMENT PROCESS	• Technical tools (plans for succession, career committees) • Objective performance analysis	• Exam • Based on knowledge • Ranking and repercussion on future career	• None	• Evaluation by results • Importance of strategic capacity	• No method • Free choice of people • Revocability
PRINCIPAL CHARACTERISTICS	• The executive taken in hand by a process built for him or her • Statistical approach (identification of a subpopulation with potential in different categories: young, senior, managers, etc)	• Equal opportunity • Meritocracy • Objective evaluation • Postings according to statutes and formal rules • Mandatory mobility	• Total independence • Importance of training and environment	• Personal mobility • Independence and risk of market and competence • Competition	• Dependence on (and by) boss • Global view • Importance of performance • Emulation with teams • Subjectivity and personal relations
REPRESENTATION OF POTENTIAL	• Individual: planned according to company's needs • Approved by experts	• Outlined and known • Approved by exam success	• Unimportant in relation to education • Birthright • Approved by experience	• Not applicable • Only immediately important • Approved by experience	• Random, traced by boss • Approved according to boss's appreciation
SOCIAL DYNAMICS	• Individual progress • "Scientific" • Differentiation from peers • Model of competition at any stage of career	• Rite of passage • Strong stratification by status • Irreversible • Model of competition at time of exam	• Importance of human qualities • Wisdom more important than speed or initiative • Respect	• Network management • Image management • Encourages originality	• Like-minded groups • Importance of "old-boy" network' • Unstable position • Model of seduction

methods. Their own professional success will be interpreted as a validation of the chosen strategies and work methods of the entire company.

The meta-model implies constant reflection on one's limitations in order to perpetuate the dynamics set in motion by the different levels of intervention (or nonintervention!). Indeed this system should not become the only route of access to the top jobs, otherwise one of the six other systems will develop in its place. In its openness to the unforeseen and its expression of unity and diversity, local and global issues, formal and informal methods, this system makes a dynamic coexistence in a field fraught with tension easier by maintaining a balance.

Table 4.1, created with the assistance of Frank Bournois, attempts to highlight the key points of the five models. It is obvious that no company will present a single, stereotyped model as the models used will always be put into the context of the firm's stakes, social, technical, and organizational characteristics, thus necessitating a mix of the different models.

Management literature unsurprisingly concentrates on the instrumentation of career management, particularly the management of potential. This development corresponds particularly to the growth of human resource management between 1975 and 1990.

The limits of the technical centralized homogeneous systems became apparent in the crisis of the 1990s with globalization of companies and markets. They are no longer perceived as capable of meeting the requirements of various environments or ensuring the necessary adaptation and flexibility. Open systems that integrate the different areas of tension have to be invented.

To manage the diversity that characterizes the present period, it is necessary to understand each different route of access to top jobs and appreciate the internal coherence of each type so that a new system can be developed to integrate and complement them. For any given company, this means making changes that can be seen as progress, integrating any breakdowns created in the process of taking stock of its past.

Over and above strategic wills and technical tools, it has been the aim of this study to show how the management process influences the selection and training of future managers. This brief presentation should make it easier to identify the system used in any branch or firm and thus find one's place either as an executive or as an agent of change, if the consequences for actions and skills are not those desired.

Looking at how a company identifies and develops high-potential executives and prepares directions reveals the way it is run in terms of dynamics and influence on behavior and consequently on the training of personnel.

REFERENCES

Bauer, M., and B. Bertin Mourot. 1987. *Les 200: Comment devient-on un grand patron?* Paris: Seuil.

Bourdieu, P. 1979. *La distinction, critique sociale du jugement.* Paris: Minuit.

Bourdieu, P., and J. C. Passeron. 1966. *Les Héritiers: Les étudiants et la culture.* Paris: Minuit.

Bourg, J. F. 1989. Le marché du travail des fest balleurs: Dualisme et rapport Salarial. *Economie et Humanisme* 310: 47–61.

Brunstein, I. 1996. Pour une sociologie de l'activité solidaire. *Les Enjeux de l'Emploi.*

d'Iribarne, P. 1989. *La Logique de l'honneur: Gestion des entreprises et traditions nationales.* Paris: Seuil.

Freud, S. 1913. *Totem et tabous.* Paris: Payot.

Hall, E. T. 1979. Au delà de la culture. Paris: Seuil.

Ibarra, H. 1993. Network centrality, power and innovation involvement. *Academy of Management Review* 36: 471–501.

Roussillon, S., and F. Bournois. 1995. Lyon. *Collection CNRS.*

Suleiman, E., and H. Mendras. 1995. *Le recrutement des élites en Europe*. Paris: La
    Découverte.
Watzlawick, P. 1978. *La réalité de la réalité: Confusion, désinformation, communication*.
    Paris: Seuil.

5

The Management of High Potential— U.K. Perspectives

Noeleen Doherty and Shaun Tyson

In the United Kingdom, high-potential management trainees are often identified by a number of labels including *highfliers, fast trackers*, and *high potentials*. Such individuals are normally recruited from a high-quality graduate population and are often developed rapidly. The underlying assumption is that they will become the future cadre of senior managers, destined to lead the company and are, therefore, essential to future organizational success. Such fast-track recruitment and development for employees believed to have high potential have a long history in the United Kingdom. In the nineteenth century the British Civil Service began the formal process of fast-track recruitment for those civil servants destined for senior policy-making roles. By the 1930s there were well-established management development programs for graduate entrants within "blue chip" private sector companies such as ICI, Courtaulds, and the oil companies. In addition, many "professional" occupations operated a kind of apprenticeship model to foster talent, and the philosophy of recruiting and developing high-potential people became and remained a pervasive practice in many U.K. organizations.

The desire to create a highly qualified work force has been underpinned in the United Kingdom by government policy, designed to promote a rapid increase in the provision of university courses and to encourage more people to seek higher education (Scott-Clarke and Byrne 1995). During the 1990s an increasing number of graduates in the labor market and the "graduatization" of many jobs previously filled by nongraduates led to a glut of prospective candidates and increased competition for high-potential positions. This began to focus attention on the changing nature of the graduate labor market and career opportunities for graduates (Report highlights 1993; Swim or sink 1994).

Prevailing market conditions did appear to have an impact on graduate recruitment trends, but even in the face of recessionary pressures to cut costs and increase effectiveness and efficiency, the financial and human resource investment in the recruitment of high-potential through a graduate recruitment drive remained a priority. The recession of the early 1990s in the United Kingdom resulted in a slight decrease in graduate recruitment. There was an increase in graduate vacancies, conservatively estimated by the Association of Graduate Recruiters (AGR) at about 4.2 percent in 1994 (Thatcher 1994). This cyclical trend continued, with a small reduction in vacancies in 1999. Companies such as Marks and Spencer, which had traditionally recruited a graduate cohort, cut back on recruitment during 1999 (Welch 1999). However, demographic trends and an expansion in demand from all sectors of the economy, together with the continuing significance of graduate populations to longer-term business success, encouraged a growth in numbers of recruits in 2000 and an increase in graduate salaries, four times the rate of inflation (Association of Graduate Recruiters [AGR] 2000). The recruitment process is becoming more complex with fewer opportunities on dedicated graduate schemes but many graduates finding a route into companies through the general recruitment drives (AGR 2000). Graduate recruitment has been aided also by the growing use of the Internet in recruitment in the United Kingdom (RCI 2000). The structured and systematic recruitment of significant numbers of candidates is facilitated by the Internet as it is highly suited to managing information such as qualifications, details of degree level, major subjects studied, and personal aspects of the curriculum vitae (CV).

THE FAST-TRACK ROUTE

Traditionally, the management of high potential has been based on a rational long-term career philosophy. This philosophy relied on the notion of career as hierarchical, whereby people were often assisted by rapid development, supported by succession planning, and rewarded by ever-improving income prospects. This system drove the human resource strategies, policies, and practices that have been designed to identify, select, recruit, induct, train, develop, reward, and manage the careers of high-potential people. However, organizations have faced many changes as a result of environmental pressures and internal reorganization. Within the labor market there has been a move toward short-term contracts and a casualization of managerial work. It is now common to find temporary executives and "interim managers" in previously permanent senior positions. There has been an increase in midcareer change; increased flexibility in working hours; more work intensification and home working; entry of more women in the ranks of graduate trainees; flatter organizational structures, with more self-employment, Europeanwide working; and new occupations. But with these changes have come greater uncertainty, fear, and stress.

These changes in organizational life have produced changes in the concept of career (Adamson, Doherty, and Viney 1998). There has been a general reorientation of the employment relationship with different definitions of career. This has led to more fluid career progression and varying opportunities for career development, and shifting career prospects for all employees (Goffee and Scase 1992; Stroch and Reilly 1994; Herriot and Pemberton 1995). There have been shifts from careers to jobs, from long-term to the short- and medium-term employment terms, which now include a range of "deals" and contracts for all. The fundamental nature and impact of these changes were becoming apparent throughout the 1990s (Hirsh and Jackson 1996; Jackson et al. 1996; Herriot and Pemberton 1996; Arnold 1997).

It has been suggested that there has been a shift in psychological contracts between employer and employee (Herriot 1995; Herriot et al. 1997). The deal of the 1970s was loyalty and compliance by the individual, repaid by security and promotion from the organization. The contracts of the 1990s, however, focused on individual accountability, flexibility, and long hours, in return for a job (not a career). Herriot has argued that in the future, the psychological contract will be based on a trade-off between the employee's willingness to be flexible and intention to leave and the employer's offering "employability" and flexible contracts, in return. The employability deal produces benefits to the individual through experience and development, which improve the CV and personal career prospects. Thus, many organizations are no longer offering security and a job for life in return for loyalty and commitment. This negation of the *old deal* has impacted noticeably on senior managers and professionals who have until now enjoyed the security of a psychological contract that was based on mutual commitment and trust over the long term (Herriot and Pemberton 1995, 1996). As a consequence, career management policies and practices within organizations are reflecting these changes (Hirsh, Jackson, and Jackson 1995).

The initially slow move toward "objective" criteria in the selection of high-potential staff, in particular within the Civil Service, shifted the concentration away from "Oxbridge" graduates (Fulton Report 1968). Other changes to fast-track development schemes that have been driven by the widespread appointment of better educated staff to all levels, many with first degrees, included the acceptance that existing staff could be seen as having the same potential for development as graduate recruits appointed to management training schemes (HMSO 1993; HMSO 1994; Clarke, Wiseman, and Graven 1994).

For the individual regarded as being high potential, we can characterize the changes from recruitment for long-term development to a system of recruitment into a pool from which some will rise to senior management roles. One might anticipate a corresponding shift in attitudes to career. The old definition of career as "the image of oneself in process," in Everett C. Hughes's (1937) words, reminds us of the importance of self-image derived from career status and the relationship between the objective and the subjective career. More recently, Jackson, Arnold, Nicholson, and Watts (1996) emphasized the importance of the notion of career as a way of facilitating individual development over time. Thus, the expectation of a "career," based on long-term development with progression through a series of roles and positions that guarantee improving income prospects, is closely associated with personal development and the context of "self." In contrast, the organizational context of uncertainty about future labor force needs and the new perspectives on career threaten to undermine organizationally derived self-concepts. There is a time lag between awareness of this reality and the expectations of graduate hopefuls on university campuses (Modic 1989; Lockwood, Teevan, and Walters 1992).

As career research entered the 1990s, theorists argued that the major focus of attention for organizations would be the effective integration of career development programs with corporate strategy and individual career strategies (Feldman 1989). This required synergy in recruitment drives, matching recruitment efforts with human resource planning and succession planning requirements and with the needs of individuals. The subsequent revolution in labor markets, employment structures, organizational practices, and educational provisions led to the suggestion that careers were in a state of profound change (Jackson et al. 1996). Within the organizational context such changes meant a rethinking of the management of careers across all levels, not least for those who are the high-potential managers of the future.

In both public and private sector U.K. organizations, recruiting and developing high-potential people remain a pervasive practice. High intellectual ability and the potential to develop managerial and interpersonal skills are the core competencies needed in such individuals. These needs have focused attention on the identification and recruitment of graduates as the pool of talent, which will be developed for future managerial positions (Strebler and Pike 1993). However, many organizations now wish to devote their resources to a broader population, to develop potential in all their employees, while still identifying those who are high performers through appraisal schemes, as, for example, in the case of Procter and Gamble. This debate is reflected in the question of whether development center or assessment center approaches are to be used. Perhaps the practice of not publishing the names of high potentials helps the company to prevent the self-fulfilling prophecy.

There is a related need to maintain the motivation of high-potential staff. To meet this need British and other European companies use a range of techniques. These include secondments (temporary assignments to gain experience, not necessarily in the same company) and opportunities to attend special training/education programs such as sponsored MBA programs. High remuneration or more extensive fringe benefits and opportunities to learn, including more latitude in making mistakes, and opportunities for challenging work, for example, running a small business unit at an earlier stage than most managers, are offered.

HUMAN RESOURCE PLANNING

Fundamental to fast-track recruitment is the need for business planning and succession planning which is tandem with a strategic vision for the organization

Figure 5.1
Civil Service Fast-Stream Recruitment Model

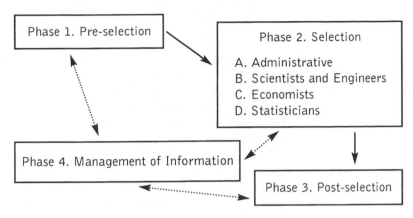

that shapes the requirement for fast-track populations. Rothwell (1995) suggested that human resource planning, although an essential feature of human resource management (which should match estimates of demand and supply from external and internal sources), has been given a low priority as a result of economic uncertainty. She suggested that there is a long-standing need for more effective planning for people, yet there is little empirical evidence to suggest that rigorous planning is being undertaken to any extent. The apparent lack of human resource planning may be a consequence of the degree of global change impacting on organizations currently or as a result of the reality of organizational life, which is ever changing. However, a high-potential philosophy is underpinned by the development of potential from within and as such requires human resource planning and succession planning strategies that identify how many people are needed for senior roles and the competencies required for the future. Also, the effective planning of such movement within the organization and the development of individuals require tracking and monitoring of attrition rates and of achievements as people progress.

Personnel management in the U.K. Civil Service has been based on a model of best practice with policies and practices often in advance of those in organizations in the private sector. Many organizations in the private sector have emulated these models and adopted practices initiated in the public sector (Doherty 1994). There have also been attempts to adapt and integrate private sector practices into the public sector (Morley 1993). The rigor with which the public sector addresses fast-track recruitment highlights many of the issues around the management of this population. The Fast-Stream Recruitment process in the Civil Service is illustrated by the model shown in Figure 5.1. At the preselection stage, the Recruitment Service manages information, which stems from the feedback from previous selection exercises, allowing adjustment of advertisements, criteria, and process. After the selection exercises, the outcomes are also reviewed, to see how the quality of the candidates and the processes match up to the requirements. These key elements of policy and practice remain central to the management of high potentials.

RECRUITMENT AND SELECTION

Selection and assessment are increasingly seen as critical to large-scale processes of organizational change (Iles and Salaman 1995). Organizations seek to recruit and select staff in order to support the achievement of strategic objectives. It is argued that the recent changes in organizational systems and structures are commonly associated with the search for recruits from within or outside with new attitudes, skills, and experiences, as organizations make significant changes in their key competencies. Recruitment and selection are components of one set of strategies that are increasingly important to the delivery of results that will support organizational strategies. The managerial competencies approach, it is argued, fundamentally influences any return on investment in both human and material capital.

Competencies are typically defined as the personal characteristics required to perform a job effectively. Since the days of Boyatzis (1982), there has been a continuing interest in the definition of high performance through competence language (Tyson 1988; Jacobs 1989). The systems for selecting highfliers frequently utilize assessment-center techniques, in which the predesigned exercises are intended to reveal whether or not the candidate possesses the competencies required for high potential. The problem with such approaches is that there is a presupposition that these competencies can be determined, although it is difficult for future performance to be established from existing performance. The degree of change is now so rapid that there is no method for determining which future competencies would be needed (Fulmer 1993). The way around this problem has often been to move to generic, broad competencies, which are person- rather than job-centered, such as "critical thinking abilities," "tolerance of uncertainty," and "interpersonal skills." These abstract qualities, such as Shell's famous "helicopter quality"—the ability to oversee all major management areas and to see how they interrelate—have been used by some organizations for many years.

Research on twenty U.K. organizations, including British Gas and W. H. Smith, which recruit a large number of graduates, was conducted by the Human Resource Research Centre at Cranfield School of Management (Doherty, Viney, and Adamson 1995, 1997). There was a great deal of convergence in the methods and processes used in recruitment and selection as 90 percent of participating companies used the "Milk Round" process, whereby selection teams visit colleges and universities to present the career opportunities for fast-track graduates, with the intention of attracting high-potential students who are about to graduate. This is traditionally the main recruitment effort to attract graduates. Some organizations were selective in the universities they targeted. Rather than a blanket effort they focused on specific centers of expertise in relevant subjects and concentrated recruitment efforts with these specific universities. Also, by the late

1990s, the dramatic expansion of higher education and changes in the graduate population required campus recruitment programs on an ongoing basis (Arkin 1999).

The issue of obtaining the level of quality required was the focus of attention in the recruitment process since the graduatization of the labor market had resulted in a very-wide-quality spectrum. Organizations were looking for a needle in a haystack, which had become bigger. This is a trend that has persisted. In 1999 employers were reported to be finding that many graduates still did not have the vital skills required (Moody 1999).

Doherty, Viney, and Adamson (1995, 1997) drew attention to the seemingly subtle shift in what graduates were being offered. Although over three-quarters of the companies studied had not explicitly changed their fast-track philosophy, many appeared to be subtly changing their career management philosophy. Over a third indicated that they did not use the term career or had no definition of career. A subtle change in emphasis had moved the offer away from the guarantee of a career to the offer of a long-term opportunity. Graduates were being offered the conditions under which they could increase their employment capacity and enhance their commercial value in the marketplace, which were embodied in the notions of continuous employability, marketability, and adding of value to the business. The emphasis in the language focused on development and opportunity as the key phrases for graduates.

Many organizations were striving to be more frank and honest about what they were offering, trying to convey an impression of organization culture: what it is like to work here and the way we do things around here. This was an attempt to communicate more realistic expectations to graduates, a major challenge for these organizations. The majority of companies also reflected a more discriminating approach to the management of graduates, indicating that they did not actively encourage an *élitist* culture, in order to reduce the differentiation between fast-track populations and other managerial populations. Hence, there was a growing emphasis on graduates' being recruited into real jobs and a move for some to fixed term as opposed to permanent contracts.

This research indicated that companies were attempting to shift the nature of the psychological contract for high-potential employees to a new deal that embodied different expectations from the organization and a different offer of employment. The nature of the new psychological contract is one of a transaction rather than a relationship, with more explicit offers and expectations from the organization (Herriot and Pemberton 1995).

High potentials are an increasingly discerning pool of individuals, who may view this new deal as an opportunity for training and development and use it as a stepping stone in their personal career development, with no commitment or loyalty to the company. Previous work has uncovered an increasing number of violations of the psychological contract that created unmet expectations among graduate management populations, leading to a lack of trust, lower satisfaction, and greater intentions to leave the organization (Robinson and Rousseau 1994). The balance of power appears to have shifted away from the employer and toward the employee. Employees, particularly those with appropriate technical skills and expertise, are now being aggressively headhunted, offered "golden handshakes," for example, in the form of share options and shorter routes to partner status to tempt them into companies (Gracie 2000).

Paradoxically, organizations need to engender some sense of organizational commitment in order to reap the return on investment in high potentials as future assets (Viney, Adamson, and Doherty 1997). Organizations in the United Kingdom now face the challenge of maintaining a high-potential philosophy within the constraints of structure and opportunity, in order to strike a workable deal for both the organization and the high-potential individual. Traditional graduate recruiters such as banks and consultancies are now reintroducing longer-term career development packages to stem the drain of talent to the new dot-coms and to encourage the graduate recruit to commit to the company for a specified period (Gracie 2000).

The management of high potential and the changes impacting on organizational policy and practice are clearly highlighted by the case of the Midland Bank (see Text Case 5.1).

WILL THE "HIGH-POTENTIAL" CONCEPT SURVIVE?

From our discussion so far there are many pressures that raise questions within organizations about the future of those policies that seek to develop high-potential managers through a fast track. The changing nature of careers is not just a consequence of flatter structures and business uncertainty. The reciprocal response from those who believe they can sustain their own career concept independently of an organization—those who have bought into the "employability" bargain, who are likely by definition to have the most to offer in the conventional sense—is to take control of their own destinies. These people are the intellectually able, in their twenties and thirties, who can build their careers between organizations.

The portfolio career is a legitimate aim for such individuals when they reach their forties and fifties, by which time they will have gained a wide range of experience, a network of contacts, and insight from their own experiential development. These are the high potentials for whom fast-track schemes were designed and developed but who now no longer need organizations to manage their careers. They are the population that has been taught how to survive in the corporate jungle and how to do "deals" as a way of achieving a sense of career within the changing organizational context. It could be argued that such bright stars will not remain as committed company men and women.

However, the demand for good corporate citizens remains. Promotion potential is prized, developed, and utilized in many large organizations, from the Civil Service to Shell, the big banks, insurance, and other blue chip companies, and many senior managers seem to continue to strive to find suitable successors.

Text Case 5.1
The Management of High Potential at Midland Bank

MANAGING HIGH POTENTIAL IN THE MIDLAND BANK

Before the merger with the Hong Kong Shanghai Banking Corporation (HSBC), Midland Bank had a traditional view of career as a job for life with hierarchical progression. This approach to career operated within a self-development ethos that promoted individual responsibility for career development and progression with local patronage and sponsorship. HSBC on the other hand have operated a more centrally driven and directive approach to career management, an approach that is now being adopted within Midland. The career strategy/policy of Midland is now essentially a dual-career system with different policies for managers and nonmanagers. The general philosophy is to create all-around general bankers with the objective of growing managerial talent from within. The careers of managers (middle and senior) are managed from the center, while all nonmanagerial employees are managed at the functional level by line managers within branches of the bank, who are responsible for career reviews and discussions.

There are a range of methods of recruitment, selection, induction, training and development to meet the needs of different populations of employees. All graduates join the Midland Executive Training Program, a year-round recruitment program. However, this program is also open to nongraduates who can fulfill the selection criteria, providing the opportunity to identify and develop talent across all employees, to generate a group of potential managers with appropriate skills throughout the organization. Assessment of potential is based on the demonstration of job-specific skills and competencies as outlined in the Jobs Guide, a comprehensive profile of the competencies and training and development required for all positions within the bank.

Line managers identify high potentials against a list of criteria: scope for growth, capacity to take on responsibility, value to the business, unique skills and breadth of skills. Employees are judged against these criteria and divided into quartiles. A team of senior directors and business managers (the Executive Development Forum) monitors the development of individuals in the upper quartile. Such high potentials are supported in their development in both professional and nonbanking skills. A central data base of information on managerial groups is used to create profiles of high-potential individuals that can be matched against vacancies within the business.

Source: By permission of the Midland Bank.

Succession plans are not now just a matter for a few senior executives at the top. The management development activity, if there is a central human resource (HR) function, is usually charged with the responsibility of ensuring that there is a pool of talent available in all the strategically important business areas such as marketing, finance, and operations management. Without a high-potential concept this could only be achieved through the management of a sophisticated internal labor market, with all the attendant policies on appraisal, assessment, and development. Such policies if applied throughout the organization are only able to help the "cream rise to the top" if all line managers are actively involved in the process, as reported by Poole and Jenkins (1996). In a major survey, they found that managers have "more responsibility than personnel/human resource departments for most training and development issues" (1996, 9). The increasing use of 360-degree appraisal schemes means there are wider constituencies involved with evaluating the performance of high potentials, sometimes across national boundaries.

Our doubts about the survival of the high-potential concept rest on trends that are influencing many of the changes in career and career management. There is a move to take responsibility for one's own career and life while the notion of the corporate self is changing. Alongside these there is a clear move to line management's assuming responsibility for all the major human resource management practices. These trends focus on individual responsibility and autonomy. These remain only doubts, as the need for succession is very powerful and top management still views this as essential for the continuance of the company. The recruitment, development, and management of high potentials seem to be among the most likely functions to retain the support of the top management team (Tyson 1995).

The reconciliation of these potentially conflicting forces, the desire for the control over one's own future and development and the corporate need to control the careers of high potentials, may be achieved by policies that encompass life-long learning, career breaks, sabbaticals, secondments, horizontal development, and challenging learning programs. The concept of the corporate self now includes personal assets such as knowledge, skills, contacts, family-friendly resources, and liabilities such as mortgages, debts, personal failings, and skill deficits, all of which imply an instrumental attachment to work. But this fits well within the current concept of organizational career. Organizations are becoming looser confederations of interests, with indeterminate boundaries between suppliers, staff, customers, and shareholders. Pluralities of competing interests and shifting alliances now constitute the organization. Who will be better placed to cope in such an environment than the inner-directed, instrumentally motivated, high-potential individual, who builds his or her own career by taking advantage of the development opportunities of job enlargement, broadly defined career progression, and continuous learning and then moves on to new adventures elsewhere?

REFERENCES

Adamson, S. 1997. Career as a vehicle for the realization of self. *Career Development International* 2(5):245–253.

Adamson, S., N. Doherty, and C. Viney. 1998. The meanings of career revisited: Implications for theory and practice. *British Journal of Management* 9(4):251–259.

Arkin, A. 1999. Campus Mentis. *People Management* 5(2):38.

Arnold, J. 1997. *Managing Careers into the 21st Century*. London: Paul Chapman Publishing.

Arthur, M. B., D. T. Hall, and B. S. Lawrence, eds. 1995. *Handbook of career theory*. 4th ed. Cambridge: Cambridge University Press.

Association of Graduate Recruiters. 2000. *Graduate salaries and vacancies 2000*. Warwick: AGR.

Boyatzis, R. E. 1982. *The Competent Manager: A Model of Effective Performance*. London: John Wiley.

Clarke, D., L. Wiseman, and I. Graven. 1994. *Review of east stream recruitment*. London: Cabinet Office OPSS, HMSO.

Doherty, N. 1994. Managers of the future: Public and private sector strategies for fast stream recruitment. *British Academy of Management Conference*. Lancaster. September.

Doherty, N., C. Viney, and S. Adamson. 1995. *What is on offer? The graduate career management challenge*. Human Resource Research Centre Report. Cranfield University School of Management.

Doherty, N., C. Viney, and S. Adamson. 1997. Rhetoric or reality: Shifts in graduate career management. *Career Development International* 2(4):173–179.

Feldman, D. C. 1989. Careers in organizations: Recent trends and future directions. *Journal of Management* 15(2):135–156.

Fulmer, R. M. 1993. Anticipating learning: The seventh strategic imperative for the 21st century. *Journal of Management Development* 12(6).

Fulton Report. 1968. *Committee on the Civil Service*, Vol. 1 report. London: Command 3638 HMSO.

Goffee, R., and R. Scase. 1992. Organizational change and the corporate career: The restructuring of managers' job aspirations. *Human Relation* 45:363–385.

Gracie, S. 2000. Share options, designer offices, company flexible hours—employees want it all. *Director* 53(121):40–46.

Herriot, P. 1992. *The Career Management Challenge: Balancing Individual Needs and Organizational Needs*. London: Sage.

Herriot, P. 1995. The management of careers. In S. Tyson, ed. *Strategic Prospects for HRM*, pp. 184–205. London: IPD.

Herriot, P., W. E. G. Manning, and J. M. Kidd. 1997. The content of the psychological contract. *British Journal of Management* 8(2):151–162.

Herriot, P., and C. Pemberton. 1995. *New Deals: The revolution in managerial careers*. Chichester: John Wiley and Sons.

Herriot, P., and C. Pemberton. 1996. Contracting careers. *Human Relations* 49(6):757–790.

Hirsh, W., and C. Jackson. 1996. *Strategies for career development: Promise, practice and pretence*, IES Report 305. Brighton.

Hirsh, W., C. Jackson, and C. Jackson. 1995. *Careers in organizations: Issues for the future*, Brighton. IMS Report 287.

HMSO. 1993. *Career management and succession planning study*. London: Efficiency Unit Cabinet Office.

HMSO. 1994. *The Civil Service continuity and change*. White Paper. London.

Hughes, E. C. 1937. Institutional office and the person. *American Journal of Sociology* 43:404–413.

Human Resource Research Centre. 1993. *A study examining the feasibility of market testing recruitment to the Civil Service fast stream*. Report presented to the First Civil Service Commissioner.

Iles, P., and G. Salaman. 1995. Recruitment, selection and assessment. In J. Storey, ed. *Human Resource Management: A Critical Text*. London: Routledge.

IMS. 1992. Large firms losing their grip on graduate market. *Personnel Management* 24(11):85.

Inkson, K., and T. Coe. 1993. *Are Career Ladders Disappearing*? London: Institute of Management,

Jackson, C., J. Arnold, N. Nicholson, and A. G. Watts. 1996. *Managing careers in 2000 and beyond*. IES Report 304. Brighton.

Jacobs, R. 1989. *Assessing management competencies*. Ashridge: Ashridge Management Research Group.

Kanter, R. M. 1989. The new managerial work. *Harvard Business Review* 67(6):85–92.

Lockwood, J., P. Teevan, and M. Walters. 1992. *Who's managing the managers? The reward and career development of middle managers in a flat organization*. London: Institute of Management Research Report, Institute of Management/ER Consultants.

Modic, S. J. 1989. Motivating without promotions. *Industry Week* 238(12):24–27.

Moody, M. 1999. Back to basics: We expect today's graduates to be tomorrow's high flyers, but employers are still finding that new graduates do not have the vital skills. *The Director* 53(2):31.

Morley, D. 1993. Strategic direction in the British public sector. *Long Range Planning* 6(3):77–86.

Nystrom, P. C., and A. W. McArthur. 1989. Propositions linking organizations and career. In M. Arthur, D. Hall, and B. Lawrence, eds. *Handbook of Career Theory*, pp. 490–505. Cambridge: Cambridge University Press.

Pool, M. and G. Jenkins. 1996. *Back to the line? A survey of managers' attitudes to human resource management issues*. IM Research Report.

RCI. 2000. *The recruitment confidence index special report on Internet recruitment*. Cranfield School of Management, Daily Telegraph and TMP (worldwide).

Report highlights need for rethink over traditional career paths for graduates. 1993. *Personnel Management* 25(4):79.

Robinson, S. L., and D. M. Rousseau. 1994. Violating the psychological contract: Not the exception but the norm. *Journal of Organizational Behaviour* 15:245–259.

Rothwell, S. 1995. Human resource planning. In J. Storey, ed. *Human Resource Management: A Critical Text*. London: Routledge.

Routledge, C., and C. Elliot. 1982. Organizational mobility and career development. *Personnel Review* 11(3):11–17.

Sadler, P. 1993. *Managing talent: Making the best of the best*. London: Economist Books.

Scott-Clark, C., and C. A. Byrne. 1995. Degree of dismay. *The Sunday Times* (London), 28 May.

Steele, B., J. Bratkovich, and T. Rollins. 1990. Implementing strategic redirection through the career management system. *Human Resource Planning* 13(4)241–263.

Storey, J., ed. 1995. *Human resource management: A critical* text. London: Routledge.

Strebler, M., and G. Pike. 1993. Shortlisting the best graduates. *Institute of Manpower Studies Report* 253.

Stroch, L., and A. Reilly. 1994. Making or buying employees: The relationship between human resources policy, business strategy and corporate re-structuring. *Journal of Applied Business Research* 10(4):12–18.

Swim or sink is the harsh world for the high-flyer reveals future top managers survey, 1994. *Journal of Managerial Psychology* 3:ii–v.

Thatcher, M. 1994. Statistics conceal the full extent of the recovery in graduate jobs, AGR told. *Personnel Management* August: 63.

Tyson, S. 1988. Detecting management training needs by examining management qualities. In S. Tyson, K. F. Ackermann, M. Domsch, and P. Joynt, eds. *Appraising and Exploring Organizations*, pp. 178–194. London: Croom Helm.

Tyson, S. 1995. *Human resource strategy: Towards a general theory of HRM*. London: Pitman.

Viney, C., S. Adamson, and N. Doherty. 1997. Paradoxes of fast track career management. *Personnel Review* 26 (3):174–186.

Welch, J. 1999. Marks and Spencer axes its graduate program. *People Management* 5(11): 14.

6

Highfliers in Germany

Michel Petit and Christian Scholz

INTRODUCTION

The concept of executive highfliers or high-potential executives[1] is currently being used in scientific publications in Germany. Recent publications on human resource management in Germany deal with the topic, especially in terms of the dramatic change from old economy to new economy. But for a long time, business managers tended to be generally reserved about the use of this term. So does this mean that the notion, which is the central theme of this present book, has no place in the Federal Republic of Germany? Indeed, such a claim would oversimplify the situation. Our aim in this chapter is to show that in Germany the situation reveals a variety of different tendencies.

First, we attempt a definition. Many Germans, at the first encounter, automatically associate the notion of executive highflier with that of an elite. In addition, the notion of executive in Germany requires a clear definition. We will show that the notion of high potential contains a double ambiguity.

Second, we describe certain guidelines for high-potential management within the area of industrial policy. The contemporary German firm is very committed to the concept of functioning within "fair partnerships" (*Partnerschaft*). They seek to ensure equality of opportunity both in training and promotion, while acknowledging the slow but sure transformation of values that is taking place at the different levels of the firm.

Third, we present and comment on the empirical facts met with in career management within German firms. The main emphasis is on those who have executive responsibility.

Within German companies, ensuring the supply of first-rate management executives is a major concern. But the question may well be asked whether the creation of a specific category of highflier executive corresponds to basic German managerial values.

PROBLEMS OF DEFINITION

What Is the Situation of the Elite in Germany?

We get a definite general impression from our discussions with human resources managers from large German companies, who prove to be rather reserved when the term highfliers is used for executives. For them this term is largely associated with an elitist notion. Now, as soon as elitist concepts are mentioned, the foreign interviewer detects a feeling of vague uneasiness, sometimes even distrust, among many German managers. Sometimes they simply reject the notion. Let us attempt to define the reasons for this attitude and to examine the validity of such an association between highflier and elite.

The Painful Aftermath of the Second World War

The ideological and material collapse of the Third Reich left Germany with a gaping wound and gave rise to the most anguished doubts. How could Germany sink to such a level? Who bears the blame for this historic catastrophe and its unspeakable atrocities? On what basis can the future be conceived?

Germans soon developed a distrust of everything: of the German language perverted by Nazi propaganda and ideology, of certain great philosophers who had been glorified by the national socialist movement, and, of course, of those members of the elite who had approved of this perverted system or who, through lack of perception or courage, had allowed this terrible mechanism to get under way. So all groups constituting an elite were regarded with shame: the intellectual and scientific elite, the political elite, the economic elite, the military elite, and so on. They were accused of failing to enlighten the nation culturally, and above all of failing to build up an opposing force. In this respect, they had shared, up until the Second World War, in the great prestige that power and authority (*Obrigkeit*) had enjoyed in Germany since Martin Luther (1483–1546), the founder of Protestantism.

In short, the Germans[2] put into doubt the whole of their cultural heritage, and abroad people suspected all Germans, without taking into account the passionate debates that took place in Germany about the very foundations of democracy. This debate is still going on, questioning the legitimacy of power, the efficacy of counterchecks and of opposition power, as well as the respect due to all human beings. It has led to an unfavorable image of any elite.

After the Second World War, the Germans were indeed alone in two senses: they were cut off from their own culture and despised by the rest of the world. Yet they had to keep going.

The Premises of the German Miracle

German reconstruction was based on the economy, built up on an industrial foundation much less destroyed by the war and the bombings than is generally believed. Of course, most firms had participated greatly in the Nazi war effort; their managers had been forced to cooperate with the Nazis; some did so voluntarily, others to save their skins. Many managers were reinstated (Berghahn 1990, 125), because qualified executives were scarce and the cold war was threatening, which considerably slowed up the "denazification" process being carried out by the Allies, particularly the Americans.

In short, this renaissance of the German economy was to involve neither the reinstating of cartels that had dominated Germany since the beginning of the century nor a return to authoritarian management methods stemming from Prussian military traditions. The new German economy was to be built up on an original synthesis of certain cultural elements and some borrowed from other economic and industrial traditions imported from America.

It was no longer a question of an elite, but of a spirit of professionalism and cooperation centered on research and development, of technology, of the deutsche mark, and of the control of inflation and the trade balance. Industrialists and business leaders behaved with the greatest discretion and reserve, both in politics and in the world of the media.[3]

Matters have changed over the last two decades. There are in Germany now a certain number of very charismatic business leaders. It is nonetheless true that economic decision makers tend to keep clear of politics, the influence of the state and of its civil servants.[4]

The Uncertainties Bound up with the Elite

The notion of a leadership elite involves two types of qualifications: (1) the legitimacy of an elite, and (2) membership in the elite.

An elite is the result of a dichotomy that appears in a social group; there are the "best" and the "less good." What basis of selection has been used? Certain bases can today be considered outmoded or unsuitable, for example, birth or privilege. Others are quite normally applied: academic results or acceptance by some professional group. At the academic level, such a dichotomy logically involves a separation of the education system into two parts: the privileged highways leading to an elite and the less prestigious ways that lead away from it. And who can prove that the so-called privileged highways are really the best ways possible? And who is up to reforming them? Only those who have been along them, and who therefore belong to the elite. The elite who are the judges of the system that conferred on them the status of elite are also the judged! For this very reason, such a system can become closed on itself and give rise to mediocrity.

The elite is composed of individuals with a level of performance distinctly superior to the average. But how long will they maintain this standard of energy and motivation? Such may vary greatly over a whole professional lifetime. Can one—indeed should one—be excluded from an elite if one's performance falls off? In theory, yes, but in fact, what happens in reality is quite different. In practice, an elite creates an esprit de corps, an association that ensures solidarity among its members, whom it defends against the rest of society.

In short, an elite tends to perpetuate itself without being able to reform itself and so runs the risk of becoming a caricature of itself. In this case, it loses its legitimacy (its excellence) and since it is not subject to democratic control, it becomes dangerous.

Surely the solution is to reject the notion of a leadership elite. Many Germans agree with this conclusion and advocate an education system, both secondary and university, that is adaptable, accessible, and flexible. Thus they are opposed to the creation of "Grandes Ecoles" in the French sense, whose "old boy" associations try to monopolize prestigious jobs, in both the public and private sectors.[5]

For these same Germans, the firm should behave with the same objectivity as the education system. No distinction should be made a priori between the graduates of any university-level institution; and, what is more, opportunities should be given to employees who are graduates of short training courses (apprentices, for example) to go on to longer, higher training courses to give them access to higher places in the hierarchy. Such a system exists in a number of firms in Germany. We give an example later in the chapter.

Are Highfliers an Elite?

In Germany, the suspicion and rejection that were obvious in the case of certain of those whom we interviewed seemed to stem from the association of the notions of highfliers and elites. We attempted to show that this association of ideas is largely due to the consequence of major historical events that were specific to postwar Germany.

To consider highflier executives as necessarily an elite seems exaggerated to us, as long as certain conditions are applied:

• It is to be a transitory state, and so limited in time.
• This status may/must be repealed if not justified by results.
• It is not the only way of rising to top executive posts, only a way of speeding up the careers of those who are eligible and willing.
• The existence of high-potential executives is not justifiable for its own sake; it depends on a management strategy aimed at developing new and important qualities.
• The management of high-potential executives must be part of a differentiated system of career management. Under no conditions should it be the only method for the development of executive careers.

Between highfliers and an elite, the discussion is far from over, and the arguments put forward are rich in interest. But in any case, the essential point at issue is the capacity to ensure a supply of top business managers. This can no doubt be done in different ways, and, in this respect Germany occupies a rather original position that we are now going to explain.

The Concept of Executive (*Führungskraft*)

The system applied in Germany divides the active population into five categories, by the criterion of "professional position held" (*Stellung im Beruf*): Those who are independent (*Selbständige*) (about 9 percent); paid family members (*Mithelfende Familienangehörige*) (about 2 percent); public servants (*Beamte*) (about 9 percent); employees (*Angestellte*) (about 41 percent); and workers (*Arbeiter*) (about 39 percent).

The category employees is subdivided into ordinary employees, intermediate employees, superior employees, and leading employees (*leitende Angestellte*).

The notion of executive (*Führungskraft*) really corresponds to a subgroup within the employee category. The limits of this subgroup are not very clearly defined.

Only the leading employees are specifically defined in the law concerning the internal organization of firms (*Betriebsverfassungsgesetz*) of 1972, modified in 1988. The criteria used in the definition (Welge 1992, 939–941) are partly based on management concepts (hiring and firing of staff, capacity to act in the name of the firm, responsibility for the defining and applying of company strategy) and partly based on remuneration. The leading employees also have a special body to represent them within the firm known as the spokesmen committee (*Sprecherausschuss*), which is part of the Participation in Management scheme (*Mitbestimmung*).

So the executives as such are not very clearly defined, even though the term (*Führungskraft*) is in current use within the firm. And it must also be understood that being an "executive" in Germany does not mean belonging to a clearly identified socioprofessional group that can be defined in sociological terms. In this respect, the media and publicity are very revealing: unlike in France, the executive class of the population is not used as a specific target for publicizing products or services. In the press there is not a great deal of reference made to the state of mind, the attitude, or the life-style of this particular category of the population.

In conclusion, then, it is evident that the executive class is much less significant in Germany than in France. In fact, it is not really possible to differentiate between an average executive and a qualified foreman. Yet the Germans give as much significance to the different executive functions fulfilled by the different categories of the staff as the French and others do. This German particularity is well illustrated by Beate Krais in the article "Why are there no executives in Germany?" (*Sociologie du Travail* 1992, 4: 497–506).

The Notion of Highfliers

If this term is considered from a linguistic point of view, a contradiction becomes obvious. Since something that is potential is by definition not yet real, we find ourselves in the realm of probability, even of speculation. Linked to this first uncertainty, we find that the adjective the *high*, linguistically speaking, contrasts with the adjective *low*, which could imply a dichotomy: on the one hand, there would be the "highfliers" and on the other the "lowfliers." However, no one would dare to use, above all in writing, the term "lowfliers." Thus, you either are a highflier or are not a highflier. You are either a member of the group or not. There is no half way possible. And this, in spite of the uncertainty about the potentiality's ever being objectively recognized as a reality! Since linguistics has for some time now evolved from its early manichean state of antonyms and developed a series of intermediary states, the most reasonable range of definition to adopt is to consider the concept of potential high-flier as a continuum stretching from an absence of potential to the maximum potential. Thus we find ourselves with a scale ranging from the least to the most, or, inversely, a scale on which the categories can only be marked off by convention: in other words, by the criteria inherent in the culture.

Summary

It must be said, in conclusion, that the term *highflier* is not very precise; it can lead to any number of interpretations, one of which could well be more or less elitist. It can also be seen why the interpretation of this term could pose particular problems in Germany, since the notion of executive is rather tenuous and all forms of elitism are often seen as suspect.

That, no doubt, is why German managers prefer as a rule to take the full range of potential into consideration and not just one end of this range.

We are now going to describe the German vision of potential within a firm and how it develops, concentrating on the upper part of the range. We shall be defining *highfliers* in the broadest sense of the term.

THE PRESENT SITUATION AND FUTURE TENDENCIES

Germany at the present time is going through a restructuring phase, perhaps the most important one since the end of the Second World War. And this applies as much to the transformation of values within society as to the transformation of structures within the German economy, and particularly to the organizational transformation within German firms. Thus, the transformation is taking place at several different levels and so must be viewed as a whole. The strategic areas of today are taking shape within two contexts: the society itself and the business world.

We now attempt to describe the present situation and the future tendencies in terms of their influence on the function and the role of highfliers.

The General Context of Social Policy

The Transformation of Values at the Sociopolitical Level

In Germany, all state-run organizations are built up essentially on two basic principles: equality in the eyes of the law and equality of opportunity. This has produced the following imperatives: protection of minorities and measures to encourage and support those in difficulty and/or at a disadvantage within society. For example, the basic social rights that are guaranteed by the Fundamental Law (*Grundgesetz*), and, stemming from this, there is social legislation and administrative requirements such as employing handicapped people in public departments and paying a tax of DM 200 per month for any post reserved for handicapped people. In this way, a type of social market economy (*soziale Marktwirtschaft*) has been developed since the end of the Second World War with the powerful trade unions and a series of worker participation laws, for example, the management-participation law of 1952 in the coal and steel industry and the law of 1976 governing the internal organization of a firm. These laws gave more rights to job seekers and increases to low wage-earners.

After the first signs of collapse at the beginning of the seventies with the oil shocks and then with the beginning of the eighties, it became patently obvious that the principle of sharing economic advantages from the top to the bottom of the scale, which can work in a period of prosperity, had become quite inadequate. That is why in 1982, when there was a change of government, the Christian-Liberal coalition did not want just a simple change in the economic and social policy, but an overall change of direction (*Wende*) at the intellectual and moral levels, emphasizing more strongly such values as performance (*Leistung*) and competition (*Wettbewerb*), according to the motto *Leistung muss sich wieder lohnen* (Performance must be rewarded again).

However, many classes of society remained unaffected by this renewal of values launched by the politicians; they remained dubious about the notion of a society based on performance and competition and in some cases rejected it totally, because it does project a persistent image of a society in which everyone is always jostling for position (*Ellbogengesellschaft*), in which everyone tries to get on in life by using the cyclist technique: cringe to those above and pedal those below into the ground. It is undeniable that the CDU/CSU (*Christlich Demokratische Union* [Christian Democratic Union]/*Christlich-Soziale Union* [Christian Social Union]) and FDP (*Freie Demokratische Partei* [Free Democratic Party]) government, confronted by a strong trade union reaction, could not manage to get a discussion on the role of an elite under way and so did not convince the citizens that such a thing is sometimes necessary. The reason for this is perfectly clear: an elite is still seen today as a privileged class, in direct

Text Case 6.1
FDP

> In its program for the 1994 elections, the FDP is even more explicit:
> "Education, science and research are our society's most important
> investments. . . . Education policy must be able to be assessed by the cri-
> teria of a society based on performance. . . . We want competition
> between different schools at the pedagogical level, between universities
> at the research level. In the future, private schools must also receive
> state aid. Every individual, and also society as a whole has a very real
> interest in seeing that the greatest number possible of people can fully
> develop their individual potential. We need specific talent not only at
> the scientific and artistic level, but also in practical professional life. In
> all sectors of education and continuing education, we need to support
> the high-fliers and those whose performance makes them part of an
> elite. We want to encourage the elite among technicians and unskilled
> workers."

conflict with the concept of equality of opportunity and equality in the eyes of
the law.

Aware of this rejection, political economists and public education authorities
still hesitate to speak openly about the shortcomings that are beginning to show
up in all fields of research, in the educational system, and in managerial practice.

In the meantime, it is abundantly clear that special attention must be given
to highfliers in schools, universities, and the world of business.

The Education System

In Germany, the education system is also founded on the basic values of
equality of opportunity and equality in the eyes of the law. These values are
particularly championed by the Social-Democrat Party (SPD), which won 36.4
percent of the votes in the legislative election on October 16, 1994. The
Christian-Democrats (CDU/CSU), who won 41.5 percent of the votes, and even
more so the Liberals, actually include the question of performance and competition in public education in their political platform (Text Case 6.1). Unlike
the SPD, these parties propose that special support be given to those "whose
performance puts them in the elite" (*Leistungséliten*). It seems very unlikely that
these concepts will be adopted in practice, since questions concerning education
are dealt with by the member states (*Bundesländer*) and any reform would have
to be approved by the regional governments, which were dominated by the SPD,
after being accepted by the Standing Committee of the Ministers of Education
and Culture (*Ständige Kulturministerkonferenz [KMK]*).

Comparisons carried out in Europe regularly point to the very high quality of
public education in Germany. The system is made up of the following:

- Schools of general education: primary schools (*Hauptschulen*), junior secondary schools (*Realschulen*), senior secondary schools (*Gymnasien*)
- Technical schools (*berufspezifische Fachschulen*)
- The higher education system: further education (*Berufsakademien*), polytechnics (*Fachhochschulen*), universities (*Universitäten*)

This system has proved its worth, according to many experts. Others fear, with good reason, that German scientific research is below international standards, since the democratic system based on the principles of equality of opportunity and education for all has its weaknesses: the highfliers, those with special aptitudes and talents, do not receive sufficient attention in this kind of system. Furthermore, this structural weakness cannot be compensated for by opening some elitist universities (*Élite-Hochschulen*), because only a thorough reform of the whole system, the need for which is no longer denied by anyone today, could ensure a lasting improvement.

In this respect, it is extremely important for the future to decide to what extent management training should be more practically oriented to answer the needs of the business world. It is clear that this tendency is developing in two directions:

- Toward a vertical differentiation in studies and academic training at different levels
- Toward a horizontal expansion in the range of disciplines taught

In the context of vertical differentiation, a university degree will no doubt be introduced in the future at the end of the first study cycle (*Grundstudium*) with emphasis on practical training: this would mean a shorter period of study with courses of improved quality. The second study cycle would exclusively train future research specialists and lead on to the doctorate (*Promotion*) and senior professorships (*Habilitation*).

The horizontal expansion in the range of disciplines taught points, for example, to the setting up of new postgraduate courses offering varied university disciplines (Afheldt 1986; Fisch 1986; Kremla 1992). As an example, the postgraduate course on European economies opened in the University of Saarland could be quoted. This course deals with the challenges the European Union presents to businesses. Looked at generally, Germany should follow the same evolutionary pattern as the rest of Europe: there will be more and more small, very mobile business schools, which will be in competition with the well-known American schools. They will be characterized by their customer-oriented approach (*Kundenorientierung*), their adaptability, and their ability to innovate.

The General Context of the Industrial Policy

The Transformation of the Structures

"Everyone must have his chance"—this was the watchword of those who had established democratic structures in the firm during the period of prosperity and who were responsible for the development of future executives. Today, in the era of business reengineering, the requirements as far as executives are concerned and the conditions under which their careers develop are radically different. For instance, organizational transformations within the firms at present are doing away with whole categories within the hierarchy, leading to a reduction in the number of executive posts. And this does not involve only those beginning their career, but those who have already risen in the hierarchy and who see their prospects of development threatened or even disappearing (cf. Schlichting 1994). In the short term and looked at from the point of view of the firm, this is a positive development since it lessens the payroll. But in time this policy will create problems in the field of human resources management. The blockage in recruitment and the reduction of staff tarnish the firm's image and make it more difficult to find highly qualified and motivated young executives. It is seen as an organization that offers few prospects for development and that treats its personnel as a pool of workers that can be increased or diminished as the need arises. The highfliers themselves, who are sure of keeping their jobs, suffer from the bad feeling within the firm and no longer feel inclined to devote all their potential to the service of the firm.

Within the range of the structural and organizational changes taking place in firms, the human resources management departments are also being restructured and their function and responsibilities are undergoing transformation. The human resource management (HRM) departments with a high level of specialization will from now on find themselves more and more decentralized, even becoming profit centers. They will concentrate more on controlling and verifying, for example, the efficiency of training programs. Identifying and developing highfliers will probably involve rethinking this principle of decentralization to a certain extent.

The Transformation of Skills

Organizational transformations, of course, entail changes in the type of executive required for the future. Business reengineering, for instance, involves specific requirements as far as management by objectives at every level is concerned and an intensive application of project management techniques. This could pose problems.

Executives who have always followed a single-strand career development or who have gained promotion simply through seniority (*Kaminkarriere*) cannot cope with an increased range of responsibility resulting from the reorganization and streamlining of the different departments. In this situation, widely trained executives and self-reliant employees who have had varied experience in the most diverse sectors of the firm must be sought.

Increasing staff management duties and responsibilities mean that executives need more than just sound technical competence; they primarily need a high degree of social competence. The transformation of values within the firm and the rapid technological developments require a constant reviewing of executives' qualifications. "These changing tendencies in the type of qualifications sought for do not mean that the traditional qualifications are no longer required. The traditional is completed and modified by the new" (Sarges 1990, p. 30):

- From the specialist to the generalist
- From the functional manager to the leader
- From the ethnocentric to the international and intercultural

Under the heading of "social competence," Hoets (1993) includes:

- The capacity to work as a team
- The ability to communicate
- Dealing with conflictual situations
- The ability to impose oneself
- The ability to delegate
- The desire to accept management responsibility

Further requirements are

- The sense of innovation
- Creativity
- Mobility (geographical)
- Flexibility (dealing with time)
- The desire to take risks

As a result of the complexity of an ever-changing environment, executives must not only be up to preparing the firm for all possible scenarios, but also be capable of introducing the change and integrating it into the firm and its environment.

This is only possible if the executives are keenly aware of the interdependence of the political and the economic aspects, if they fully understand the local particularities, and if they can calculate the risk involved in the different possibilities available (Fischer 1992).

This applies particularly to the high-technology industries, which are in a very competitive sector, and for which any advantage gained from developing or introducing a new product is much greater than that derived from the standard financial and market-based growth techniques.

The majority of executives who are at present responsible for staff management are sadly lacking in these additional qualities required; that is why human resources managers must have the highfliers well in mind when recruiting new executives, so that these weaknesses and shortcomings can be rectified.

Incentive Schemes

Highfliers are obviously much more efficient than the average, as a general rule, but they are not ipso facto prepared to give their best at all times.

The incentive schemes in German firms are essentially based on money and are rather standardized. A survey carried out by the IOO/EBA (International Organizational Observatory/European Business Analysis) showed that German firms often propose moderately priced insurance policies, an addition to a pension, price reductions on the products sold by the firm, loans at moderate interest rates (often for building, which encouraging the employee to stay put), as well as savings bonds issued by the company. However, many firms now realize that in the future they will have to devise a more supple and a more individualized remuneration scheme for their executives, for example, a system based on the "cafeteria principle," in other words, self-service.

Becker (1995) points out that the traditional incentive schemes are above all of an operative kind and so they encourage an operative, short-term style of thinking. That is why he calls for more strategically oriented incentive systems that encourage a more reasoned, long-term attitude toward them and so build up the stability of the company.

"When the values change in a firm and so alter the attitudes of the individuals in the firm, different styles of incentive must be introduced, which will motivate the individuals in their own private life and also in the work place" (von Rosenstiel 1995). Thus, the incentive schemes must not only correspond to the new objectives, but they must also be adapted to the new realities of the environment and to the new values. Zimmer (1987) comments that in Western Europe incentives of a material kind are less important than the following:

- A professional activity that is satisfying, interesting, and varied
- Dialogue and participation in decision making
- Autonomy and acceptance of responsibilities
- Prospects for personality development
- Frankness and confidence in interpersonal relationships

On the other hand, Wagner (1993) concludes his study by claiming that at the present time executives are once again very keen on material incentives, for example:

- Company cars
- Additional pension rights
- Financing of insurance policies
- Sharing in the capital of the firm
- Special concessions (financial and fiscal)

Summary

In the present state of German society, equality of opportunity and loyal business relationships are certainly compatible with values such as performance and competition, but they do not produce an elitist education system that provides privileged conditions, for example, a specific baccalaureate degree or admission to certain selective "grandes ecoles."

The increasing number of candidates for higher education in Germany results in excessive student numbers at university level. A reform of university education has been under discussion for a long time now, but there is no indication that highly selective courses that will lead to more prestigious degrees than others will be introduced.

At a general level, German society will no doubt continue to live by its egalitarian principles and will refuse to select its future leaders at an early stage.

At the economic level, Germany is subject more than ever to international competition. The high price of its labor, the progress that must be made in the economic sectors, and the significant strengthening of services have repercussions on the structure of firms and the specific requirements in their executive personnel, who must now be more concerned with acquiring managerial qualifications, as opposed to technical qualifications, than they were in the past. These new executive profiles are not produced by the university system but directly by the firms themselves through their continuing education schemes. We now describe certain characteristic aspects of German executives.

The individualized ways of organizing time with sabbatical periods, flextime, early retirement, extra holidays, and other adaptations of the time budget are not so important to the Germans.

This apparent contradiction is easier to understand if the dates of these surveys are taken into account. In periods of economic prosperity, the staff has an unconscious feeling of job security and so is more concerned with nonmaterial values. On the other hand, during a period of recession they are much more anxious to protect themselves from all eventualities.

CERTAIN EMPIRICAL FACTS

We refer to certain practical facts published by the IOO/EBA study (for this see Scholz 1994a; Scholz 1994b). Through the International Organizational Observatory and European Business Analysis, the University of Saarland is responsible for research on Germany. The aim of IOO/EBA is to study organizational structure, company strategy, and human resources management in European firms. Part of this has been a study carried out in Germany of the sixty-two largest German industrial firms. A summary of the results that have a bearing on the current topic follows.

Age, Seniority, Specialization

As a general rule, the age of top German executives is much higher than that in other countries. Only a small group (7 percent) has reached this level before the age of forty; 36 percent of those on the board of directors or in management committees are already over fifty-six.

It is the same so far as seniority in the firm is concerned. Of board of directors/ management committee members 41 percent have been working for more than twenty years in the same firm, 65 percent for more than ten years.

If the overall experience of executives as a whole is considered—and this is important to the understanding of the statistics that follow—it turns out that about one executive in two has worked in only one sector of the firm and therefore has had a rather specialized career. The situation is the same thing for those who change firms: in 40 percent of the firms analyzed, those who were on the board of directors or management committee had worked for only one firm.

In general, only those executives who have worked in several firms and who know several professional branches have varied experience: 47 percent of executives have worked exclusively in one given sector of the firm and 41 percent for only one firm; 42 percent have worked in several firms but always in the same professional branch.

Jochmann (1990), who predicted a higher staff turnover during the 1990s caused by a lack of executives in the labor market and advocates that firms encourage their staff to offer suggestions for their own development to facilitate executive recruitment. This did, in fact, happen.

The Recruitment Process

Langer (1992) considers the different selection criteria for executives seeking a job. On the basis of these considerations it stands out clearly that senior executives (*leitende Angestellte*) positions are the final phase in the professional career of highfliers. That is why it is so interesting to take a closer look at the recruitment process of this category of executive: the personal interview with a senior in rank is the decisive step in the process. Work certificates (*Arbeitszeug- nisse*) come with work experience; psychological tests are rarely used. In the context of the recruitment process, it is not unheard of for an applicant on the short list to be asked to take aptitude tests in addition to the interviews run by members of the personnel and other departments. All this kind of testing is often referred to as the "assessment center," and, of course, the style of these tests varies from one firm to another. In comparison with other methods, assessment centers seem to be rather convincing (cf. Thornton et al., 1987, p. 56). Certain firms use certain specific evaluation techniques. Table 6.1 shows that one firm in four has used an assessment center in the past (7.5 percent very often and

Table 6.1
Selection Methods Used with Staff

METHOD USED	SENIOR EXECUTIVES		OFFICE WORKERS		WORKERS		N
	Intensive Use (%)	Infrequent Use (%)	Intensive Use (%)	Infrequent Use (%)	Intensive Use (%)	Infrequent Use (%)	
Personal Interviews	92.5	5.0	92.9	4.8	85.0	15.0	40
Work Certificates	70.0	25.0	73.8	23.8	72.5	22.5	40
Final Diploma Grades	42.5	42.5	40.5	47.6	37.5	42.5	40
Formal Criteria	40.0	47.5	45.2	38.1	32.5	45.0	40
Group Interviews	30.0	32.5	26.2	35.7	10.0	32.5	40
Biographical Questionnaires	20.0	10.0	21.47	14.3	27.5	7.5	40
Psychological Test	7.5	20.0	2.4	21.4	2.5	7.5	40
Assessment Center	7.5	17.5	4.8	31.0	0.0	2.5	40
Graphological Tests	0.0	12.5	00.0	2.4	0.0	0.0	40
Knowledge Tests	0.0	7.5	0.0	19.0	0.0	20.0	40
Intelligence Tests	0.0	7.5	0.0	14.3	2.5	0.0	40
Other Methods	2.5	7.5	2.4	7.1	0.0	2.5	40

Source: Used by permission of Dr. Christian Scholz.

17.5 percent infrequently); it must be borne in mind that only 29 percent of the participants took the test. This is explained by the relatively high cost of this method, which consequently cannot be used for all recruiting.

It is interesting to note the purposes for which the assessment center (AC) is used. Overall, 36 percent of firms claim they use this method to recruit their employees, but only 25 percent use it to select their senior executives.

Since staff recruitment has become such an important challenge over the last few years, a large number of methods have evolved to ensure that the right candidate is appointed to the right post. As this is concerned there are only marginal differences between staff categories—workers, clerical staff, senior executives.

The inquiry highlights the crucial importance of the following variables: the personal impression, quantifiable results (work certificates and final diploma grades), and formal criteria. The tests measure knowledge and intelligence; graphology (writing tests) and psychological testing are very rarely used: in only 5 percent of cases is a graphological assessment called for. At this level, the differences from methods used in other countries, in particular France, are probably considerable. The detailed results of the study can be seen in Table 6.1. Generally speaking, the AC cannot be used in every case—for example, when selecting top executives, since the applications must be treated confidentially, and in awarding promotions in medium-sized firms, since there are few candidates and the cost is high. And besides, many other factors impede the efficiency of the AC (cf. Ausmüller, Beutel, and Fischer 1993):

* Too much emphasis is given to the specific characteristics of a precise executive post, turning the assessment of potential qualities into a kind of selective examination.
* Senior executives do not differentiate enough between the different candidates at the short-listing stage.
* The results obtained in an AC are not always reliable indicators of what will happen in reality—the long-term effects of negative results gained during the assessment of potential are unknown.

The relatively high cost level, the likelihood of negative effects on the day to day work, and the fact that the results obtained are not guaranteed to be reliable have given rise to a certain amount of criticism, which means that firms use the AC less frequently and in more precise ways.

For integrating senior executives into the team, the briefing interview (*Einarbeitungsgespräch*) is the method most used, closely followed by the different training programs. In the firms we took as our sample, the idea of appointing a mentor and guide and the use of formalized programs were not very evident.

Career Management

When promoting someone, particular attention is paid to his or her range of abilities—particularly in the "generalist" area—and the results he or she has achieved. Apart from this, such considerations as mobility, professional experience, the range of competence (particularly specialized know-how) are important, whereas membership in the firm is not of great importance. At present, the concept of seniority is losing more and more credibility in German firms.

There is a special kind of promotion, described by Priewe (1989), which is to grant symbolic privileges to encourage particularly promising candidates to wait until a suitable post for them is available.

It must be noted that there are no clear separations between these different criteria, considering the great variety in the range of abilities offered by the different individuals. The differences between the different countries could also be taken into account when the results are analyzed at a later date.

For staff promotion in general (excluding that of senior executives), the results obtained and the individual range of abilities play an important part. In the case of senior executives, their "generalist" abilities are of prime importance; in 92 percent of firms, this was one of the three main criteria (see Table 6.2). In the case of workers and office workers, their specialized skills are considered more important.

The catchword that "Managers must be mobile" is borne out by this survey. For workers, mobility is not a promotion criterion in 94 percent of the cases.

Table 6.2
Criteria for Promoting Senior Executives

SEVEN MAIN CRITERIA FOR PROMOTING SENIOR EXECUTIVES	SENIOR EXECUTIVES(%)	OFFICE WORKERS(%)	WORKERS (%)	N (%)
Range of abilities (particularly "generalist" abilities)	93.2	42.3	17.6	52
Results obtained	67.3	84.6	84.3	52
Mobility	38.5	13.5	5.9	52
Professional experience	36.5	65.4	31.4	52
Range of skills (particularly specialized skills)	34.6	53.8	31–41.7	52
Length of service	1.9	13.5	21.6	52
Other criteria	25.0	13.5	7.8	5

Source: Used by permission of Dr. Christian Scholz.

The same applies to office workers (87 percent). Yet, this criterion is taken into account, among others, by 39 percent of the firms.

When deciding on training programs, the range of abilities takes the lead. Of secondary importance are general education, mobility, and professional experience. Once again, length of service in the firm does not count for a great deal.

The same can be said for career development criteria. The range of abilities is again the most important factor, followed—at a fair distance—by professional experience.

In the management training program field, the range of abilities of those concerned is a determining feature. General education, the university degree, and mobility are of equal importance, but in second place.

It is not surprising that top executives mainly choose training courses that last a maximum of two weeks. Only a small minority have an MBA, which represents an added professional achievement.

The vocational training program is varied. Firms in the main (84 percent) concentrate on management functions and management techniques. They then choose course content that is specific to the different requirements. Courses in oral expression and the teaching of foreign languages also arouse a great deal of interest.

Summary

Using the results obtained from this human resources management survey and particularly the facts relevant to top managers, we can build up a typical profile of the highflier in German companies:

- Considerable experience in one professional branch
- A specialized career in one, sometimes in several sectors, of the same company
- A rather limited experience of working abroad
- Qualities such as patience and stamina, since the road to the top of the pyramid is long
- The need to get on well with the immediate superior, whose good opinion is essential for promotion
- The necessity of having good results in previously occupied posts
- A taste for geographical mobility

These managers seem above all to be acknowledged specialists who gradually acquire managerial skills. Highfliers in German firms are trained in a system of executive career management that meets the needs of the firm without creating a fast-track category for high-potential executives. They build up their careers patiently and methodically within the same professional branch. They work in a general atmosphere that is unfavorable to the elitist concept, and therefore, by an association of ideas, to the swift advancement of executives showing high potential.

GENERAL CONCLUSION

Let us express our feelings in one single phrase: basically, the notion of the high-potential executive does not correspond to present German values.

Seeking a new form of stability, as they are at the moment, after the reunification and in view of the firmly held ideals of equality of opportunity, equality of treatment, and protection of those who are at a social disadvantage, Germans could not be expected to accept a new category of young executives, gifted and enjoying privileged treatment.

As for German firms, this philosophy is quite legitimate because their image is the very opposite of elitist categories: they are seen as fulfilling a social function, training the young, allowing every employee to participate in a concerted effort for the common good. In some respects, firms take on the attributes of a family that tries to preserve its cohesion by overlooking certain differences. This is how enterprises (*die Unternehmen*) become firms (*die Firmen*) with its emotional connotations; this is how those employed by Rowenta or la Dasa become *Rowentaner* or *Dasianer*.

This is not to say that there are no more bosses or subordinates. Authority is always highly respected in a German company, but it is legitimated by the many years, the decades of working together, by the communication and interaction between the executives and the employee representatives (*Betriebsrat*). In this context it is difficult to imagine the appearance of a category of executives who change from one firm to another, from one professional branch to another, motivated only by the drive for power, to become the all-powerful leader of a firm, any firm!

In Germany, the "divinely appointed" business leaders have disappeared. Outside appointments to the board of directors are not usual and parachuting senior civil servants and graduates from internationally prestigious institutions is very rare. Unlike France, with its grandes écoles (École Polytechnique, École Nationale d'Administration), there is no privileged path in Germany for becoming chairman of the board of directors (*Vorstandsvorsitzender*).

Under these conditions, one must take one's time and not try to force the pace.

Priority is given at every level to the evaluation of potential. The opportunity is then given to everyone to develop that potential at his or her own pace, by respecting each individual's choices, encouraging communication at all levels, and building up training programs.

As time goes by, potential is developed, each person's range of abilities becomes surer, and agreement is reached on his or her professional development. After a long and gradual process of selection, one becomes—or one does not become—the chairman of the board of directors.

In any case, it will be difficult for the new chairman to wield power in a personal, exclusive way. Team spirit is a highly valued quality in the German world of management. Furthermore, the firm that one manages always represents the leading value, even if it requires lobbying the government and the parliament in Berlin, even if it necessitates going to the other side of the world to sell the products manufactured somewhere in Germany.

In this respect, the decentralizing effect of federalism is clearly seen. It is always giving rise to tensions between the central authority (*Bund*) and the sixteen member states (*Bundesländer*)—between the member-states and the local region where every German and every German firm is firmly rooted both geographically and culturally. This feeling of "polycentrism" that arises naturally from federalism is found in the thinking of firms and individuals. It expresses itself in various intellectual patterns. In order to become effective, federalism requires that certain attitudes develop, such as team spirit, conflict management, and arbitration procedures.

Let us return to considering German managers, who are, as it were, high-potential executives. Observers largely agree when it comes to defining them (Joly 1996, Scheuch 1995):

- They are not management professionals, but specialists—economists, lawyers, engineers—who have progressively qualified as "general managers."
- They are not only professionals in a firm, but professionals serving a firm.
- They are not "divinely appointed" leaders, but have been elected within an organization.
- They are not very keen on public appearances and not tempted by a political role.
- They do not have particularly extravagant life-styles.

In short, these business leaders appear rather as a functional elite and not as a social elite. It is difficult to speak of an elite in Germany, and it does not seem that this situation is likely to change very rapidly. Indirectly the highfliers suffer the general feeling of disapproval reserved for all those who stand out too much from the norm: they are not reserved enough.

In the end, it is no easy task to resolve this conflict concerning highfliers, because first an answer must be found to the underlying question, What kind of top executives will we need in the future?

The First Response

We shall need rigorous administrators, with a thorough understanding of their firm and its basic functions, completely integrated in a professional branch and dedicated to the success of the organization they are in charge of. It might well be said that German firms are in a good position, because they are able to mold their own leaders. The point must be made, however, that the development process of this internal potential is a little slow and there is a risk of inbreeding.

The Second Response

Intuitive and spontaneous team leaders must be produced. They should be expert in communication, creative, and highly aware of intercultural factors. In this case, German universities will have to reform their management training strategies and German firms will have to change their concept of business leaders.

Some will perhaps consider that the surest response is to make a synthesis of the two preceding ones. Economists will say that the question posed is not of great importance, since it is the market, or the markets, that force the hand of business leaders. Intercultural specialists will yet again emphasize the strong link between national cultures and corporate cultures in spite of the internationalization of organization and the globalization of markets.

And furthermore, they will be very careful not to recommend any particular system of executive career management as a model to follow, be it German, French, American, or Japanese.

We conclude this study by quoting a very wise principle that holds good for all international comparisons: avoid making value judgments at all costs: Nothing is better, nothing is worse, everything (or almost) is different.

NOTES

1. The two terms *executive highflier* and *high-potential executive* are used interchangeably as synonyms by the translator through the text.
2. This problem was most openly dealt with in the German Federal Republic, because

a democratic way of life was set up. Since the German Democratic Republic had been taken over by the Russians, the Communist ideology imposed a grotesquely biased, simplistic explanation of these same events, preventing the East Germans from interpreting this essential event in their national history in any other way.

3. Except for the outspoken intervention of business leaders against the economic policy of the Brandt-Scheel government and for the Christian Democrats (1972), which, however, ended in a complete fiasco. cf. Berghahn (1990, 134–135).

4. It should be understood that in Germany there is very little to-and-froing between ministerial posts and managerial posts in business, whereas this is quite usual in France; cf. Bauer and Bertin-Mourot (1993, 14).

5. *Wirtschaftswoche* (April 22, 1994) clearly illustrates this point of view in the article (p. 28) *Schwere Fehler* (Bad mistakes), in which are recounted the dismal failures of some former students of L'École Polytechnique or L'École Nationale d'Administration when placed at the head of great French industrial or banking firms, without any apparent effect on their future careers! The article concludes by saying that in the context of the internationalization of the economy, the influence of such schools should be lessened.

REFERENCES

Afheldt, H. 1986. "Das Anforderungsprofil an Führungskräfte im Jahr 2000: Prognosen und Szenarien." *Konstanzer Blätter für Hochschulfragen* 23 (March) Heft 2–4, 82–94.

Annandale-Massa, D., and H. Bertrand. 1990. "La gestion des ressources humaines dans les grandes banques européennes, Quelles stratégies?" Bernard Brunhes Consultants, *Economica* 1, 126.

Aumüller, R. Beutel, K., and H.-P. Fischer. 1993. "Die Post-Assessment-Center Ära— Vorgesetzte wählen Führungskräftenachwuchs aus." *Zeitschrift für Personalforschung* 7, 64–76.

Bauer, M. and B. Bertin-Mourot. 1993. "Comment les entreprises françaises et allemandes sélectionnent-elles leurs dirigeants"? *Problèmes Économiques* no. 2337, August 11.

Becker, F. G. 1995. "Strategische Anreizsysteme (Überblick)." Scholz, C., and M. Djarrahzadeh (Eds.), *Strategisches Personalmanagement: Konzeptionen und Realisationen*. Stuttgart: Schäffer-Poeschel, 185–200.

Berghahn, V. 1990. "Die Wirtschaftséliten in der Politik der Bundesrepublik." U. Hoffmann-Lange et al. (Eds.), *Éliten in der Bundesrepublik Deutschland*. Stuttgart, Berlin, Cologne: Kohlhammer, 124–141.

Berthel, J. "Führungskräfte-Qualifikationen (Teil 1)." *Zeitschrift Führung und Organisation* 206–211.

Berthel, J. 1992b. "Führungskräfte-Qualifikationen (Teil 2)." *Zeitschrift Führung und Organisation* 279–286.

CDU/CSU. 1994. *Wir sichern Deutschlands Zukunft: Regierungsprogramm von CDU und CSU zur Bundestagswahl*. Bonn.

Dahrendorf, R. 1965. *Gesellschaft und Demokratie in Deutschland*. Munich: Piper.

F.D.P. 1994. *Liberal denken: Leistung wählen: Das Programm der F.D.P. zur Bundestagswahl*. Bonn.

Fisch, R. 1986. "Innovation und Ausbildungssystem." *Konstanzer Blätter für Hochschulfragen* 23 (March), Heft 2–4, 57–65.

Fischer, H. 1992. "Warum Manager umdenken." *Gablers Magazin* (11–12), 14–17.

Friedrichs, P. 1992. "Die Vision vom Manager" *Gablers Magazin* (6–7), 27–31.

Föhr, S. 1994. "Zur Vorteilhaftigkeit von Cafeteria-Systemen." *Zeitschrift für Personalforschung* (8) 58–86.

Hoets, A. 1993. "Förderung sozialer Kompetenz als Aufgabe der Personalentwicklung—Instrument der Anpassung, insbesondere von Frauen?" *Zeitschrift für Personalforschung* 7 (1), 115–133.

Hoffmann-Lange, U. (Ed.). 1992. *Éliten, Macht und Konflikt in der Bundesrepublik.* Opladen: Leske Budrich.

Jochmann, W. 1990. *Berufliche Veränderungen von Führungskräften.* Stuttgart: Verlag für Angewandte Psychologie.

Joly, H. 1996. *Patrons d'Allemagne: Sociologie d'une elíte Industrielle 1933–1989.* Paris: Presse Nationale des Sciences Politiques.

Kets de Vries, M.F.R. 1995. "Dysfunktionale Entscheidungsfindung und organisatorische Pathologien." Scholz, C., and J. Zentes (Eds.). *Strategisches Euro-Management.* Stuttgart: Schäffer-Poeschel, 247–258.

Knebel, H. 1994. "Auswahl und Belohnung von Managern: Krisenverursacher oder Erfolgsfaktor?" *Personal* 46, 357–363.

Krais, B. 1992. "Pourquoi n'y a-t-il de cadres en Allemagne?" *Sociologie du travail* 4: 497–506.

Kremla, M. 1992. Massenuni. *Störfaktor* 5, 72–78.

Langer, C. 1992. "Die Organisationswahl von Führungskräften." Diss. Univ. d. Bundeswehr Hamburg, Hamburg.

Limpens, E. 1994. *Leistungsorientierte Differenzierung von Führungskräften: Probleme—Bedingungen—Wirkungen.* Cologne: Wirtschaftsverlag Bachem.

Lüthje, J. 1995. "Élite statt Bildung?" *Der Spiegel* (27), 180–181.

Maccoby, M. 1976. *The Gamesman: The New Corporate Leaders.* New York: Simon and Schuster.

Miller, P. 1995. "Strategischer Wandel in Europa als Managementproblem." Scholz, C., and J. Zentes (Eds.). *Strategisches Euro-Management.* Stuttgart: Schäffer-Poeschel, 277–292.

Mungenast, M., and P, Finzer. 1993. "Auswahl von Führungskräften durch Assessment Center." *Personal* 45: 336–338.

Priewe, J. 1989. "Aufwärts, aber ohne Beförderung." *Management Wissen* 12:98–112.

Sarges, W. 1990. "Wie man Führungspotential identifizier." *Gablers Magazin* 4(2): 29–32.

Sauerhöfer, M. 1992. "Wie Führungskräfte Unternehmen prägen." *Gablers Magazin* 6 (6–7):16–18.

Scheuch, U., and E. K. Scheuch. 1995. "Hochadel auf Zeit." *Manager Magazin* 3:191–201.

Schlichting, C. 1994. "Karriere im schlanken Unternehmen." *Personalführung* 27:386–395.

Scholz, C. 1994. *Personalmanagement. Informationsorientierte und verhaltenstheoretische Grundlagen.* 4th ed. Munich: Vahlen.

Scholz, C. 1995a. "Runderneuern oder ausmustern?" *Personalwirtschaft* 22 (6): 30–34.

Scholz, C. 1995b, "Strategisches Euro-Management." Scholz, C., and J. Zentes (Eds.). *Strategisches Euro-Management.* Stuttgart: Schäffer-Poeschel, 31–55.

Scholz, C. 1995c. "MBA an der Uni—eine Alternative?" *Management & Seminar* 22 (7–8): 34–36.

Scholz, C., Y. Michels. 1994. "Struktur und Verhalten deutscher Unternehmen." 1991: 1. *Deutscher IOO Ergebnisbericht, Diskussionsbeitrag Nr. 34 des Lehrstuhls für Betriebswirtschaftslehre.* Insbesondere Organisation, Personal-und Informationsmanagement an der Universität des Saarlandes. Saarbrücken.

Schuppert, D. 1990. "Aus der Kraft der Verantwortung—'Face-to-Face Leadership' Nachdenkenswertes über Coaching." *Zeitschrift für Sozialpsychologie und Gruppendynamik* 15(4): 20–49.

Simon, H., and K. Wiltinger. 1993. "Führungsnachwuchs von morgen: Der Kampf um die Besten." *WISU* 1: 763–764.

SPD. 1989. *Grundsatzprogramm der Sozialdemokratischen Partei Deutschlands: Beschlossen vom Programm-Parteitag der Sozialdemokratischen Partei Deutschlands am 20 Dezember* 1989. Berlin: SPD, December 20.

Statistisches Bundesamt (Ed.). 1994. *Statistisches Jahrbuch 1994 für die Bundesrepublik Deutschland.* Wiesbaden: Metzler-Poeschel.

Stein, V. 1995. "Betriebswirtschaftliches Universitätsdiplom: Gut genug für die Unternehmen von heute und morgen"? Der Karriereberater 19 (7): 139–154.

Thornton, G. C., B. B. Gaugler, D. B. Rosenthal, and C. Bentson. 1987. "Die prädikative Validität des Assessment Centers"—Eine Metaanalyse." Schuler, M. and W. Stehle (Hrsg.), *Assessment Center als Methode der Personalentwicklung.* Stuttgart: Poeschel, 36–60.

von Rosenstiel, L. 1995. "Wertorientierungen im Personalmanagement." Scholz, C., and M. Djarrahzadeh (Eds.). *Strategisches Personalmanagement—Konzeptionen und Realisationen.* Stuttgart: Schäffer-Poeschel, 210–216.

Wagner, D. 1993, "Cafeteria-Modelle in der Unternehmenspraxis." *Personalwirtschaft* 20 (3): 53–56.

Welge, M. K. 1992. "Führungskräfte." Gaugler, E., and W. Weber (Eds.). *Handwörterbuch des Personalwesens,* 2nd ed. Stuttgart: Poeschel, 937–947.

Westerwelle, A., and A. Westerwelle. 1995. *Die besten Universitäten und Fachhochschulen für Wirtschaftswissenschaftler: Deutschland—Österreich—Schweiz.* Vienna: Ueberreuter.

Zimmer, D. 1987. "Rahmenbedingungen erfolgreicher Managemententwicklung." *Personal* 39: 186–190.

7

Leadership Italian Style

Luciano Traquandi and Patrizia Castellucci

INTRODUCTION

Our study of high-potential management (HPM) addresses the ways in which Italian companies identify and develop new managers. The study is divided into four sections:

- The first section discusses the ideas, assumptions, and beliefs (both conscious and unconscious) that influence HPM strategies and practices. In particular, we consider the impact of certain aspects of Italian managerial culture and context.
- The second section evaluates the advantages and the risks inherent in any HPM policy, with a specific focus on Italian companies.
- The third section reviews the range of HPM practices—including the policy of deliberately avoiding highflier management altogether—found in Italy.
- The fourth section details specific policies within four large Italian companies.

In conclusion, we add some suggestions derived from our experience within Italian companies and from our work as consultants and researchers.

BUSINESS IN ITALY

Small to Medium-Sized Companies

The most significant aspect of the Italian business world is the unusually large number of small to medium-sized companies (SMSCs). About 70 percent of

Italian companies are small or medium-sized, with sales ranging from between 1 and 80 billion Italian lire (ITL). SMSCs produce 70 percent of the country's gross national product and employ 75 percent of Italians working in private industry. Because of their predominance, SMSCs contribute to the character of Italy's business climate far more than do larger companies.

Many of these SMSCs are family-owned, and the large majority are run by male family members—although there are some exceptions, particularly in those parts of the country where matriarchal traditions are strong. Not surprisingly, each small company is strongly influenced by the behavior and personality of its owner. Because of the idiosyncrasies of individual owners, even companies with similar profiles or products may vary widely in management practices. SMSCs do share a few common characteristics, however, and those characteristics influence HPM policies.

Common Traits of SMSCs

The flexible nature of moderately sized companies leads to one of the common characteristics. Free from the rigidities of larger corporations, SMSCs can quickly take advantage of changing conditions. When niche markets and new markets arise, or when the rates of exchange become temporarily favorable, SMSCs can move quickly to exploit these opportunities. However, this flexibility conflicts with the basic premise of high-potential management: that it is possible and worthwhile to invest in well-chosen employees in the present— with the expectation that these employees will play important managerial roles in the future. In a fast-moving and unpredictable entrepreneurial business environment, it is difficult for companies to invest in this kind of long-range strategy. Instead, it is often easier—and sometimes safer—for a company to wait until a situation arises, then to find someone, either inside the company or outside, who is capable of handling it. Later, when important changes again occur, this person may well be replaced by someone with a more appropriate profile. In many cases, high flexibility comes into conflict with a long-term HPM policy.

As mentioned before, another common characteristic of Italian SMSCs is that they are run by owner-bosses. Although these owners have distinctive management styles, they generally share a common trait: they like to be in control. It is true that the company many benefit when the owner is directly involved in all decisions and all aspects of management. But in extreme cases—which in Italy are not at all rare—an obsessive hunger for control may do damage. Whether an owner's need for power is mild or excessive, any authoritarian climate of control will influence the development of new managers, who must adapt to the whims of the owner in order to fit in.

At the same time, a strong and determined high-potential manager, one with a high level of initiative, may chafe under the control and may represent a threat to the controlling owner. When faced with such a situation (or even with the possibility of having authority questioned), the owner may choose one of two options. He may decide that an "insider" will be more reliable and therefore groom a relative or friend to assume a crucial management position. Or he may introduce an "outsider," thinking that someone outside the family may be more controllable and manageable than his kin would be. Either way, the owner's need for control will naturally ensure the probability that his key managers— those in line for the top positions—will have personalities and goals that are similar to his own. In short, such an owner tries to "clone" a leader like him rather than empower a strong alternative future leader.

The grooming of the owner's successor may well be the highest form of high-potential management practiced in such companies, although it is not necessarily planned. Because of this, the owner's expectations for his successor may be suddenly shattered. It is particularly shocking, and also difficult, when an owner realizes that the "anointed" member of the family cannot suitably fill the assigned role. Whatever the plan was for succession, a failure of expectations could signal the end of a family enterprise.

Cultural Aspects of Italian Companies

In addition to the factors of flexibility and owner control, existing cultural backgrounds affect highflier management in SMSCs. In fact, cultural factors have an important effect on companies of all sizes. Certain common aspects have a significant impact on HPM policies in Italy.

The Expectation of Devotion, Effort, and Sacrifice from Employees

Managers, especially those at high levels, must demonstrate that they consider the company their highest priority. They must consistently work overtime, accept unwelcome assignments, and put their work above family and other personal interests. When a lower-level manager willingly puts the company first in this way, these actions give strong evidence that the employee may be a future high performer, suitable for key roles in the company.

Those who give first priority to personal interests, on the other hand, may not be considered for key positions, even though their overall performance may be excellent. In Italy, it would be fatal to one's career to take even a short leave of absence to care for a new baby or pursue another interest. With such a damaging performance evaluation, it would be virtually out of the question to expect to be hired by another company.

The Expectation That Men Will Be the HPM Candidates

Because companies expect employees to subordinate personal interests, men are more likely to be HPM candidates than are women; at the same time, and for the same reason, Italian women generally do not find it interesting to be HPM candidates. With some exceptions, this division of roles is considered a

Figure 7.1
High-Potential Management (HPM) Systems in Italy

Level 1	Level 2	Level 3	Level 4	Level 5
No HPM	Relatives and close friends	HPM's in key roles	Actual potential	"Leopard Stains"

natural situation by both sexes. Undoubtedly, this attitude stems from the Catholic culture, which, although it is slowly fading in Italy, still influences unconscious behavior and personal decision making.

The Value Given to Personal Creativity, Initiative, and Leadership

An employee who shows extraordinary initiative and leadership may be able to overcome deficiencies in background. Strong personal qualities may override the lack of a proper college degree, low social status, or even a previously average performance, and the employee who demonstrates highly valued abilities could become an HPM candidate. Conversely, a person who holds all the "good cards" could slip out of the fast track if he fails to show initiative, creativity, and an aptitude for leadership.

Those ambitious employees who are conscious of these points realize that they must not only work for results, but also sell a certain image to the right people. They must display their leadership qualities in public, selling themselves in an appropriate way, one that is assertive but not exaggerated or overemphasized.

COMMON HPM POLICIES AND PRACTICES IN ITALY

Because of the large number of small companies in Italy and the large differences in management styles, it is nearly impossible to describe a typical Italian HPM system. Nevertheless, we have tried to classify approaches, ranging from Level 1, in which no HPM policy is applied, to Level 5, found in companies that have systematically adopted an HPM policy for all management positions, as demonstrated in Figure 7.1.

Level 1. At this level, HPM policy is purposefully ignored. Strangely enough, this approach is taken in companies of all sizes. Some owners of small companies proudly deny the need to identify and cultivate promising managers. At the same time, a prominent Italian high-technology company, which employs twelve thousand people, has adopted formal HPM policies but often chooses to ignore them.

There are various possible reasons for the "do nothing" approach. For one thing, owners of small companies tend to rely on their own capabilities in scouting out needed human resources. A sense of independence, a need for control, and a pleasure in making absolute, nearly despotic decisions may lead the owner to forget rationality and economic interest and ignore the problem (or opportunity) of HPM. Although the company may suffer from this total absence of HPM, the personal values of the owner take precedence.

The high-tech company mentioned has employed the "do nothing" approach in significant cases—although it has not been the rule. Sometimes an important position becomes vacant and remains unfilled while management tries to find candidates among people who are not too busy. The approach taken by management and the personnel department is to ask, Who is not doing anything important right now? This approach is not always a failure, however. In one case, an important role in international marketing was offered to a young engineer who, because of his independent spirit, had been previously classified as "not reliable for important roles within the company." But in fact, this person, who had been excluded from the HPM list, took the offered position and embarked on a brilliant career.

In both small and large companies, the alternative to an HPM process, which is admittedly slow in producing seasoned managers, is to rely on the "free market," as it is called in Italy. For the small company, the free market is external, typically including people working for competitors. For big companies, the free market can also be internal and can include the reservoir of unsatisfied people in low-level jobs or those who are looking for a more fulfilling opportunity. The truth is, the results of this non-HPM approach are sometimes comparable to those of an efficient HPM policy.

Level 2. Members of the family or quasi family are selected and groomed for key positions. In companies that adopt this method of filling strategic roles, positions are often filled by relatives. For example, eleven of the twenty-four employees in one company were family members, and they filled all of the key positions. In such companies, the owner (assisted sometimes by other family members) may begin monitoring the young people in the family at an early age. He may test and observe them by giving older children summer jobs or easy full-time jobs. This informal selection process generally leads to the selection of specific young people as potential managers for crucial positions. In addition, a special family member will be recognized as the probable successor to the owner—although as long as the parent has any part in the company the succession will be in name only, even after the son has been named chief executive officer (CEO).

Educationally, the young managers-to-be may follow various paths, ranging from graduating in philosophy from the Sorbonne in Paris to receiving a degree in mechanical engineering from a school in northern Italy. Many parents would encourage the latter option, keeping the son or daughter close to home and family control. However, other families may frown upon education altogether. In these families, the owner (whether parent or relative) may believe that time spent not working for the company is time wasted. Or he may feel that a family member may be intellectually corrupted by university study; for example, the student may discover a different professional interest. Consequently, the high-potential relative will be looked at in the context of the owner's beliefs and the company's culture. These attitudes are fading in Italy, but they are still alive. Remember, in Italy, the family generally has long-lasting control over all life and work decisions.

Sometimes bigger companies approach the problem of succession in ways similar to those found in family-owned companies. Even when no blood relative is available, a division director can "clone" and develop a "quasi son" to give some continuity to his management style and objectives. If the division director is promoted to higher positions, the "son" will carry on his work, embodying the director's personality, belief system, and behavior. This approach is neither good nor bad. It does simplify the process of changing leadership, and it provides a cultural stability in that part of the company.

Level 3. HPM is created to cover key roles. This approach is typical of larger companies. When, according to the perception of top leaders, the company's architecture creates some roles that are more crucial than others, the company may conceive and apply a specific policy of HPM for these key roles only. These roles may involve the business the company is involved in, the balance of internal powers, or the relationship with external entities, particularly in the case of state-owned companies, which tend to be strongly influenced by the government in power at the time.

Position titles for these roles may be as ordinary-sounding as central research director or Far East general manager. But within the architecture and power structure of a particular company, these ordinary positions may be highly important. Sometimes it is not easy to find formal evidence of an HPM process for filling these positions. Since this type of highflier management involves unique and specific positions, the policy can be kept at a quasi-confidential level. Naturally, the process of filling these crucial roles internally requires a great deal of time and energy, and the free market is always available to those companies that want to skip the HPM process.

Sometimes in bigger companies the clan of "companions in adventure" arises. These are people who together founded a division, were involved in difficult projects, survived a tough reorganization, achieved important results, or know important and confidential aspects of the company life. This group can provide candidates for the key roles. In other words, in these cases, the high-potential pool has been naturally formed through a Darwinian-type process. Generally, the members of the clan are skilled in their ability to navigate within the company culture. They are able to exploit the best ideas and resources and are wise enough to avoid useless or harmful initiatives. It sometimes happens that during a severe reorganization, possibly due to a takeover, the new board will use these kinds of people to ease the transition.

Level 4. The company relies not on a specific high-potential system, but on actual potential. This type of HPM is not rare in Italian companies that have a certain critical mass of people. In this system, the company does not correlate its future high performers to a specific need, plan, or characteristic of the company. Instead, the "good" qualities of the employee automatically qualify him or her for highflier status. In extreme cases, no role may exist in the company that corresponds to the qualities of the employee. Yet the company feels it should recognize employees who exhibit interesting skills, attitudes, and behavior, it decides to take note of these people and follow and manage their careers. In the Fininvest Group (now known as Mediaset), the motto has been, "We hire the right person for an undefined job." The corollary of this philosophy is "Sooner or later, someone with good potential will wake up and make an important contribution."

Companies with this attitude experience a great flexibility in human performance and are likely to find new talent. In the case of the Fininvest Group, some people with backgrounds as artists have proved to be good organizers, strategists, and managers; at the same time, ordinary professional people have demonstrated unexpected artistic capabilities and have overcome conventional and cultural barriers to succeed in a new field.

Level 5. The company systematically seeks to discover and develop future high performers (HIPOs), are scattered throughout the company in a "leopard-stains" pattern. In Italy, this is the frontier for HPM; a more comprehensive type of HPM is very rare. At this level, companies look for certain characteristics in people working within functional areas of the company. These characteristics, which vary from company to company, include a well-balanced blend of managerial attitudes. For example, the right attitudes mentioned by an electronics company were creativity, leadership, initiative, and personal sympathy. Faithfulness and loyalty were also important, but not when these qualities grew into compliance or "yesmanship." The ability to say no was appreciated when the nos were not merely personal reactions but important to the company interests.

In this company, the leader of each functional group is encouraged to identify high potentials, and even to identify those who may belong to other groups. The human resources department keeps a record of these individuals, and these records are used to influence salary decisions. At lower hierarchical levels, high-potential employees cannot expect to receive large salary increases, but they may be assigned to delicate missions, often within task forces. After a few years of this HPM policy, the company had created a "leopard-stains map" of high-potential employees scattered through nearly every functional area and geographical site.

Further levels of HPM complexity may be found in other companies. But in general, when an HPM approach becomes too systematic, it becomes expensive and may be difficult to manage for long periods. Overapplication of HPM may lead to some of the negative results outlined previously.

HIGH-POTENTIAL MANAGEMENT IN LARGE ITALIAN COMPANIES: SOME EXAMPLES

HPM policies within large companies may resemble any of the five levels we have outlined. In order to show the diversity of highflier management styles in Italy, we have studied the policies of four internationally known Italian companies. Each of these companies is also important and highly visible within the national economy.

Pirelli

A manufacturer of tires, Pirelli was founded in 1872. Today, the company employs thirty-eight thousand people and makes some ITL10,000 billion in profits.

Traditionally, Pirelli has given particular attention to both human resources and the managerial culture. Special emphasis is given to employees' development—a concept that is often subscribed to in theory but not often put into practice. Although it is fashionable for Italian companies to say they are interested in employee development, Pirelli is one of the few that actually try to implement the theory. The traditional philosophy at Pirelli is that through policies designed to foster talent and through the attention of management high performers will spontaneously emerge to cover important managerial roles as needs arise.

However, the company has also formulated and put into practice a formal system of HPM. The goal is to give maximum development to all future high performers within the company. This HPM policy is a tribute to Pirelli's dedication to offering equal opportunities to all its employees; at the same time, the policy supports the company's strategic vision toward human resources. In Pirelli, the aim of HPM is to increase the diversity and number of future high performers by identifying those bright employees whose contributions could be lost if not developed through a specific, systematic, and proactive approach.

The monitoring and evaluation process is centered on three key stages of an individual's career. Initially, persons are evaluated after two or three years of working for Pirelli. Most of these are recent college graduates. After five years, those who have reached quasi-managerial positions (*quadri*) are reevaluated. After ten years, an evaluation is made of those managers (*dirigenti*) who could rise to top positions within the executive group.

There is no formal assessment center where these evaluations are made, but rather they are made through deep involvement in the process by people in contact with the high-potential employee: his or her manager, the higher-level leaders, and other people, such as customers, who may be able to give important information about the candidate. In making the evaluations, the company considers the candidates' alignment with Pirelli's values, their achievement on the job, and their personal skills and capabilities. In addition, the HPM appraises how each candidate performs in certain fundamental managerial skills. These include innovation, risk taking, speed of reaction and initiative, ability to create economic value, integration (ability to cross borders and work with others), management of collaborators, sensitivity to human resources, external relations, flexibility, and ability to learn.

Pirelli's HPM system obtains information for evaluation in two ways. Interviews of the candidate, managers, and others are one method, which is systematically and extensively used as a means of evaluating individuals. The other selection method is to hold campaigns or self-promotion contests for a group of professionals (for example, the administration people campaign or the researchers campaign). Those identified as highfliers receive training appropriate to their level of experience.

The Pirelli HPM system mostly follows the leopard-stains model of highflier management (Level 5). This can be seen in the systematic attention it gives to college graduates, who are scattered everywhere within the company. The leopard-stains model is also apparent in the effects of campaigns by professional groups, which have resulted in the identification of high performers in different areas of the company. Pirelli's system also contains aspects of the actual potential model, or Level 4. Performance on the job could be considered a way to test an employee's actual potential, insofar as it is congruent with Pirelli's basic value system.

Montedison

The industrial conglomerate group Montedison, which is involved with chemistry, engineering, and energy, has created a comprehensive system of HPM. The intent of the system was to empower and make available managers for the whole group of companies, through the internal exchange of high-potential employees. But this systematic HPM policy was interrupted from 1990 to 2000 as the group made some important structural changes. Core business practices, technology, stockholders, and management styles have all shifted, affecting HPM along with all other areas of the corporation.

Because of this interruption in HPM, some highfliers quit the company, necessitating new hires. Although at first glance this appears to be a negative result, the arrival of newcomers may have facilitated the process of change, allowing a quicker adaptation to the new paradigms within the company. Naturally, the newcomers accepted change more easily than those who were entrenched in the old system. Besides, as the company stabilized, some of the "lost potential" people rejoined Montedison, introducing fresh managerial vision from the organizations where they had been employed during the interval.

Despite the long interruption of a corporate HPM, most of the companies in the group kept the HPM mentality alive and maintained some semblance of highflier management within the system. High-potential people still emerged and made important steps in personal growth and diversification (moving, for example, from pharmaceutical research to marketing, finance, or management). This less-official HPM system continued to produce high-potential human resources, people who were employed inside the discovering company, within other companies in the group, or at the corporate level. The highfliers were from several levels of hierarchy, both low and high.

A flexible approach to HPM helped the company move through a period of important changes, when continuous adjustment was required by managers. By its very nature, the informal system of HPM helped overcome the dangerous reaction that sometimes occurs in times of change: an attitude of rigidity and attachment to the status quo. Most likely, a systematic HPM would not have been possible during such a time. It might even have been dangerous when changing events inevitably would have led to inconsistencies in its application (causing the "broken promise" effect on employee morale).

The experience of Montedison suggests that during times of significant reorganization lasting over an extended period a global HPM is difficult to apply. Moreover, because a successful HPM seems to require some stability, companies might benefit by suspending HPM during such times of change. If it is suspended, there may be negative results as some people quit the company, but HPM practices will tend to remain spontaneously active.

When Montedison had a formal HPM policy, it seemed to be based mostly on the actual potential (Level 4) model; the highfliers within the group had diverse careers and were easily transferred between companies in the group.

ST Microelectronics

ST Microelectronics (ST), a producer of electronics and semiconductors, is perhaps Italy's largest high-tech company. Located in thirty-two countries, it employs twenty thousand people and produces about 4500 billion lire in profits. The company was formed from the merger of two state-owned companies, the Italian SGS and the French Thomson. Although in many ways integration within the corporation has been strong, HPM policies and management have remained decentralized and in the hands of single companies. For this reason, there is a specific Italian approach to HPM within ST.

In Italy, it was nearly impossible to find experts in semiconductors who were not already within ST, so it was crucial from the beginning to select people for key roles quickly: solid-state researchers, designers, production experts, and even marketers. Because of the high level of innovation and changing scenarios in the semiconductor market, being able to fill new roles has become crucial. Managers also have to be ready for fast vertical growth as new business units, new geographical areas, and new activities require new leadership. Because of these needs, ST must find its technical and managerial people internally, and it must maintain a reservoir of high potentials that is strong in both quantity and quality. A continuous and intensive HPM process, incorporating an assessment center and using group leaders as talent scouts, helps keep that reservoir filled.

The traits that ST looks for in its highfliers are as follows:

- Personal ambition
- Achievement in his or her present position
- Efficiency and ability to act rapidly
- Ability to take responsibility
- Ability to make decisions
- Willingness to "stand out" (*esporsi*, which means to "decide and act," becoming visible as a daring person)

The identification of highfliers is followed by a planned development path giving the person experience in all managerial aspects, including international experience. Career plans are created and implemented on an individual basis and take into account the abilities and possible managerial level of each candidate. The main result of the HPM system is that ST in Italy is considered a challenging place for "the best and brightest" of the young technical graduates— but at the same time offers a stimulating environment, with opportunities for personal growth and change that are not possible within other high-tech companies.

In terms of our model, the company's HPM system resembles the leopard-stains model (Level 5).

AGIP

AGIP is an important company within the ENI Group, a state-owned conglomerate with the mission of guaranteeing national access to energy and raw materials. The trend within ENI is toward privatization (about 30 percent of the group is now offered on the stock market). AGIP deals in energy, mainly in oil and gas, and has thirteen thousand people working worldwide. The entire ENI group has HPM policies that take into account the operational characteristics of each separate company within the group.

As a result of the nature of AGIP's business, basic careers within the company are classified according to two categories: domestic or international jobs and technical (also called "professional" in Italy) or managerial jobs. The HPM policy takes these fundamental divisions into account. It's important that AGIP quickly establish, with surgical precision, which career options are most appropriate for a promising employee and develop an appropriate path for him or her.

There are two times when the company appraises the potential of a young graduate or a middle manager. The first assessment occurs after three years of work in the company; the second, after five or six years. Three kinds of competencies are appraised: problem solving, personal and managerial interactions, and achievement on the job. This process of appraisal, which is widely applied, leads to a companywide map of distinctive competencies within the various career categories (managerial-technical, domestic-international). An important side benefit of this mapping is that the company can, by evaluating common elements within various occupational streams, establish its global models in terms of professional profiles. This model is defined at two levels: the company-wide or corporate model and the professional families model.

The HPM policy at AGIP is oriented toward the company's values and its perceived mission; candidates are evaluated both on professional performance and correspondence of their actions and work with company values. One of these values is confidentiality, and the HPM system seeks to ensure respect for the individual during the evaluation. The assessment center keeps all personal information confidential, and an external consultant ensures that the HPM process respects each individual's more intimate information.

A wide reservoir of highfliers must be identified and developed for key human resources needs within the company; of these, a small number are identified as very high potentials. These are those who can aspire to top positions and functions. They may even transcend company borders and reach important positions within the larger ENI Group.

Because the competence mapping at AGIP is extensive, highflier management at this company is highly intensive, even transcending leopard-stains. Because of the example of AGIP, it may be necessary in the future to add a Level 6 category of Italian HPM to our model.

SUMMARY

Italy's business climate is characterized by many small to medium-sized companies. Most of the SMSCs focus on a high-potential management style that (1) requires the complete devotion of employees, (2) is flexible, (3) values creativity, and (4) is male-oriented.

Five levels of Italian-style HPM can be identified. At Level 1, no conscious HPM policy is adopted. At Level 2, only family members and quasi-family members are considered for leadership positions. Level 3 HPM creates a policy only for certain key roles, those that have particular significance within the company's architecture. A company adopting a Level 4 approach values the actual potential of employees; instead of grooming a specific high performer to fill a specific need, such a company gives highflier status to anyone with valued skills, attitudes, or behavior and trusts that these qualities will be useful to the company sometime. Companies that operate at Level 5 systematically locate and develop high potentials throughout all areas of operation.

Italy's SMSCs tend to remain at Levels 1 and 2 in their high-potential management, but larger multinational corporations more often function at Levels 3 to 5. The case of AGIP suggests that a Level 6 may be emerging, with high-potential management that resembles the more traditional corporatewide systems common in American multinationals.

CONCLUSION

From our experience as consultants and researchers, and given our belief that the world is based on a humanistic culture that is technically and operationally oriented (a kind of grounded humanism), we believe that overly planned and scientific approaches to human behavior are flawed. What is important in high-potential management is the vision of what talented people can and should become, not the system for managing this.

HPM principles and practices are based on several assumptions. The most significant are that human attitudes can be monitored, at least indirectly; that behavior of human beings has some kind of stability; and that companies can significantly influence the development of people and direct their professional growth. It is useful for companies to act as though these assumptions are true, but they must also remember that there are exceptions. Case histories show instances of people who, because of a bad performance, were considered by one company to have very poor potential, but who then had brilliant careers in other companies, or who went on to found successful companies of their own. Managers must keep in mind that they cannot determine once and for all the potential of another person.

One approach that helps us to integrate our thinking about HPM is to put it within the conceptual framework of transactional analysis (TA). According to Berne's theory, the human ego is composed of three states: the Child, the Parent, and the Adult. The first two states are formed during the first years of life and are relatively stable. Nearly unchangeable is the Child Ego State. When this state of personality is active, the person is in touch with his or her deepest emotions and is most able to create and to satisfy inner needs. The Parent State, which can change in response to important events, is the depository of an individual's beliefs and prejudices, and the ability to protect and prohibit. The Adult State changes throughout life in response to new information and increased awareness. This part of the personality deals with the *here and now*.

The ideas of Transactional Analysis can provide useful insights into human behavior for human resources managers. Using TA, we understand the "wholeness" of a person, his or her deep characteristics and attitudes, in terms of the unchangeable Child State of Ego, which governs how the person reacts in times of stress, creativity, and other basic conditions. The rarely changing Parent State tells us what a person's values are and also how great his or her sense of duty is.

Too often, HPM focuses on the Child and Parent States. This is especially true in Italian organizations whose owners and managers are trying to clone a surrogate. In an attempt to change the unchangeable Child State, these owners create rigid prescriptions for how a person must act when experiencing stress, when creating, and when feeling emotions. These controlling owners also try to mold the high potential's Parent State into a duplicate of their own. The high-potential employee is expected to act exactly as the authority or parent figure does. He must develop similar values and let duty prevail.

But the ever-changing Adult State clearly shows the weaknesses of this or any rigid HPM system. We cannot determine once and for all the characteristics of the Adult State; nor can we control its activity: it can decide to grow in different directions in response to new experiences and new awareness. HPM systems should therefore focus on this aspect of the personality. Although not completely controllable and predictable, future leaders acting as adults have the capacity to grow and develop continuously. They learn to learn and consequently to make dynamic decisions based on ever-changing external realities and new internal awareness. An Adult State approach to HPM requires a fluidity that encourages people to advance, move sideways to new growth opportunities, leave the company for better options, or come in from outside the enterprise to fill important positions.

Although no person can be controlled, talented individuals with leadership potential are able to form serious commitments to an enterprise that values their performance and encourages them to give their best to the job at hand. The myth that the behavior, growth, and development of high potentials must be carefully controlled should be abandoned. A new psychological contract of mutual gain, based on negotiation and the determination to treat talented individuals as adults, should be at the heart of a high-potential management system.

8

Grooming Leaders in the Netherlands

Daniel F. J. Vloeberghs

INTRODUCTION

In recent years, globalization, diversity, technology, and social changes have simultaneously provided opportunities and threats for career management. Organizational growth has increased opportunities for individual advancement, but flattened organizational hierarchies have resulted in fewer occasions for promotion. Career awareness has become a major topic and concern in the development process of high potentials. In order to assess the identification of high-potentials (HIPOs) and their management development in an internationalizing environment, this chapter focuses on the changing management development (MD) system in a Dutch company, DSM Heerlen.

Career management is briefly outlined at the beginning of the chapter in the context of general management development. A conceptual and more concrete model of career management, together with a reference to the cultural influence on MD systems, lead to an introduction of DSM and its general background, as well as a brief history of its changing HIPO and leadership approach. The new challenges facing human resource management (HRM) at DSM—such as continuous employability, organizational culture, internationalization, and competency profiles—are assessed on a strategic basis, followed by the important shifts and developments in MD that have occurred during the past thirty years. The chapter concludes by proposing measures necessary for DSM's survival in the future.

CAREER MANAGEMENT IN THE CONTEXT OF MANAGEMENT DEVELOPMENT

With hiring and training, career management can be seen as another aspect of competence management in organizations. It helps maintain the core competency of organizations and increases the involvement, development, and motivation of employees. Today employees are responsible for their own career development and growth, and organizations offer the necessary facilities and support. This mutual responsibility for career development can be described as a changing psychological contract. Drastic changes in the economic and social environment have led to a rethinking of the implicit agreement between employers and their employees. Workers can no longer expect job security in exchange for acceptable levels of job performance and loyalty. Nowadays, employers expect their people to perform to the best of their abilities, show commitment, be flexible, and above all be employable at different levels and in different functions within the company. Employees expect fair compensation, but the respect, recognition, support, and participation of the organization are equally important.

Management development is a special form of career management that focuses on specific personnel who fill strategic positions in the organization. Four types of MD can be distinguished according to their target groups (Bergenhenegouwen et al. 1998, 347):

- Executive development: the development of the organization's top-level leadership
- Management development: the development of middle management and HIPOs
- Leadership development: the identification and development of professionals and managers with specific leadership qualities
- Human resource development: the consideration of all employees, including middle management and high potentials

In *Career Dynamics: Matching Individual and Organizational needs* (1978), Edgar Schein, a frequently cited career-management authority, presents the concept of an overall system of human resource planning and development (HRPD) from a managerial and organizational perspective. Since it is complex and dynamic, an effective approach to HRPD demands accurate matching of individual and organizational activities. Although this model is conceptually rich and clarifying, it requires creativity, determination, and vision to translate the tuning of individual and organizational needs, expectations, and activities into concrete organizational forms and structures.

In contrast with Schein's model, which lacks practical application, Vloeberghs and Kog (1995) set up a typology in which they distinguish three kinds of career management models, namely, a control model, a plan model, and a stream model. They attempt to explore the concrete manner in which organizations shape their career policy—focusing in particular on higher and middle management and how they rethink and reorient future prospect.

- *The control model* of career management mainly occurs in bureaucratic organizations that lack a connection between actual performance and criteria for appraisal and promotion. Decisions concerning applications and promotions are made at the top without taking individual needs and expectations into account because the higher organizational interests are seen as top priority. The model involves a minimally planned, reactive approach that leads to appointing employees by seniority. This control model occurs in static organizations that are acting in a reasonably stable environment. Furthermore, the role of the personnel department (if present) is restricted to administratively managing systems and files. The control model, lacking long-term or strategic properties, is often applied in government organizations such as ministries, schools, hospitals, universities, and prisons.

- *The plan model* is found in organizations that are systematically trying to bridge the gap between the available and necessary future leadership through long-term and strategic planning. Amplifying vertical mobility with horizontal and diagonal movement broadens career possibilities in such organizations. Top-down career management is still in order, although career development is also prevalent. Here a systematic approach to management development becomes obvious. But despite the emphasis on matching the organization and its individuals, in reality the organizational needs and imperatives are the main priority. The plan model exists in a less stable environment; therefore, strategies are formulated on the basis of middle-term or even short-term predictions and are often applied in divisional organizations with a strong bureaucratic approach where organizational control is still obvious.

- *The stream model* makes mobility possible in all directions: vertical (up and down), horizontal (rotation), and diagonal. The coherence between career flows and other human resource tools receives a great deal of attention. Setting up programs and initiatives such as counseling, coaching, advising, inplacement, mentoring, and outplacement makes room for career guidance. Open internal and external communication, continuous employability, and pluralism (initiatives concerning older employees, women, newly hired employees and their coaches, migrants, and minorities) are also important issues. Values such as innovation, flexibility, competitive strength, learning capacities, and competence development play an important role because of a fast changing, uncertain, and chaotic environment. This organization type is linked to a flat and more flexible structure where line management is integrated in the MD policy. The personnel department evolves toward human resources and is mainly active as an internal consultant advising individuals about career management.

Confronted with the challenge of translating these models into organizational realities, the people responsible for MD in six large multinationals (namely, Shell, Philips, Hoogovens, AKZO, DSM, and Unilever) developed for their divisions in the Netherlands a platform for exchanging experiences and developing joint training for MD staff. They emphasized MD as a process of planning and systematically tuning the interests of the organization with those of the employees. Their definition of MD is striking (Vloeberghs 1998, 161): "MD is a process of systematically matching the needs and possibilities of employees, resulting in an individual career plan and linked activities—a process that aims for continuous and adequate manning of managerial and specialist functions and for optimal development opportunities for co-workers." Describing MD at one of these companies—DSM (the Netherlands)—illustrates the importance of MD as a strategic human resource tool.

An analysis of its MD history shows that DSM currently operates under the plan model. The top-down character of management development has essentially dominated the company in the past, but a more systematic approach to MD is beginning to evolve. Rapid acquisitions (many of them international in scope), reengineering, downsizing, and an uncertain environment have led DSM to decentralize its MD activities, integrating line management. But the individual influence on career management is still minimal and not systemized. Strategic MD tools other than management and leadership training are hardly explored or used. Currently, MD policy at DSM tends toward the stream model, although it still requires some changes. In general DSM has evolved since 1967 from a total control model (merely focusing on hiring and firing) toward a plan model (whereby the individual's performance and potential are measured objectively). The need for an MD structure has now become obvious. The company will need to adopt the stream model if it wants to survive in the twenty-first century.

The cultural influence on MD systems should not be underestimated. Evans, Lank, and Farquahr (1989) divide MD systems into four categories according to their national/cultural stereotypes: the Japanese model, the Latin-European approach, the Germanic tradition, and the Anglo-Dutch model. It would take too long to analyze each approach, but it is clear that the Anglo-Dutch model applies to the DSM case. Strategic high-potential development in this company consists, among other aspects, of carefully monitoring HIPOs by management review committees, matching up performance and potential with requirements for short-and long-term job development, and emphasizing a management development staff (Sparrow and Hiltrop 1994, 372–373).

GENERAL INFORMATION ABOUT DSM

DSM describes itself as a global company with increasingly international dispersion, a wide product range in materials, fine chemicals, and synthetic fibers), and worldwide leadership positions—a company seeking more internal synergy, striving for less susceptibility to economic fluctuations and products with a higher added value, and aiming for more financial solidity across cycles.

In 1997 the enterprise embraced thirteen business groups organized into four activity areas: hydrocarbons and polymers, basic and fine chemistry, resins and synthetic materials, energy and remaining activities. In 1995 a turnover of 9.822 million DFL (Dutch guilders) was realized, with a net result of 1.071 million DFL; 16,990 staff members were employed worldwide, 10,317 of them in the Netherlands. A part of DSM's strategy is to increase the geographical spread of its operations. The acquisition of Vestolen, Germany in 1997 and Gist-Brocades in 1998 furnish proof of this tendency. DSM has roughly two hundred locations throughout the world and is represented in almost forty countries. Most of its operating companies are in Western Europe, but DSM is also strongly represented outside Europe (in the United States, Canada, Mexico, Brazil, China, and Singapore). About 75 percent of sales are realized in European countries and 16 percent in the United States.

Currently DSM has grouped its activities into three clusters, life science products, performance materials, and polymers and industrial chemicals. The company considers the life science products cluster to be the top-priority growth area. It comprises the business of DSM Fine Chemicals, DSM Specialty Intermediates, and the former activities of Gist-Brocades. DSM expects this cluster to meet its growth objective through autonomous growth and acquisitions or alliances. The performance materials cluster includes high-value-added business in various end markets with global customers. Here DSM focuses on expanding business potential in the United States and Asia. The polymers and industrial chemicals cluster comprises DSM's petrochemicals business and gas-based activities. The main goal in this area is to retain its place among the European olefins and polyolefins producers.

DSM originates from the Dutch States Mines, established in 1902. In 1973, however, the last coal mine was closed in compliance with the 1963–1973 plan. Since then, the company has been confronted with various internal and external changes as a result of its growth from a small chemical company into a medium-sized international chemical group. DSM has now become an international chemicals group with annual sales of nearly NLG 15 billion (approximately $7.6 billion in 1997) and a work force of over twenty-three thousand. About 45 percent of those employees are based in countries other than the Netherlands. During the past decades a strong reduction of the work force became necessary (e.g., from forty-two thousand between 1960 and 1970 to approximately thirty thousand today).

New organizational structure within the company necessitated a new culture and recruitment system. The way in which the different DSM organization components developed mutual cohesion is important for a good understanding of the strategic significance of management development. Table 8.1 is an extensive representation of the evolution of strategy, structure, culture, and recruitment, over forty years, from 1965 (when the mine company closed) up to and including the projected future situation in 2005.

A CHANGING CONTEXT FOR MANAGEMENT DEVELOPMENT

Although it appears that the approach regarding MD and HIPO at DSM had not fundamentally changed by 1985, Table 8.1 shows how much external and internal surroundings, especially since 1989, have been accelerating. Their ef-

Table 8.1
The Tuning Issue at DSM

	1965–1974	1975–1984	1985–1989
STRATEGY	• Closure of the mining company • Reconverting South Limburg • Construction Chemistry Holland	• Built out of bulk chemistry (synthetic fibers and chemical products) • Diversification of building and the making of synthetic materials • Gradual internationalization	• Maintenance of competitive position in bulk activities (rationalization) • "Specialties" and "high performance" products • Participating in oil-winning

STRUCTURE	• Functional organization:
	  • Emphasis on production, technique, logistics
	  • Limited commercial experience, only distribution
		• Divisional organization structure:
		  • Combination of markets and products in 7 divisions
		  • More autonomy per division
		  • A number of divisions with special diversification assignment
			• Further decentralization to divisions of the "running" business
			• Stronger concern influence as to new development programs
			• More focused acquisitions and joint ventures (Japan, USA . . .)

CULTURE	• Dominance of technique and production • Heavy and rather official system	• Construction of a commercial system and experience • Market-focused and competitive • Division to sub-cultures, depending on the nature of the division	• Stimulating the "technology push" and innovative ability • More flexibility
STAFFING HIGHER LEVEL	• Technical-organizational management • A lot of rules • Low diversity of management styles	• Diversity of functions, need for regular job rotations (production, commerce, business development) • Growth and career possibilities	• Need for highly qualified specialists • Need for general managers and risk-taking

Table 8.1 (*cont.*)

1990–1995	1996–2005
• Focusing (back to the core business) • Aiming for either European or world leadership • Eliminating noncore activities	• Selective expansion in fine chemistry and materials • Further internationalization
• Further decentralization (from 6 divisions to 13 business groups) • Reduction of staff and services • More business-focused staff and services • Re-engineering processes in different business groups • Applying new management information systems	• Maintaining of the decentralization trend • Worldwide application of management information systems • Evolution to a more market-focused organization • How to enlarge the synergy between the business groups/new approaches on the synergy question
• Toward a more businesslike style • Accent shifts in culture: e.g., more result-focused, more of a "do-it"-culture, more empowered employees	• From "push" (doing what the manager asks) to "pull" (the manager facilitates, coaches, gives a vision, empowers) • Initiative, empowerment, feedback (360°) • More responsibility to the employee for his/her career • Team spirit and creativity • Increasing the organizational ability to be a learning organization • Integrity; ethics of the undertaking • The importance of the employee survey as a barometer of social climate • Need for top managers with a clear strategic view and inspiring abilities
• Outplacement and outsourcing • Need for more management quality	• Need for more managerial abilities (broader, integral view) • Multicultural functioning managers • Broadly employable staff (limited number of specialists) • Risk behavior • More horizontal movements: growth is more a matter of quality than of vertical promotion (attention to social intelligence)

fects and implications will without doubt influence the MD system of the future. We first examine the most important moments, then map out the influence on HRM in general and MD in particular.

DSM's approach regarding MD and HIPOs had not fundamentally changed before 1985; the following list highlights external and internal influences that have accelerated the growth of MD at the company since 1985:

- 1989: new strategy DSM 2000, focused on leadership. This internal strategy project predicted DSM's position in the year 2000 and defined how to achieve such a position.
- 1990–1994: outlining a project, Concern 2000, with great attention to structural aspects, such as the establishment of business groups and the abolishment of the former divisional structure and the outsourcing of parts of services and staffs (reducing staff).
- 1995: new organization introduced. The company established thirteen business groups (BUGs) that report directly to the board of directors.
- 1996: attention to HRM as well as management and work style. The purpose is to emphasize results and customers with corporate components as the cornerstones.
- 1997 and on: MD's thirtieth year at DSM. Management development is scrutinized, leading to a critical rethinking of the MD system and to a reorientation of the MD instruments.

NEW CHALLENGES FOR MANAGEMENT DEVELOPMENT

Strategic note CPO 1996, "HRM in a Competitive and Ever Changing Environment," represents and investigates four crucial areas that present challenges to MD at DSM. Through intensive cooperation and consultation between corporate personnel and the various business groups, the notice underscores the need to decentralize the HRM policy.

Continuous Employability

Employability consists of a shared responsibility between the organization (usually the manager and the management) and the employees, who need the assurance that there will always be employment, either in their current positions or in future positions. This approach aligns with the fact that a company is no longer able to guarantee lifelong employment for every member of its staff. Thus there is no longer room for less effective workers (in the past these were described as "social cases," now often coldly removed as "dead wood" or "supernumerary"). Connected to this is an unambiguous demand for firmer support from managers for training and development. At the same time, the need for continuous employability points out the possible positive role of personal development (with built-in forms of self-assessment), besides the more traditional skill training.

Organizational Culture

Although a general company direction was clearly defined between 1990 and 1995 (in the company mission statement), the business groups obviously felt the need for a more operational approach. This is found in a strategic note from 1996 in the form of three activity fields. The organizational culture is described as one of "responsible care," acknowledging that coworkers are essential for the success and continuity of the firm. At the same time, care for continuous employability also offers the best guarantee for optimal employee motivation and involvement in company activities. Furthermore, it aims for an open, direct, and clear relationship. A few radical changes have occurred in management and leadership style, which mainly concern the delegation of responsibilities, a more supporting and coaching role of managers, mutual communication, and team work. The introduction of "empowerment" on lower levels is crucial in the competitive struggle. The difference between successful and less successful or unsuccessful enterprises is eventually determined by their capacity to answer changing market demands within a shorter space of time. The role of the future leader shifts away from control and decision making to the creation of optimal working conditions and coaching of employees through the realization of their "tasks, authorities, and responsibilities" (TARs).

New criteria are gaining importance in the selection of executives, such as the following characteristics of the "new style" DSM manager: external orientation (knowing what is happening in the market and what is important for the customer), leadership (having a clear vision, being able to transmit it, searching for synergy, and coaching employees), and a focus on performance (paying attention to costs and the adding of value, as well as creativity and a sense of renewal). Training sessions, which directly address the new leadership style and indirectly address other HRM areas, are offered through "corporate management courses" and extensively attended by managers in the framework of their management development. They mainly entail courses in creative expression, creative leadership, and mobilizing of teams. As for employee style, the emphasis in on an entrepreneurial attitude, appearance as real "professionals," personal responsibility for continuous employability, and learning in teams, by which they contribute to the concrete realization of a "learning organization."

To provide adequate recruitment for management and specialists in a strongly changing environment, DSM designed a management development system targeting both top and higher levels of the entire firm. Table 8.2 is the form DSM uses to evaluate HIPOs within this system.

Internationalization

In the future, more DSM activities will be situated outside the Netherlands, and even outside Europe. Certain planning scenarios project that around the year 2010 about 75 percent of the activities will be situated outside Europe. At pres-

Table 8.2
Cohesion between Strategic Goals and Work Fields

	High				Low	
I. Inflow Transfer						
Recruitment and selection, introduction	1	2	3	4	5	6
Placement	1	2	3	4	5	6
Outplacement	1	2	3	4	5	6
II. Personnel Development						
Training, education	1	2	3	4	5	6
Career interview	1	2	3	4	5	6
Evaluation	1	2	3	4	5	6
Career planning	1	2	3	4	5	6
Continuous selection	1	2	3	4	5	6
Expatriate policy	1	2	3	4	5	6
III. Working Conditions						
Job evaluation	1	2	3	4	5	6
Individual judgement	1	2	3	4	5	6
Consultation	1	2	3	4	5	6
Working conditions	1	2	3	4	5	6
IV. Organization						
Job descriptions	1	2	3	4	5	6
Working structure	1	2	3	4	5	6
Working conditions	1	2	3	4	5	6
Organizational development	1	2	3	4	5	6
V. Personnel Information						
Reporting administration	1	2	3	4	5	6
VI. Welfare Care						
Care-activities	1	2	3	4	5	6
VII. Internal Communication						
Media, newsletter	1	2	3	4	5	6

ent the highest priority is to create a real international management framework. The company needs to play catch-up in order to send a number of DSM managers to other countries as expatriates in an accelerated period. On the other hand, a number of non-Dutch high potentials should be identified and developed as well. Working conditions for expatriates as a whole should be designed and tested worldwide. A simple international information network can provide a clear view of the available supporting services in these countries.

Competency Profiles

Executives of the business groups and corporate personnel worry about the quality of the available management. Several of the factors mentioned previously[1] create the need to strengthen human resource competencies in both recruitment and management development. The concrete procedure represented here is primarily a set of HRM standards that operationalize the profile of a "good" leader at DSM. A number of explicit, measurable performance indicators that require regular reporting are connected with more normative competency criteria, for instance:

- The "we want optimally trained employees" norm can be concretized by a (minimum) number of days of training per employee.
- The "we need new blood in the organization" norm can be expressed in a policy of recruiting middle and even higher management outside business groups and even outside the DSM organization.
- The "we need a more international and cross-cultural executive population" utterance can be evaluated through the number of coworkers in expatriate positions (e.g., 125 in 1999 instead of 75–80 in 1997) and the number of non-Dutch people in the group of high potentials.

The corporate management development (CMD) department plays an integrating role in promoting MD at DSM, and a team of four supports three cross-departmental connections. A business group MD commission meets approximately eight times every year and is active per part of the firm (business group or staff). Branch commissions for functional sectors like marketing, technology and production, human resources and organization, finance, economy, and information technology (IT) follow up on developments in question, translate these into function profiles, and advise with respect to nominations. These sector groups consist of business and functional managers from the business units and the corporate organization. Geographical MD commissions strive for synergy in the human resources policy of the four most important DSM countries (United States, United Kingdom, Germany, and France). These country commissions meet two or three times yearly in the country concerned under the authority of a senior president or managing director.

Finally the president of the company, who, in this structure, is the chairman of the group top executive development (TED), plays a crucial role. This group prepares the most important top nominations. The managing director Corporate Personnel and Organization (CPO) acts in this structure as chairman of the executive development commission, which arranges the nominations directly below the top. The other cross-connections report via CPO.

In this way and in the framework of an extremely light corporate structure, policy components that otherwise would have been overseen in the decentralized organization receive extensive attention. Moreover, a direct connection with the strategic decision-making process is built in. We mention as well the consistent supporting role of the (limited) CMD department, which focuses mainly on guarding the process and the quality of performance at the different levels and on the application itself for the approximately 250 top employees.

SHIFTS AND DEVELOPMENTS IN MANAGEMENT
DEVELOPMENT AT DSM

Management development (MD) activity has always been an important point of attention at DSM. On April 14, 1997, the organization even celebrated its thirtieth anniversary. Economic activities, strategic options, and social challenges have repeatedly exerted their influence on the manner in which the MD system has been shaped. At first, vacancy filling in the growing company was almost exclusively stressed. Mobility was considered synonymous with promotion, and the whole approach could not keep up with the actual situation. From the beginning of the seventies, a certain broadening and expansion occurred as the maintenance and search for real management potential were at the core of MD activities. During the eighties, more attention was given to a larger differentiation into several target HIPO groups, like "fast growers" and "solid citizens." Complex career building increased, approximately half of the new employees gained a second specialty and about an equal number ended up in several functions (from supervising specialist to depth specialist). Around the same period, there seemed to be a need to let manager profiles connect as closely as possible to specific life phases, product groups, and product developments.

New developments and challenges occurred during the nineties. Workshops held on the occasion of the thirty-year MD symposium already pointed to the following direction:

- MD and cyclical sensitiveness: in its starting phase, economic fluctuations and the following reorganization and decentralization trend slowed fast development of MD at DSM. Market conditions will force MD to apply a hiring policy that follows economic cycles. In this matter, the past turbulent years of acquisitions, expansions, and rationalizations, closely bound with market conditions, have forced DSM to hire a considerable amount of new and inexperienced employees.

- MD and decentralization: before 1967 a strong HRM function and hierarchic structure characterized DSM. But since the strategic note of 1967, which pointed out the responsibilities of managers concerning a well-functioning system for hiring, planning, and training, high potentials are managed by decentralized MD commissions. Because of the still ongoing decentralization, the current MD policy needs to maintain synergy by allowing internal transfers.

- MD and employability: DSM has its activities in business sectors that require long-term investment, long-term research, as well as long-term employee relations. Therefore MD needs to focus on the long-term capacities, knowledge, and employability of DSM's employees. High potentials should be given the opportunity to leave their business units in order to advance their growth and employability in the firm. They need to be supported in their choices to take action that opens up new opportunities.

- MD and internationalization: the continuously growing internationalization is without any doubt of crucial importance. Whereas in 1990 the relationship between the Netherlands and foreign countries, in terms of employment units, was 60/40, the prognosis for 2000 showed a relationship of 40/60. This elicited more and more the question of the extent to which a number of policies, concepts, and tools developed in the south of Holland would also be applicable in Singapore, Shanghai, Chicago, and other places.

Furthermore, DSM is working toward a concrete realization of a cultural turnover in a more explicit manner than in the past. The whole company is attempting to acquire a number of specific characteristics and skills. The leadership training sessions essentially focus on all (higher) staff members. This new culture will lead to an approach that enlarges the impact of individual employees. Different policies and programs like empowerment, more undertaking and risk behavior, 360-degree performance evaluation, cross-cultural influence, work in project teams, electronic network structures, and stress on employability will undoubtedly emphasize the necessity for new directions and a new MD system. HIPO management will be different.

FUTURE ACTIONS

It can be said that DSM has built a solid tradition in the area of management development between 1967 and 2000, although some criticism still exists. For instance, management training has received too little attention in the past. The individual development of high potentials was mainly a matter of job rotation, and other HIPO development tools were hardly used. Furthermore, the lack of sufficient reserves or a talent pool led to an MD crisis, and the risk of filling vacancies through chaotic ad hoc decisions became a reality. International MD in its turn needs more attention if the MD system wants to run parallel with DSM's strategy.

For the future, the following policies should be reconsidered and reshaped:

- Development of new leaders and coworkers: too little time is spent discussing and explaining necessary improvements and the learning required to overcome limited knowledge, experience, attitudes, and behavior (as mentioned in the critical report). Analysis and discussion of the judgment reports by the MD commissions are seriously considered, but afterward, too little time and attention go to concretizing improvements. Agreements concerning career training and behavioral changes should be specified in a "contract" formulated by the manager and the employee.

- Ranking of MD: decentralizing often results in insufficiently developed professionalism as well as only a remote emphasis on management development. Currently MD is not a priority in some areas because the MD profession is not appropriately developed. MD tasks are often seen as peripheral by decentralized working personnel officers. However, decentralized personnel staff must also be able to investigate reports on development and improvements and stay informed about the possibilities in the larger organizational context. This leads to little real expertise in the HR function.

- Flexibility between business groups: business groups tend to hoard their HIPOs, thus obviously not facilitating a broad career perspective and potentially having a prejudicial effect on MD as well as on individual career planning. Transferring across the borders of business groups is thus getting more difficult and can only be advanced through informal personal contacts and influence.

- Opportunities for employees to influence the MD process: employees currently have limited possibilities to influence the process. It is becoming apparent that the company needs to increase its openness about employee potential, to contribute to two-way feedback and give employees an awareness of their own competencies as judged by the company. Increasing the influence of employees fits into the development of a learning organization and the framework of employability.

- Criteria for leaders: leaders should be defined less in terms of knowledge and more in terms of skills and behavior, such as coaching, communication, building and maintaining relations, and ability to share power in a flat organization. Personal traits can turn the scale in promotion possibilities, as a result of both social changes (more independent employees) and organizational development (as delayering leads to more intensified relationships).

- New role of the managing board: changing people's behavior in the organization is a slow process that requires great effort but will certainly continue in the twenty-first century, together with the implementation of a few new MD tools. The goals of the DSM managing board are to complement the strengths of the MD system that existed when MD was founded in 1967 and during the cyclical storms up until 2000, and to adjust and renew the system, keeping the challenges of the millennium in mind.

SUMMARY

The identification and development process for high potentials is without any doubt a key element in linking strategy, culture, and the human resources in an organization. Individual learning must be considered within the context of organizational learning. The DSM case demonstrates the major influence of organizational development on MD systems. During recent years, a rapid succession of acquisitions, internationalization, and rationalizations have led DSM to decentralize its MD activities and increase the influence of line management. However, management development is obviously not yet a stable part of DSM, and certain measures, mentioned earlier, are necessary to ensure its role for sustainable competitive advantage. At present, management development at DSM does not sufficiently take environmental developments into account, and therefore it risks being too narrow and too unadapted to survive in the future.

NOTE

1. Such as (1) higher demands due to the disappearance of the divisional level (2) the introduction of a flat organizational structure with the disappearance of promotional opportunities and possible position blocking by current but less qualified personnel, (3) the need to function as a learning organization connected with the demand for more delegation, (4) empowerment and more (mental and functional) flexibility, and finally (5) the challenge of increasing internationalization.

REFERENCES

Bergenhenegouwen, G. J., E.A.M. Mooijman, and H. H. Tillema. 1998. *Strategisch opleiden en leren in organisaties.* Deventer: Kluwer Bedrijfswetenschappen.

Bournois, F., and S. Roussillon. 1997. Identification and development of potential for management and executive positions in France. *Career Development International* 2(7):341–346.

Bournois, F., and S. Roussillon. 1998. Préparer les dirigeants de demain: Une approche internationale de la gestion des cadres à haut potentiel. Paris: Éditions d'Organisation.

Burack, E. H., W. Hochwarter, and N. J. Mathys. 1997. The new management development paradigm. *Human Resource Planning* 20(1):14–21.

de Vries, M., and A.C.M. Wanders. 1997. MD bij DSM, 30 jaar en verder, brochure, DSM N. V., Heerlen.

Ebadan, G., and D. Winstanley. 1997. Downsizing, delayering and careers—the survivor's perspective. *Human Resource Management Journal* 7(1):79–91.

Edelstein, B. C., and D. J. Armstrong, Jr. 1993. A model for executive development. *Human Resource Planning* 16(4):51–68.

Evans, P., E. Lank, and A. Farquar. 1989. Managing human resources in the international firms: Lessons from practice. In P. Evans, Y. Doz, and A Laurent, eds. *Human resource management in international firms: Change, globalization, innovation.* New York: Macmillan. Pp. 113–143.

Feldman, D. C., and M. C. Bolino. 1996. Careers within careers: Reconceptualizing the nature of career anchors and their consequences. *Human Resource Management Review* 6(2):89–112.

Hall, D. T. 1995. Executive careers and learning: Aligning selection, strategy, and development. *Human Resource Planning* 18(2):14–23.

Nelson, D. L., and Q. J. Campbell. 1994. *Organizational behavior: Foundations, realities and challenges.* Minneapolis/St. Paul: West Publishing.

Schein, E. (1978). *Career Dynamics: Matching Individual and organizational needs.* Reading, MA: Addison-Wesley.

Sparrow, P., and J. M. Hiltrop. 1994. *European human resource management in transition.* New York/London: Prentice-Hall.

Sullivan, S. E., W. A. Carden, and D. F. Martin. 1998. Careers in the next millennium: Directions for future research. *Human Resource Management Review* 8(2):165–181.

Vaughn, R. H., and M. C. Wilson, 1994. Career management using job trees: Charting a path through the changing organization. *Human Resource Planning* 17(4):37–54.

Vloeberghs, D. 1989. Human Resource Management: Visie, Strategieën en Toepassingen, ACCO, Leuven-Amersfoort.

Vloeberghs, D. 1997. Handbook Human Resource Management. Managementcompetenties voor de 21ste eeuw, ACCO, Leuven-Amersfoort.

Vloeberghs, D. 1998. Management development in a context of drastic changes. *Journal of Management Development* 17(9):644–661.

Vloeberghs, D., and E. Kog. 1995. Van loopbaanbeheer tot loopbaanbegeleiding. *Economisch en Sociaal Tijdschrift* 4:591–622.

9

Selecting Leaders in Poland During the Transition Period

Czeslaw J. Szmidt

CONTEXTUAL FACTORS

When examining the process of managerial selection in Poland, it is necessary to understand the nation's political, economic, and social conditions before attempting to analyze human resource management.

Poland was doubtlessly the first country in either Central or Eastern Europe to experience the economic and social change that led to the collapse of communism. The Solidarity Union was set up in August 1980, and so-called progress forces managed to introduce two laws in September of the following year, just months before the government's December 1981 crackdown on Solidarity. Thanks to these laws, which concerned state-controlled companies and the self-management of personnel, anti-Communist forces (the Solidarity movement and the Works Council) reached an immensely significant objective: they were able to influence the election of general managers in state-run companies (at the time there were around eighty thousand companies in Poland, two-thirds of which were government-controlled). For the first time in a Communist country since 1945, domains reserved for political leaders, their allies, and the secret services were being infiltrated. By 1988, a year before the roundtable talks that brought together all the country's political parties and social forces, Polish records showed 250,000 employed managers, excluding chief executive officers (CEOs).

Before 1981, the Communist Party committee nominated candidates for managerial positions (in public administration organizations, political parties, and unions as well as in companies) without consulting persons inside the organization. It was said, during that time, that managers were "delivered to companies in a closed briefcase." Clearly the most important criterion for professional advancement was membership in the Party, or at the very least, the "right" political ideals. A Polish expression from that period proclaimed that a manager should be "BMW"—not representing speed in decision making or technical efficiency, but rather signifying three Polish words: *bierny* (passive), *mierny* (mediocre), and *wierny* (faithful).

Theoretically, the Party's human resources were considerable, and the system for managing them particularly efficient. In the mid-1980s, the Polish United Workers' Party boasted 3.65 million members, and one of its satellites, the United Peasant Party, had 500,000. The Democratic Party (with 100,000 members, Poland's second largest party) and the Socialist Youth Party (50,000 members) accounted for a good portion of the rest of the working class. This battalion of 4.3 million Party members, mixed among the nations' 38 million inhabitants, affected the jobs of 17 million employees. In other words, 4.3 million voters wielded enough power to distribute managerial and executive positions to hand-picked individuals.

However, it should be noted that the Party's structural flaws made it weaker than it could have been. For instance, many people never accepted Party "dignity" (membership), even if it would have saved their career. What is more, in the early 1980s, the Party suffered a serious crisis—membership dropped by approximately 25–30 percent (6 million members in 1980, 4.3 million in 1985).

A UNIQUE WAY TO RECRUIT MANAGERS: THE "CONTEST"

The social atmosphere at the beginning of the 1980s paved the way for "compulsory contests" for executive positions. Starting on September 25, 1981, contests were officially held; this law remained unchanged and in effect even during war years (1981–1984).

From the time the contest was initiated, the right to nominate a company director belonged to the Works Council (fifteen to twenty people elected for a period of two years); the exception to this rule is new firms' first directors, who are chosen by a government ministry. In this last case, the whole procedure of the contest (particularly the evaluation of the candidates) is carried out by a jury, the composition of which evolves in keeping with Poland's political situation.

Since the birth of the leadership contest in 1981, the composition of the jury has tended to reflect large-scale social forces rather than the normal "stockholders" common to Western companies (employees, suppliers, shareholders, customers). Between 1981 and 1990, Polish leadership juries were made up of the following:

- A representative of the ministry
- A representative of the company's primary financial institution
- A representative of each union in the company (in practice, there were always at least two: the Solidarity Union and the Post-Communist Union; often, though, there were as many as five or six)
- A representative of each political party inside the company (usually just the Polish United Workers' Party, though in certain firms were found the United Farmers' Party or the Democratic Party)
- A representative from the Socialist Youth Party (rarely a representative from Rural Youth)
- A representative of the firm's central engineers and technicians.
- Three representatives from the Works Council—a significant portion of the eight to sixteen total jurors

In general, larger juries existed in larger companies. The larger the jury, the greater the number of representatives from the Communist Party and its partisans—a situation that allowed the Party to keep political control over the personnel of the largest and most strategic companies. The system was designed to allow a conglomerate political party to take control of the other parties, youth groups, and former unions.

Very often, the decision of a jury that included three representatives of the Works Council and one from Solidarity depended completely on the engineering and technical representative. So, in order to strengthen its own position, the post-Communist left wing apparently revived a vassal organization that had been either inactive or ineffective for several years. This kind of manipulation was easier to achieve in large companies because the Works Councils more or less upheld the letter of the law in smaller ones.

In most cases it was the Works Council that initiated the search for a new director and that publicly opened the contest. Then the jury (which included only three representatives from the Works Council) was to lead the evaluation of the leadership candidates and, on the basis of the jurors' political alignment, make the final choice. The jury had to choose between a simplified procedure (one stage) and a "full" procedure (two stages). The single-stage procedure, carried out solely by the jury, required candidates to attend an interview and submit, a few days before the meeting, a presentation of their views regarding company management. During the two-stage procedure, external consultants could be enlisted to evaluate the applicants' competency. But since the presence of consultants led to a more objective evaluation process, certain jurors attempted to block the participation of such advisers in order to ensure the selection of a politically advantageous candidate.

These actions deprived most jury members of objective information, of clear alternatives, and of the power to influence the contest's proceedings. Furthermore, jury members (except the representatives of the ministry and occasionally the delegates from the company) rarely had previous experience with personnel management questions. Consequently, the ministry's representatives were often able to use their position to steer fellow jurors away from making sound human resource decisions.

A typical manipulative technique often surfaced during the contest's final stage. A scale with a maximum of 100 points was used in this phase to evaluate each candidate, and most members of the jury awarded all candidates the same number of points, more or less. However, one or two jurors would award 100 points to their favorite and none to all the others—regardless of their qualifications. Thus the contest was rigged to fit the wishes of the manipulators. And since the contest's votes were made by secret ballot, no one could question the results.

After the elections in 1989, the ban on Communist Party intervention in companies, together with shifts in Poland's political layout, led to a change in jury composition. From 1990 and on, juries were made up of five people: three representatives of the Works Council and two from the ministry. This change is evidence for the victory of Solidarity forces. But in 1992, the party's divided political forces and administrative consolidation (which took place despite numerous protests from Works Councils and trade unions) led to the alteration of this jury composition. In the end, ministry envoys were given three votes, and two votes belonged to employee representatives. The other general rules of the contest remained unchanged from their original 1981 drafting.

Above all, the contest for the position of company director required publicity. In the first place, the law required organizers to announce the contest to the company's staff and then to place announcements in at least two newspapers. In practice, the largest companies attempted to attract good external candidates by running contest advertisements in six to eight newspapers, on a variety of dates, and in several regions. Following the advertising period was the application deadline, generally two weeks before the contest started.

The Contest for Senior Management Positions

The principal qualifications for leadership candidates are rather typical of all cultures undergoing transitional management. They are generally the following:

- A university degree (master's or doctorate) in a technical field, technology, economics, or law
- Professional seniority of at least six to eight years
- Managerial experience of at least three to four years
- Qualification in management, economics, trade, or international trade
- Knowledge of foreign languages (mainly English); since linguistic skills are still relatively weak in Poland, ads tend to include the expression "knowledge [of foreign languages] desirable"
- Good health

• A maximum age of forty-five: the jury cannot admit an applicant above that age because this would necessitate the revision of the entire procedure in order to maintain
fairness; the rules of the game and the recruitment strategy have to be established
before the contest opens

An applicant's file consists of

• A personal questionnaire (a document with standard information, such as date of birth,
family status, date of marriage, number of children, qualifications, profession, distinc-
tions, foreign language skills, professional history, and political party membership)
• A biography (younger candidates submit a Western-style résumé)
• References from previous employers
• A medical certificate, dated within the last three months and affirming that the candidate
is fit for a managerial post
• University diplomas and other certificates
• A certification of language skills

Because certificates, diplomas, and references are not yet as highly regarded in
Poland as they are in more stable social systems, it is necessary to confirm that
candidates possess the skills necessary for a managerial position.

A typical approach to determining this is to test the following:

• Theoretical and practical knowledge of organization, company management, personnel
management, finance, marketing, accounting, foreign languages, and general culture
• Psychological factors—personality and intellectual aptitude

The results of this testing have considerable weight: around 95 percent of
juries' final decisions conform to the results of consultants' examinations. Consultants, then, are extremely influential in the selection of modern Poland's future leaders.

Another key event in the contest is the interview. In the "short" procedure,
it is one of the decisive elements. In the "long" version, two interviews are
generally organized: the first, with all candidates who have qualified for the
contest; and a second, for candidates who have made the first cut. The first
interview aims to ascertain the details of the candidates' file, as well as candidates' general knowledge. The jury members then award points in various categories, rating each candidate on a previously determined scale.

The second interview generally covers two issues, which are dealt with simultaneously and more briefly in the "short" procedure. The first is the potential
manager's proposed method for administrating personnel policy and managing
relations with unions, work councils, and subordinates. The second issue is the
candidate's concept of company management from economic and technical
standpoints.

TRENDS SINCE THE MID-1990s

The greatest changes since the mid-1990s are these:

- Candidates' average age is dropping. Firms are hiring new managers aged between twenty-eight and thirty; in the past, new employees were typically over forty.
- Nobody dares ask (in fact, it is formally forbidden to ask) whether the candidate belongs to a political party. Candidates, then, are no longer questioned on their political beliefs.
- Applicants are generally more qualified, thanks to numerous business and management training courses. Candidates' files are becoming "copious"; more and more, they contain postgraduate diplomas and certificates from specialized workshops and developmental experiences either in Poland or in foreign countries.
- More and more candidates master foreign languages, computers, and quantitative managing techniques.
- Recruitment areas are expanding geographically because candidates are more willing to assume positions far from home.
- Today's juries can include company supervisors, company owners, or owners' representatives.

The contest, with its strictly defined rules, was still compulsory in state-controlled companies in 1997. But despite the fact that partially or entirely privatized enterprises were not obliged to use this technique, the contest is still the best known and most widely used recruitment method in Poland.

ILLUSTRATION: DEVELOPING HIGH-POTENTIAL EXECUTIVES IN A LARGE POLISH BANK

The advances in human resource management can be illustrated by a large Polish bank and its network of branches, an organization that has had a human resource director since 1995. When this bank was created, the managers were almost all chosen from within the company—an obvious sign that confidence and seniority ranked high on the list of selection criteria. This method was quite suitable at that time, when the bank hired about one thousand employees at once; jobs were not threatened, and long-term careers were virtually guaranteed. Since 1990 the bank's number of employees has grown fivefold, a trend mirrored in other banks. The geographical area covered by this particular establishment also grew, its 36 branches existing in 1989 increasing to more than 150 by 1997.

Under these new, larger-scale conditions, it was not feasible to use the same methods of human resource management as in the 1980s, so the bank modified its policies. During the effort to identify and develop high-potential executives, a different kind of contest was developed to suit the vast need for managers to fill positions in newly created branches.

When hoping to find good candidates from within the bank, "closed" contests were organized, and the participation of certain individuals was solicited. This technique created a system of promotion for young, aspiring managers, and it helped to expand the scope of the bank's annual employee evaluation interviews. In this setting, it was possible to investigate applicants who applied of their own spontaneous will as well as the applicants nominated by senior staff members.

On the other hand, for new jobs and technical positions (known as *terrae incognitae*), the contest was open to everyone. Well-organized "open" contests usually attracted a significant number of candidates—between five and twenty-five people—if the organizers could guarantee a fair procedure and an objective decision.

The president of the bank, with the help of the human resource director, made the final decisions for branch manager positions. A human resource manager and the branch managers, in turn, made final decisions on subordinate positions.

CONCLUSION

In conclusion, the recruitment procedure that originated in the 1980s in Poland has evolved much, but its basic elements currently remain unchanged. A national "school" has now been created to help consultants in their work, in effect preserving the way they evaluate candidates. In some ways, this newly established form of recruitment is contributing to an original, nationwide personnel management policy.

Since the West has so deeply impressed upon Poland its scientific and cultural principles, it would seem that management recruitment tools would be similarly passed on. Actually, the contest is unique to Poland—no other Eastern European country has anything quite like it. The contest's presence in Poland serves an important dual role: it is not only the beginning but the heart of executive management, and it allows interaction among hitherto alienated individuals, such as public authorities, consultants, labor representatives, and unions. There are, of course, many variations on these contests and on the way their roles are carried out, and though perhaps there are as many slanted contests as there are objective ones, overall progress is being made.

Understanding how Poland is shaped by the same large-scale forces (politics, economics, unions, etc.) that drive the "contests" is essential for grasping the way personnel management policies are structured and future leaders are developed.

REFERENCES

Bournois, F. 1991. *La gestion des cadres en Europe* Paris: Eyrolles.
Brabet, J. 1993. *Repenser la gestion des ressources humaines* Paris: Economica.
Jamroga, J. and B. Nogalski. 1989. "Kariery zawodowe polskiej kadry kierowniczei." *Doskonalenie Kadr Yàerowniczychn* 7/8: 11–19.
Kasten, M. 1989. "Nomenklatura," *Doskonalenie Kadr Kierowniczych* 7/8: 3–11.

Kostera, M. 1993. "Role Spoleczne menedzera." *Przeglad Organizacji* 7:10–12.

Lachiewicz, S. 1983. "Specjalista w przedsiebiorstwie przemyslowym. Warsaw: PGE.

Louart, P. 1991. *La gestion des ressources humaines* Paris: Eyrolles.

Rocznik Statystyczny GUS, 280–282.

Szmidt, C. 1984. "Konkursy na stanowiska dyrektorow." *Organizacja i Zarzadzanie* 15: 69–83.

Thevenet, M. 1992. *Impliquer les personnes dans l'entreprise* Paris: Editions Liaison.

10

Leadership Commitment, Women, and the Japanese System

Mami Taniguchi

THE PURPOSE AND RESEARCH QUESTION OF THIS STUDY

There are few women managers in Japan. According to a 1995 survey of the Labor Ministry Japan in 1995, the percentage of women at general manager level is 1.5 percent, and at section manager level it is 2.0 percent (Ministry 1995). Even though many women have the academic background and have demonstrated their ability on the job, they are unable to be managers in Japanese firms. Then, what are the conditions, besides the two mentioned, necessary to be promoted to management in Japan. Studying women managers and their relationship to the Japanese style of management may clarify some points of Japanese management that have never come into the limelight.[1] This is the fundamental research question of this study. Its purpose is to give some insights toward answering this question.

In order to clarify the research question being considered, Itami's "employeeism" is applied as the theoretical framework. Whereas in capitalistic companies it is considered that a company belongs to its shareholders, in Japanese companies it is recognized that a company belongs to its employees. This idea is what Itami calls employeeism. It is adopted by many Japanese companies; in them employees who commit themselves to the company for a long period become core members of the company. For that reason, part-time employees and women who retire after a few years cannot be core members of Japanese companies (Itami, Kagono, and Ito 1993). Since many women retire after a few years, principles applied by Japanese management do not apply to women em-

Figure 10.1
Personnel Composition of a Japanese Company

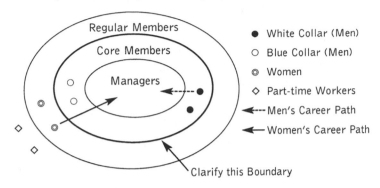

ployees; women cannot become core members in "employeeistic" companies because one must work in them as long as he or she can contribute unique management resources to the company.

To sum up, *core members* are those to whom the principles of Japanese management apply and who have a chance to be managers in employeeistic companies. In this study, the term employeeism and *Japanese management system* are synonymous.

The term *commitment* can be defined as "devoting oneself to the company." Japanese companies regard male employees as having a commitment to the company from their initial hiring, but in the case of female employees, it is hard to know in the early stages of their career whether they have the same commitment. Most new female employees require more time than their male counterparts to become committed to the company. For that reason, in companies adopting the Japanese management style, there exists a difference in the starting point of the career path between male and female employees.

Figure 10.1 shows the personnel composition of Japanese companies. It is assumed that women start from outside the boundary, as noncore members; later some of them can become core members, and still later managers. Men start inside the boundary, as core members, and some later become managers. The boundary between men and women in initial status draws a line between those to whom Japanese management practices should be applied and those to whom they should not be applied.

If we study the situation of a woman working for a company adopting employeeism and carefully investigate details about how she changes her status from noncore member to core member, to manager, we may be able to clarify the nature of the boundary and the restrictions that it produces.

The author considers that there are five characteristics that distinguish whether an employee has commitment or not. If the employee is willing to perform all five, the company regards him or her as having commitment. These five items are the following:

1. The employee shows the intention to continue in service for a long time and subsequently remains in the firm for a long time.
2. The employee does not refuse overtime work.
3. The employee socializes with the other people in the company.
4. The employee socializes with appropriate people outside the company.
5. The employee does not refuse a sudden transfer of post even though the locality is remote or undesirable.

These items used to measure commitment are the characteristics of personnel appraisal in Japanese companies and are quite different from those used in Western companies, which only take into account one's ability and business results. It is assumed that in appraising employees commitment to the company is heavily weighted in Japanese companies (Kumazawa 1997).

METHOD AND RESEARCH DATA

In this study, surveys were employed for quantitative analysis, and case methods were utilized in the conclusions. A questionnaire examined the company's personnel division (one personnel manager for each company answered; there was a valid response from 148 companies and the valid response percentage was 20.2 percent), women managers (one woman manager for each company answered, valid response of 102 managers, valid response percentage of 14.5 percent), and subordinates of women managers (one subordinate for each woman manager answered, valid response of 178 subordinates, valid response percentage of 24.2 percent).

In two of these surveys conducted, on a company's personnel division and on women managers, questions about the "items to measure commitment" (serving continuously, working overtime, socializing with people inside the company, socializing with people outside the company, accepting transfer to a remote locality) were included. The responses to these questions revealed the following facts.

The average length of service of women promoted to management positions is much longer than that of male employees, to say nothing of the average for female employees as a whole. Furthermore, many had the intention of working long term from their entrance into the company and have continued to serve in the same firm, all the while remaining single and having no children. Also, they had been working overtime before they were promoted to manager status, and the amount of overtime work was about the same as or more than that of their male counterparts. These women consider socializing with people in the company more important than do their personnel managers, and they frequently had drinks after work with their colleagues during their years in the company. However, few women managers had a transfer to a remote locality and did not consider a transfer to a remote company branch as directly affecting promotion.

The results of these surveys show the following facts about Japanese women managers. They have served continuously, worked overtime, and socialized with people inside the company. The amount of hours and frequency of overtime work are equal to or greater than those of male employees. It is clear that they show devotion to their company in these actions. On the other hand, there were only a few women managers who had a chance to socialize informally with customers or clients (so-called *settai*) or who were transferred to a remote locality.

In this research, case analysis have also been conducted among three Japanese companies (Aisin-Seiki, an automobile parts manufacturing company; Nippon Telegraph and Telephone, a communication services company; and Familiar, a child textile manufacturing and wholesale company).

In choosing three Japanese companies as subjects of case analysis, the following three characteristics were considered:

1. A company in which the percentage of male employees is larger than that of female employee and job categories are assigned by gender
2. A company that has a benefit system for women who continue working; as a result, women's length of service is close to that of men
3. A company in which the percentage of female employees is larger than that of male employees, which therefore allows women an opportunity to demonstrate their business ability

Companies of type 1 draw a line between men's and women's jobs. Women are usually limited to assisting male workers. Examples of those can be seen in key industries such as manufacturing or construction. In such companies, male employees take the initiative to socialize, work overtime, and have receptions for clients. In investigating a company with this characteristic, it seems to be clear why few women are promoted to management.

In companies of type 2 continuous service can be expected without reference to gender, so the effects of the other four items to measure commitment on promotion to management are considered.

Companies of type 3 have appointed women as supervisors in the past. For that reason, in such companies, there are relatively many women managers. Companies with this characteristic have often been the object of long-term case analysis.

Two foreign companies were chosen as subjects of case analysis. One is a nonpharmaceutical manufacturing and wholesale company (Procter and Gamble); the other is a computer related tools manufacturing and wholesale company (Olivetti). These two companies are well-known foreign companies in Japan, which have more than one thousand employees. The industrial categories of these two are different, as are the nations in which their headquarters are located, the United States and Italy.

One-on-one interviews were conducted with each personnel manager, a woman manager (a subject of each case), her superior who had some influence on her appointment to management, and colleagues and subordinates. For each company range five to nine persons were interviewed.

The results of the case analysis made clear the following two characteristics of Japanese companies compared to foreign companies. First, a sexual division of labor exists in Japanese companies; jobs are divided by gender and male and female employees are assigned different jobs. In not only type 1 companies but also types 2 and 3, a perception of gender roles still exists. In company 3, whose chair person is female, female employees are expected to work in sales or design and can be promoted only in these sections. However, company 2 differs from 1 and 3 because women who have graduated from universities have been treated the same as men. In other words, they can follow the same career path.[2]

Second, Japanese companies checked women's commitment before promoting them to management status.[3] There is an *informal* screening system for commitment in Japanese companies. It takes superiors time to consider females as core members equal to male employees or to determine whether they intend to work as men do.

In the case of Japanese company 1, the superior asked the female to work continuously, as men would, even if she married in the future, when she was about age thirty. Then he started to provide on-the-job training for her, to see whether she had the intention to work comparably to men. After one year, she would have a chance to change her occupational category from a clerical position (*Ippanshoku*) to a career position (*Sogoshoku*). Then she could follow the same career path as men, in other words, be a candidate for a management position. Similarly, the woman manager of the Japanese company with characteristic 3 could not become a full-time employee, and therefore could not become a manager, unless her superior appraised her attitude toward her job, commuting between Tokyo and Kobe every week and socializing with clients. These two cases show that the commitment level of these female employees was checked before their status changed. In the case of the woman manager of Japanese company (2), although she did not change her job status before being appointed as chief operator, it was confirmed whether or not she would accept night duty and whether she intended to maintain networking relationships in the workplace. In addition to that, before she was promoted to chief manager in a personnel division, a position in which the majority are men, the company intentionally placed her in a division in which hard work, such as overtime work, is required to let her experience a hard job, to see whether she could work as her male colleagues did.

In most cases, such commitment screening is implicit. The female, regarded as an object, does not know that she is now in a period of commitment screening. As I mentioned before, there is a boundary in Japanese companies (see Figure 10.1). When a female crosses the boundary, commitment screening occurs. One of the superiors whom I interviewed said that he arranged his female subordinates' commitment screening period at around the age of thirty, when the probability of her quitting the job was reduced.

Tadao Kagono characterizes this commitment screening system (*trust checking system*, in his work) as a *hostage system* (1997). According to Kagono, male employees in Japanese companies are in a hostage system from their initial hiring until their retirement. Except for their very first years, from the beginning of their company lives to the middle stages, they are paid less than their contribution to their company merits. However, in their latter stages, most employees in a hostage circle are supposed to be paid more than their work productivity would call for. They work continuously even though they are underpaid relative to their contributions, preparing for their overpaid period: *investing invisibly* in the lifetime employment system. This is the Japanese hostage system that Kagono describes.

To use Kagono's term, companies check a female's commitment before allowing her to enter this *hostage circle*. If a female without commitment became a manager, she would prevent core members from working as a team, since her life would not be taken hostage and she would not *invest herself invisibly* in the company. The attitude of commitment plays an important role with respect to mutual trust among employees in a hostage circle.

Commitment screening is also done for male employees. Males are supposed to be checked for commitment every time they are asked to undertake a new assignment, and the number of times they pass these screenings influence the level to which they can be promoted. However, commitment screenings are not necessary for them to be core members or for Japanese management practices to be applied to them. Males continuously have their commitment to the company evaluated even after they become managers. They have to compete with other male managers continuously. I also consider that companies require more commitment of men than of women, but most men are not aware of it, because they can provide it.

On the other hand, in the case of foreign companies, there is no need for a confirmation of commitment, and female employees expect to be treated in the same way as male employees. Why is there no confirmation of commitment in foreign companies? The following two explanations can be considered. First, foreign companies may expect less commitment because they do not consider long-term employment as important as Japanese companies do. Second, foreign companies are able to determine whether females intend to work in the same manner as males before employment. Females who do not want to follow the same career men do will not look for jobs in foreign companies. They tend to work in Japanese companies in clerical jobs until marriage and are willing to accept their position under the division of labor by gender.

FINDINGS OF THIS STUDY

One of the main findings of this study is that Japanese management is biased toward male employees. Focusing on the commitment of women managers to their companies reveals not only that they start their career outside the boundary to be applied to the principle of Japanese management, but also that a division between core employees and noncore employees exists in each company. More-over, the commitment of women is confirmed before they pass the boundary.

Another main finding of this study is how large a burden it is to work in a Japanese company that adopts Japanese management style. Not only job per-formance, but attitude toward the job and relations with company employees are included in personnel appraisals. Before appointing women to management Japanese companies place on them burdens that are manageable for male em-ployees but unmanageable for female employees. Family responsibilities, such as performing household duties, raising children, and taking care of parents, are generally accepted as women's duties, and thus obstruct female employees from fulfilling the expectations of Japanese management. This is the reason why there are only a handful of women managers in Japan.

CONCLUSION OF THIS STUDY

This study has helped make clear the point that female employees traditionally have been lacking in company commitment and that women who have been appointed to management positions have shown commitments to their respective companies. However, at the same time, this means that these women managers are among the minority who were able to survive the screening for commitment in Japanese firms in general. For female employees, to serve continuously in a Japanese company and be appointed to management means to bear the burdens set up by Japanese management. Of course, to increase female managers it is desirable that the division of labor by gender be changed somehow in Japanese society and that burdens on women, such as household responsibilities, be light-ened. But more important, unless the burden imposed by Japanese management is lightened, it will remain difficult for Japanese companies to have women as core members and to appoint them to management roles.

The author believes that there is an opportunity to reform the Japanese man-agement system, lightening the burden of Japanese management, recognizing women as core members, and appointing them as managers.[4]

In order to explain how to reform the Japanese management system, I will discuss my thoughts on the type of managers in Japanese companies. Figure 10.2 shows four possible combinations of conditions relevant to becoming a manager in a Japanese company. On the X axis is Commitment, which increases from low to high. On the Y axis is Job Performance, which also increases from low to high. Employees in the pc cell (that is, low performance and low com-mitment) cannot be managers in Japanese companies. Although male employees in the Pc cell can become managers, the number is very small. Only in the PC cell can both male and female managers be promoted to the top management level, since they fill both requisites for promotion. In pC (that is, low perfor-mance but high commitment) only male employees can be promoted. Most Jap-anese companies have offered this type of employee lower management positions. That seems to be unusual in Western companies. Such managers give

Figure 10.2
Combinations of Conditions to Be Managers in Japanese Companies

PERFORMANCE

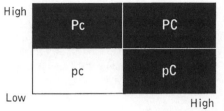

pc: unable to be managers
Pc: men managers (but rare)
PC: women managers
    men managers can be executives
pC: men managers can be seen at
    lower levels of management

COMMITMENT

messages to other employees such as "Even if you cannot get results on your job, everybody knows you were doing your best, and companies evaluate the process not results. You could have a chance to be a manager." In other words, they give messages that commitment is rewarded, which play an important role in unifying employees in the long term.

Increasing the number of Pc (that is, high performance but low commitment) managers may reform the Japanese management system. However, what is important is that making the standard of commitment screening lower for women and increasing the number of women managers in this cell (that is, large P, small c) may also reform the Japanese management system.

NOTES

This chapter was taken from *Studies in Commemoration of the 30th Anniversary of the Founding of Hiroshima University of Economics* (March 1998), pp. 325–339. Used by permission.

1. There are several factors contributing to the present condition of the scarcity of women managers in Japan: (1) the Japanese management system, (2) accepted ideas that performing household duties, raising children, and taking care of parents are women's duties, (3) lack of institutional (child care facilities, etc.) facilities, (4) regulations (for example, a tax system that prevents many women from working), (5) women's tastes and academic backgrounds (preference for majoring in literature or home economics, preference for clerical jobs), (6) family conditions. In this study I have focused on the factor of the Japanese management system.

2. Company (2) had been a publicly held firm. It is known that public organizations have assigned those holding bachelor's degrees from the more elite universities a different career track; thus they can be managers at an early age regardless of gender.

3. Commitment is one of the factors that influenced their promotions. Taniguchi (1995) indicates that five conditions are required for females to become managers in Japanese companies: (1) a companywide or company executive intention of increasing the number of female managers, (2) adequate commitment of the employee, (3) employee job performance, (4) the employee management ability, (5) superiors' willingness to

consider the employee a potential manager. (Superiors arrange a commitment screening period only for females who have management ability and requisite job performance.)

4. There are two dimensions of the Japanese management system. One is positive; it includes the principle of equality and participatory management. As I have mentioned, these practices apply not to females but to males. The other dimension is negative; it includes imposing excess overtime work, so that employees must neglect their private lives. The Japanese management system has been criticized for requiring this kind of employee overcommitment to the company. Of course, such overapplication of the system needs to be reduced. Studying women managers helps to make the negative aspects of Japanese firms more evident.

REFERENCES

Brinton, M. C. 1993. *Women and the economic miracle: Gender and work in postwar Japan.* Berkeley, CA: University of California Press.

Chalotte, L. S., and G. O'Kelly. 1987. Barriers and constraints to the recruitment and mobility of female managers in the Japanese labour force. *Human Resource Management* 26(2):193–216.

Itami, H. 1987. *Employeeistic companies.* Tokyo: Chikuma shobo.

Itami, H., Kagono, T., and Ito, M. 1993. *Japanese corporate system.* Tokyo: Yuhikaku.

Kagono, T. 1997. *Resurgence of the Japanese style of management* Kyoto: PHP Research Institute.

Kumazawa, M. 1997. *Meritocracy and corporate society.* Tokyo: Iwanami.

Lansing, P., and K. Ready. 1988. Hiring woman managers in Japan: An alternative for foreign employers. *California Management Review* (Spring): 112–127.

The Ministry of Labour, Japan. 1995. *Summary of actual labor market for women.*

Simon, H. A. 1969. *The sciences of the artificial.* Cambridge, MA: MIT Press.

Taniguchi, M. 1995. Women managers in Japanese companies: Constraints under Japanese management system. *Rokkodai Ronshu-Keieigakuhen* 42(1): 21–36.

Taniguchi, M. 1995. A subordinate perspective on female managers. *Rokkodai Ronshu-Keieigakuhen* 42(2):1–19.

Taniguchi, M. 1995. Japanese management through women managers' eyes. Monograph series Graduate School of Kobe University, no. 9503.

Taniguchi, M. 1996. Japanese management and women managers. Ph.D. diss. Graduate School of Kobe University.

11

Managing Talent in China: Confucian Origins

Changjun Dai and Zhi-guang Zheng

INTRODUCTION

The modern ethic of management in China derives its principles from more than two thousand years of Confucian thinking. With its emphasis on conformity to communal values—moral obligations to society and people—the Chinese ethic of management is not only about institutions, rules, or code books: it is a social management approach aimed at regulating relations between managers and managed. It maintains distinctions between good and evil, justice and injustice, fairness and partiality, honesty and dishonesty, and so on. So the ethic of management is about appraising good and evil as well as prescribing a standard of behavior. It reflects and defines the nature of relationships between the managers and the managed, making moral judgment an indispensable element in managing behavior.

Central to this ethic of management is the idea of managing talented people. Confucius and his followers persistently considered talent as a key to the success of any enterprises. In fact, correctly and successfully fitting people to positions is emphasized in China's traditional Confucian writing.

In this chapter, we examine the ideas of managing talented people as reflected by the ancient Chinese philosophy, the practice of those ideas in China historically, and the impact of those ideas on modern management practices in China as well as in countries where Confucianism has a long tradition.

CONFUCIAN VIEW OF TALENTS

The theory of managing talent in Chinese history is closely related to the traditional Chinese perception of human beings, in which Confucius's view oc-

cupies a central position. Confucius was the first man in Chinese history to end
the ruling class monopoly on education by opening the first private school,
where his theory of humankind was gradually developed in his lectures. Confucius thought that "benevolence is a characteristic element of humanity. . . .
Righteousness is the accordance of action with what is right, and the great
exercise of it is in honoring the worthy" (Legge 1971, Doctrines, 405–406). A
man who does not respect talents is not worthy of respect from other people. A
worthy man is, in the first place, a benevolent man. And benevolence is an
inseparable part of one's talents. The Confucian theory of humankind was presented more than a hundred years before that of Western philosophers such as
Aristotle and Plato.

Confucius's theory that people are by nature good influenced early Chinese
writings, which used *man* and *the worthy* interchangeably. *Records of Historians*
said that running a state "depends on man"; "one is wise if he understands man"
(Qian 1957, 77). The first book that distinguished man from the worthy is *Shan
Shu*, in which kings are advised that "appointments of offices are only for the
worthy" (Shu 1816, 120). It was not until the Han dynasty that the word *talents*
came into official language to describe those who "know the past and future,
and are able to see a thousand miles beyond" (Xian 1983, 110).

Meng Zhu, a Confucius disciple, gave a definition of what could not be
counted as worthy people: those people whom "if you would blame them, you
find nothing to allege, if you would criticize them, you have nothing to criticize.
They agree with the current customs. They consent with an impure age. Their
principles have a semblance of right heartedness and truth. Their conduct has a
semblance of disinterestedness and purity. All men are pleased with them and
they think themselves right, so that it is impossible to proceed with them to the
principles of Yao and Shu (both of them great and virtuous kings in ancient
time)" (Legge 1970, 500–501). Both Confucius and Meng Zhu thought that such
people do not speak from their heart. They cannot distinguish bad from good,
they want to please everybody, and they are the enemy of virtue and righteousness.

Mo Zhu, another scholar in early Chinese history, is the first person to develop
a systematic view on worthy people. In his essay *Honoring the Worthy*, Mo Zhu
says that worthy people are those who possess righteousness, virtue, and talent.
Appointing those people to official positions is extremely important to the stability and prosperity of the state. Mo Zhu advocated a respect for the worthy
people and he said that only they are entitled to the crown of the state, a direct
criticism of the hereditary rule of the royal family at that time. Mo Zhu was
actually challenging the political system of his country. He said that "the fundamental of politics is respecting the worthy people." Not only the king should
be selected on the basis of his worthiness: all state officials should also be
selected on a merit system regardless of their family, wealth, and social background. "When the state is run by a lot of worthy people, the rule of the state
runs deep, when worthy people are few in a state, the rule of the state becomes

superficial." Mo Zhu's book about the worthy can be regarded as a succinct summary of the views about talented people during the Warring period in China's history (Yiran 1954, 25–38).

In the Han dynasty, a dynasty immediately following the Warring period, the importance of talents was further recognized by people in both official positions and the academic world. Shima Qian, one of the most outstanding historians in Chinese history, wrote *Record of Historians*. In this magnificent book, Shima, among other things, examined the reasons behind the rise and fall of consecutive kingdoms in earlier history. Adopting an individualistic approach in his analysis of history, he drew people's attention to the importance of those worthy people in history who helped bring about the important events and changes in China's history. By doing so, Shima, from a historical point of view, contributed many penetrating insights to our knowledge of talented people.

In the late Han dynasty, Wang Chong, also a scholar in the Confucian tradition, emphasized that the differences in people should be taken into account when one wants to employ their talents. He noted that "people with different talents should not be treated the same" (Heng 1979, 22). He argued that no one was born with knowledge. There was no such thing as being born a wise man. "Sages can only learn to be the sages" (Heng 1979, 1; 498). Knowledge, as contrasted with basic intelligence, can only be learned and equates with wisdom. So he paid particular attention to experienced, aged men in his definition of talents and asked rulers to seek advice from such men. Wang considered age and experience to be the essential components of talent. He used an analogy to describe talented people. In a society they are just like big rocks. To move those rocks requires a lot of strength. It is the responsibility of rulers to exert their strength and move those rocks. Talented people are to a state, according to Wang Chong, what pillars are to a building (*Heng* 1979, 1: 570–1575).

This view of talented people was accepted and practiced by politicians during the late Han dynasty period, illustrated by *The Story of Three Kingdoms*. The late Han dynasty was characterized by an extremely weakened emperor at the center of the government and an uneven distribution of power among various local warlords. From this group of local leaders emerged three brilliant politicians who quelled widespread local riots and divided the empire into three kingdoms. This division of the Han empire was followed by a fierce fight among the three politicians who tried to succeed the emperor of the Han dynasty and become the sole ruler of the whole country. The writings by and the deeds of those politicians have greatly enriched the ideas of Chinese high-potential (HIPO) management and have provided politicians and businessmen many empirical examples of HIPO management.

China's feudal society reached its peak in the Tang dynasty. "The Rule of Zhen Guan" is considered the most prosperous period in China's history, in part because of the emperor's philosophy of managing talented people. The ruler, Emperor Tai Zhong of Tang, attached great importance to high-potential selection in securing his rule and in governing the state. He said that "the first priority in running the state lies in finding the right person." "Only those who win the heart of talented people can conquer the world." He said that by comparing oneself to a talented person, one would better understand oneself. "Using bronze as a mirror, one can dress himself up. Using history as a mirror, one can know the successions of history. Using man as a mirror, one can correct himself" (Guopan 1979, 393–394). Without this emphasis on promoting and protecting talented people, the prosperity and stability of the Tang dynasty would have hardly been possible.

Han Yu, a famous writer and scholar during the Tang dynasty, developed the idea that influenced China's thinking about managing talent. Han said that although talented people are important to society, even more important is the person who knows how to find talented people. He noted that high potentials, or in his words "winged steeds," were more prevalent among those who knew how to distinguish high-potential people from others. If the discovery of the talented were not protected, the winged steed or the talented would end up toiling in the field, driven to do farm work, in which they are not particularly effective. Thus, people capable of discovering the talented are of great value, as winged steeds are more prevalent than those who recognize them (Tite 1980, 236–238). By stressing the importance of such talent selectors, Han Yu opened a new way of thinking in the theory of Chinese talent management history.

Wang Anshi is the first thinker in Chinese history who clearly advocated that education, selection, and full use of the talented should be integrated into a coherent strategy for managing high potentials. A politician described by Lenin as the "Chinese reformer of the eleventh century," Wang Anshi represented a political force during the Song dynasty that championed legal reform of the corrupt political system that was quickly collapsing. In one of his writings to the emperor, Wang stated that "teaching, nurturing, obtaining and appointing talented people should be consistently pursued. Otherwise, the talents in the world would be ruined and wasted" (*works of Anshi* 1974, 3).

Prior to the Qing dynasty, the talented people were usually those who excelled in military, state government, or artistic fields. During the Qing dynasty, however, scientists were considered by the emperor to be talented people who required special protection. Emperor Kang Xi gathered some scientists with potential to the court for special training, after which some were appointed to high positions. This practice demonstrated the emperor's recognition of the importance of scientific advancement to the enhancement of state power amid the increasing infiltration of Western influence and industrialization.

This brief review of the evolution of Chinese thought about managing talented people indicates that the concept of having potential has gradually expanded over time. Confucius believed that some of the competencies needed to have potential were benevolence and virtue. Since Confucius' time, many new dimensions have been added to this theory. But one theme remains unchanged: talented people are central to the stability and prosperity of the state, or any other enterprise, and identifying and managing talented people are prerequisites for prosperity.

IDENTIFYING, SELECTING, APPOINTING, AND EVALUATING THE TALENTED

Identifying those with potential is the first step toward successful talent management. Ancient Chinese thinkers persistently tried, generation after generation, to remind us to use caution when fitting people to positions.

Confucius emphasized that one must understand the person throughout. He said, "I will not be afflicted by men's not knowing me; but I will be afflicted that I do not know men" (Legge 1971, *Analects*, 145).

To discover talented people requires some skills. *Yi Chou Shu* (The Remnant of the Chou Dynasty), one of the earliest history books in China, devoted a whole chapter to discovering talented people, in which six methods were identified: observing sincerity, appraising words, listening to sounds, observing expressions, observing hidden signs, and appraising virtue.

Observing sincerity focuses on one's personal characteristics and feelings; *appraising words* uncovers a person's intended meaning; *listening to sounds* and *observing expressions* focus on finding personal qualities by studying facial expressions and listening to voice inflections. *Observing hidden signs* strips off the disguise to reveal character traits. Finally, *appraising virtue* evaluates the whole person, using the five other methods, to make an overall estimate of the person's potential.

Liu Shao of the Han dynasty developed seven methods focusing on emotions and behavior in identifying a talented person: (1) determine with whom the person associates; (2) identify the person's motives; (3) observe changes in emotion to validate the person's integrity; (4) analyze the person's levels of expertise; (5) observe the person's interaction with others; (6) ascertain whether the person is modest and polite; and (7) discover the person's strengths through his or her weaknesses.

Liu Shao also said a talented person could be misjudged. He criticized the practice of judging a person by fame or fortune without analyzing the emotional makeup or virtue of the person. When judging a person, a line should be drawn between methodical and arbitrary thinking, between creativity and recklessness, between caution and incompetence, and between principle adherence and intransigence (Records 1983, 27–35).

Zhuge Lian, a well-known politician and strategist during the Three Kingdom period, summarized from his own experience seven principles for judging a person's potential: (1) test reasoning and analytical skills by asking conflicting questions; (2) test the person's ability to debate an issue by repeatedly arguing with him on the same issue and see how he approaches the problem; (3) test decisiveness by letting him make a decision and see whether he is capable in his analysis of the situation; (4) test level of commitment by assigning him or her a difficult task and by clearly informing him of a danger or difficulty, then see how brave he is and how willing he is to make self-sacrifice; (5) test the level of self-control by making him drink alcohol and examine his ability to exercise self-control; (6) provide him with access to something of worth and see whether he is corruptible or acts with integrity; and (7) assign an important task to measure/test dependability. These Zhuge Lian principles reflect the Confucian standard for judging potential and character (*Complete Works of Zhuge Lian* 1986, 100–112).

Talent identification is a precondition to talent selection. Following the teachings of Confucius, Chinese scholars and politicians have regarded personal virtue as the first criterion in selecting someone for an official position. Personal virtue always precedes ability. Confucius said, "A horse is called a thoroughbred horse not because of its strength, but because of its virtues" (Legge 1971, *Analects*, 288). Mo Zhu stressed that among all the principles for selecting officials, the first priority is the adherence to virtuous behavior. Overpowering with virtue far exceeds overpowering with strength (Yiran 1954, 27).

Emperor Tai Zhong of Tang also noted that the top priority in politics is to have the right person for the right service. He said, "There should be no haste in selecting an official. Once you employ a virtuous man, all virtuous men would come to your service; once you employ a mean man, you will be surrounded by mean men" (Guopan 1979, 394). Shima Guang expressed well the relations between virtue and ability as he said "ability is the endowment of virtue while virtue is the commander of ability" (Zizhi 1987, 15).

The practice of selecting officials in China has taken several forms, including boss or supervisor recommendation. Confucius said, "Raise to office those men you know. As to those you do not know, will others neglect them?" (Legge 1971, *Analects*, 263). Meng Zhu developed this idea further by suggesting that after a recommendation, it is necessary to make an investigation and make sure the recommendation reflects reality. He suggested also asking high potentials to make their own recommendations. Those recommendations, made on the basis of one's family background, social status, or personal relationships, should be carefully scrutinized. Otherwise, the state would be run by an exclusive, not necessarily qualified, group (Legge 1970, 166).

In addition to supervisor recommendations, direct recruitment is a suggested method for selecting talent. This was usually done in two ways. The ruler either issued an order inviting people who thought they were qualified to go to the court for an interview or granted a courteous interview to those with outstanding talents.

The third way of selecting talent in ancient times was for rulers to condescend and receive ordinary people, treating them with respect. This method proved quite effective in attracting talented people. "The sacred king often condescends himself to show his inferiority to the talented," said Meng Zhu. He contended that rulers should go out of court to search for potential. In doing so, they must not assume an air of royal dignity and require that the talented people enter service by the order of "his majesty." If rulers can descend to a less formal and dignified level in receiving common but talented people, they can "get the virtuous people and talented people at their will" (Legge 1970, 380–390).

Recognition of Chinese competencies is another important aspect of talent management used historically in China. Chinese literature has provided ample evidence on how to make the most efficient use of talented people with varied strengths and weaknesses. First, different levels of talents should be rewarded accordingly; the key is that the job requirements be met in a way that best suits the character of the person. If "one lets a steed plough the field, the steed will not be as good as an ox."

Second, one cannot expect talented people to be perfect. Confucius said: "Pardon small faults and raise to office men of virtue and talents" (Legge 1971, *Analects*, 263). He also said: "Without some great cause, do not dismiss from their offices the old officials. Do not seek in one man talents for every employment" (Legge 1970, 338). Success in one area does not necessarily equal competency in another. Being talented does not make one a saint. The talented are also ordinary people. Good politicians never fuss with small character faults or shortcomings. "No gold is a hundred percent pure, and no person is perfect."

The third idea in using talented people is that HIPOs require vision and courage—once the person is employed, there should be no doubting. Sticking to this principle is important in drawing out full potential. If a ruler decides to use a person for an important mission, not only must he not doubt the person of his choice, he should also prevent other people from expressing doubt, even if his views run counter to opinions of the majority. Full confidence and complete trust are considered prerequisites to using the talented effectively.

Constant evaluation is a fourth component in talent management. Guan Zhong, a well-known politician in China's history, once said that "talented people should be first tested and tried out before being employed" (Qian 1957, 102). Early history books have recorded that in the earliest dynasties in China, officials were evaluated every three years (*Shan Shu* 1816, 34). During the Tang dynasty, a government ministry was organized to evaluate officials on a regular basis. The process was open, fair, and democratic. The evaluation standards varied from time to time, but they were all aimed at rewarding qualified officials and removing unqualified ones.

Normally, the evaluation process requires that the standards in assigning punishment and rewards be fair, reasonable, and stable. They must also be widely publicized and repeated so that people know the sanctity of the law. Officials doing the evaluating must exercise impartiality and be righteous themselves. Decisions on rewards or penalties made on personal biases should be prevented at all costs. Additional scrutiny should be given to those who are relatives of top officials, who are fond of women, who are susceptible to changes in their wealth or social position, or who love rumors and enjoy cultivating informal personal relations within the court.

Talent training is also fundamental to talent management. Confucius was among the first to recognize the importance of this. By opening China's first private school, where he spent most of his life teaching and tutoring, he tried to cultivate and develop potential in his students to prepare them for service to the state. He first raised the idea that "By nature, men are nearly alike; by practice, they are wide apart" (Legge 1971, *Analects*, 318), meaning that people are not born with their talents. The differences among people are the result of education and learning. Confucius held that "in teaching, there should be no distinction of classes" (Legge 1971, *Analects*, 305). He wanted all people, regardless their family background or wealth, to have access to education. Confucius developed many teaching principles and methods that are currently valued by people in the teaching profession.

Confucius's idea of talent management has influenced his descendants. Generation after generation, many educators in China followed his steps and took the cultivation of the talented as their lifetime career. Han Yu, as a writer and governor in the Tang dynasty, was an ardent supporter of education. He wrote many articles elucidating the methods of teaching. One of his famous sayings is "Expertise comes with diligence but becomes rusty in play and sport. Action succeeds in thinking but aborts in conforming" (Tite 1980, 143). Kan Youwei was a famous advocate of political reform in the late Qing dynasty. He spent most of his life trying to save China from degenerating into a colony of Western powers. He insisted that if China wished to prevent being colonized, top priority should be given to equipping a large number of people with advanced modern ideas and technology through education. Only then could China be developed economically and politically, able to confront the continuous threat from foreign powers. He stressed that learning should be combined with practicing; learning was for the purpose of using.

This brief review illustrates that the evolution of the concept of identifying, selecting, and managing talent in China was deeply rooted in the Confucian tradition. Its implications are not confined to state governing. On the contrary, the ideas implicit in Confucianism are considered widely applicable to modern enterprise management as well. In fact, Confucius' perception of human beings is the source from which many other principles in management in China are derived.

CONFUCIANISM: GREATER THAN CHINA

Confucian thought is not exclusive to China. Many surrounding countries also regarded Confucianism as part of their cultural heritage, which has influenced management strategies. In fact, Confucius's writing was introduced to Japan as early as the third century. Southeast Asia is the place where Western culture and Chinese culture meet. As these countries become more modern, more and more people of Chinese origin are beginning to rediscover the values of their cultural roots. Many scholars from these countries are attributing the economic take-off to the traditional Confucian ethic. Lee Kwan Yew, the former prime minister of Singapore, said, "Our history did not start with the arrival of our ancestors in Singapore. It started more than five thousand years ago with the rising of Chinese civilization. This is part of our history. We are the inheritors of this system and culture." He also declared that the Confucian ethic is the government's guiding principle in running the state.

In 1989, under the sponsorship of the United Nations (UN), an international symposium was held in the hometown of Confucius in memory of his 2450th birthday. Experts from more than thirty countries around the world attended the meeting. They discussed various aspects of Confucius thought and their impact on the contemporary world. Some American scholars noted that many social problems such as family violence, juvenile crime, and drugs, all of which are associated with postindustrialization society, cannot be solved through legal proceedings. These problems are partly due to an absence of efficient communication among people. Confucianism offers one possible direction in which to work for a possible solution to some of these social problems.

At the UN conference, this view was echoed by a German scholar who observed that the West has been overdeveloped. With the help of advanced scientific technology, said the German, many people from the West thought they could control the world and nature as God does. Western people should learn from Confucius to restrain themselves from pursuing unlimited or indefinite things. Confucius once said: "Riches and honors acquired by unrighteousness are to me as floating clouds" (Legge 1971, *Analects*, 200).

In Japan, Confucianism is deeply integrated into the Japanese culture. A former Japanese prime minister said, "Japan should combine democracy, liberalism and Confucius' teachings together, using Confucius's thought as guiding moral principles." In a letter to one of the authors, a Chinese scholar stated that former U.S. president Ronald Reagan was reported to have said, "Not only Chinese people, but the whole humankind have benefitted from Confucius's noble behavior and great thinking and moral principles."

Confucian influence is part of management practices in East Asia. Many enterprises in those countries established a set of values based on Confucius' idea of "relying on the people." Combined with Mencius's idea of benefiting and enriching people, Confucius's idea of the ethical man is regarded as a foundation upon which the goals of enterprises are determined. Companies such as Panasonic of Japan, Taiwan Plastic Company, and Samsung of South Korea successfully integrated Confucian principles with entrepreneurial spirit, while establishing enterprise goals, such as fostering a cooperative spirit, maintaining a sense of security, and adopting the same set of values.

Eiichi Shibusawa, "father of Japan's capitalism," wrote *Analects and Calculus* many years ago, emphasizing the relationship between Confucius and business management. Shibusawa established "Parity of virtue and profits" as his management principle and energetically implemented it within his five hundred enterprises. Ryoji Yokoyama, another famous Japanese entrepreneur, thought that lifetime job security and seniority are the reflection of Confucius's notion of propriety and trade unions are an expression of Confucius's idea of "priority of harmony." Yokoyama's management philosophy is based on Confucian notions of "benevolence" and "righteousness." He follows the idea that "one who loves everyone will be loved forever by everyone; one who respects everyone will be respected forever by everyone." The Mitsubishi company claimed that the doctrine of the mean or middle is the highest moral standard for the company's management. Namihei Kodaira, the founder of the Hitachi Company, said "harmony" and "sincerity" guide the company. The motto of the board director of Toyota is "Heaven, earth, man, knowledge, virtue and courage," adopted from Mencius's idea that "opportunities of time vouchsafed by heaven are not equal to advantages of situation afforded by the earth, and advantages of situation afforded by the earth are not equal to the union arising from the accord of man" (Legge 1970, 208), as well as Confucius's saying, "To be fond of learning is to be near to knowledge, to practice with vigor is to be near to virtue, to possess feeling of shame is to be near to courage" (Legge 1971, Doctrines, 407) Confucius's ideas were widely applied in the practice of management in Japan.

Today, a group of multinationals in Japan have designated a list of Chinese books as required reading for people new to business. The *Book of Sun Zhu* offers theoretical advice to managers handling adverse situations. *The Story of Three Kingdoms* offers lessons and experiences to teach people how to handle trying/difficult interpersonal relations. In most Japanese companies, employees are required to read *The Story of Three Kingdoms*. One scholar from the Research Institute of Society and Industry of Japan said that for Japan to be more competitive both domestically and internationally, it must study and apply the strategies and techniques employed in *The Story of Three Kingdoms*. He thought that the book provided inexhaustible wisdom and advice to those entrepreneurs engaged in fierce international competition.

The influence of Confucian ideas is also widely felt in Singapore. The Confucian notion of management has made a positive contribution to Singapore's economic development. The dominance of Confucian thinking in the management is the result of the triumph of native culture deeply rooted in Confucian tradition in its clash with Western culture from overseas. In the early 1980s, Confucian Management Ethics was a required class for junior and senior high school students in Singapore. Experts specialized in Confucian studies were invited to lecture in the classes and participate in the government planning to design a curriculum of Confucian studies in schools. In an attempt to make Singapore the world's leader in Confucian studies, the Singapore government also founded the Eastern Asia Philosophy Institute and regularly recruited Confucian scholars from around the world to conduct research in Singapore. Because of this government sponsored promotion, Confucian management ethics have been widely endorsed by many enterprises in the country.

South Korea also has a tradition of Confucianism. During the 1960s, rapid economic growth gave rise to a utilitarian tendency in South Korean society. Massive material production has made it difficult for the traditional culture to play a role in restraining people from excessive pursuit of material goods. That tendency prompted some Korean management experts to reconsider the direction of the development of the state economy by reasserting moral principles of Confucian thought. Beginning in the 1970s, a study of Confucian influence on society and economy in Korean history caused Korean management experts to focus on the Confucianism style of management. They set up the Eastern Research Institute of Confucian Management at Korea University and worked out an outline for integrating the native Confucian management ideas with the state economic development. This intensive research project produced a series of articles in 1978 analyzing Confucian thought and its influence in Korea and other Eastern Asian countries. The common theme of these articles was that the Confucian style of management (focusing on the ethical man) was, is, and should be the real ideological foundation for Korean enterprises.

This Confucian style of management with Korean characteristics, together with the successful stories of Korean economic development, have attracted the attention of international academics. The application of Confucian ideas in management practice in Korea has won approval and positive reactions from many Western management scholars and practitioners.

The influence of Confucian management philosophy has spread from China to many of its neighboring countries. Many of its ideas have been reformulated to adapt to local conditions. But one condition remains constant: Confucius style of management is a human centered philosophy. People from all over the world are becoming interested in studying how those ideas contained in Confucius thought can be applied to contemporary management practice. It is certain that the theory will continue to attract the attention of international researchers for years to come.

CONCLUSION

History has shown that the Confucian philosophy of management has made great contributions to the practice of China's modern management. But that does not mean that modern management practice should neglect the use of scientific methods in management. On the contrary, the present backward status of China's management is partly due to the insufficient use of scientific methods in managing enterprises. Management based on scientific methods such as specialization, standardization, or quantification in China is yet to be strengthened. Scientific methods are the hardware in modern management; corporate culture is the software. A combination of both constitutes the only effective means to a successful management strategy.

This chapter has examined the Confucian concept of the ethical man, which defines the standard by which high-potential management is determined. According to Confucius, the most important talent a man can possess is virtue. Being virtuous, which constitutes being talented, was the criterion most often used in selecting and evaluating officials in China's history.

This Confucian idea of humankind has influenced the way in which management in China is perceived. Rather than focus on Western ideas of management, which emphasize competition among individuals and a "star" system, the Confucian approach centers around harmony, conformity, and community. Some well known Chinese entrepreneurs were the pioneer practitioners of the Confucian management philosophy. Their exemplary style of management has set a definitive standard for the Chinese approach to management.

Confucian ideas have also been practiced by foreign entrepreneurs in some Eastern Asian states, such as Japan, South Korea, and Singapore. Despite their differences, Asian entrepreneurs accept the idea that human beings are at the center of management. They also consider conflict prevention a top priority in their dealings with employees and agree that individuals should place their private interests behind collective interests. Confucius ideas are vital components of the corporate culture of many East Asian countries—they are a part of their national culture and traditional heritage. Confucian philosophy of management combined with modern management methods will go far to advance a Chinese management system and a special Chinese (Asian) high-potential management orientation.

NOTE

This chapter is part of a series of research projects on the study of Human Resource Management conducted at Nankai University. The project is sponsored and funded by the Chinese National Natural Science Foundation (CNSF); its approval number is 79270057. Professor Changjun Dai, the director of this project, provided basic ideas and the theoretic framework for this chapter.

REFERENCES

Complete works of Zhuge Lian. 1986. Beijing: China Book Publication.
Gupoan, H. 1979. On Emperor Tai Zhong of Tang. In *Essays on History of the Tang Dynasty, the Sui Dynasty and the Five Dynasties.* Beijing: Reading and New Knowledge Publishing House.
Legge, J., trans. 1970. *Mencius.* New York: Dover Publications.
———. 1971. *Analects: Analects, the great learning and the doctrines of the mean.* New York: Dover Publications.
———. 1971. The doctrines of the mean. *Analects, the great learning and the doctrines of the mean.* New York: Dover Publications.
Lun Heng. 1979. Vol. 1. Beijing: China Book Publication.
Qian, S. 1957. *Records of historians.* Beijing: China Book Publication.
Records of People. 1983. *New collections of Confucian classics*; Vol. 6. Taipei: World Book Publication.

Shan Shu. 1816. In *Notes and Commentaries of Thirteen Confucian Classics*. Beijing: Publishing House of Art and Literature.

Tite, T., ed. 1980. Miscellaneous discourse four. In *Selected Works of Han Yu*. Beijing: People's Literature Publishing House.

———. 1980. On Teaching. In *Selected Works of Han Yu*. Beijing: People's Literature Publishing House.

Works of Wang Anshi. 1974. Shanghai: Shanghai People's Publishing House.

Xian, L. 1983. Huan Nan Zhi. In *New Collections of Confucian Classics*. Vol. 7. Taipei: World Book Publication.

Yiran, S. 1954. Honoring the worthy. In *Mo Zhu and Commentaries*. Beijing: China Book Publication.

Zizhi Tongjian. 1987. Shanghai: Shanghai Ancient Book Publishing House.

12

From Revolutionaries to Political Entrepreneurs: Selecting Leaders for China's Modern State-Owned Enterprises

Xuchuan Yang

INTRODUCTION

Amid the impressive success of economic reform in China, Chinese state-owned enterprises (SOEs) stand out as a stark reminder that China's economic reform still has a long way to go. In fact, profits in the private sector are continuously overshadowed by the rising deficit of SOEs. Although the Chinese Communist Party (CCP) has repeatedly attempted to rejuvenate SOEs since 1984, two-thirds of Chinese SOEs are struggling—just barely surviving. Top political leaders view SOEs as the greatest stumbling block to a sweeping success of their reform program.

One reason for the chronic inefficiency of China's state industry lies in the management of SOEs. Under the traditional central planning system, SOEs are publicly owned. The party exercises the supreme control over SOEs, but it delegates the management and supervision of routine operations to individual factory managers. So, in Chinese SOEs, as in other Communist countries, factory managers are no more than government employees. Acting more as bureaucratic administrators than as business entrepreneurs, managers perform their duties strictly according to the directions of the superior party officials. Managers have more responsibility to please the party than they do to create profit.

Accordingly, the pattern of developing HIPOs in Chinese SOEs is heavily influenced by the Chinese political system and cultural traditions. The criteria for selecting HIPO managers reflects the party's emphasis on political reliability and conformity. This politicization of HIPO identification and selection is the result of the party's wish to maintain its grip over every aspect of industry in China.

In this chapter, I try to answer the following questions:

1. To what degree has economic reform changed the practice of HIPO manager selection and recruitment in China?
2. Has this practice of HIPO recruitment and selection facilitated or undermined the current drive to improve SOE efficiency, and how has it done so?

This study is a result of fieldwork done in China between September 1996 and January 1997. During the course of the fieldwork, I interviewed factory personnel, distributed questionnaires, and collected written materials of various kinds. I visited six SOEs, all of them large or middle sized, located in Tianjin, Shanghai, and Hunan province.

HIPOS DURING THE REFORM

During the economic reform, which began in the early 1980s and which is still under way, the old system of HIPO identification and promotion had to be shattered to make way for the emergence of a new type of SOE manager. As the priority changed from political conformity to economic development, the criteria for SOE manager identification and promotion also changed significantly. Whereas the old system had placed party loyalty as the top priority, managerial skills and education became equally important as, if not more important than, political correctness in selecting HIPOs.

During the reform, the party specified four criteria in HIPO promotions: revolutionalization (*geminghua*), expertise (*zhuanyehua*), youth (*nianqinghua*), and knowledge (*zhishihua*). These four standards clearly indicate that the party has made a remarkable change in its practice of selecting factory managers. Revolution, or political loyalty, alone does not qualify one for a top managerial position in an SOE, although it still is the top criterion. In fact, in many places, political conformity has become secondary in the promotion of HIPOs. This is evident in several ways.

First, party membership has become a less important if not irrelevant factor in HIPO promotions. As the top priority of SOEs is now the improvement of factory efficiency and profit, a manager's ability to fulfill production targets counts more that political conformity to the party ideology. In six sample factories, three top managers were not party members. What is more, when I asked those top managers about the importance of party membership in selecting lower- or middle-level managers, five of the six said that personal talents and skills are the primary factors that influence their promotion decisions. One top manager even said that the issue of party membership never crossed his mind in his promotion decisions.

Second, the definition of political conformity has changed. Prior to the reform, one's trustworthiness was judged by his or her compliance with the ruling ideology. Now that compliance has changed to compliance with economic policies. This compliance determines one's acceptability as well as upward mobility. Under this situation, a HIPO's competitiveness for promotion is measured by how capable and faithful the person is in implementing the party's reform policy, lowering the factory's deficit, and increasing efficiency. In my interviews with factory managers, nearly all said that they would attribute their career success to their accurate implementation of reform policies made by the top leaders. These policies include the responsibility system, the shareholder system, and the separation of the party from management.

Third, level of education has assumed a particularly important role in identifying HIPOs within Chinese SOEs. In fact, government agencies in many places have arbitrarily drawn a line demanding a certain level of education for certain levels of managerial positions. Those who fail to meet the qualification would be automatically excluded from promotion consideration, regardless of their working skills. This has created a "heat of diploma" in the society. Many potential HIPOs were forced to enter college and earn a diploma just to meet that minimum education requirement line for promotion. Increasingly the tendency in China is that the higher the educational level, the more likely one will be promoted. In Shanghai, one of the most vibrant cities in China, nearly all government officials above the level of director or chief of administrative bureaus have postgraduate degrees; a bachelor's degree does not suffice for a government managerial position.

Yet despite this shift of emphasis from politics to knowledge and skills in Chinese SOEs, one factor has remained unchanged throughout the reform period: personal networks are still a critical element in HIPO selection and promotion.

In fact, the concept of HIPO is a highly elusive and ambiguous one when applied to China's practice of recruitment of top factory managers. The meaning of this concept varied in different periods. In Mao's era, a HIPO was judged in the basis of political reliability; during the reform, a HIPO is primarily determined by how a person can accurately and creatively implement the top political leader's reform policies. These different standards of HIPOs have produced different kinds of SOE managers. But when translated into the concrete practice of daily SOE activities, these standards all boil down to one final standard, which runs through each political period, unaffected by the changing political climate and always proving decisive in HIPO identification and promotion. This standard is the personal loyalty of HIPOs to the specific leaders charged with making promotion decisions.

As a result, there is no objective or impartial rule governing HIPO identification and promotion in China. The judgment is as highly elusive as it is unpredictable, completely subject to the personal discretion of the decision makers. As one interviewee described, quoting a well-known Chinese saying: "If the leader says you are talented, then you are talented. Even if you are not talented, you are still talented. If the leader says you are not talented, then you are not talented. Even if you are talented, you are still untalented." Hence, the ability to please the leader and win the leader's appreciation is the first quality that a potential manager must possess. A candidate who is independent and insensitive to human relations will always be the first to be dropped from the top leader's potential candidate list, regardless of talent or skills.

This human relation–centered approach to promotion and recruitment sows the seed of personal networks in Chinese SOEs. In order to climb up, ambitious HIPOs often have to court favor of the top leaders by throwing themselves at their service. This courtship behavior can take a variety of forms, from sending of gifts on important days and help to leaders' children in finding jobs to blatant bribery or direct solicitation.

At the other end, such behavior is often encouraged, welcomed, or rationalized by the leader, who considers it the only way to determine who will most reliably implement his decisions. It is the most natural thing, as the argument goes, that no one will appoint one who, instead of helping the leader, would undermine the leader's efforts to achieve his goals. No matter how talented a potential appointee is, if that person cannot be trusted with work he or she is assigned to do, that talent only backfires. This is why reliability and personal loyalty always come first, before everything else, in the HIPO recruitment and promotion process.

IDENTIFICATION AND PROMOTION IN CHINESE SOEs: THE OLD WINE IN A NEW BOTTLE

The necessity to assure personal loyalty based on a good private relationship between the promoter and the promoted has contributed to a distinctive Chinese pattern of HIPO identification and promotion. In my fieldwork, I found three factors that were used by top leaders to gauge the reliability of HIPOs. These factors included education, geographic location, and past working experience.

Education

One characteristic of Chinese SOEs is that they are not only producers, but also welfare providers for their employees. This welfare function of SOEs makes them responsible to their employees for a wide range of material services: housing, medical care, child care, education, and transportation, to name a few.

As a direct result of this welfare function, many large or middle-sized SOEs in China have their own technical schools. Owned and financed by the SOE, these schools recruit and train young high school graduates and turn them into future employees. Because of their limited purpose, these are usually two-year schools with small student bodies. For each SOE, the graduates of its technical school only constitute a small portion of its employee size, normally between

Table 12.1
Educational Background of Managers A and B

	No. of middle level cadres	No. of technical school graduates	Managers with other backgrounds	Ratios of technical school cadres to other cadres %
A	150	105	45	70:30
B	210	130	80	61:59

Source: Yang (2001, Chapter 1).

10 and 30 percent. Of the six SOEs I visited, four have such schools, with a yearly turnout of graduates from 50 to 150. In those sampled factories, the percentage of these school graduates to the total employees in the factory also varies from place to place. In one SOE, the number of employees who are graduates of that SOE's technical school is about 200, approximately 18 percent of the total number of the factory employees. In an SOE with 5,800 employees, about 500 are graduates of the factory technical school, less than 10 percent of the total working force. In another SOE in Shanghai, its technical school graduates constitute more than 60 percent of the total working force in the factory.

However, this variation of ratio between technical school graduates and total factory working force across these three SOEs does not hide one fact: in these factories, the majority of the top or middle level managers are graduates of the factory-run technical schools. Table 12.1 shows the educational background of middle-level managers in the first two large factories, A and B (A is a textile machinery factory in Shanghai with forty-five hundred employees and B is a chemical factory in Hunan province with fifty-eight hundred employees).

This tendency to recruit managers from among graduates of factory run technical schools reflects a practice of HIPO promotion that emphasizes similar education levels and experience (Child 1994, 32–35; Lockett 1988, 475–496). This practice stems from a perception of top SOE leadership that graduates of these schools are more reliable than graduates of other schools. The knowledge they learned in the school is also readily applicable to the factory production. Often, only after this group has been groomed for possible promotion will the top leaders set their eyes on other factory employee groups, such as college graduates or skilled workers, in their search for potential candidates.

So a vicious circle has been created by this practice, in which factory managers educated in the factory technical school first promote those who are graduates of the same schools, and these people for the same reason also first select their successors from among school's alumni. The tendency to promote employees with the same educational background underscores the uncertainty SOE managers feel about the personal loyalty of "outsiders" and about the willingness of outsiders to faithfully carry out factory policies.

Even more important to this practice of school-based discrimination in HIPO promotion is the fear of top SOE leaders that they themselves will be overshadowed by those with more education. These leaders are very reluctant to promote those with higher education to important positions because they believe that, first, more education does not always translate into more talents; second, they, although less educated, are not necessarily inferior to those college graduates in their capabilities; third, their career will be negatively influenced if those with higher education outperform their superiors and make them look bad in the eyes of their superiors. As a result, SOE leaders perceive college graduate turned managers as a threat to the security of their career and an uncontrollable group of employees. So, HIPO managers with not only the same school background but the same educational level of top leaders often have a much better chance of promotion than their better educated colleagues.

This preference for factory-trained employees does not necessarily conflict with the factory's need for highly educated management candidates. If a job requires some college training, top managers will first consider sending these factory school graduates to college. When, after two or three years, they return with a diploma, these people will be appointed to leading positions in the factory. In this way, the dilemma of having to appoint an employee with only an associate degree to a position requiring a full college education can be avoided. A personal familiarity with the factory school graduates and a strong confidence in them as faithful followers are the two main reasons why top managers choose these people for HIPO recruitment.

Geographic Location

Another consideration underlining promotion decisions is the geographic background of HIPOs. Many scholars have noted that people in China have a natural tendency to form personal connections with those who have the same geographic roots (Pye 1989; Lieberthal and Oksenberg 1989; Nathan 1977, 34–66). In Chinese SOEs, geographic connections are widely used by ambitious HIPOs to cultivate relationships with top leaders—and for good reason. The identification and promotion of HIPOs are deeply influenced by geographic considerations. This geographic connection does not necessarily require that people share the same birthplace so that they are countrymen (*laoxiang*). Working in the same place in the past is also a sufficient condition to attract two people to each other. Similar geographic background can bind two parties into a strong emotional bond based on a common recollection of happiness and hardship that each went through with the other in the past. As a result, a strong sense of trust and confidence emerges between the two parties.

This pattern of promotion based on geographic affinity was manifested clearly at a textile factory located in Shanghai (sample factory C). This factory was originally built by local government, in part to solve the unemployment problem of young people after the Cultural Revolution. During the Cultural Revolution, these young people were sent to different rural regions in the country to engage in forced labor as part of Mao's reeducation plan. These areas include Yunnan province, Helongjiang province, Inner Mongolia autonomous region, and Anhui province. When the Cultural Revolution ended in 1976, these young people swarmed back to their hometowns from all corners of the country. The local government was forced to invest to build this factory just to create enough jobs to absorb the unexpected influx of labor from the countryside.

When the factory was started, the local government appointed a person who returned from Helongjiang province as general manager. By doing so, the local government inadvertently started a two-decade tradition of factory rule by those who returned from Helongjiang Province.

In the first organizational chart of the factory in 1979, 15 middle level managerial positions were created for a total of 860 employees. Of these 15 positions 8 went to those from Helongjiang province; 5 were assigned to those from Yunnan province; and the remaining 3 were given to people from other parts of the country. With the general manager of the factory returning from Helongjiang province, the Helongjiang group took a majority of the managerial positions in the factory. When asked how important it was to have been in Helongjiang province in order to obtain a management position, the director of the Personnel Division said that it was crucial. At that time, not only middle-level positions were occupied by people from Helongjiang province: so were many administrative positions. People with other geographic backgrounds were assigned to operate machines on workshops or to do other kinds of menial work. The only force capable of challenging the dominance of the Helongjiang group was the Yunnan group. Table 12.2 shows the distribution of managerial positions in the factory during the 1980s.

However, the challenge by the Yunnan province group to the Helongjiang group did not become real until the general manager was promoted to work in the county government and left the factory. With his departure, many other Helongjiang group members also left the factory, leaving behind a huge power vacuum. This time, the county government appointed a member of the Yunnan group to succeed the Helongjiang manager.

The ascendancy of one of the Yunnan group to the top managerial position ushered in a new period for the factory, in which members of the Yunnan group dominated the factory elite. Here the pattern of HIPO selection and identification repeated itself. Factory employees with Yunnan background were favored over non-Yunnan members. This practice of HIPO selection based on geographic similarity persisted right into the reform. It was not until the county government appointed an outsider as the general manager that these old personal networks were broken apart and a more balanced power distribution appeared in the factory. With a full knowledge of the decade of the geography-oriented networks and their potentially damaging effects, the new manager sought to counterbal-

Table 12.2
Distribution of Positions in C

DISTRIBUTION OF MANAGERIAL POSITIONS IN C			
	Total Number	Top Positions	Middle Level Positions	Percentage to All Positions
Heilongjian Youth	156	5	10	65
Yunnan Youth	143	1	3	17
Anhui Youth	18	0	2	8.5
Inner Mongolia Youth	N/A	0	2	8.5
Total		6	17	

Source: Yang (2001, Chapter 4).

ance the dominance of the Yunnan group by promoting people of other geographic roots to the middle-level positions. Only then did this practice of HIPO promotion subside.

Past Working Experience

The third factor influencing HIPO identification and selection in Chinese SOEs is a person's work history. In this case, decision makers identify HIPOs from among those with the same or similar work experience.

Traditionally, employees in a Chinese factory can be classified into four categories: (1) administrative staff (*xingzheng*), which consists of those who work in the factory offices as managers or administrative assistants; (2) technical workers (*jishu*), who perform scientific research on new products for the factory; (3) workshop workers (*chejian gongren*) who are directly engaged in machine operation and product manufacturing on the floor; and (4) political workers (*danzheng*), who are professional party workers such as party secretaries, trade union workers, and propaganda workers, who are charged with protecting party leadership in the factory. These political workers are inserted into the various levels in the factory hierarchy and work under the direct supervision of the party committee, headed by the party secretary of the factory.

Usually, if a top leader has attained his position by working his way up through one of those four channels, it is very likely that he will believe that those with similar working experience are the most suitable to succeed him and are thus more qualified for promotions. This pattern of using similar working experience to identify and select HIPOs is based on a conviction that those with similar experience will share the same ideas and be more reliable in implementing the leader's policies. With like-minded people in power, the top leader will be less worried that his decisions will be distorted, delayed, or misinterpreted in the implementation process. In fact, those potential appointees and top leaders have often established close working and personal relationships long before the top leaders attained their positions. The promotion of the former by the latter is only one way to confirm this special relationship between the two.

In one sample factory I visited in Tianjin, I found evidence of this pattern of HIPO selection in my interviews with factory middle or top-level managers. The factory has a general manager, but the real power is in the hand of the party secretary. Because of the supreme authority of the party secretary, selection and recruitment of HIPOs heavily favor those who have had the experience of political work in the factory.

I had the chance to review the personal information of some 60 of the total 120 middle-level managers in the factory. I found that 40 of those 60 managers, or nearly 70 percent, have had various amounts of political work experience in the factory. These people not only occupy important positions in the political arena, but also take a lion's share of administrative and technological positions. These positions include directors of workshops and managers of the Human Resources Department, Planning Division, and research labs. When I asked the manager of the Human Resources Department why there was such a heavy concentration of political workers in the factory's middle-level management, the manager—who himself also was a political worker by career—told me that this was a result of some thirty years of dominance of the party secretary of the factory. This secretary had reigned in the factory for such a long time that he had established a strong and complex personal relationship permeating every corner of the factory. With the exception of the general manager, who was appointed by the factory's superior government agency, all the other important positions, from the associate general manager to the foreman on the workshop floor, were filled through the party secretary's recommendation and direct involvement. The few middle-level managers with little political work background were all close associates of the party secretary during his brief tenure as the general manager from 1982 to 1986.

When I interviewed the party secretary of this auto factory, he told me directly that the employees are indebted to him for what the factory achieved in the past. His leadership, he said, had steered the factory through the most difficult time and made it one of top-ranked SOEs in Tianjin. Now the factory is one of the most technologically advanced enterprises in the city, and its employees have some of the highest salaries in the area. He proudly claimed that one of his legacies in the factory was the appointments of many middle-level managers who, he believed, would ensure that his policies would continue after his retirement.

Overwhelming influence of the party on HIPO selection is not peculiar to this Tiajin auto factory. In every SOE in China, there are two offices that handle the recruitment of factory employees. One is the Human Resource Department, the other the Organization Division. The former is directly responsible to the general manager, charged with recruiting workers and preparing payrolls, among other functions. The latter is under the direct leadership of the party secretary. Its functions consist mainly of supervising and promoting managers in the factory. Promotion decisions are made by the party committee and issued in the name of the Organization Division. The Human Resource Department has a very limited role in the political careers of factory workers. In this Tianjing factory, the party's total control of the career development of middle-level managers is reflected by the supreme and unchallenged power of the party secretary.

POLITICAL ENTREPRENEURS: CHINESE-STYLE HIPOs?

In public, the criteria of HIPO selection in China have changed significantly during the reform. Prior to the reform, political loyalty and conformity were the top prerequisites for many promotions. In the reform, the ability to implement reform policies faithfully and deliver desired profits became the primary standards. Yet in private, personal relationships and connections have always played a critical role both before and since the reform, influencing the fate of many ambitious and capable HIPO candidates. In both periods, personal loyalty of a potential appointee to the person who makes appointment decisions continues to be one of the main criteria for attaining upward mobility.

This emphasis on personal connections in HIPO selection and promotion does not necessarily conflict with another important quality of a potential appointee, the ability to create enough profits, but it certainly affects his or her accountability. When a factory manager feels that his grip over the factory and his continuous upward mobility depend more on his superior's appreciation of his submission than on the production numbers and profit rate, then his effort will be directed more toward pleasing his superiors than pleasing his employees. He will spend more time in devising ways to court the favor of the leader than in finding ways to improve factory productivity. When these two goals are mutually exclusive—if a good personal relationship with the leader provides a greater guarantee of continuous upward mobility than job performance—there is a strong incentive for HIPO managers to be more responsive to the personal needs of top leaders than to the needs of the factory.

So a HIPO "policy" based on personal loyalty often encourages, or at least tolerates, indifference to job performance among HIPO managers. As long as these HIPOs think their personal relationship offers better assurance for them to get what they want, there is not much incentive for them to concentrate on improving their job performance. And when production does decline, these managers can always blame external conditions such as markets for causing efficiency to lag (Huang 1990, 431–459).

This pattern of HIPO management has become a source of low productivity in the factory. When a manager is more concerned with his superior's attitude toward him than with market signals, the first likely victim will be factory efficiency. Achieving factory efficiency requires that the manager be more responsive to market relations than to human relations. It also requires that the manager be held more accountable for the outcome of his job performance than for his superior's opinion of him. However, the Chinese political and cultural systems have turned factory managers, especially SOE managers, into political entrepreneurs—business executives who owe their career success more to their ability to serve the interests of the political leaders than to their ability to deliver profits to the factory.

That explains why so many Chinese SOE managers spend so much of their working time among government officials in government offices instead of in their offices. One study has shown that of all working hours an SOE manager spends, one-third is devoted to external communication (*wailian*) (Huang 1996, 12–13). This external communication includes dealing with government leaders in finance bureaus, banks, tax offices, superior professional agencies, street committees, energy bureaus, and so on—all of whom are important to a smooth production environment in the factory.

But of these external contacts, the most important is the communication with the top government officials. Among the phenomena that often intrigued me on my field trip were the effort and enthusiasm that many SOE managers put into inviting or even cajoling top government leaders to visit their factories. It is obvious that a visit to the factory by a top political leader will boost the factory's reputation among the public. But one manager's hidden agenda is to use such visits to promote his own image to the top leaders. As one middle-level manager admitted, a visit by a top political leader often indicates that leader's personal recognition of the manager and his achievements. Such a face to face meeting is the most effective way for the factory manager to get the attention of the top leader and to begin to build a good personal relationship (Lampton 1992, 33–58). Usually, careers of HIPO managers depend on how well they impress these leaders during their visits.

Much stronger evidence that the pattern of HIPO selection and recruitment in Chinese SOEs is likely to hurt factory efficiency is one of my findings in the field work. In all the big SOEs I visited, I identified a similar pattern of productivity fluctuation: the highest productivity number tends to be concentrated in those years when visits by top political leaders from both local and central levels occurred most frequently. Again taking SOE A and B as examples, Table 12.3 shows their profit rates, number of top leaders' visits, and promotion of factory leaders during a seven-year period.

The table reveals that most visits by the top political leaders usually occur in the year when the factory profit reaches one of its peaks and has increased dramatically from that of the previous year. In addition, promotion of factory managers also occurs right around this time, and continues after the peak period, regardless of the economic conditions of the factory. In fact, the career of the general manager at A illustrated this point. In 1992, one of A's peak years, the manager was transferred to another large textile factory as the top manager. In 1994, when the production of that factory plummeted, he was appointed general manager of a major textile complex. At the time I was there, this textile complex

Table 12.3
Leaders' Visits and Promotions

COMPANY A	1989	1990	1991	1992	1993	1994	1995
Profit*	3505	3402	5455	13553	18638	7407	4500
Nat'l Leader Visit	3	5	17	12	5	3	2
Local Leader Visit	5	5	7	4	2	0	1
Promotion	0	0	0	2	1	1	1

*profits in ten thousand RMB unit
Source: Factory Book of A over the last ten years

COMPANY B	1989	1990	1991	1992	1993	1994	1995
Profit*	209	122	218	480	205	2104	1302
Nat'l Leader Visit	2	0	0	4	2	11	1
Local Leader Visit	3	1	0	5	2	1	3
Promotion	0	1	0	1	1	1	0

*profits in ten thousand RMB unit
Source: The Record of Important Events of B of this Period

Source: Yang (2001, Chapter 5).

was in serious financial trouble, but the manager was poised to become the vice chairman of an important political organization controlled by the Communist Party.

CONCLUSION

Patterns of HIPO selection and promotion in China are deeply embedded in a political system that is characterized by one-person rule. Human resource management in Chinese SOEs has, just as in other societies, emphasized three types of capital: human capital (education, skills), political capital (political loyalty, party membership, and ideological conformity), and social capital (interpersonal connections). But different political periods prioritized one kind of capital over another. Consequently, the criteria for evaluating HIPO managers also differ from one period to another. Before economic reform, political capital was considered the most important asset in HIPO promotion. Recruitment was primarily based on political loyalty and conformity of potential appointees. This emphasis on a political virtuocracy reflected the priorities of Mao Zedong, who considered a continuous revolution in a socialist country the paramount task facing the Communist Party. This continuous revolution, characterized by incessant class struggle to root out any capitalist or feudalist remnants in the society, required political conformity as the top criterion for any HIPO selection and promotion.

During the reform, this emphasis on political capital was replaced by an emphasis on human capital. HIPO managers are identified and selected on the basis of their managerial skills and education. This shift of focus was prompted by a shift in priority that occurred with the ascendancy of Deng Xiaoping. Deng discarded the old political doctrines and made economic prosperity the primary task of the Communist Party. As a result, virtuocracy has given way to meritocracy as the key factor in HIPO selection and promotion in Chinese SOEs. Managers who faithfully implement reform policies and significantly improve the economic conditions in their factories are favored in promotion.

But the positive effects of this human capital–centered approach have been undermined by a persistent emphasis on social capital in the selection process. Chinese cultural emphasis on compliance with authority and social harmony discourages any behavior that deviates from publicly recognized and approved norms and values. Superiority still is a source of authority and respect. Such traditions hardly changed under Communist rule. Indeed, they are reinforced by the authoritarian nature of Communist rule (Child 1994, 29–30).

In the cultural context, it is not surprising that social capital assumes such an importance in the HIPO selection and promotion process in China. Economic reform has not reduced the importance that leaders attach to personal loyalty and conformity in selecting managers. Although stress on social capital does not necessarily lead to a slowdown or recession in SOEs, it certainly holds SOE managers more accountable for their patron's goodwill than for their own working performance. When a conflict of interests does arise between personal loyalty and economic conditions of the factory, HIPO managers will be encouraged to rely on the protection of their political mentors—at least as long as they continue to believe that pleasing the authorities offers the best hope for political survival and upward mobility in the power hierarchy.

REFERENCES

Child, J. 1994. *Management in China during the age of reform*. New York: Cambridge University Press.

Huang, J. 1996. Some research notes on the contract system. *Enterprise Management* (Qiye Guangli) 24: 12–15.

Huang, Y. 1990. The web of interest and patterns of behavior of Chinese economic bureaucracies and enterprises during the reform. *China Quarterly* 123: 431–459.

Lampton, D. 1992. A plum for a peach: Bargaining, interest, and bureaucratic politics in China. In D. Lampton and K. Lieberthal, eds. *Bureaucracy, Politics, and Decision Making in China*. Berkeley, CA: University of California Press, 297.

Lieberthal, K., and M. Oksenberg, eds. 1989. *Policy making in China*. Princeton, NJ: Princeton University Press.

Lockett, M. 1988. Culture and the problems of Chinese management. *Organization Studies* 9: 457–496.

Nathan, A. 1997. A factional model of CCP politics. *China Quarterly*, 53: 34–66.

———. 1997. From native to work place: Labor origins and outcomes of China's Danwei system. In X. Liu and E. Perry. *Danwei: The Changing Chinese Workplace in Historical and Comparative Perspective*. New York: M. E. Sharp.

Pye, L. 1998. *The Mandarin and the cadre*. Ann Arbor: University of Michigan Press.
Yang, X. 2001. Power, material distribution and labor productivity in China's state owned enterprises. Ph.D. thesis in political science. University of Utah, Salt Lake City.

13

Developing Future Leaders for Vietnam's Market Economy

Nguyen Ngoc Hoang

"Bach nien chi ke, mac nhu thu nhan" [The best century-long plan is to plant human resources].

—Confucius

During the first thirty-two years of Communist rule in Vietnam, from 1954 to 1986, the regime imposed a Soviet-style command economy on the country. As in other Communist countries before the breakup of the Soviet Union, the state strictly planned and controlled all aspects of Vietnam's economy. Business activities were performed by state-owned enterprises (SOEs), which were run like government offices and were staffed with "civil servants" who had been selected primarily on the basis of political loyalty and Party connections.

Since 1986, however, Vietnam has moved toward a market economy, and the state no longer supports SOEs as it formerly did. Although the public sector is still large, an SOE is now supposed to be a "real" business, concerned primarily with profits. Yet the long practice of appointing approved Party members as managers has hindered Vietnam's efforts to foster viable businesses and to build a strong market economy. Most notably, the former system has created a serious shortage of managers with enough training and experience to create viable, competitive SOEs and capitalist-style businesses.

The following points summarize the Vietnamese Communist system of promoting leadership in SOEs:

- The candidate is basically a civil servant. No business-related experience is required, although such experience may be preferable. In certain cases, only a minimum level of education is required.

- *Hong* (red, loyal to the Communist Party, preferably with a proletarian ancestry) and *chuyen* (competent) are still important considerations in selecting candidates for executive positions in SOEs. The criteria for successful candidates are largely based on records dealing with one's personal and family background—infamously known in Vietnam as *chu nghia ly lich*—and not on observation of performance or on any tests or trial periods. The candidate's political background is the underlying factor in any decision on his or her suitability.

- In many cases, a job must be created for an "influential" candidate.

- The kind of training the candidates receive may be highly irrelevant to the jobs they will be given later.

- There is no trial or monitoring period for the candidate after "graduation."

- Last, but not least, the Organization and Personnel (O&P) officers, who have the chief responsibility in this grooming process, are unable to appraise the competence and enterprise of candidates because they do not know how. These officers are in their own positions for political reasons, not for any competence. As a result, the process of grooming the leadership for SOEs or ministries does not take into consideration the specific needs of the enterprise but is instead a blend of oriental feudalism, French bureaucracy, and Soviet classism. So instead of the management of headhunting to improve current leadership and to select future leaders, it seems that the heads are the hunters for the favor of O&P decision makers.

THE SEARCH FOR A NEW SYSTEM OF MANAGEMENT

In 1986, the Party leaders decided to switch Vietnam's economy to a market-oriented system. Since the change, the toll to the state sector has been heavy: about ten thousand quasi SOEs (under government control, but receiving no government funds) have been declared to be in rigor mortis; and almost six thousand of the twelve thousand officially established SOEs have dissolved. Many of these SOEs became privatized—particularly when powerful Party members embezzled government property and took control of factories and machinery for themselves. Under the changing conditions, graft and corruption in the country increased, and the rate of failure for SOEs accelerated, slowing only after government intervention in 1994, when the Party finally decided that the state sector should remain the "leading" sector of the economy (Nugent 1996).[1] In order to strengthen this policy, the Party ruled that only foreign investors could undertake joint ventures with SOEs and that only the state could export goods.

This does not mean that all surviving companies are viable and can withstand the test of the market economy. According to one estimate, at least 70 percent of the remaining SOEs, most of them small-scale, provincial- or district-level enterprises, are at the brink of insolvency and collapse. At the central level, the government has done its best in the past several years to help bigger companies stay strong. But the measures that it has employed have invited criticism from foreign observers that the government has failed to live up to its policy of equality for all economic sectors. And the government measures have apparently fostered corruption. Many of the cases of insolvency, fraud, and financial abuse brought to trial since the introduction of market-oriented economic reforms in 1986 have involved big SOEs and state-controlled banks, both of which have traditionally enjoyed strong support from the government.

Various reasons have been discussed for the constant business losses, insolvency, and bankruptcy of SOEs. Some commentators blame the market economy, implying that if there were no competition from the private sector and from foreign goods, and if the consumers had only one choice, many SOEs would not have collapsed. But in fact, the blame seems mainly to rest with poor management. Many top managers of SOEs still feel ill at ease with the challenges of the market economy. As the country's market system develops through the embryonic stages, these managers have yet to grasp the full meaning of the change. They also have yet to understand the problems they will likely face and to learn how to cope effectively with these problems.

Of course, such understanding requires both knowledge and experience. But these managers are lacking in both. Either because business education is inadequate in Vietnam or because the present learning curve is too steep, these managers seem actually unaware of both the changes and the problems. In other cases, some SOE managers have stumbled because they have tried to run before learning to walk—with disastrous consequences. One example is the megalomaniacal practice of merging several smaller companies into a "state-owned conglomerate" (similar to the Korean *chaebol* or the Japanese *zaibatsu*), only to find that managing a company of one thousand employees is not the same as running one with fifty—nor is it the same as simultaneously managing ten companies of one hundred employees each (National School 1995). The experience of the market economy has shown that most SOE executives, at all levels, are hopelessly inefficient. In fact, the more an SOE is exposed to the market, the worse its management seems.

Although the old system of promoting corporate leadership appears to be stubbornly fighting for survival, it obviously has become totally inadequate. The seemingly inexhaustible reservoir of competent young candidates that existed under the old system has become totally drained as talented people have headed to the private sector. To deal with this predicament, many SOE directors encourage their staffs to take evening courses in English, computers, foreign trade, business law, accounting, foreign investment, and so forth. They have also started hunting for managers who are experienced in working with foreign traders and international investors and who know how to manage a market-driven company.

International organizations and foreign firms have also offered specialized courses in the stock exchange, insurance, auditing, and international marketing. Although these courses are always welcomed by companies, they seem to lack effectiveness. Because the contents of the courses are seldom adapted to the Vietnam situation, they often benefit trainees in only a limited way. At the same time, the students are usually not well enough prepared to absorb what they are taught.

Obviously, people with knowledge of and experience in market economics are really scarce in Vietnam. It simply has not been possible to gain a strong background in business within the country, and of those people who learned about the market economy in the south before 1975, not many remain. So far, training programs have been unable to fill the gap. Young graduates of the newly opened schools of business cannot learn much practical information from instructors who have not been properly educated in market economics themselves.

Serious students now go to schools in the United States, Australia, and Japan instead of Communist countries. And very few of these students return to Vietnam; if they do return, they usually prefer working in the private sector, and for good reason: SOEs can provide neither adequate financial rewards nor the high positions that are still being denied to those outside the Party. Besides, if they were to work in government SOEs, they would be considered "overseas Vietnamese"—that is, inferior to those who never left.

Actually, few educated people are interested in working in SOEs these days. Many competent staff members, having lost interest in the lifetime employment system in SOEs and in the lack of future that they perceive there, have departed. As a result, instead of succeeding in enlisting the best and the brightest, many SOEs are suffering from a brain drain.

In response to this situation, foreign governments (United Kingdom), nongovernmental organizations, or international institutions like the United Nations Development Program (UNDP) have designed programs such as TOKTEN (transfer of capital and technology programs) to recruit "voluntary" foreign and overseas Vietnamese technicians to work with SOEs for brief periods as "advisers" or "business planners." The result of these programs, however, is questionable, because managers at Vietnamese SOEs have not been enthusiastic in supporting them. These managers believe that they are not yet big enough to need outside help, and they resent intruders.

A common criticism of many state companies is that they have been so preoccupied with short-term objectives that they have often ignored long-term development issues. This observation is true, but it is also true that of the six thousand surviving SOEs,[2] most are now preoccupied with simple survival, besieged as they are either by production problems or by a serious exhaustion of capital. As far as building future corporate leadership is concerned, the critical need to find people to handle current problems is already too overwhelming a task. Developing human resources to meet future development needs must seem an elusive luxury to these companies.

Four factors must be present before Vietnamese SOEs can afford to systematically develop future leaders. First, there must be faith in the long-term future of the business itself. Second, the company must be large enough to afford this kind of human investment. Third, there must be a clear sense of direction. And finally, there must be an enabling institutional framework that not only encourages such an endeavor but also ensures that it can be a meaningful effort.

Even if building corporate leadership is not a pressing issue in smaller-sized state companies, it is an acute need in bigger SOEs, especially in what national leaders prefer to call "business groups." A business group is something like a "conglomerate," "holding company," or Korean-style *chaebol*. The formation of business groups is one of the most cherished ideas of Prime Minister Vo Van Kiet, who became greatly impressed by the chaebols in Korea and the trading corporations of Japan. Kiet came to believe that the public sector of Vietnam should also develop "big business groups," which would have a twofold purpose: they could be strong enough to counter the challenge of foreign companies, and they would represent a large share of the national economy in order to maintain the "leading role" of the state-controlled sector. Kiet planned to form his big business groups by gathering all of the businesses within a particular industry and binding them together. Within a conglomerate there could be a bank, a foreign trading company, various manufacturing companies, training services, a science and technology research center, and so on. Each company within a business group would be an "autonomous" unit, but it would work under the direction of a common board of directors, which would consist of directors of all member companies and of representatives of various government agencies.

The Vietnamese experiment with conglomerates began first with centrally administered industries in major fields like steel, coal, electricity, petroleum, construction, telecommunication, civil aviation, railways, food, sea products, cement, tobacco, and coffee. Big cities like Ho Chi Minh City[3] and Hanoi, determined not to be outdone by the central government, are following suit with their own "business groups." Before long, other big cities, like Da Nang, Hai Phong, Dong Nai, Vung Tau, and Can Tho, will no doubt be tempted to follow suit.

Skeptics point out that this new model of incorporation is in no way comparable to existing models of Korean chaebols or Japanese zaibatsu. Rather, they say, this idea of "powerful business groups" is simply a resurrection of the once-favorite and now totally bankrupt Soviet-styled model of *lien hiep xi nghiep* (union of enterprises). But what Vietnam's economic architects may not be ready to divulge is that they realize it will be a long time before Vietnam can support big joint stock companies. In the absence of these big companies, they may reason, these state-owned business groups demonstrate that Vietnam can think big and act big anyway; besides, the presence of the groups also may encourage the private sector to set up large joint stock companies.

At the very least, the establishment of these business groups has made clear the need for HIPO development in Vietnamese SOEs. These business groups not only need to find capable managerial executives for various member companies and departments, but also must provide long-term training to the line-and-staff executives of the group so that they can handle increasingly complicated business tasks. In the course of expanding their cooperation with foreign partners in joint venture projects, these groups have sought foreign help with skill training. Vietnam Civil Aviation Corporation, Petro-Vietnam, and Saigon Tourism have all developed training schools of their own. Although senior managers may take these training programs only to show that they can still learn, they do acquire new managerial skills there. However, these training programs are less institutionalized than those in other countries, and they are a long way from being the comprehensive programs for developing managers that are seen in more developed economies.

Change is also coming to Vietnamese enterprise through totally foreign-owned enterprises or those enterprises operating in cooperation with foreign firms, such as foreign-invested companies or those operated by business cooperation contracts (BCC companies). Although the government is encouraging the establishment of Party cells even in these companies, neither the control nor the influence of the Party in these enterprises is important. Foreign-owned companies have introduced what seems a radical system of personnel recruitment and promotion. Party membership or participation in the war is rarely considered a plus; instead, employee evaluations are based on merit and tested competence. Of course, the Vietnamese partner in a joint venture may be able to plant its own choices in certain high positions, but in most cases, the Vietnamese partner recruits local employees under the supervision or approval of the foreign partner. In these foreign companies, employees are often highly paid and are given re-training opportunities. Those who are considered highly capable are often sent to Singapore, Thailand, Japan, or Australia for short-term training.

Of the private companies that are primarily Vietnamese, many are set up as actual family businesses, and these too are more willing than SOEs to employ the best and the brightest workers they can afford. Whereas leaders of Communist SOEs never seem to consider the problem of continuity and what will happen when they leave, owners of private companies are more likely to have a long-term vision and to be concerned with choosing and training the most reliable among their children to take over the business someday. Because the rights and responsibilities of a director of a SOE are still not defined clearly, he often does not have a long-term interest in the company, but the owner of a private company has full rights over his business, and he alone is liable for this company's performance.[4] His management is likely to continue improving, while the that of the SOEs stagnates.

As the private sector grows, it obviously poses a challenge to SOEs, with their poor record of developing corporate leadership. The Vietnamese government tends to dismiss the importance of the private sector in comparison to the public sector.[5] But considering the fact that private companies were officially permitted to come into being only in 1986 and the fact that the government is still treating this sector inequitably, the strength that the private sector has gained is in no way negligible. Private companies are especially strong in domestic and foreign trade, services, and small manufacturing. Whereas SOEs have to rely on the state to set up cooperative relations with foreign companies, many private companies have natural ties with foreign counterparts, especially with overseas Vietnamese and with the Chinese in Hong Kong, Taiwan, Thailand, Singapore, and even China.[6] These ties facilitate the transfer of not only capital but also technology and managerial skills.

VIETNAM'S HIPO DEVELOPMENT: MEGATRENDS

Sesto Vecchi, one of the best-known American business consultants in Saigon before and after 1975, also notes, "Vietnam will be a far different place in 2010 than it is today."[7] This is no doubt true, but the quality of the change remains to be seen. Not a few observers hope—along with nervous Communist leaders—that Vietnam will become another Asian dragon. Yet if this dream is to come true, several tasks must be accomplished during the intervening years. The government must demonstrate, through concrete action, a firmer commitment to market reforms and economic democracy. If the public sector is to remain the leading sector of the national economy, it must not be by compromising the basic rules of market economics, nor must it be at the expense of other sectors.[8]

In fifteen or twenty years from now, SOEs may still exist, although perhaps not on the present scale; nor will they be run by their current managers. But the questions of who the new managers will be and how they will be promoted have not yet been answered. Ideally, they should belong to a new generation of SOE executives: they should have adequate education, time-enriched experience, high managerial skills, and an enterprising spirit. But those managers are still fictional in the Vietnam of today. At this moment, there seems to be no visible bridge between past practices and a future of sound SOE management.

It is generally believed that the current trend toward a market economy is irreversible. The change may be slowed, but not shifted. It is to be hoped, however, that as the market economy develops, Vietnamese managers in general, and those running SOEs in particular, will create a business culture (still unidentifiable in Vietnam) and a unique, typically Vietnamese business management style. In particular, they must become more aware of the need for *thu nhan* (cultivating human resources), and they must devote more organized effort to HIPO development.

One hopeful sign for HIPO development is that business education in Vietnam is improving. Many business schools are realizing that they cannot teach much—and students are also discovering that they cannot learn much—without radical reform in the educational system. Therefore, schools are beginning to seek to establish cooperative ties with foreign universities in order to improve the curriculum, acquire more able instructors, and gradually modify the teaching method. Successful education reform could do much to change perceptions and practices within the business community; better educational opportunities can foster not only the desire to study but also the wish to improve the system with well-trained people.

Another hopeful sign took place in mid-1996, when the National Assembly passed a law that provides for radical reform in the status of state enterprises. Much time will be needed to put the law into effective practice, but some positive measures have already been taken, although not universally. The reform provides for the assignment of state capital assets to SOEs for autonomous management, the abolition of the parental role exercised by ministries and local administrations over SOEs, the establishment of boards of directors, and the definition of managers' powers and responsibilities. Under this system, chief executive officers (CEOs) can really control the resources of their companies. They will have more power to use these resources as they deem necessary, and—theoretically—they can assume the sole responsibility for employment and compensation policies. In essence, SOEs must now be run as private companies are.

With better business education and a more attractive and challenging corporate environment within SOEs, young talents and ingenious executives will likely emerge in greater numbers. These young executives will have more than adequate opportunities to prove themselves as prospective leaders of their corporations; they will, in fact, become the corporate heroes of the new era. In other words, they represent a new generation of business executives, comparable to their Asian counterparts.

But if Vietnam is to become a minitiger in two decades, there will have to be tens of thousands of these competent business executives who have been developed by then. As the demand curve for trained executives grows increasingly steep over the next twenty years, the need for HIPO development will be enormous. Business education will continue to be the most significant factor in this executive training, but other reforms must also be intensive. Corporations, especially conglomerates, must play a more active role in developing HIPO employees; to accomplish this, managers at all levels must identify such individuals and channel them through effective systems of promotion.

Effective business reform within Vietnam will also require government reforms. Observers hope that within twenty years, businesspersons will achieve a real and direct influence within the power system of the state, and their input will steadily influence more sensible political and economic policies. If this occurs, then Vietnam will have acquired an entrepreneurial class that plays a significant role in society.[9]

As Vietnamese businesses work to establish models for HIPO development, they will have to deal with the former, nonproductive policies. Of course, *chu nghia ly lich* (the policy of employment based on family/social background) will need to be eliminated, even at SOEs. Similarly, the "red" factor must become much less important in any hiring or promotion. The personnel office (O&P) will survive, but it should become more capable of tailoring human resources development to corporate needs. Therefore, the O&P should not be staffed by those with connections to the police or security; nor should it be staffed by people without any business or management skills.

At the same time that corporations try to modernize their approach to hiring and promotion, it is vital that they base their reforms on a foundation of accepted traditional values. As with many Asian countries, Vietnam is a nation that traditionally accords high respect to intellectuals and talented people. It has been generally believed that "learned men" (*si*) understand the nature of things and hold the key to social development. This is reflected in a system of social hierarchy that ranks educated people at the top of society.[10] As a result of these attitudes, which were influenced by Chinese Confucianism, the Vietnamese have traditionally cared greatly about education. Investment in education was given the highest priority, both within families and within the society as a whole. In fact, in the traditional family, a man's only duty was to study and earn a degree, while the rest of the household was to labor and make any sacrifice necessary to finance both his studies and the high cost of examinations. Confucianism calls this *thu nhan* (human planting, or investment in human resources).[11]

So, now that the Communist system is being called into question, companies are again giving heavy consideration to the education level, expertise, and business skills of candidates for employment or promotion. Vietnam's traditional social values are being restored, in a way, through a renewed emphasis on education and on an individual's competence in "social building." On the other hand, the country has spent more than two decades witnessing intellectuals' unsuccessful attempts to make history, and the Vietnamese have perhaps become more pragmatic. Most likely, a university degree will become less and less important to managers involved in identifying, selecting, and grooming management candidates. Although the nation will continue to produce a large number of degrees, during the next ten years companies will probably look less carefully at education and more closely at a candidate's proven abilities in diversified business and leadership skills.

Logical casualties of the former system will be lifetime employment and seniority-based promotion. Lifetime employment has been a tradition in Asian countries, but now, even Japanese, Korean, and Chinese companies are less willing to be bound by guarantees of employment. Asian workers are also losing interest in the old system. In Vietnam particularly, educated people have come to dread the Communist promise of lifetime employment, which to many workers seems to be a life sentence. Younger, more educated employees prefer instead the flexibility that will enable them to explore other opportunities. Besides, these younger individuals have become increasingly ambitious and more impatient at having to wait for persons in positions above them to be promoted or to retire.

There is another reason that many Vietnamese employees no longer find job security—and the promise of promotion after ten to fifteen years—as attractive as they once did. During the years of central bureaucratic and paternalistic planning and administration, lower-echelon staff members developed a pattern of distrust and contempt toward management. The promotion of incompetent Party members often sowed discontent among employees—especially those with considerable education. Mediocre management, combined with rampant corruption among top executives of many SOEs, further damaged the respect of young staff for their bosses.

Now, as Vietnam emerges from decades of dormant torment, these young people have acquired high expectations. Understandably, they often assume that great opportunities will be available and plentiful, but these expectations can easily become frustrations if "golden" opportunities turn out to be elusive. Large, well-established, highly reputable companies[12] that offer generous pay packages are naturally favorite choices for capable and self-confident young people. But even smaller companies can attract promising candidates if the management cares about building up an image that will appeal to the most capable candidates. HIPO individuals prefer to work with a management that is approachable, communicative, and willing to create opportunities for its employees. Also considered an "agreeable land for a bird to perch" is a firm with a charismatic top executive, one who is well trained and highly connected, who has cultivated extensive relationships within both domestic and foreign business circles, and who is committed to developing a corporate culture based on respect.

Capable employees may also be attracted by a company with a "family" style of management. Vietnam has had a tradition, influenced by Confucian teachings and Chinese culture, of managing business enterprises as though they were families. The feeling was that only in this context would each employee have a sense of belonging and want to contribute to the fullest of his or her abilities. Subordinates were expected to work with order, discipline, respect, and absolute submission to their superiors. Managers, on the other hand, demonstrated love and care for the "younger generations" and sacrificed for them. Under the family-management concept, the enterprise was seen as a larger roof providing safety and security for the smaller families of each employee. The enterprise had a close relationship with their employees' families, and it took care to promote each member of the company in accordance with his abilities. When the time came for power to be transferred from one generation to another, the process was quite peaceful, as a result of a carefully planned system of selecting, training, trying, apprenticing, sharing power, and finally passing power to heirs.

Unfortunately, this tradition has been severely affected by the constant wars and internal conflicts that have plagued Vietnam for more than a century. During this difficult period, the influence of Confucianism waned dramatically,[13] a decline that accelerated during the Communist rule since the 1950s. The intent of the Communist system was to undermine the family as the basic unit of social development. By destroying the traditional family of husband, wife, and children who lived together in the common pursuit of happiness, the Communists sought to transform the "socialist firm" into a new family for the people.

But as capitalist ways replace the old Marxist system, and as Vietnam's neighboring countries return to the traditional Asian style of business management, there is a growing awareness that Vietnam should also move back toward family-style business management. In most cases, private firms with visionary management could easily groom their HIPOs in ways similar to the traditional management styles. And they should. The technologically sophisticated managers who are emerging in Vietnam are no longer civil servants who desperately need the blessing of ranking Party members in order to advance. Since these employees are "talents" in the traditional sense of Asian cultures (and a talent is hard to find!), they should be treated as *ke si* (intellectuals), with dignity.

SOEs may find it more difficult to make the shift to the traditional management style, however. For one thing, their attitudes toward HIPOs are often bureaucratic and patronizing. Besides, bad habits die hard, and the bureaucratic, "favor given, favor received" mentality of many senior SOE managers will not simply vanish overnight. But the system must be changed. A fair and systematic plan for developing HIPO managers, based on ability, not connections, could generate more trust among employees, as would a process of training, testing, retraining, and retesting. In addition, the person who oversees the selection of suitable candidates should also oversee their development, at least in the early phases of grooming.

How long the grooming process would last and what the specific stages would include depend primarily on the size of the enterprise in question and on the degree to which management is affected by "foreign influence." Some managers might adopt the Chinese way of building up succession, whereby the "apprentice" works closely and industriously with the incumbent manager. Or, since the Japanese have made it clear that they want the Vietnamese to learn something from the "Japanese model of management," local businesses may try the Japanese strategy of recruiting young graduates from universities and giving them varied exhausting experiments that allow only those with fortitude to survive. On the other hand, Vietnamese managers could also try the American model, which is more "systematic and comprehensible" to Vietnam's business students. No matter what model is adopted, the process of grooming HIPO executives in Vietnam is likely to be shorter than the practice normally observed in other countries with a time-tested tradition of developing "talents." And once a candidate is chosen, he or she can be sure to be the "heir apparent" of the system. To be realistic, in the foreseeable future, promotion opportunities are still not open to everyone, or to most people. This means that until an efficient free and democratic system is established in the country, it will remain a "class society" in which some people are more equal than the others. But Vietnam is in the process of rapid change. There is good cause of hope for positive evolution in the years to come.

CONCLUSION

Several international observers of Vietnam have concluded that the future of the country—whether or not Vietnam can prevail in its battle against poverty and backwardness—depends on the success of the entrepreneurial class and its growth as a force within the country. But this success is dependent on the government's commitment to market reforms, and the pace with which it is willing to institute reform. Unfortunately, the country's prospect is less than encouraging because of a kind of near-sightedness. Despite some reforms, there continue to be in Vietnam a schizophrenic containment of market development, an excessive fear of "peaceful evolution," and only listless reform in education. Many in power still fear that they themselves cannot survive the suspension of the current system of political patronage. These attitudes are an impediment to the kind of reform that will be required to build a viable business environment.

And there are other obstacles to overcome. For one, the main problems in many transitional economies are, beyond any dispute, intolerance and political and economic selfishness. Vietnam seems to have more than its share of these properties. In addition to these factors are domestic and foreign policies that more often raise the eyebrows of possible economic trading partners. Some actions of the Vietnamese government are quite frustrating. For instance, while it was trying to persuade the United States to normalize economic relations between the two countries and grant the Most Favored Nation status (also known as the Normal Trading Relations/NTR) to Vietnam, it hosted in June 1997 a conference of activists from Asian and Pacific nations to discuss support for Cuba in the face of the continued trade sanctions by the United States. There is also cause for fear that the process of change may be unnecessarily prolonged. But if political leaders can come to realize that they have already missed too many opportunities and that Vietnam cannot develop in total disregard of current worldwide trends, the nation's economic and business environment will continue to progress.

NOTES

1. Nicholas Nugent has dealt with the most recent developments in Vietnam's pursuit of *doi moi* (renovation) policies.

2. According to a report of the World Bank published in 1994, there are fewer than three thousand SOEs operating in industry. One-fifth of these are at the central level, though not all central-level companies are large and well equipped. The remaining SOEs are trading and services companies.

3. Take the case of Hochiminh City, for example. In 1994, the vice chairman of the city, Le Nfinh Chau, decided to set up a "business group" called Satraco by combining all state-owned domestic and foreign trade companies into one, in spite of strong opposition from the public and from these companies themselves. He was forced to retire in June 1996 over a political case, but his "business group" remains.

4. "It [the Vietnamese government] is slowly moving towards more accountability by state-owned enterprises," remarked Sesto Vecchi, an American lawyer with much experience in Vietnam, in the article "Take the long view on Vietnam," published in *Far Eastern Economic Review* May 1997, 160(21):36. This sense of accountability, however, stems from the fact that the government no longer can subsidize the business of an SOE, rather than from a system in which a director of an SOE is held responsible for poor performance and any wrongdoing in his company.

5. Vice Premier Phan Van Khai told a news conference in May 1995 that the Vietnamese government will proceed with its "corporatization plan" in its own way because "the private sector in this country is not strong enough to absorb de-nationalized SOEs."

6. Vietnam's most important foreign investors are from Hong Kong, Taiwan, and Singapore. It is believed that "unofficial investments" from the overseas Chinese in these countries are of no less importance.

7. Vecchi, *Far Eastern Economic Review* 160(21) (May 1997): 36.

8. To date, leadership in Hanoi still gives lip service to Marxist-Leninist theories and passes all blame for social vices such as corruption, drug trafficking, and prostitution to the market economy. *Far Eastern Economic Review* 160(22) (May 1997) said, "When official corruption is unearthed, the inclination is to blame the market and not the government." The *Deseret News* also published a Reuters story on June 14, 1997 (p. 7), stating that a senior leader of the Communist Party called upon the regime to be "highly vigilant" in relation to the threat of markets by studying more about Communist doctrines.

9. At present, the influence of business in both the Central Committee of the Communist Party and the National Assembly, or even in local People's Councils, is negligible, although the ruling party and its government have repeatedly pledged to seek advice from business people to formulate their economic and business policies.

10. Vietnam's social culture, heavily influenced by the Chinese philosophers Confucius and Mencius, ranks intellectuals first among the four main social strata: *si* (intellectuals, or learned men), *nong* (farmers), *cong* (craftsmen), *thuong* (merchants).

11. A famous saying of Confucius is, The best one-year plan is to plant rice; the best decade-long plan is to grow forest; the best century-long plan is to plant human beings *(Nhat nien chi ke, mac nhu thu coc; thap nien chi ke, mac nhu thu moc; bach nien chi ke, mac nhu thu nhan)*.

12. During the 1980s, a job with a trading company was the number-one target of Vietnamese job seekers. In recent years, working with a foreign company or a foreign-invested firm seems to be everyone's dream.

13. Tran Te Xuong, a famous Vietnamese poet in the nineteenth century, lamented, "Cai hoc nha nho da hong roi/Muoi nguoi di hoc, chin nguoi thoi" (The learning of Confucian thoughts is a failure already; of ten people going to school, nine would soon quit studying).

REFERENCES

Forbes, D., et al. 1991. *Doi Moi, Vietnam's renovation policy and performance.* Canberra, Australia: Australia National University Press.

Harrison, J. 1982. *The endless war: Fifty years of struggle in Vietnam.* New York: Free Press.

Harvard Institute of International Development. 1994. *In the direction of the flying dragon: Economic reforms in Vietnam* (Vietnamese edition). Cambridge, MA: Harvard University Press.

Hoang, N. 1996. *Vietnam Doi Moi in perspective.* Quy Mai, Vietnam.

Karnow, S. 1983. *Vietnam, a history: The first complete account of Vietnam at war.* New York: Viking Press.

Mya, T., and L. H. Joseph Tan. 1993. *Vietnam's dilemmas and options.* Singapore: Institute of Southeast Asian Studies.

The National School of Public Administration Alumnae Association Magazine. 1995. *Vietnam: Recommendations for the future.* Berkeley, California.

Nugent, N. 1996. *Vietnam, the second revolution.* London.

Pacific Basin Research Institute. 1993. *Toward a market economy in Vietnam: Economic reforms and development strategies for the 21st century.* Rockville, MD: Pacific Basin Research Institute.

World Bank. 1994. *Vietnam's transition toward a market economy* (Vietnamese translation).

14

The Role of the Army in Developing High-Potential Israeli Executives

Daniel Rouach

From many points of view, Israel is unlike any other country. From 1950 to 2000, the country has lived under the weight of enormous military pressure, which has affected cultural, social, familial, and economic life.

Firms operate in a permanently disturbing climate due to the troubled political context. The risks of war and the threat of a sudden major (quasi-unexpected) crisis are part of daily life.

Thus, methods of organizing and managing business, systems of external recruitment and internal promotion, staff behavior toward each other and the outside, the appointment and departure of managers, the choices made by teams and their methods of operation, and so forth, are all influenced directly or indirectly by two factors at the same time: the army and the Americanization of mentalities. The latter is little spoken of by analysts and outside observers. If there is one single country that holds an extraordinary attraction for Israelis, it is the United States.

Nothing had appeared at the approach of the year 2000 to counterbalance this attraction for Israelis, who have become extremely dependent on the United States in matters of politics, economics, finance, and culture.

In this chapter, we are not going to focus on the process of Americanization, the cultural origins of company managers (Ashkenazim or Sephardim), on areas and regions where the elite of the country are to be found, on the influence of religion in the choice of managers, nor on the growing impact of Russian scientists who have emigrated to Israel. All this would mean specific and detailed research (Klatzmann and Rouach 1995).

Here we attempt to answer two key questions: who are the elite who run the country, and what role does the army play in their development?

THE BUSINESS ELITE IN ISRAEL

The time seems long off when, in 1987, the Israelis discovered alternative business values and were scandalized by the $40,000 monthly salary of Ernest Yafet (former president of the Leumi Bank). When he left his pension was $56,000 per month in a country where the minimum wage was 40 percent lower than the French equivalent.

The past fifty years have brought great development to Israel. The new image recently promoted by the Israeli media is that of a new elite, largely Ashkenazim (Jews of European origin), who live mostly in reserved areas (Ramat Hasharon, Savyon, etc.) and who go out of their way to copy American fashion and culture. One Israeli TV series, *Ramat Aviv Guimel*, has even parodied the practices of this "new elite" with its peculiar life-style.

Such a life-style may be new to Israelis, but it does not seem to be influenced by the army. Israel does not have a military elite; rather, it is a citizens' army made up of draftees and reservists. Since so many are in the army, it is not surprising to find highly ranked officers in various political and business elites.

THE PIONEERING SPIRIT OF FUTURE LEADERS

The role of the army has always been crucial, and it is important to remember that before the Yom Kippur War in 1973:

- Defense was the absolute priority and elite units were the backbone of military command.
- Common values were accepted by all Israelis. The kibbutz (Hebrew for collectivity; a communal farm) was very influential.
- The elite was "motivated by a moral spirit."
- The question often debated was, Is a state of war the ideal state?
- There was a view of the army as being "the sacred spearhead of the nation."
- The philosophy of Ben-Gurion still existed. He had always sought to inject a pioneering spirit into the army: an idealistic mentality in the officers, army participation in agriculture on the borders, total devotion, and an eagerness to volunteer. Ouri Ben Eliezer of the University of Tel Aviv stated that Israel had become an "armed nation" immediately after the creation of the state. The close ties among the political, military, and industrial elite were one of the dominant characteristics of this society. These elite groups all have a mutual influence.

GENERATIONS OF ENGINEERS AND INVENTORS, TRAINED BY THE ARMY, CREATING THEIR OWN COMPANIES

During negotiations for the preparation of an industrial strategy, the army mentality is never far away. At the age of eighteen, all young Jews (except the ultraOrthodox) pass through the military. No Israeli can spend three years in the army and leave it intact. The tension that reigns in the elite is extreme, sleepless nights are frequent, and death is always around the corner as attacks can be deadly. According to certain commentators, the atmosphere in some units in South Lebanon is like the situation in Vietnam at its worst.

In this context, the culture of the economic and political elite is strongly affected by a military dimension. The Israeli army, which influences the attitudes of Israeli managers, is an army of movement, made up of small units and commandos who react rapidly and flexibly. The extension of these qualities is obvious in the community.

During many assignments in Israel with French industrialists, we have noticed that the latter always seem surprised by the rapid reactions and quick decisions made by our managers. They are also surprised at the wealth of knowledge Israelis have about their competitors.

The article, "A Land of Tech and Money," (Newsweek, April 2, 1996) states: "Israel boasts the greatest number of start-ups outside Silicon Valley. The founders are engineers and scientists inspired by elite units of the army of projects linked to Defense."

There is no respite for the many who join the elite. The Israeli must carry out his milouim (reservist activities of thirty to forty-five days a year) up to the age of forty-four. He therefore knows his fighting companions perfectly well and often considers them as his family. The army is a place of socialization that structures the business community. Women spend two years in military structures between the ages of eighteen and twenty.

Company organization is informal, and professional relations are less hampered by conflicts with superiors since these have been previously handled in the army. Interactive learning is favored. Technological innovation in both civil and military sectors is always praised in Israeli culture and media and is considered to be indispensable as a driving force for the future of this country celebrating its fiftieth anniversary.

MILITARY ROLE IN EDUCATION

So, the elite in Israel is deeply marked by army culture. Other training routes exist for the elite—the kibbutz, school, and university—but nothing replaces the influence of the military experience had by young adolescents. Because Israel is a melting pot of successive waves of immigrants who have made the country, Tsahal is the quintessential social and cultural integration system. Tsahal is a very erudite army.

The Israeli defense forces constitute the biggest school in the country. The number of soldiers taking courses in the variety of subjects taught in the military academies and vocational and paramilitary schools is easily the biggest collection of students in any institution or group of institutions. The influence of the army on education is deliberate, rather than an indirect result of the environment. Educational activities are systematically organized.

The army extends beyond traditional education to instill certain universal values such as love of country, loyalty and dedication, solidarity with the world's Jews, and identification with the Jewish people's past and the Zionist ideal. All levels of schools, all courses, and all publications participate in developing these values. Opinions may vary as to the success of all these activities, but nobody can contest the impact the army has in the instillation of national, Jewish, human, and civic virtues.

THE MODERN ELITE

After a stint in the army, the future managing executive goes to the university. The company elite arrive already mature and with the firm desire to study rapidly so as to enter professional life at the age of twenty-five to twenty-seven, these qualities are instituted by the military. The universities, however, are structured according to the American model; most professors have studied in the United States and the American way of thinking reigns supreme. Those who studied in Western or Eastern Europe always have the impression they have missed out on something special by not spending time in the United States.

Most Israeli postdoctorate students go to the United States or Canada, where North American laboratories welcome them warmly. This trend accentuates the very real brain drain in Israel. Indeed, very few large laboratories in New York, Boston, Los Angeles, Chicago, Toronto, Montreal, and Vancouver are without Israelis on their staff. The best Israeli professors perform research in conjunction with laboratories in other countries and participate in the race for publication in English-language journals, on which their future largely depends.

In order to give this theory a real dimension let us present the true case of Ruben as an illustration. Ruben has the typical elite profile. The army has left its mark on him; he is Ashkenazi, is married, and has three children. He is a senior executive who specializes in industrial litigation and works for a conglomerate. He was born in Israel and is a Sabra—a native-born Israeli—a name Israelis give themselves to describe their "thorny outside, but soft inside." Ruben is an only child; his parents were imprisoned in the Nazi concentration camps, and that knowledge has had a profound effect on him. The Holocaust haunts his view of life and shapes his view of Israel's security. After brilliant studies and pushed by his parents, he took the "royal way" and became a lawyer. Israel has a ratio of lawyers per inhabitant higher than that of the United States. Before becoming a lawyer, he did his military service in the commandos despite his mother's protests. In Israel, only sons (often the case for families of former deportees) are allowed to serve in less-exposed units. Wounded in the Yom Kippur War, he escaped serious physical injury. His social life is intense. It is no accident that Israel has a record number of mobile telephones for the number of inhabitants: more than 1.5 million phones in circulation! Every Friday evening (the eve of Shabbat, or Sabbath) he meets with childhood friends, military friends, work colleagues, and neighbors, as do most Israelis. His neighbors are part of his family. In Israel your neighbors know everything about you and lives intertwine in apartment buildings. His living standard corresponds to that of the new elite: a villa, two cars, three computers, one mobile phone per person, and two trips abroad per year to escape from the pressures of living in a region of constant drama. This way of life bears no resemblance to that of the former elite.

THE NINE LAWS OF THE COUNTRY'S ELITE

The country's elite are not isolated. They live in a universe where the economy undergoes rapid changes. The beliefs of the elite are easily spotted, and a common denominator links the country's leaders. The following outline the nine main points of consensus on which the country's industry and managerial behavior rests.

Company Elite Groups Are Associated with the Strategic Stakes of the Country: To ensure the future, industries that are vital to the country's security receive top priority: computer technology, nuclear industry, aeronautics, robotics, biotechnology, and medical instrumentation. Clearly most Israeli technology is developed for the defense sector. Creative and innovative technology and its role in boosting the economy have always been considered vital for all Israeli managers.

An Elite at the Forefront of Training: Education, university, and research will always be the country's priorities because they help to ensure defense. The diffusion, improvement, and appropriation of foreign technology must also be permanent. With a view to the country's security, Israeli leaders are convinced that only gray matter superior to that of neighboring countries will ensure victory in the case of war.

A Fighting Elite: The speed of aggressive commercial activities in international markets reinforces the importance of reaction time. In the face of technological change, competition and any kind of opportunity must be developed. Israelis, as we have already stated, are influenced by the military mentality.

An Internationally Minded Elite: Building international technological alliances with the United States and Europe in particular will be continued. Companies must be obliged to compete with the best multinationals.

An Elite in Research: Israel will be built in a zone of technology, and investment will be made in R&D as well as the scientific potential.

The Elite as a Play in Resolving the Country's Conflicts: We will bypass the conflict in the Middle East and limit the impact of the boycott by focusing on the Asian and Eastern European markets.

The Elite and Management Innovation: Improved productivity, quality of management practices, and long-term international marketing prospects will help the Israeli economy expand.

The Elite's Social Responsibility: Privatizing highly symbolic public companies and encouraging free enterprise while limiting inflation and public debt are our goals, as well as maintaining unemployment at its current acceptable level and reserving better integration and jobs for Russian Jewish immigrants.

The Elite and its Diplomatic Influence: The elite must preserve relations with the United States, source of $3 billion a year, and Europe, in order not to lose the advantages of technological cooperation and public markets.

Israel is marked by its concentration of economic power in the hands of groups drawn together in solidarity and living in symbiosis with the rest of society: universities, the army, political power, banks, trade unions, administration, and the kibbutz.

Since the beginning of the 1990s the army has been losing its influence, and younger generations no longer hesitate to find new markets to point the way to the future. Right up until the 1980s a young Israeli who was refused by the army for military service bore a stigma that could affect his entire career. Although this is now less frequently true, the military influence continues to provide the structure for the country's networks of senior executives and managers.

REFERENCES

Bendelac, Jacques. 1995. *Israël à crédit, l'Harmattan Comprendre le Moyen-Orient.* Paris: PUF.

Cabrillac, Bruno. 1994. *L'économie du Moyen-Orient: Que sais-je?* Paris: Presse Universitaire Française.

Chambre de Commerce et d'Industrie Israelo-Française, 1996. Israël petit pays grand marché, vol. 5. Paris.

Dun and Bradstreet International. 1995. *Israel's leading enterprises 1995.* Tel Aviv: Dun and Bradstreet International.

Israël à l'aube d'une ère nouvelle. 1995. *La lettre diplomatique*, numéro spécial.

Klatzmann, Joseph, and Rouach Daniel. 1995. *L'économie d'Israël: Que sais-je?* Paris: Presse Universitaire Française.

Remaking Israel. 1997. *Business Week*, February 17.

Revue Française de Coopération Economique avec Israël. 1997. No. 165 (August–September): 57, 58.

Rouach, Daniel, and Bisraor, Léon. 1992. *Israguide—Le Guide pratique des affaires avec Israël.* Tel Aviv: RI International.

15

Preparing African Leaders

Evalde Mutabazi

Political tensions are ravaging many countries all over the world; in Africa alone, several political leaders are being ousted. In this context, contributing to the academic debate on "identifying high-potential executives" fills me with equal measures of enthusiasm and revulsion.

The subject excites me not only because this work has been initiated and coordinated by my colleagues, but also because it deals with current situations in Africa and on four other continents. Despite my enthusiasm, participating in this enterprise disgusts me in certain ways. Although the subject has always been at the heart of crucial social issues, we observe today that certain communities have dismantled centuries-old mechanisms for educating managers and have replaced them with imported systems. Thus, the majority of African expertise in this field has been buried under the rubble of wrecked ancient social orders and has been replaced by Western systems.

In the end, my excitement eclipses my revulsion because, in Africa and elsewhere, the management question—that is, determining which characteristics make up an effective manager—needs a new edge as we pass from the second to the third millennium. The fact that this question is again open for discussion results partly from the dawning of the twenty-first century, which is indisputably marked by the emergence of world markets, by the interdependence of national economies, and by the widening of the gulf between rich and poor (on both an international and an interpersonal level). And since this irreversible globalization is brought about by companies rather than by political or diplomatic institutions, the managerial question must be examined. My thoughts are based on several studies done in France and in six African countries that deal with the clash between cultures and management models in firms and governments of differing cultural backgrounds.

ABOUT THE STUDY

My interviews with several companies in nations throughout Africa (Congo, Ivory Coast, Nigeria, Senegal, Rwanda, and Democratic Republic of Congo [ex-Zaire]) have confirmed these ideas, as have my observations of several French-based multinational firms (Mutabazi 1998). Although it had not been my intention to compare them, I was surprised by the ideological similarities among the eight multinational companies set up in France, their eight African subsidiaries, and the eight public companies and eight smaller, private companies in Africa.

These similarities surface in the answers to two general questions, on which 82 percent of African and French managers were in agreement:

- How can we better manage business globalization, cultural differences, and the interdependence among national economies?
- What skills do managers need to develop in order to reconcile economic demands with the development of more tolerant and beneficial international relations?

Seventy-eight point six percent (78.6 percent) of interviewees (African and French alike) believed that the manager's role should include greater cultural and social breadth and should take into account the recent overlap between economic and political affairs. This opinion indirectly repudiates the separation of economics and politics, and consequently the separation of companies' economic and social gains from local political issues.

These ideas have become a reality: numerous managerial associations, such as the European Roundtable, are being set up all over the world. The mission of such organizations transcends the activities of individual member companies, their economies, and their places of origin. Although they do not replace regional structures like the European Union, Mercosur, and so on, most of these associations are interested in, among other topics, a variety of cultures, management models, and methods of training future managers (Calori and de Woot 1994). Among the skills often cited is the ability to work across cultural boundaries as partners, members of management teams, and operators from mixed cultural backgrounds.

AFRICA: *PRIMUS INTER PARES* VERSUS "COCONUTS"

The purpose of this chapter is not to compare African and Western methods of preparing managers but to present two concepts: (1) the factors common to African companies' top management approaches and (2) local employees' expectations of their superiors. This analysis should further the evolution of the business world; it should not look to the past, assign blame for failures in the relations between Africa and the West, or point out blunders made by African firms and their managers (Paul 1993). While highlighting the fact that African managers are often categorized according to their ethnic and tribal (M'Bokolo 1995) background, the study suggests that via the firm we can reconcile local tradition with ideas from other continents—a goal that lies at the heart of management training in Africa.

Although today's modern African corporations may be similar to those in the West in terms of technological and financial globalization, African managers operate in an economic, technological, political, and cultural context that is clearly different and demands conflicting, if not diametrically opposed, priorities (Cabanes and Lautier 1996). From this deviation must spring the two contrasting leadership profiles for effectiveness in running African firms: *primus inter pares* (or first among equals) and "coconut" (i.e., black on the outside, white on the inside).

These leadership competencies have maintained an uneasy coexistence since colonial administrators introduced their Western methods of government. The friction between traditional management values and those learned from Western schools and churches has led to several problems. Since this conflict lacks a framework for reconciliation, it often puts African companies in a position of ambivalence. Indeed, although the majority of local employees are profoundly attached to the *primus inter pares*, which is the traditional African profile, managers in public and private subsidiaries of Western firms favor the coconut profile taught in their organizational cultures. Informal and mutual recognition between the two schools of thought has led to increased tolerance, but the disharmony between these two profiles is apparently one of the main sources of problems in modern African firms.

Africa has always been ruled by chiefs. However, African history since colonization has been stained by the disturbance of the traditional principles that govern sociability and intercommunal relations. Certain communities do not know which way to turn, so their leaders develop behavioral patterns in harmony with their own personal values—instead of being either *primus inter pares* or coconuts.

In view of the events that are currently ravaging several nations on the African continent, it is clear that several types of leadership profiles have been formed, deformed, and reformed, but none of these can replace the ancestral *primus inter pares*.

If we are to avoid sending Africa into harmful regression, as Philippe d'Iribarne (1990, 28–39) asserts in his article on decentralizing public companies in Africa, it is clear that any imposition of managerial models and profiles from the outside must integrate local tradition and experience. A new profile would be even more efficient if it were based on the most pertinent aspects of local mentality. In other words, in order to enjoy complete integration, managers of African companies must be able to reconcile the demands of business globalization and its effects on international relations with the expectations of native employees.

This observation raises extremely difficult questions. How can observers with insufficient knowledge of African and Western cultures analyze one of these leadership profiles or the other in the context of multicultural work phenomena? How can we identify the underlying forces that shape the behavior of African employees and managers? Which values and work standards motivate workers, and which hinder them? Which standards help employees exercise creativity, and which inhibit them?

In order to identify the skills necessary for today's African managers, I suggest we examine African firms' key characteristics and traditional methods of managing interregional relations, as reported in the studies of Jean Kizerbo (1972) and Christian Potholm (1981). This paradigm will not only reveal the social structure that has shaped African mentality since precolonial times; it will also anticipate, without comparing the differences between Africa and the West, modern companies' difficulties in balancing local traditions with corporate culture assumptions. More precisely, our aim is to demonstrate which local traditions are retained, which Western ideas are adopted, and which of both types are rejected or altered through local companies' policies.

PRIMUS INTER PARES: THE TRADITIONAL PREPARATION OF AFRICAN LEADERS

My detailed studies in Nigeria, Ivory Coast, Congo, Senegal, Rwanda, and Democratic Republic of Congo are supplemented by my findings from other trips (to Burundi, Uganda, Tanzania, Kenya, Mali, Ghana, Benin, etc.). As background, it should be pointed out that before colonization most African countries were made up of small clans and kingdoms. In most cases power was centralized around one or more kings and regional clan chiefs. Before the Napoleonic model was introduced in French-speaking Africa, for example, the regions that are now countries were divided among many independent kingdoms.

Though several countries in the lakes region had already adopted variations on monarchy, they all incorporated elements of clan-style government. For example, Rwandan patriclans (groups of people dependent on a patriarch who passes on his name to his descendants), including the Bega, Banyiginya, Basindi, and Bagesera, often enjoyed a certain autonomy that allowed members to make decisions without taking matters before the chief. The same system applied to regions of Democratic Republic of Congo or ex-Zaire (among the Bakongo, Baluba, and Bashi).

In almost all countries studied, the success of a leader (whether head of a family, clan, or kingdom) lay in his capacity to listen well and to put his community's interest first. In order to cultivate these essential qualities, future chiefs were taught from a young age to examine social issues and their effects on the community. Moreover, they learned from experience how to represent and defend community interests without provoking the anger of the high king or of other clans. The Mandes and Senoufos of Ivory Coast were autonomous to the extent that their representatives could reject propositions—whether the king's or other clans'—that worked against their own clan's welfare.

Although centralized monarchies had governed some regions (such as the kingdom of Mali) since time immemorial, other regions (notably Burundi and Rwanda) were introduced to monarchy only at the beginning of the twentieth century, when colonial administrators and European missionaries imposed it for developmental and ethnocentric ends. The monarchical form of social organization differed from the previous one in that a single king wielded much of the power and divided government positions among his clansmen. Placed in a position of superiority, the quasi-deified kings often abused their power by reigning in an autocratic or even bloody way—to the detriment of many citizens. The heirs of these kings learned their role by hunting and accompanying their fathers to the decapitation of vanquished opponents and other enemies of the kingdom. But such incubation of tyranny did not exist in older, established kingdoms such as Benin or Mali. In these kingdoms, central power was under the control of a committee of wise men who not only aided the king but also questioned his decisions when he veered off-course.

A third form of government, a segmented structure, existed among the Krous and Ibos of Ivory Coast and the Tekes of ex-Zaire. This variation was more decentralized than the previous two. The sacred nature of its royal power was based on religious rites that, rather than placing the king above other citizens, unified the community (e.g., the Baoules, Lobis, and Bakoues of Ivory Coast). Thus, the chiefs were trained to lead a conglomerate power structure formed of equal representatives from all clans. Through religious rites, the chosen king acquired extraordinary power, but he could keep it only by respecting his subordinates. The chief was essentially trained to be wise; he learned to surround himself with enlightened advice on which he could base his decisions without being swayed by the general mêlée. He was even prepared to renounce his royal decision-making prerogatives in order to guarantee the collective good.

In line with the observations of M. Fortes and E. E. Evans Pritchard (1964), our interviews in different countries revealed that Africa's diverse, ancestral forms of organization all used several principles that deeply affect the African mentality even today. The common ground that we found in these administrations were the social principles that governed interclan and interpersonal relations before colonization. Unlike today's conflicts, often based on self-interest, these cultural values led to openness, tolerance, and integration—not to exclusion and rejection. In the case of serious conflict between clans, negotiation (using the counsel of historians, elders, priests, and medicine men) was preferred to war.

COMMON SOCIAL PRINCIPLES IN AFRICAN LEADERSHIP

In countries across Africa, the values and skills that leaders have traditionally developed are strikingly similar. Despite the diversity of countries and com-

Table 15.1
Traditionally Essential Values in African Leadership

Four Main Lines of Thought	Elements of Internal Cultural Coherence	Humankind's Ultimate Goal
People's relationship with life	Concept of life as a universal current	Prolong and protect life
People's connection to nature	Unitarian concept of nature • The universe is not a dichotomy: there is no rift between the natural and supernatural or the material and spiritual	Be an integral part of nature and live in symbiosis with it • Activity must respect the timelessness of nature and human community • Take the time to live fully
People's relationships with other humans	Vertically organized moral order • Rites of passage and harmonization of relations among the living, the dead and the gods • Power based on age and interpersonal skills • Principles of inheritance	Respect community norms • Reciprocity of duties and rights • Shared knowledge • Transmission of knowledge through rites organized by elders • Search for cohesion and recognition: a society of friends
People's relationship with God	God is the Father of fathers, the Ancestor of ancestors • Heaven and earth are inseparably linked by ancestors	Harmony in body, mind, and spirit through a balanced relationship with the other elements of the universe

munities, all Africans interviewed—whether executives or peasants, philosophers or company managers, teachers or business advisers—agreed on certain social principles that in the past have been at the heart of leadership-oriented education. As we will see, these beliefs and values constitute *common ancestral traits* in attitudes and behavior. This observation confirms the hypothesis of Pierre Erny (1987) and other authors that maintains that African cultural unity significantly transcends national and local diversity in communities from the Mediterranean to Cape Town, from Somalia to the Atlantic.

Among the key organizational characteristics analyzed, only those common to all African kingdoms will we consider pertinent to Western management and economic globalization. After we attempt to identify the lessons taught by *primus inter pares* of the past, we will show how the tension between these principles and Western ones has produced managers whom the Africans themselves, with a certain irony, refer to as "coconuts."

Table 15.1 presents the main elements of community systems[1] of cultural coherence as studied in six different countries. It also lists the common cultural values and behavioral norms thought to be essential in educating and preparing leaders. This chart derives from our investigations in Africa (a detailed study of fifty interviews with "experts" of local traditions—ex-village chiefs, religious chiefs, company executives, and professors of history and human sciences) and from several specialized works on Africa (Fortes 1949; Fougeyrollas 1987; Cohen 1961; Brameld 1955; Parin 1966; Read 1960; Temples 1949; Elungu 1987).

By cross-referencing our data, we noticed that the first line of thought, "people's relationship with life," pervaded the other three as well. It concerns all Africans, but particularly those destined to occupy positions of responsibility within their society. Here, in a few words, are the qualities that correspond to people's relationship with life:

* Strong attachment to life and nature
* A concept of life as a powerful breath that transcends and nourishes all the elements of the universe—whether human, beast, plant, or stone
* Recognition that, since this breath is eternal, the existence of life is absolute proof of the human species' link with the rest of the universe.

In African countries, life cannot be conceptualized and compartmentalized (into professional life, family life, life on Earth, afterlife, etc.) as it can in the West. Given that life is rooted in the distant past (with preceding generations) and that it branches out into an equally distant future (including both the living and the unborn), it is quite naturally lived in continuity. Since death is a perfectly natural step in this ceaseless process, Africans can weep for their dead without being terrified at the prospect of their own life's end. Making the most of life through senses, rituals, myths, words, and daily experience with others is part of humankind's vocation and mission on Earth.

The chart suggests that the vertical nature of human relations is fundamental to the development of chiefs' convictions, attitudes, and behavior. If life is a central, unifying process that bonds all the elements of the cosmos, chiefs should recognize their position in the never-ending cycle while helping others to identify theirs. In almost all the countries studied, by linking generation to generation, young to old, and living to dead, this powerful cycle of life gives the present an eternal importance that places it above both past and future. Seen in this way, life is inexhaustible both individually and collectively. Life is greater than individuals and groups, and chiefs of all ranks should encourage the members of their communities to love and respect it.

The second formative principle in African leadership is "humans' connection to nature." This relationship is closely related to the first and is made up largely of the following elements:

* In all countries studied, one of the primary tasks of leaders is to establish harmony with their community and environment. We noticed evidence of this harmony in the fact that no traditional African communities had irreversibly damaged their surroundings through overexploitation. Africans have long benefited from their environment— using wood for housing, longboats, clothes, and cooking; and mining gold and copper—without harming it. The destruction of the countryside (as in Rwanda and Congo) was initiated by Western companies' abuse, which included the mass extraction of gold, diamonds, tungsten ore, copper, and tin.
* Before the colonial period, local communities preserved nature because their leaders' first priority was to supervise communal respect for nature. Farming and handicrafts

were environmentally sound activities used to provide for the local community—not to amass wealth.

- Contrary to popular belief, Africans do not worship trees and animals or believe that nature contains supernatural elements. Although they were not venerated (as were the cow in India and certain trees in Togo), several locations and animal and plant species were protected because of their particular function in the balance with nature, their rarity, or their medicinal properties. For example, certain forests are used for meditation, for communication with the divine, for religious rites, and for the initiation of the young.

- As a general rule, humans are an essential part of nature; their superiority does not allow them to abuse their knowledge of animals and plants. On the contrary, it should lead them to protect nature and use it to meet their needs. With this in mind, all leaders should supervise production (agriculture, animal breeding, handicrafts, fishing, and so on), verifying its environmental legitimacy and putting it at the disposal of the community as a whole. Finally, nature, a gift given to all, demonstrates the fact that the fruits of human labor must be shared in order to preserve communities and the friendly ties between them.

Even more central to Africa's quest for a new leadership profile is the third point: "interpersonal relations." It reveals Africans' aspirations, expectations, and disappointments regarding the attitudes, behavior, and management styles developed in certain companies today. Interpersonal relations influence leaders' attitudes toward work and determine the productivity of entire organizations. Good management of interpersonal relations leads to success and motivation—in companies as well as in society itself.

As previously mentioned, African principles of interpersonal relations help individuals to develop certain attributes, as the following points illustrate:

- In all the communities studied, social organization was based on interpersonal relationships. A chief's first priorities are to protect social energy and to encourage interaction among different communities. This function seems even more important in light of D. Desjeux's comment, "This human energy is made up of men, women and children and is thus constantly threatened by death and disease" (Desjeux 1987, 60–97). In this context, where social energy circulates and fluctuates, knowing one's ancestry is a main focus of African education. Ancestry is a great stabilizing force; it enables individuals to establish their own place in the dynamics of the community and to benefit from their clansmen's protection. Family and clan ties, whether matrilineal or patrilineal, unite individuals and groups through common ancestors.

- Western notions of individualism and collectivism did not exist in any of the communities we observed. In fact, such terms often do not exist in traditional local languages. These communities' fundamental method for managing human relations, then, is cosubsistence—among individuals and among the concentric circles that make up a clan or community. As for newcomers to this system, they are not rejected or dominated but are welcomed and perhaps even integrated in the community.

- African management of human relations is generally not characterized by the development of technical skills, but by the gradual adoption of a philosophy of universal fellowship, which is maintained by initiation and other religious rites. It would be useful here to recall the objectives of these rites:

- To transmit activities, services, and specialized knowledge from older to younger members of the community.

- To serve the community by allowing it to take advantage of specialized members' expertise, ensuring that distinctive skills, such as healing, do not remain the exclusive property of a single individual or clan. This responsibility belongs to the leaders (elders, medicine men, or religious figureheads) who organize the ceremonies. Since the rites are shared by all initiated members, individual knowledge—including the medicine man's—is given up to the community.

- In rites of transition, to encourage cohesion and harmony between age groups and to prevent intergenerational friction.

- In initiation, to set participants apart from the group while making them full members of the community; to allow individuals to gain new knowledge in order to serve the collective good.

- Again in initiation, to preserve the social order and instill a common moral code in all individuals and groups (peer groups, professional groups, colleagues, neighbors, etc.), ensuring the primacy of the community. So, the community has supreme and legitimate authority over behavioral norms, over community management and organization, and over individuals themselves.

- Contrary to the widespread notion that community spirit kills off individuals' personality and initiative, the social system we have just examined uses a vertical cultural framework in which individuals occupy a precise station and submit to mandatory rites of passage as they progress from childhood to youth, from youth to adulthood, from adulthood to old age, and finally on to the world of the ancestors.

- One of the leaders' main responsibilities is to ensure respect for a fundamental principle of community life: harmony must be preserved between generations, between professions, and between community members' different levels of status.

- Whereas Western society has tended to endorse personal gratification, many Africans are community-minded, having a profound respect for the central rules of society. Pressure to obey the rules is exerted not only by the living, but also by vigilant ancestors, who are omnipresent in community life through myth recitals and social gatherings organized by elders and religious leaders.

- Since it is recognized that the community is more important than the individual, excessively egocentric attitudes are swiftly condemned. Anyone exhibiting this behavior is perceived as a threat to social unity and to the community's survival and is subject to ostracism. Since ostracism from the community can mean social and even physical death for those who suffer it, egocentrism is relatively uncommon.

Before presenting the final cultural aspect that Africans share, it is perhaps important to underscore the fact that the vertical human relations analyzed here are balanced by horizontal relations among peers (i.e., people belonging to the same age group or status level). This balance endows older members of the

community with significant power and prevents the vertical hierarchy from en-
trenching community life in a backward-leading rut.

The lessons that older generations teach are of great value. A Rwandan prov-
erb says: "Autarebye ahavuye ntamenya aho agana" (One never knows where
one is going without comparing progress with past experience and roots). In
other words, the past is only as important as the insight gained in weighing it
against the current dynamics of local communities. This is why leaders-in-
training learned the history of communities and kingdoms—not to reproduce it,
but to analyze it and apply those lessons in preparation for future conditions.

As the following pages will demonstrate, several practices imported from
Western management—such as evaluating individual short-term rather than collective long-term performance and valuing technical skills above seniority—are
in direct opposition to the heritage that still pervades African mentality. This
conflict obviously stems from differing ideas about time management; contrary
to the widespread Anglo-Saxon adage "Time is money," these temporal elements
differ in Africa. This clash is the origin of numerous misunderstandings between
local staff members and Western expatriates—problems regarding project dead-
lines, work schedules, business forecasts, and planning activities.

Africans often chuckle at Westerners' never-ending preoccupation with the
future, and Westerners, in turn, sometimes see Africans as carefree children
living in an eternal present. But if we look beyond these stereotypes, we will
find that the two cultures also differ in their concepts of work and its results,
time, social principles, and people's relationship to life. For example, the Western expression "to waste time" (as if it were an object) has no meaning in Africa,
since every event and accomplished action is a bearer of time. As C. N. Biguma
and J. C. Usunier stress, "Time is never wasted in Africa as it simply cannot be
wasted. It is in constant transformation as an energy of life. Time is lived in
one form or another; nobody can take it away, not even death. There is a time
for everything, even to die" (Biguma and Usunier 1989).

Given the religious diversity in the six countries studied, the phenomena
brought about by the fourth line of thought in African culture (humans' relationship with the divine) are more difficult to observe and categorize. However,
as Africans familiar with traditional ceremonies, we have been able to observe
certain phenomena and investigate the importance of religion in African leaders'
education and behavior.

As previously illustrated, the supreme chief is a religious figure who is en-
throned through certain rites. In traditional social structures, the king was considered sacred. In order to promote behavior befitting his supreme status, the
king was prepared from a young age to know and respect his culture's myths
and taboos and to observe the religious rites that spread and revived them
throughout the community.

As a representative of the community's ancestors, the leader had a duty to
bring about harmony between the living and the dead by entreating protective

divinities. According to experts and elders, all gods are connected to other elements of the universe, particularly to humans. This means that the gods are present in family life, in plants, in animals, and in daily actions at work—whether in an office or in the fields. The belief that deity is omnipresent does much to explain the rites and prayers performed to obtain the guidance, energy, and protection necessary to complete difficult or risky projects, such as hunting expeditions, career shifts, or factory machine replacements.

In these cultures, a thorough knowledge of the divinities was very important. For example, the inhabitants of countries such as Democratic Republic of Congo, Togo, and Benin worshiped specialized gods (divinities of the harvest, the sea, fertility, and so on), as did the Egyptians. Familiarity with divine personalities was equally important in countries such as Rwanda, where worshipers addressed one supreme god, Ryangombe, through certain ancestors or mythical characters. Generally, in this African understanding of the universe, God is the Father of fathers, the Ancestor of ancestors—a belief that explains the importance and respect Africans have traditionally given him in the education and training of their leaders.

THE COCONUT LEADER: FRUIT OF THE COLLISION BETWEEN AFRICA AND THE WEST

How do African employees perceive company managers and their managerial practices? At the present time, these impressions surface in employee behavior and sentiment regarding certain newly implemented Western-style values and norms. Given the ingrained nature of the African mind-set, it would seem that including Western techniques in local management would do nothing but cause daily disappointment, frustration, and tension for African employees. Rather, the clash between two models from completely separate cultural universes leads African employees to sort through the Western and local contributions to their company, categorizing each as good or bad, pleasant or unpleasant, advantageous or harmful, a failure or a success, and a credit or a discredit to company managers.

Our field observations tended to show that this openness to multicultural reality resulted not only from daily experience with production techniques and formal company norms. An even more important factor was the quality of social interaction permitted by the management system. As a general rule, local employees' behavior- and attitude-shaping relations within their company were characterized by the following factors:

• Leaders' roles are determined more by experience with on-the-job relations than by formal procedures imported by modern companies. Interestingly, the principles implemented in this way often directly oppose the values and behavioral norms developed by community leaders.

• The way leaders juggle their various roles depends on how they plan to fit Western management values in with the African social structure. This clash leads to tension for employees, who are caught between the cold world of organizational logic and the warmer, relationship-based world of their native communities.

• In general, the formal separation of the firm from local community life corresponds neither to the expectations of local employees nor to the reality of running a concrete business in Africa. This gap between the formal and informal, between being at one point in time within an organizational boundary and at another in personal life space, forces the employees to withdraw psychologically and attempt somehow to live by two diametrically opposed ideologies.

In all countries and firms, this work versus nonwork life tension seems to cause a general dissatisfaction with local managers and their management styles, particularly in branches of Western-based multinationals. In many African firms, employees converge en masse to denounce those aspects of their managers' behavior that do not conform to life outside work. Some managerial practices and procedures are even rejected as being contradictory to local values and aspirations—hence Africa's current desire to develop new management values.

On this subject, one of the hypotheses validated by our multinational research indicated that Western business techniques and "coconut" managers are tolerated only when they allow community culture to remain intact. But in practice, fear of unemployment and poverty forces employees in most countries passively to accept anything the company imposes—even norms that grind against local values. This is, of course, one of the origins of African firms' problems.

African firms—especially, as previously stated, some public firms and branches of Western-based multinationals—frequently find themselves in this incongruous situation. In fact, 86.04 percent of African firms' native employees (and 92 percent in branches of multinationals) believe that their companies' managerial practices clash with their own work values. This overwhelming majority underscores the crucial nature of the management question. After all, the running of any company, African or not, is achieved by people and the mobilization of people. But to obtain the latter, managers need qualities and skills that meet the requirements of the individuals to be mobilized. This is where "coconut" managers fall—they are so preoccupied with respecting formal procedures and rules that they often neglect pragmatic company management and work's social aspect and values, which are so essential among Africans.

So in an organizational sense (organization of space, internal regulations, working hours, division of labor and power, working procedures, and so on), the "modern company"[2] generally pays little attention to the managerial values and preferences of African employees. Fundamentally Western, "coconut" policy, as well as mixed African-Western policy (which is even worse in this setting), totally confuse the employees who must live with these contradicting experiences. To the surprise of many Westerners, when African managers disregard traditional management values in favor of Western styles, adverse results sometimes follow.

By closely observing the behavior of African employees, we noticed that some employee-manager relations were based on local values and some on Western rationale. Although the Western version may seem to be nothing more than a harmless cultural adaptation, the principles underlying these two models of labor management often cost local firms dearly. For instance, this is the case when employees pit themselves against local values while lacking dedication to Western ideas.

Certain African executives—even directors—drag their companies down when, for whatever reason, they pretend to forget that powerful social rules shape the behavior of their "brothers." According to these rules, every self-respecting African, on or off the job, has the duty to create, maintain, and nurture ties of friendship; to offer assistance; and to respect others' rights and duties.

A traditional African norm is at the root of gift and favor exchanging, of visits to family and friends, and of phone calls to clansmen and friends from other communities. Currently, expatriates or "coconuts" tend to reject this norm, which they see as contrary to their own management values.

Rather than seeking to understand this African behavior in depth, these expatriates label it as laziness, corruption, nepotism, or lack of professional conscience. For example, the African manner of holding a meeting is judged only on its outward appearance and is often thought to be, in the words of a Belgian expatriate interviewed in Zaire, "a useless and interminable palaver, a waste of time which costs the company and society too much" (Mutabazi 1999, 398).

EMERGING MANAGERIAL ATTRIBUTES:
OPEN-MINDEDNESS AND A SENSE OF IDENTITY

The clash between African and Western philosophies seems to be the greatest obstacle to the success of African business management. It teaches that, unlike Anglo-Saxon culture, African culture strives first to develop human relations, an investment necessary to generate productivity and ultimately financial profit. In practice, it is not easy to take this conceptual difference into account when one is preoccupied by short-term productivity and performance, and the practice that even seems contemptible and unproductive appear in an interesting light when observed more closely.

African interpersonal behavior and social conduct transcend both local traditions and Western logic. In other words, African employees are not less human, less rational, or less strategic than their Western counterparts; instead, they have a wealth of multicultural business and administrative experience on which to draw. The very fact that managers have so often rejected the African social attitude demonstrates that it has never been thoroughly understood or evaluated through practical application in other countries and continents.

The vast majority of African employees—even including "coconuts"—never completely Westernize themselves. This is true even among those workers who, having been trained in the West, help diffuse (Mucchielli 1992) the North American "one best way" with almost evangelistic zeal. Because they can see the detrimental effects of imported models, most of them truly adhere to Western-style management only for strategic reasons. However, the observation of sixty executives (ten from each country studied) showed that attitudes were divided between the two extremes:

- A great number of African managers shut one eye to the behavior of their collaborators who conform to local traditions, albeit in contradiction to the formal requirements of their firms or public institutions.
- Far fewer managers are currently attempting to reconcile local cultural values with managerial demands; these few realize that African companies can escape neither local cultural dynamics nor the pressure of globalization on today's markets
- As previously stated, this second attitude is emerging principally in private, local companies and is more widespread in the informal sector, where managers have implemented original, flexible, and sometimes very productive solutions.

For example, African managers who sympathize with the local mind-set are tackling absenteeism by developing management procedures that allow sociability instead of imposing traditionally ineffective formal sanctions. As Alain Henry (1996) observes, there are probably several models of African management that combine local and foreign business techniques.

With this in mind, several observations demonstrate how local company managers are taking into account African workplace values. Particularly in the informal sector, developmentally minded managers have invented original business solutions that are largely ignored by the West because they step outside the bounds set by company directives and accepted management techniques. Although structural adjustment programs initiated by international financial backers often impose imported management models, some local company founders work toward "cultural adjustment" (Manguele 1993) by introducing prenegotiated methods for organizing work and for dealing with problems (such as absenteeism).

A CASE STUDY

Combining management skills acquired in a Parisian business school with a general education from his native community, thirty-six-year-old Kitenge set up and developed his own innovative business on the fringes of Kivu in 1985. In order to avoid the complications of local political rivalries, Kitenge decided not to appeal to his politically powerful uncles for financial backing—a procedure that would have been entirely acceptable in his community. Consequently, Kitenge could afford neither high-quality equipment nor well-trained employees. Still, even with these disadvantages, the company enjoyed remarkable prosperity, which continued until Kivu's last sociopolitical upheaval. This success was based partly on Kitenge's harnessing of the African social mentality, which induced the employees to be more involved in their work. Kitenge pointed out during our interview that he had understood the African notion of human relations to be a bonus—not an obstacle.

As he interviewed his first five employees and questioned them about their network of friends and neighbors, he saw what he called "an inexhaustible reservoir of potential." Kitenge reflected, "It was as if my little company [should employ] seventy-five people, not five." And after performing many interviews and exploring the possibilities in detail, Kitenge decided to run his cheese factory with all of them—not just the five he had originally hired.

From the first day, Kitenge had negotiated with his employees in order to find an immediately operational work force from this reservoir to deal with uncertainties inside and outside the firm. Among the unforeseen circumstances he wanted to control were the unexpected rise in orders (notably from European consumers, who created a significant market for the region) and the problem of employee absenteeism. The management style Kitenge adopted ultimately turned out to be as useful for coping with these obstacles as it was for solving other operational problems.

Two analyses of Kitenge's experiment, one in 1989 and one in 1993, revealed that his management system was based on two principles: operational versatility (sharing job-related knowledge and experience) and the reciprocity of rights and duties among company members, their communities, and their friends.

In practical terms, this system of management meant that four months after starting work, employees responsible for a step in the production process could learn a second job as well. In addition, right from their second year in the firm, employees could train a friend, brother, or cousin to fill their jobs so they could be replaced efficiently during sicknesses and other absences. This system worked successfully up to our last meeting with Kitenge, which was during the outbreak of the war in Rwanda in 1994.

In order to help his system to run smoothly, Kitenge held weekly meetings with his foremen. This gave them an additional opportunity, aside from their normal daily interaction, for mutual exchange of personal work experiences. In this way, the foreman in charge of collecting milk could become aware of the problems faced by his colleagues in manufacturing and selling the cheese, and vice versa. Another aim of these meetings was to develop community spirit in the three foremen, who would then spread this awareness among their workers, discouraging clannish behavior and promoting unity throughout the whole company.

Each of the three foremen then had to organize a relatively short weekly meeting with his team in order to take stock of their daily working experiences and suggest improvements for their activities. The foremen met in the morning and at the beginning of the week with the boss; the meetings with the workers took place every Friday, at the end of the day. In this way, they could meet outside the workplace—in the village of one of the foremen or even at Kitenge's house. By setting up such a system, Kitenge hoped not only to open up his company to local community life, but also to benefit from the citizens' ideas. Thanks to discussions among permanent employees and other workers or potential hirees (friends, family, and clan members) several company problems were solved.

Such was the case in 1992, when Kitenge decided to install a simple computer system for managing accounts and following up sales. In 1991, after visiting a Parisian trade fair that impressed him with its computer demonstrations, he decided to buy a particular program, along with the necessary equipment. But he had no computer specialist. Kitenge realized that some local, public companies had experienced maintenance problems with Western technology, and he was apprehensive about depending in this way on a third party. He wanted to hire a local specialist capable of installing the system and running it to fit each staff member's needs. In other words, candidates not only had to have adequate technical skills; they also had to integrate all of the company procedures into the computer system.

On returning to Zaire (now Democratic Republic of Congo) from the trade fair, Kitenge presented his plan to the foremen and explained which skills he was looking for in a candidate. Having lived for several years near Paris, he was naturally wary of Westerners. For one thing, he had noticed that machines in African factories became rusty from disuse and misuse because few Western suppliers provided sufficient training for local personnel to maintain them. Plus, through friends from student days and his own internships in French and English companies, he knew that Western specialists were reluctant to share their knowledge without getting something in return. Consequently, he did not want to recruit a Western expatriate; he preferred to search out an African who could meet his requirements, which included the ability to train a substitute. Talking to the foremen and tapping the community grapevine, Kitenge quickly found such a person.

Integrating the African social mind-set into the administration of his company enabled Kitenge to find rapid, efficient, and productive answers to management problems in many areas—not just in recruitment. For example, absenteeism, which is so devastating to most African companies, did not exist in Kitenge's company. Furthermore, having interwoven the principles of community spirit and sociability with the demands of a productive company, he did not have to be present every day. Since the company had quickly become the employees' business (and by extension, their villages' business), it ran on their synergy, working in almost perfect harmony with the surrounding communities.

This analysis would not be complete without underlining the process Kitenge used to take advantage of community spirit and implement the principles of business productivity at the same time. As he discovered, a "mix" of African and Western cultural contributions is not only possible; it can be desirable, when handled correctly. Both philosophies contain valuable lessons for training managers in light of the current trend toward global economies and multicultural businesses.

Kitenge's case shows that community spirit and competitiveness are not mutually exclusive in African companies. This is why, for example, human resource management depends on the ties between workers and their communities. Kitenge strictly applied the following principles to tackle the problem of absenteeism:

- *First principle.* Substitutes are acceptable only if they are members of an employee's community or circle of friends. Substitutes' status as friends or clansmen easily lends itself to oral confirmation, given Africa's traditionally dense social networks. These networks are developed and maintained on a daily basis according to the principle of mutual knowledge and assistance, which is central to African social ideas.

- *Second principle.* As long as they have not completed their apprenticeship and are not responsible for a work station, potential substitutes maintain an external status, though they are still considered "friends" of the company. Although neither legally employed nor paid for the duration of their apprenticeship—which varies from one week to one month according to the complexity of the tasks involved—they are already part of the active network of company members. And since the company maintains close contact with local communities, the apprentices develop even stronger ties with the other employees from their region.

- *Third principle.* When established employees unexpectedly leave the firm, substitutes are nominated by trainers, the foreman, and other team members who have had the opportunity to get to know them and to observe their apprenticeship. After Kitenge's decision, the nomination team has the right to express its dissatisfaction with new employees. However, this opposition will take effect only after a four-day observation period, during which the substitutes must demonstrate their ability to work and integrate themselves into the company. True to the principle of reciprocity of rights and duties among members of friendly communities, such opposition occurred in Kitenge's company only twice in five years, both times after conflicts between candidates and team members. In both cases, the candidates had uncorrected problems outside the firm that caused their problems inside the firm. Thanks to Kitenge's employees, the failed candidates' community leaders were able to meet together and quickly resolve the situation.

- *Fourth principle.* Substitute workers are hired only if they accept certain commitments. In the presence of a community member (not employed by the company) and two established employees representing the company, they must agree to loyalty and solidarity in the firm and among its employees, and they must agree to share their expertise with coworkers. Except in cases of illness, in which the company automatically bears the cost, substitutes agree to work at three-quarters of their absent colleagues' regular wage. The remaining quarter is used to cover the less effective use of time, to foot the cost of apprenticeship, or to throw a company party for an accomplished employee. If substitutes' work is unsatisfactory, they are paid at a rate much lower than the permanent employees' wage.

- *Fifth principle.* The company seeks to put absent employees to work as soon as they return, but it favors substitutes over other candidates if the absentees do not return or if another, similar job opens up.

This efficiency in dealing with employee absence and in mobilizing the entire work force demonstrates that African social ideals are not in unresolvable conflict with Western business logic; interviews with Kitenge, his foremen, and their workers support their conclusion. In other words, the reciprocity of rights and duties on which Kitenge relies could be successfully implemented in all African companies, since these principles are at the heart of a common cultural background. In a number of associations (Henry 1991) (such as the African *tontines*³) and in most cases of community action, this principle is even more pertinent because it creates whole new relationships among employees, their companies, and the communities they deal with.

CONCLUSION

To conclude, the solution to Africa's current management problem lies in learning from those managers who successfully find a happy medium between African culture and their companies' demands for productivity. That is not to say, however, that we should overlook the wisdom that the majority of managers have to offer—even if these managers ignore negative behavior caused by the clash between Africa and the West. Nor should we fail to learn from Western subsidiaries and public companies that oppose local social values by imposing objectionable work regulations.

Contrary to popular stereotypes and sometimes hasty media generalizations, corruption is no more a part of the African business mentality than it is in any other region of the world. Indeed, corruption goes directly against the grain of many key principles of African culture. In Africa as elsewhere, if public funds are embezzled, if managers misappropriate company capital, or if heads of state squander national income, it is a question of personal materialism—not of African culture as a whole.

As a number of facts in Africa show, most individual and collective misbehavior including certain political scandals results from the ideals of mutual assistance and free access to community knowledge, not from the individual hedonism imported from the West. Our analysis of several social phenomena, which supports the theories of Desjeux (1987), shows that ancestral traditions have even helped to incite some coups d'état aimed at ending the abuse of communal property by political leaders such as Sékou Touré in Guinea, Amin Dada in Uganda, Jean-Bedel Bokassa in the Central African Republic, and Sese Seko Mobutu in then Zaire. Considering the social context of these men's ascension to and fall from power, one realizes that Africans are similar to the other peoples of the world: they prefer to be ruled by leaders with integrity and a high respect for the common good. Community has always been more important than the individual; African history shows that most of these leaders have come to power by working for the common good and fallen from power by ignoring it. What is more, this same principle applies not only in government, but also in nonpolitical *tontines* and other associations.

When training future African managers, one can no longer ignore the fact that their mentality is affected more by the ideal of the common good than by the importance of individual performance, which has been imported from North American management models. Since rejecting this logic leads to costly problems for the company and local public administrations, managerial training programs should not omit to mention that many African employees readily give up their own wages in order to participate in important community events. In other words, this cultural principle impacts behavior so strongly that, instead of stubbornly resisting it, managers would do better to learn how to harness its energy and put it to work alongside the demands of global economies.

The behavior patterns observed in this study prove that using outside-the-culture methods in business is counterproductive when managers do not correctly utilize the community spirit and its principles of reciprocity.

In reality, this principle constitutes an impressive force and can be a factor in progress when it is used well, opening the company up to society and integrating it in the community network. Confronted with the pressures of competition in a global economy, African managers like Kitenge have been developing the capacity to produce "returns on [the] investment" of utilizing community spirit and giving advantages and other privileges to "brothers."

As far as hiring is concerned, companies in several of the countries studied reduce social costs by shifting community pressure away from the company whenever possible. For instance, nepotism in the recruitment process (hiring relatives of top community officials or powerful clansmen) has declined; instead, companies occasionally supply material or financial aid to their communities. This aid is generally granted at planned times to projects that personally involve the managers (children's education, building of a house, starting of a small business, marriages, funerals, etc.). Rather than yield to the endless pressures to hire certain individuals, these managers accomplish good for their community while retaining the right to determine when and how much to aid their fellows.

In the recruitment process, many managers of privately owned companies favor locals who possess the same skills as applicants from other communities. When these candidates do not have the necessary skills to fill a job vacancy, the company either trains them or helps them to find another job. Training is much appreciated by the candidates and their communities, who do not wish to lose respect (especially in jobs of responsibility) or expose their few members to failure. In other cases hiring decisions cannot be explained by community pressure, but by the managers' goal to surround themselves with more faithful and loyal workers. Even in these cases, however, the candidates are hired only if they are truly part of the community or company network and are capable of mobilizing these networks when faced with various challenges such as confronting trade unions, mobilizing workers on the shop floor, making financial negotiations, leading publicity campaigns, and so on.

Our study included a brewery of European origin that had established itself in all six countries in question. Managers of its local branches considered the launch of new products an ideal opportunity to generate return on investments—giving products to employees or granting privileges (in hiring, funding associations, or assistance in building collective equipment for villages) to neighboring communities. During our stays in Rwanda and Zaire we discovered that the brewery's principal advantage in competing with other breweries was its employees' capacity to rely on word of mouth and on their cooperative networks of friends from their native communities. As the firm's marketing director for Central Africa stated, "To promote product and corporate image in Africa, word of mouth and the little promotional bottle sent to our employees' communities far outweighs the efficiency of local press or national radio and television because it is more direct, friendly and community-minded than the cold communication of western advertising media" (Mutabazi 1999, 444).

From these different elements we can conclude that the main challenge for modern African companies is not absenteeism, embezzlement, apathy, or any of the problems that critics attribute to Africans without understanding the problems' origin and local context. If these different behavioral patterns exist, the real challenge—particularly for businesspeople—is to make sure that companies are no longer perceived as independent of their community or indifferent to its issues and expectations.

As this chapter demonstrates, African managers must integrate Western managerial logic and African social ideals—not oppose them. Instead of adhering to scientific management theories and the Anglo-Saxon adage "Time is money," African business leaders should implement more comprehensive management theories tailored to their companies' situation. In other words, our study shows that African managerial trainees should not be forced to become either *primus inter pares* or "coconuts"; it would be more profitable to educate them about the inevitable culture clash between different management models.

Africa has never been turned in on itself, and the business world's present trend toward globalization will only open it up even more to external influence. In fact, all of Africa's recent and ongoing political upheavals show that the continent is increasingly exposed to geographical, strategic, ideological, and economic rivalry. As the third millennium dawns, and with it a buildup of human and material waste from the current interregional mismanagement of relations, African managers, like managers on other continents, will be able to take advantage of globalization only if they can reconcile openness and identity, economic and social profit, community and corporate spirit.

NOTES

1. The term *system* is used in the cybernetic sense; the lines that follow are interdependent in all cultures. A major problem on one line disturbs the entire community and endangers its relationship with nature, life, and neighboring communities. It can even lead to catastrophic regression, as have the economic and religious extremists currently dominating certain regions of Africa.

2. The term *modern company* is used here to describe productive organizations, both private and public, that use Western management models as a structural basis. These companies are to be distinguished from smaller, less structured firms based on local knowledge, cultures, and traditions.

3. *Tontine*: an organization in which all workers commit themselves to the other members and bear joint responsibility for company results.

REFERENCES

Biguma, C. N., and J. C. Usunier. 1989. Gestion culturelle du temps. Paper for the IMD conference on intercultural management, Lausane, Switzerland, December.

Brameld, T. 1955. *Philosophies of education in cultural perspective*. New York: Holt-Rinehart-Winston.

Cabanes, R., and B. Lautier. 1996. *Profils d'entreprises au Sud: Les politiques de gestion face aux cultures et aux statuts*. Paris: Editions Karthala.

Calori, R., and P. de Woot. 1994. *A European management model: Beyond diversity*. London: Prentice Hall.

Cohen, Y. A. 1961. *Social structure and personality*. New York: Holt-Rinehart-Winston.

Desjeux, D. 1987. *Strategies paysannes en Afrique noire*. Paris: Editions L'Harmattan.

d'Iribarne, P. 1990. Face à l'impossible décentralisation des entreprises en Afrique. *Revue Française de Gestion* (September): 28–39.

Elungu, P. E. A. 1987. *Traditions africaines et rationalité moderne*. Paris: Editions L'Harmattan.

Erny, P. 1987. *L'enfant et son milieu en Afrique noire: Essais sur l'education traditionnelle*. Paris: Editions L'Harmattan.

Fortes, M. 1949. *The web of clanship among the Tallensi*. London: Oxford University Press.

Fortes, M., and E. Pritchard. 1964. *Les systèmes politiques africains*. Paris: Presses Universitaires de France.

Fougeyrollas, P. 1987. *La Nation*. Paris: Editions Fayard.

Fritscher, F. 1996. L'Afrique des Grands Lacs destabilisée. *Le Monde Diplomatique* 242 (April): 35–48.

Henry, A. 1991. *Tontines et banques au Cameroun: Les principes de la société des amis*. Paris: Editions Karthala.

———. 1996. Vers un modèle du management Africain. *Cahiers d'études africaines* 124:447–473.

Kizerbo, J. 1972. *Histoire de l'Afrique noire*. Paris: Presses Universitaires de France.

Manguele, D. E. 1993. *L'Afrique a-t-elle besoin d'un programme d'ajustement culturel?* Paris: Editions Nouvelles du Sud.

Maslow, A. H. 1972. *Vers une psychologie de l'être*. Paris: Editions Fayard.

M'Bokolo, E. 1995. Les ethnies existent-elles. *Revue Sciences Humaines* Vol. 48 (March): 22–25.

Mucchielli, L. 1992. Le choc des cultures: Dynamiques de l'histoire. *Revue Sciences Humaines* 16 (April): 23–26.

Mutabazi, E. 1998. Contribution à la sociologie de l'entreprise multiculturelle: Diversite des cultures et des modeles de gestion en Afrique et en France (research carried out for a Ph.D. thesis in sociology). Paris: Institut d'Etudes Politiques.

————. 1999. L'entreprise multiculturelle en Afrique: Approche sociologique. Ph.D. thesis in sociology. Paris: Institut d'Etudes Politiques.

Parin, P. 1966. *Les Blancs pensent trop: 13 entretiens psychoanalytiques avec les Dogons*. Paris: Editions Payot.

Paul, K. F. 1993. *L'entrepreneur Africain face au defi d'exister*. Paris: Editions L'Harmattan.

Potholm, C., ed. 1981. *La politique Africaine, théories et pratiques*. Paris: Editions Nouveaux Horizons.

Read, M. 1960. *Children of their fathers: Growing up among the Ngoni of Nyassaland*. New Haven, CT: Yale University Press.

Temples, P. 1949. La philosophie bantoue. Paris: Editions Présence Africaine.

PART II

Developing Leaders:
Theoretical Perspectives

16

Changing Organizations and Leadership Management

William S. Hesterly and C. Brooklyn Derr

> Giant corporations around the world are attempting to emulate small companies—experimenting with intrapreneuring, gainsharing, team approaches, spin-offs, product-line focusing, specializing, downsizing, dis-integrating, subcontracting, and decentralizing—in effect, emulating what small companies do naturally. . . .
>
> Yet, big companies will remain with us (Is Boeing soon to give way to small-scale manufacturers of jumbo jets?). Nevertheless, large companies that survive will probably be able to act like small firms . . . it nonetheless seems reasonable to expect that almost all organizations that will survive and thrive in the future will possess the best characteristics of both today's big and small successes. That is why so many well-led large organizations' efforts are being made to overcome diseconomies-of-scale by creating dozens of small, independent, manageable units.
>
> —O'Toole and Bennis 1992, 83–84

CHANGING ORGANIZATIONS: FROM HIERARCHIES TO DECENTRALIZED NETWORKS

Scholars and journalists document the pervasiveness of several trends, which, taken together, some have termed a "new paradigm of business" (Ray and Kinzler 1993; Webber 1993). An abundance of terms has emerged in recent years to describe this new paradigm. Hybrid organizations (Powell 1987), cluster organizations (Mills 1991), network organizations (Miles and Snow 1986; 1992), shamrock organizations (Handy 1990), horizontal corporations (Byrne 1993b), virtual corporations (Byrne 1993a; Davidow and Malone 1992), internal markets

(Halal 1994), strategic alliances (Kanter 1989), downsizing (Tomsako 1991), and delayering are a representative list of the trends taking place. These terms converge around a few central commonalities. First, firm size is decreasing and the size of units within firms is declining as well. This decrease reflects not a simple across-the-board downsizing as a reaction to the business cycle, however. Instead, it involves long-term changes in the role of middle managers within firms and far-reaching shifts in the way production and services are organized. Second, firms are becoming more decentralized. Headquarters units are getting smaller and divisions are enjoying greater autonomy but also more accountability. A third commonality is that firms are adopting more flexible, reconfigurable structures. Boundaries both within and between firms are more permeable as firms place more reliance on structures such as cross-functional teams and strategic alliances. Fourth, firms are turning more to shared values to facilitate cohesion and coordination than to more traditional hierarchical governance.

Why is this new paradigm emerging? One explanation points to greater demands placed on firms by environmental changes in technology and consumer needs. According to this logic, the reduction in consumer disposable income in almost all industrialized countries has led to continuing demand for better quality at lower prices. Not only are the demands more intense, they are also more turbulent as technology changes and consumer tastes shift. Consequently, firms are required to exercise more flexibility and speed if they are to survive other local and global companies operating in their markets (Powell 1987; Bahrami 1992). Another explanation for the emergence of the new paradigm focuses on the role of large shareholders (Useem 1993). As pension funds, insurance companies, money managers, and commercial banks have taken on more central ownership roles, they have increasingly pressured top executives to adjust the operations of their firms to encourage closer alignment with the interests of shareholders. Similarly, as more non-U.S. companies adopt global accounting standards and trade on American and Japanese stock exchanges, these financial market pressures become global, not just national or regional. This trend has led firms to refocus operations, reduce the role of headquarters, give more authority to operating units, and tie compensation more closely to performance.

A third, and complementary, explanation for the emergence of this new paradigm looks not at the demands placed on firms but on the supply factors such as technology and organizational innovations. From this perspective, recent innovations in information technology, in organizational design, and in performance measurement reduce the costs required to manage both outside suppliers and internal units (Milgrom and Roberts 1990; Zenger and Hesterly 1994). More specifically, information technology has reduced the cost of monitoring performance at the same time that innovations in measurement and accounting have increased the efficacy of monitoring. Additionally, information technology has dramatically reduced the cost of communicating between spatially separated units. This shift has reduced, or even eliminated, the cost advantage that internal communications have traditionally held over those that take place between firms.

Several outcomes grow out of these innovations. Firms are able to outsource more efficiently while still controlling quality. Information technology has replaced the work done by middle managers in many cases. Firms are able to collaborate more effectively with alliance partners. With greater monitoring and measurement capability, firms are able to grant greater authority and autonomy to operating units. Paradoxically, in many instances, these units may emphasize coordination with other units regardless of whether they are internal or external to the firm. Perhaps the most fundamental and overarching result of all, however, is that the shift in management costs is breaking down the traditional dichotomy between markets and hierarchies as the fundamental alternatives for governing economic activity. Hierarchies are being infused with more marketlike mechanisms such as pricing and markets are characterized by more hierarchical intervention in the form of monitoring, audits, and so on. These innovations in information technology and organization design support a stream of organizational innovations with clear underlying similarity: disaggregated structures and hybrid organizational forms that selectively combine elements of both markets and hierarchies.

Smaller Firms Organized into Smaller Units

Although the extensive research on these "new" organizational forms (Draft and Lewin 1993) tends to be more qualitative and anecdotal than quantitative, research suggests that many of these innovations promote smaller size. Large corporations have dramatically downsized (Wyatt Co. 1991; Birch 1987), refocused (Ravenscraft and Scherer 1987; Davis, Diekman, and Tinsley 1994), and vertically disaggregated (Quinn 1992; Stewart 1993). Reflecting such broad change, average firm and establishment size dropped significantly in the major industrialized nations, among both manufacturing and service firms (*Economist* 1990). An analysis of U.S. Census Bureau data offers a more detailed look at this trend in the U.S. economy. Zenger and Hesterly (1994) show a pattern of increasing firm size through the late 1970s followed by a dramatic decline in firm size by 1987. The percentage of the work force employed by large firms (over ten thousand employees) has declined by a third while employment in small firms has risen. Data also show that the average establishment size has also decreased during recent years (Zenger and Hesterly 1994); one estimate places it at 8 percent lower than in 1980 (Stewart 1993, 76).

Firms are also becoming more focused in their operations. The number of industries (Standard Industrial Classifications) in which a U.S. firm does business dropped from 4.35 to 2.12 (Stewart 1993). Since 1985, large corporations have sold off organizational units not related to their core businesses. The buyers in most of these instances were in the industries of the units sold. Firms also have become more focused vertically by concentrating on a narrower range of the value chain. In other words, they outsource more. One study found that large U.S. firms outsource more than half of their manufacturing (Stewart 1993). This trend will likely continue as scholars and management consultants recommend that firms outsource everything but their most core activities. Extreme implementations of outsourcing are best characterized as network organizations (Miles and Snow 1992, 1990). For network organizations, the primary function is not efficiently performing production, design, or marketing. Instead, the emphasis is on maintaining a network of partners that perform these tasks. Often these networks of outsourced activities take on the look and feel of an internal organization even to the point of stationing employees with partners (Quinn 1992). In some geographic areas, regional networks of numerous small firms emerge to facilitate network organizations (Piore and Sabel 1984; Saxenian 1994). The most widely noted examples of this phenomenon are in the Italian textile industry (Piore and Sabel 1984) and the electronics industry in Silicon Valley (Saxenian 1994). In these regions and industries, small firms coordinate the production, sale, and distribution of products that were once considered the province of large, vertically integrated firms (Brusco 1982; Piore and Sabel 1984; Best 1990; Saxenian 1990, 1994).

Another reason for the declining size of large companies is that many have eliminated entire layers of management and increased spans of control. An American Management Association survey of 836 companies found that whereas only 5 percent of the overall work force was middle managers, 22 percent of 1992 layoffs were middle managers (Dumaine 1993). On the basis of interviews with executives and consultants, Byrne (1993c, 33–34) suggested that the number of layers between the chief executive officer (CEO) and the shop floor should be limited to less than six, whereas the span of control of executives should be as high as thirty. Delayering and downsizing were initially aimed at cost cutting, but e-mail, shared data bases, voice mail, and other advances in information technology have reduced the need for middle managers who function primarily to collect, analyze, evaluate, and transmit information within the organization (Bahrami 1992, 34). Increasingly, firms are adopting the perspective of Bill McGowan, founder of MCI:

Most middle managers are really human message switchers. They gather information, they collate it, collect it, distort it a little bit, hold on to it a lot—because information is power; and then they distribute it. All that takes a long time and is very expensive. It stops the decision process cold. (Peters 1992, 306)

Bahrami (1992, 35) found an increasing reliance on temporary workers and consultants to enhance flexibility. This is consistent with Handy's (1989) prediction that firms will adopt what he terms the "shamrock structure," whereby a core of managers within a firm interact with outside vendors and temporary employees.

Decentralization

Related to this reduction in hierarchy is the creation of more decentralized, autonomous governance structures. Through a variety of restructuring, reengineering, and redesign efforts, the authority for decisions once the domain of headquarters have been extended to lower levels of the organization. Small divisions, plants, departments, and work teams are given greater autonomy to exchange goods, services, and information with less hierarchical coordination. Small line units have their own profit and loss statements and, in some instances, can even acquire businesses on their own (Peters 1992, 341). Asea Brown Boveri (ABB) serves as a prototype for this "radical decentralization" (Peters 1992; Bartlett and Ghoshal 1993). ABB is divided into over thirteen hundred front line companies; only one level of management exists between the managers of these units and the corporate executive committee. Another aspect of increasing decentralization is the changing role of staff units. Staff units are often dependent on the goodwill of the line units, treating them as their "customers." Staff functions that cannot be fulfilled at the level of cost and quality generated by the best providers are outsourced (*Economist* 1990; Bahrami 1992; Quinn 1992). When staff services are superior to those that can be obtained externally, these staff units are often expected to gain revenue from outside sources.

These decentralized subunits are more aggressively measured but enjoy greater operational latitude. In place of the control and coordination of hierarchy, firms employ measurement and accountability. Improved accounting measures— for example, those based on activity-based costing; new measures of nonfinancial performance; and new organizational designs enable managers to assign responsibility for well-defined measures to small internal subunits. Thus, manufacturing facilities and other functional units may be evaluated as profit centers. Indeed, anecdotal evidence suggests that firms are routinely pushing profit center accountability to units of fewer than five hundred employees (Byrne 1993c).

Another aspect of the increased decentralization of authority in firms is the changing role of headquarters units. Whereas we have noted a general trend toward downsizing, headquarters units have been disproportionally affected. Giving greater authority to operating units has led to either reduction (Useem 1993) or slower growth in headquarters staff (Lichtenberg and Siegel 1990). In many instances central staff functions have been curtailed as responsibility for areas such as human resource management have moved into the operating business units. Moreover, headquarters units have been affected by the push to make internal service providers compete with outsiders. Activities that were traditionally performed by headquarters units now are kept in-house only if headquarters "wins a contract" or requires central control for the good of the whole enterprise, as is often the case for functions such as executive compensation and management of high-potential managers (*Economist* 1990).

Flexible Structures: Cross-Functional Teams, Cross-National Coordination, and Increased Emphasis on Ad Hoc Units

Another part of the new paradigm of business are structures within firms that emphasize horizontal coordination and flexibility. Surveys indicate that a significant percentage adopted cross-functional teams in the 1980s. These teams enhance flexibility because they are based on reconfigurable rather than permanent structures. They can be formed, reformed, and disbanded with relative ease (Bahrami 1992) as market opportunities arise. Indeed, cross-functional organization is viewed as crucial in speeding the time required to put new products and services on the market (Wheelwright and Clark 1992). Bartlett and Ghoshal (1989) emphasize the importance of reconfigurable structures in their study of multinational firms in Europe, North America, and Japan. Their study suggests that flexible cross-national networks of teams within companies allow these firms to gain global economies of scale, respond to different national market needs, and develop internal capabilities. Others (Derr and Oddou 1993; Galbraith 1993) have documented the rise of cross-national task forces and problem-oriented teams as both coordinating and developmental mechanisms. These configurations introduce into the equation the issues of working across cross-national cultures and different business contexts. A more recent phenomenon is the introduction of the global franchise team in which a single business is managed across global boundaries. This emphasis on reconfigurable teams does not imply, however, that more permanent organizational structures are disappearing. Many firms have adopted a dual structure through which a formal structure of reporting relationships that changes infrequently is combined with an overlay of more temporary project teams (Bahrami 1992, 39).

The widespread adoption of cross-functional and project teams has also improved output measurement and aided the trend toward decentralizing autonomy to the lowest levels of the organization. Clustering a broad set of capabilities with a subunit allows entire processes to be reengineered around an identifiable output (Hammer and Champy 1993). This more clearly identified output makes it easier to measure and monitor unit performance. Firms can then delegate greater authority to subunits who enjoy greater latitude in decision making but also have stricter accountability for performance.

Managing Values and Purpose

Another trend that is evident in the anecdotal accounts of scholars and journalists is an increased emphasis on establishing shared purpose and values. As large multinational companies decentralize they face the potential for fragmentation. When such fragmentation occurs, coordination across units that are separated by nationality and function becomes particularly difficult. Historically, it was more feasible for firms to ensure the necessary coordination through formalized mechanisms such as standard operating procedures or close monitoring of plans and actions by upper management. However, as multinational firms face more diverse markets and rapidly changing technology combined with their decentralization into a large number of units these traditional solutions have become ineffective. Measuring outcomes and tying them to financial incentives are more compatible with the increased complexity that large companies confront, but they are often not sufficient.

The role of top managers has shifted from setting strategy to defining purpose and values (Bartlett and Ghoshal 1994; Collins and Porras 1994; Hamel and Prahalad 1994). Hamel and Prahalad (1994), for example, argue that it was a strongly shared purpose more than any detailed strategy that allowed upstarts such as Sony, Toyota, and Canon to excel despite established competitors such as RCA, General Motors, and Xerox. Such strongly shared purpose and values are essential in many instances to the creation and sustenance of competitive advantages. Strategy scholars argue that the most enduring advantages tend to be embedded in these values that constitute an essential part of organizational culture (Barney 1986; Ghemawat 1990). Thus, shared purpose and values provide long-term coherence to a firm. Shared values provide several more specific benefits (Quinn 1992, 318). They allow the trust necessary for flexibility, create group identity, facilitate teamwork, and permit the delegation without close monitoring that is necessary in a decentralized enterprise. As with decentralization, ABB serves as an example of managing purpose and values. The role of top management is to provide a philosophical framework of mission, values, and policies "within which those lower in the organization could operate and make decisions" (Bartlett and Ghoshal 1993, 31).

Other good examples are Apple Europe's three control mechanisms for the networked organization: clear sense of direction, thorough understanding of the Apple Values,[1] and two- or three-page brief reports. Also, Johnson & Johnson[2] has used its international Executive Conference and Advanced Management Programs to develop a better understanding of strategic direction, common values, and the company culture.

CHANGING ORGANIZATIONS AND HIGH-POTENTIAL MANAGEMENT

Underlying Assumptions

As outlined in the introduction and in Chapter 1, high-potential (HIPO) management traditionally has been based on the following assumptions:

- A focus on managers with potential to move up the hierarchy into key positions near the top (say the top 50–100 leadership posts): The assumption here is that future leaders will probably be general managers and future companies will most likely be large hierarchal organizations with fifty to one hundred top-level positions.

- Once a person has been designated a HIPO and successfully completed the first few entry-level assignments (some organizations have formal HIPO selection programs such as assessment centers or competency profiling systems), she is considered "corporate property": At this point, her career is carefully managed and she undergoes long-term training and development preparations for top-leadership posts. These broadening job assignments, educational experiences, and social networking activities allow candidates to gain what leaders consider essential experiences and contacts so they can be considered for advancement to higher-level positions. The assumption here is that it takes ten to fifteen years within a company to develop a future leader via a series of carefully selected developmental experiences, mostly job assignment rotations. Outsiders are hired only when there are no internal candidates. As the human resources director of one of the world's largest electronic firms put it, "We grow our own trees but we don't necessarily have all the trees in the forest."[3]

- A secret list of HIPOs at various stages of development allows top-level managers, often the Management Review Committee (MRC), which comprises high-level general managers and the head of human resources, to discuss the performance and potential of various candidates continuously and to move people on and off the list freely: Who remains on the list depends on changing leadership needs, corporate politics, and additional information as each candidate completes a new job assignment. A HIPO is often valued over time the more he learns to act as current top managers do, a pattern that leads to "cloning." Often, the HIPO system is referred to as a "tournament model" (Rosenbaum 1979) in which doing well on one assignment gives the candidate the opportunity to be part of the next game. The assumptions here are that it is desirable for one generation of leaders to groom the next, that secret lists are legal, and that good performance in today's assignment will, in fact, prepare one for leadership in tomorrow's organization.

- A group of dedicated and talented HIPOs willing to work extremely hard in every new assignment, move both geographically and functionally every two to four years to gain additional leadership knowledge and skills, and remain flexible and willing to make the personal sacrifices required to reach the top: The assumptions here are that there will exist in organizations an ample supply of talented people willing to pay whatever personal price is required to become a top-level leader and that they, as corporate property, will submit to the organization's needs.

- A governing body at headquarters, whether located in human resources or elsewhere, is empowered to design, modify, and manage the HIPO system: Depending on the developmental need of the individual, this group moves a candidate with potential from Division A to Division B or from a line position to a staff function or from a domestic operation to an international post. The assumption here is that headquarters and a central governing body (usually a management review committee) has more power than divisional or operational management and can prevent local line managers from "hoarding" their best people.

Critical Issues and Changes

Given the changing nature of organizations described in the first part of this chapter, some assumptions underlying HIPO management may no longer be valid. The "new paradigm of business," pushed by global competition, requires a hybrid market–hierarchal form of high-potential management including some more traditional concepts but also requiring new thinking for future leadership development.

The first assumption, that twenty-first-century leaders will be general managers in large, hierarchical organizations is flawed. Large companies have radically downsized, refocused, and disaggregated, and large control-oriented bureaucracies are no longer needed; nor are they responsive, flexible, and fast enough to be competitive (Harris 1993; Webber 1993). Layers of management have been reduced and fewer managers are required. And financial markets are careful to calculate productivity ratios that are based in part on the minimum number of key employees and managers. Chief executive officers are very much aware that to keep their common stock attractive to the market they must be "lean and mean" (*Fortune* 1994, 12).

"Speed," or being a superfast innovator in research and development, a superfast producer, and a superfast implementer of needed changes, is a key competitive advantage (*World Competitiveness Report* 1992, 5). The movement toward working in cross-functional and cross-national teams is, in part, an effort to speed up the process and enhance competitiveness (Parker 1994; Jones 1993; Vinton 1992).

Therefore, it is conceivable that future organizations will require not only fewer general managers, but also leaders for different kinds of enterprises and functions: smaller subunits, cross-boundary coordinating teams, and superfast respondents to diverse customer requirements. Different kinds of nonhierarchical leaders may emerge. As Dalton and Thompson (1986) discovered years ago in their work with research and development (R&D) organizations, only some of the successful leaders in the professional organizations they studied were general managers; others were technical gurus, idea innovators, intrepreneurs, and product/program champions. The notion of "opinion leader" as a key leadership function may be relevant, as is that of employee coach and process facilitator. Companies should prepare to develop different kinds of leaders than traditional corporate general managers.

The second assumption in HIPO management treats developing leaders from within and over a period (ten to fifteen years). An orientation by many of today's competitive companies toward recruiting already developed talent from the marketplace as needs change and outsourcing all but core functions brings this assumption into question. It is also difficult in this era of high-velocity change to think that the training and development received today will be relevant ten years hence.

Currently under scrutiny are the criteria used for HIPO selection. Are they based on research about how most effectively to develop leaders for bureaucratic command-and-control hierarchies? Are our assessment center criteria, our assessors (senior managers who succeeded in another organizational era), and our competency profiles still relevant and appropriate? General Electric has declared that the ability to work across organizational boundaries of all kinds (across functions, gender lines, national cultures) and international experience would be important as future criteria. Apple Computers is trying to measure one's ability to learn quickly from work experiences, even failures, as an important new HIPO selection criterion.

On the other hand, in hybrid organizations "core employees" who stay with a company, learn its norms, and have in their heads corporate memory will, if they continue to learn and adapt, be very valuable. Conceptually, the idea of developing a future leader over the course of four or five important job assignments and exposing her to coaches and mentors, as well as state-of-the-art educational events and important peer networks, is a notion tested over time. Much of the literature also comments that although future organizations will be smaller and more networked, the most important core employees will be even more valuable (Stewart 1993; Pearson 1987, Drucker 1988). The organization's most enduring competitive advantages reside in the knowledge and skills of these core employees and in their collective ability to work together (Barney 1986). We believe that the practice of selecting, training, and developing HIPOs from within will continue but that selection criteria might be modified and more HIPOs will be recruited at all career stages from the outside. The quality of the leadership may also be a factor in achieving most favored supplier status.

Third, the concept of a secret HIPO list in which it is easy for omnipotent top-level managers to move persons at will and select future leaders is problematic. A secret list in which the "old boys network" is promoted, even unconsciously, may not be legal in many countries that have equal opportunity laws. Moreover, new values and life-styles among the younger generation of HIPOs probably require them to be part of planning their own future; for many, frequent moves and subordinating personal to professional life may not be an attractive option as they may be in dual-career partnerships that require careful planning and complex relocation arrangements.

Will an ample supply of available talent exist for future leadership positions, as stated in assumption four? There is some evidence to substantiate that there is a change in values among talented employees toward greater personal/professional life balance, toward exciting work and autonomy as high-order measures of career success, and away from ascent to the top of an organization or profession or loyalty to the company (Hall and Richter 1988; Derr 1986; Driver 1980; Schein 1978).

These value shifts are part of life-style changes in which more women work and more couples and families are geographically bound to their spouse's job and their child care situation. The increased income in two-paycheck partnerships also makes individuals less dependent on the organization and less subjugated to its requirements. On the other hand, all of this is tempered by a corresponding need to learn and grow and avoid stagnation. Many recognize how important good positions are in a period of downsizing in which there may be an oversupply of talent.

Moreover, the demographics in OECD countries support the concept of a decreasing supply of talent by the year 2000. The fall in the number of fifteen- to nineteen-year-olds by the year 2000 is expected to be 6 percent in the United States of America, 10 percent in France, 14 percent in Japan, 24 percent in the United Kingdom, and 40 percent in Germany (Euorestat Data Resources). In the 1990s, the number of new job seekers under the age of twenty-five is expected to decrease 3–6 percent a year in Germany and 2 percent a year in the United

Kingdom, France, and Japan (Richman 1990, 47). Moreover, the total fertility rate of childbearing women decreased from 2.55 (1965–1970) to 1.83 (1985–1990) in the United States, from 2.33 (1965–1970) to 1.25 (1985–1990) in Germany, and from 2.00 (1985–1970) to 1.70 (1985–1990) in Japan (World Bank Population Projections).

The national politics of immigration are likely to offset a company's ability to recruit worldwide freely, even though more plants and operations will be located around the globe. Perhaps a Swedish model (Derr 1987) in which there are fewer candidates who will undergo the rigors and personal life sacrifices required of HIPOs will prevail in the future. Those who do, however, will be ready and willing to pay the price required to get to the top.

Another possibility is that different organizational requirements will promote working smarter, not necessarily harder. Working more electronically and at home (in the virtual office, which is wherever one is with a phone, a fax, and a computer linked to the company network) might also allow for more variation in assignments. It might be possible to get some international experience during a "long business trip" abroad in which one works intensively on a project or task force for three months without relocating.

Finally, newer forms of governance challenge the ideas of centrally controlled high-potential programs. Not only are companies delayering and downsizing, they are disaggregating. Characteristic of organizational reconstitution, what we have called a hybrid form of organization, are the devolution of power to line managers, the reconfiguration of organizational units into customer-focused global franchises, and the use of cross-boundary teams and business units that focus on particular customers or speed up normal business procedures. These newer organizational mechanisms can be coordinated in part by sophisticated global information systems and now require fewer coordinating managers at head office. So, local line managers and global business unit managers are more powerful and corporate staffs are less powerful as a result.

It was once possible centrally to monitor and manage the careers of high-potential managers. Powerful human resources department staffs and management review committees, along with input from very senior managers and the CEO's office, directed this process. Now many of these same staffs have been eliminated or transferred to operational business units as part of the reorganization. The role of corporate-wide human resource management is in question (Bournois and Derr 1994; Derr et al. 1992; Price-Waterhouse Cranfield Study 1991).

One organizational problem raised during this transition phase to the hybrid organization is the resultant loss of power that prevents head office from forcing independent, business-unit managers to replace their best people for the good of the whole enterprise or for a candidate's own development. The "hoarding" problem, from the point of view of HIPO management, has been worsened. Although many corporations have retained license at corporate headquarters to direct the careers of the top fifty, the old battle between the business unit director

Figure 16.1
The Career Spiral

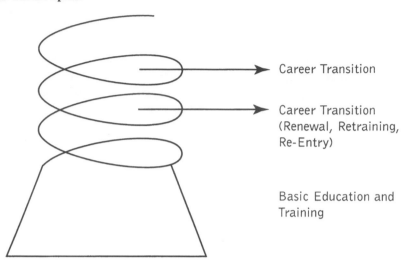

Career Transition

Career Transition
(Renewal, Retraining,
Re-Entry)

Basic Education and
Training

whose best people impact the short-term bottom line and headquarters, who need future leaders with breadth of knowledge and experience, has not been resolved.

Moreover, the changing organizational landscape has caused the most ambitious and competent potential future leaders to reassess their career strategies. No longer does it seem advantageous to stay with the same organization over the span of a career; nor does it seem wise for a talented future leader to get stuck in a traditional career path. Although the need for hard-working, career-first, and competent managers may increase, given the demographics and the shift in values among young talent, to even those who aspire to getting ahead a successful upwardly mobile future career may look more like a spiral than a linear path (see Bailyn 1989; Driver 1980).

Many view the career of the twenty-first century as a spiral model in which the problem is how to manage career transitions. Figure 16.1 illustrates this idea. Entering from a basic preparatory state, such as getting the right degree from a good university, the new brand of HIPO sees that she must get an excellent four- to seven-year placement in which she will be given an opportunity to learn, grow, stretch, develop new knowledge and skills, and become more valuable either within the company or in the external job market. Ideally the company will provide enough education, training, and experience to minimize the amount of retooling necessary for the next career transition (Waterman, Waterman, and Collard 1994).

It is evident to smart young talent, however, that the psychological contract between companies and their employees, even their most valuable people, has changed. As argued, the market is a much more powerful force in the new competitive global economy. Therefore, the HIPO candidate must also be market-oriented as well as company-centered. He also recognizes, usually, that with the rapid changes of today's organizational world, knowledge will more quickly become obsolete and lifetime learning in new critical knowledge areas will be the key component of future success.

The best and the brightest in the future may seek a company that views HIPO management as also providing learning opportunities in critical new knowledge/skill areas and helping HIPOs get specific assignments and education for the purpose of renewing, retooling, and retraining. Otherwise, the success-oriented future leader may have to take time out from an ongoing career to manage her own career transition. This process will require time and extra money.

Key elements of the career transition are (1) renewal: if one is burned out as a result of intensive hard work, travel, overstimulating new learning, lack of personal life, or other circumstances, it will be necessary to renew one's mental, emotional, and spiritual self preparatory to the next career phase; (2) retraining: if one has not had adequate cutting-edge experiences or training, it may be necessary to find a way to get needed new knowledge in, say, a technical area or a foreign language or the use of intuition in decision making; (3) reentry: whether one leaves the current organization or radically changes business units, functions, geography, or career streams, it will be important to learn how to manage starting the next career phase. This will require using past knowledge and experience to advantage while being open again to "learning the ropes" and being a junior partner in the early stages of the transition.

Also, savvy HIPOs of the future may see that opportunities are more likely to arise from being close to customers as opposed to being removed by layers of hierarchy. With customer focus such an important part of global competitive advantage, being valued by customers may be analogous to having organizational power. Choice job rotations of the future may both enhance learning and be customer-centered.

SUMMARY

By exposing underlying assumptions in pre-1990 high-potential management programs, especially in large multinational companies, questions have been raised for HIPO management in the twenty-first century.

It was pointed out that organizations of the future may need leaders other than the general managers ideal in older hierarchical settings. Future leaders will probably be recruited from outside the enterprise on an as-needed basis, but companies will also continue to develop leadership from within. The secret list of the top 100 or 150 HIPOs may continue but in some countries will certainly be resisted legally. As organizations begin to question, in this era of rapid change, how much to trust today's top management with the criteria for developing tomorrow's leadership, reliance on current managers (via assessment centers, MRCs, and "cloning" criteria) to decide on tomorrow's leaders will be problematic. Moreover, as values shift from getting ahead at any cost and as life-styles and family patterns change, there are likely to be fewer talented individuals willing to sign on for traditional HIPO training and development programs. Achievement of a future top-management position, even for the most ambitious, probably requires a different strategy from that used in the past. For the leadership-oriented, a new premium will be attached to taking advantage of personal learning opportunities, to investing in companies and jobs that enhance future marketability, to staying close to customers, and to managing the career transition in order to spiral successfully into the next career phase.

NOTES

1. As described by a senior vice president of Apple Europe an MBA in presentation at IMD, Lausanne, Switzerland, June 1990.

2. One of the authors directed the J&J Advanced Management Program at IMD in Lausanne, Switzerland, from 1990 to 1999 and is familiar with the worldwide purposes of the training program.

3. Statement by Kees Krombeen, HR director, Phillips Electronics, Human Resources Symposium, IMB, Lausanne, Switzerland, June 1990.

REFERENCES

Bahrami, H. 1992. The emerging flexible organization. *California Management Review* 34: 33–52.

Bailyn, L. 1989. Understanding individual experience at work. In M. B. Arthur, D. T. Hall, and B. S. Lawrence, eds. *Handbook of career theory*. New York: Cambridge University Press.

Barney, J. B. 1986. Organizational culture: Can it be a source of sustained competitive advantage? *Academy of Management Review* 11: 656–65.

Bartlett, C. A., and S. Ghoshal. 1989. *Managing across the borders: The transnational solution*. Cambridge, MA: Harvard Business School Press.

———. 1993. Beyond the m-form: Toward a managerial theory of the firm. *Strategic Management Journal* 14 (Winter): 23–46.

———. 1994. Changing the role of top management: Beyond strategy to purpose. *Harvard Business Review* 72 (November–December): 79–88.

Best, M. 1990. *The new competition: Institutions of industrial restructuring*. Cambridge, MA: Harvard University Press.

Birch, D. L. 1987. *Job creation in America*. New York: The Free Press.

Bournois, F., and C. B. Derr. 1994. Les directeurs des resources humaines, ont-ils un avenir? *Revue Française de Gestion* 98: 64–78.

Brusco, S. 1982. The Emilian model: Productive decentralization and social integration. *Cambridge Journal of Economics* 6: 167–184.

Byrne, J. A. 1993a. The virtual corporation. *Business Week*, February 8, 98–102.

———. 1993b. Horizontal corporation. *Business Week*, December 20, 76–81.

———. 1993c. Belt tightening the smart way. *Business Week*, October 22, 34–38.

Collins, J. C., and J. I. Porras. 1994. *Built to last: Successful habits of visionary companies*. New York: Harper Business.

Daft, R. L., and A. Y. Lewin. 1993. Where are the theories for the "new" organizational forms? An editorial essay. *Organization Science* 4: i–vi.

Dalton, G. W., and P. H. Thompson. 1986. *Novations: Strategies for career management*. Glenview, IL: Scott, Foresman Publishers.

Davidow, W. H., and M. S. Malone. 1992. *The virtual corporation*. New York: Harper Business.

Davis, G. F., K. A. Diekman, and C. H. Tinsley. 1994. The decline and fall of the conglomerate firm in the 1980s: The deinstitutionalization of an organizational form. *American Sociological Review* 59: 547–570.

Derr, C. B. 1986. *Managing the new careerists*. San Francisco: Jossey-Bass Publishers.

———. 1987. Managing high-potentials in Europe: Some cross-cultural findings. *European Management Journal* 5(2): 72–80.

Derr, C. B., and G. Oddou. 1993. Internationalizing managers: Speeding up the process. *European Management Journal* 3(4): 435–442.

Derr, C. B., J. Wood, M. Walker, and C. Despres. 1992. *The emerging role of the HR manager in Europe*. Lausanne, Switzerland: Institute for International Management.

Driver, M. J. 1980. Career concepts and organizational change. In C. B. Derr, ed. *Work, family and the career*. New York: Praeger.

Drucker, P. F. 1988. The coming of the new organization. *Harvard Business Review* 66(1): 45–53.

Dumaine, B. 1993. The new manager non-managers. *Fortune*, February 22, 80–84.

Economist. 1990. The incredible shrinking company. December 16, 65–66.

Farewell, H. Q. 1990. *The Economist*, March 24.

Fortune, 1994. Wall Street and layoffs. January 24, 12.

Galbraith, J. R., and E. E. Lawler, III. 1994. *Organizing for the future*. San Francisco: Jossey-Bass Publishers.

Ghemawat, P. 1990. *Commitment*. New York: Free Press.

Halal, W. E. 1994. From hierarchy to enterprise: Internal markets are the new foundation of management. *Academy of Management Executive* 8(November): 69–83.

Hall, D. T., and J. Richter. 1988. Balancing work life and home life. *Academy of Management Executives* 2(3).

Hamel, G., and C. K. Prahalad. 1994. *Competing for the future*. Boston: Harvard Business School Press.

Hammer, M. and J. Champy. 1993. *Reengineering the corporation*. New York: Harper Business.

Handy, C. 1989. *The age of unreason*. Boston: Harvard Business School Press.

Harris, T. G. 1993. The post-capitalist executive: An interview with Peter F. Drucker. *Harvard Business Review* May/June: 114–122.

Jones, J. W. 1993. *High-speed management: Time-based strategies for managers and organizations*. San Francisco: Jossey-Bass Publishers.

Kanter, R. M. 1989. *When giants learn to dance*. New York: Simon and Schuster.

———. 1990. Values and economics. *Harvard Business Review* 68 (May/June): 4.

Lichtenberg, F., and D. Siegel. 1990. The effect of ownership changes on the employment and wages of central office and other personnel. *Journal of Law and Economics* 33: 383–408.

Miles, R. E., and C. C. Snow. 1986. Network organizations: New concepts for new forms. *California Management Review* 28(3): 62–73.

———. 1992. Causes of failure in network organizations. *California Management Review* 34(4): 53–72.

Milgrom, P., and J. Roberts. 1990. The economics of modern manufacturing: Technology, strategy, and organization. *American Economic Review* 80: 511–528.

Mills, D. Q. 1991. *Rebirth of the corporation.* New York: Wiley.

O'Toole, J., and W. Bennis. 1992. Our federalist future: The leadership imperative. *California Management Review* 34(summer):73–90.

Parker, G. M. 1994. *Cross-functional teams.* San Francisco: Jossey-Bass Publishers.

Pearson, A. E. 1987. Muscle-build the organization. *Harvard Business Review* 65(4): 49–55.

Peters, T. 1986. *Thriving on chaos.* New York: Knopf.

———. 1992. *Liberation Management.* New York: Knopf.

Piore, M. J., and C. F. Sabel. 1984. *The second industrial divide.* New York: Basic Books.

Powell, W. W. 1987. Hybrid organizational arrangements. *California Management Review* 30(fall): 67–87.

Price-Waterhouse Cranfield Project. 1991. *International strategic human resource management.* Bedford, United Kingdom: Cranfield School of Management.

Quinn, J. B. 1992. *Intelligent enterprise.* New York: The Free Press.

Ravenscraft, D. J., and F. M. Scherer. 1987. *Mergers, selloffs, & economic efficiency.* Washington, DC: Brookings Institution.

Ray, M., and A. Kinzler, eds. 1993. *The new paradigm of business: Emerging strategies for leadership and organizational change.* Los Angeles, CA: Jeremy P. Tarcher/ Pedigree Books.

Richman, C. S. 1990. The coming world labor shortage. *Fortune,* April 9, 46–50.

Rosenbaum, J. E. 1979. Tournament mobility: Career patterns in a corporation. *Administrative Science Quarterly* 24: 220–241.

Saxenian, A. 1990. Regional networks and the resurgence of Silicon Valley. *California Management Review* 32: 89–112.

———. 1994. *Regional advantage: Culture and competition in Silicon Valley and Route 128.* Cambridge, MA: Harvard University Press.

Schein, E. H. 1978. *Career dynamics.* Reading, MA: Addison-Wesley.

Stewart, T. 1993. Welcome to the revolution. *Fortune* 128(15):66–81.

Tomsako, R. M. 1991. *Downsizing: Reshaping the corporation for the future.* New York: AMACOM.

Useem, M. 1993. *Executive defense: Shareholder power and corporate reorganization.* Cambridge, MA: Harvard University Press.

Vinton, D. E. 1992. A new look at time, speed, and the manager. *The Academy of Management Executive* 4(4): 7–16.

Waterman, R. H., J. A. Waterman, and B. A. Collard. 1994. Toward a career-resilient workforce. *Harvard Business Review* 72(4): 87–95.

Webber, A. M. 1993. What's so new about the new economy? *Harvard Business Review* 7 January/February: 4–12.

Wheelwright, S. C., and K. B. Clark. 1992. *Revolutionizing product development: Quantum leaps in speed: Efficiency and Quality.* New York: Free Press.

World Competitiveness Report. 1992. Lausanne, Switzerland: IMD Research Report.

Wyatt Co. 1991. *Restructuring—cure or cosmetic surgery: Results of corporate change in the 80's with prescriptions for the 90's.* New York: Wyatt Co.

Zenger, T. R., and W. S. Hesterly. 1994. The disaggregation of U.S. corporations: Selective intervention and convergence toward internal and external networks of small, autonomous teams. Unpublished paper, Washington University, St. Louis.

17

Toward Strategic Management for Fast-Track Executives

Frank Bournois

It is up to those currently in positions of leadership—senior managers, line managers, and resource managers—to prepare for the succession of management teams and strategic areas destined to add value to businesses and companies in the future. A few isolated authors doubt the possibility of managing fast-track executives and their career paths (Clark 1992) and fear that to do so might engender major difficulties for organizations: arrogant behavior, self-fulfilling prophesies of successful careers, blurred management criteria, partisan support of (and for) those choosing the teams, serious motivation problems for the so-called fast-track executives at times of poor growth, not to mention the disenchantment of "solid citizens," who, though their performance is good, may find that their own motivational needs and careers are neglected for the sake of the few.

In this chapter, we discuss the principles behind the design and application of a strategy for the management of fast-track executives (as defined in the previous paragraph). Like it or not, in all national and organizational cultures, an elite generally emerges, though it may go by another name: the hardcore, the relief team, the succession. We consider management to be one of the action sciences, contributing to the orientation of organized group action. Thus, the strategic management of fast-track executives (even elementary) can enable an organization to attain its objectives, to create competitive advantage, and thereby to ensure its own future.

This chapter has three objectives:

1. To display the new context in which the management of fast-track executives belongs

2. To propose a methodological guide based on our research and consulting experience, for developing a strategic approach to managing this population

3. To draw together the policies and practices of major European companies at a time when the Old World is confronted by the new business paradigm

A NEW SET OF RULES

When reading the international economic press, one cannot help but notice the range of strategic changes and shakedowns that major companies have to confront with new markets (new geostrategic phenomena, the extension of free competition laws, and the search for increased flexibility). Commentators rarely fail to insist on the central role of current and future management teams who will have to rethink and apply the required changes constantly. The examples provided today by Elf, Total-Fina, Société Générale, Paribas, and BNP are merely the precursors of much deeper phenomena. The intense conflicts that reign within senior management teams show, with some irony, that the team's solid(ar)ity is a trump card for shareholders lulled by the virtues of flexibility.

Evolution in the Management of Organizations and of Fast-Track Executives

In view of the wave of organizational changes within companies, university specialists and consultants agree that management of fast-track executives is and remains the prerogative of the senior management at the highest level of the company. This does not necessarily mean that the "fast-track" function should be centralized and managed exclusively by the headquarters, but rather that strategy should be determined, amended, and coordinated by the highest powers.

The injunctions of the 1990s for "flexible and globalized" companies have been broadly applied with major consequences for the career management of fast-track managers:

- Fewer hierarchical levels (reengineering)
- States with fewer and fewer civil servants and a general tendency toward abolishing preestablished careers (the Bank of England, for example, has only a tiny minority of civil servants in its ranks)
- A relative breakdown of the social escalator
- A rise in the number of "peripheral workers" (noncentral employees with a precarious status) as opposed to "core employees" (core permanent employees, key employees)
- The development of information technologies of which Internet is merely the most emblematic example (at a time when the acquisition of goods and services is increasingly virtual, headhunters have set up "capture sites" on a planetary scale)
- The development of new forms of network organization, such as delocalized multinational teams (we consider that network engineering [netware] has become an important means for differentiating the performance of companies)

Table 17.1
Evolution of Human Resource Director's Role, 1990–2000

Missions for the development of fast-track executives	Definition and control of the detection and development system at headquarters	Increased cooperation with operational units on this topic and development of compatible subsystems
		Development of the "Diversity-Harmonization" model
	Responsibility for nurturing an internal pool of available, loyal, motivated top executives	Responsible for nourishing a pool from both internal and external sources (competitors, suppliers). Recognition of new values for executives at work
	Definition of (secret) criteria and a confidential list of the "chosen"	More flexible criteria, greater transparency about policies, increased association between individuals and hierarchies
	Tendency towards centralizing tools, emphasis on the organization or national culture (especially at head quarters)	Recognition of cultural diversity (national, sector of activity, career)
	Concentration on the company's needs	Recognition of interdependence between levels (individual/work group/company/market/society)
	Career committee director with long-term projects (succession, career plans)	Career committee director with negotiated projects enabling internal and external employability

- Increased management of horizontal functional transversality
- An increased number of new partnerships among companies
- Increasingly porous company boundaries linked to the perception that the working relationship is increasingly fragile, in terms of both duration (the notion of a job for life or internal career path has disappeared in the countries in which it was once strongly rooted) and the strength of the legal ties between company and employee (commercial law in the place of labor law); for directors, the development of gold handcuffs or bonus withholding illustrates this acquisition of commitment to the company for a given period

NEW RESPONSIBILITIES FOR THE HUMAN RESOURCES DIRECTOR IN RELATION TO THE STRATEGIC MANAGEMENT OF FAST-TRACK EXECUTIVES

This evolution has led to a modification in the role of the human resources (HR) director, especially in the case of fast-track executives (see Table 17.1). Confronted with such tendencies, the management of fast-track executives cannot be confined to a precise action list (*how to*) to detect the best and help them evolve. A few authors insist on the need for policies and tools chosen in the light of the company's specificity. We personally ground our reflections and recommendations within the framework of a model to be constructed at the frontiers of management and psychosociology. On the one hand, the aims of the various actors (general direction, hierarchy, human resources director, the executives themselves) are not always shared and, on the other, the company cannot survive without committed executives who determine its performance.

Among the main questions that general managers and human resources directors concerned with the issue of managing fast-track executives ask themselves are the following:

- Why is it important not to confuse present and future performance (potential), and how can it be accomplished?
- How can one separate individual and team potential for developing better performance? Can only individuals develop?
- What approach should be used for determining potential? Should it be assessed in terms of the maximum position that an executive can hope to reach during a career (reference to the notion of ultimate potential) or in terms of the level reached at a specific age?
- When should one evaluate potential? It is generally recognized that one can rarely detect potential before completion of the first two positions (generally not before age thirty) even if some are convinced that they are recruiting beginners who have potential.
- How can one discourage fast-track executives from looking elsewhere? The label "has potential" increases the risk of defection. What individual measures can be taken to prevent loss of executives who have a high market value?
- How much credit should be given to the assessment of potential made by the direct superior, even when accompanied by a 360-degree assessment?
- How can the needs of the company and of the individual be harmonized, in particular with regard to personal well-being and family or private life? (Bailyn et al. 1997). The company, like the individual, may have the impression that the psychological contract has been broken if there is a lack of discussion or respect for respective characteristics or expectations.
- How much credibility should be given to detection tools (tests and assessment centers) compared to more subtle processes that enable human resources management to operate as organized social action?
- Should technology be confided to external specialists with experience in a great number of companies or rely on internal resources and the in-depth knowledge of the ground in which the policy is to develop?

There is no single right answer to these questions; they serve as a preparatory guide to developing the strategy proposed in the second part of this chapter. We now concentrate leadership development strategy on making a diagnosis of current policies as well as creating an exercise for seeking coherence among differing subsystems.

DEVELOPING A MANAGEMENT STRATEGY FOR DETECTING AND DEVELOPING FAST-TRACK EXECUTIVES

The detection and development of fast-track executives can be compared to a "risk management" approach, especially given that potential concerns, by definition, are not yet concrete. If detection and development are badly applied, the company suffers material and intangible costs: executives assigned to key posts on the basis of an assessment of potential carried out several years before that no longer corresponds to today's stakes; high investment in executives who are then lost to the competition; difficulty in defining motivating methods for remuneration; and, often, incapacity to propose positions that correspond to the individual's talents.

It may seem obvious, but we should recall that the development of a policy for managing fast-track executives belongs wholly to the senior management team. The measures taken are beyond the field of social negotiation and belong rather to a discretionary domain, protected by high confidentiality.

A review of management literature as well as our work with companies suggest that constructing a system for managing fast-track executives should be considered within a systemic perspective in which six dimensions must converge:

1. The company's organizational characteristics
2. Its strategic orientation
3. Its organizational structure
4. Its culture
5. The principal characteristics of its human resources management
6. The individual characteristics of concerned executives.

We are aware that our method is heterodox. It does not subscribe to the "fit" model, which demands that the system for managing high potential adjust itself merely to strategic orientations. Our model requires the recognition of business strategy but also other dimensions, in particular internal human resources.[1]

THE COMPANY'S ORGANIZATIONAL CHARACTERISTICS

It is important to review the central structural characteristics of an organization since these largely determine the nature and breadth of the system for managing fast-track executives. Among these characteristics we especially consider the following:

- Company size
- Sector of activity
- Age of the future company
- Nature of shareholders
- Nationality of the parent company

THE COMPANY'S STRATEGIC ORIENTATION

Management of executive potential and company strategy are closely connected and share a need for anticipation. On the one hand, the aim is to distinguish future leaders; on the other, to specify the activities in which the company will be present. The move toward strategic human resources management has broadly developed the idea that there should be strong links among the chosen strategy, the composition of the management team (Michel and Hambrick 1992), and the system for managing executive potential.

Generally, the more the company adopts a dynamic strategy for coping with a turbulent, changing environment, the more the system for managing fast-track executives requires close attention and direction. On the other hand, the more the strategy consists of managing a decline in activities or short-term modifications to adapt to environmental pressures, the less investment will be made in managing executive potential.

ORGANIZATIONAL STRUCTURE

The system for managing fast-track executives is often closely linked to the company's organization. Depending on whether the emphasis is on function, type of strategic activity, product type, or matrix, management of potential adopts different forms, especially with regard to sources of information about executives and the key actors involved in the detection and development process.

Whatever the configuration, it is important to underline that the structure defining the approach to managing fast-track executives is not overly deterministic. It is, however, important to consider the relevant level for reflection: is it the profit center, the professional family, or the country? Experts underline the need to revise the management system regularly to reflect major structural changes.

CULTURAL AND POLITICAL SYSTEMS

If one ignores the issue of power and culture within the organization, one risks creating a system that cannot function. Management literature consistently emphasizes that the management of executives is probably the most politically sensitive area of all human resources activities (Moorby 1994: 308).

Today's higher executives are the product of the culture of fifteen years ago, just as they will produce and enforce the cultural traits that will shape tomorrow. They incarnate the company's fundamental values, relaying them through their behavior and decision making (including that concerning potential).

An analysis of the biographies and professional careers of the leaders of a given company is a useful source of information about the individual characteristics valued by the organization. Depending on the country, the "fast-track" label carries a certain number of privileges, including status, level of salary, and privileged links with shareholders, but also an introduction to networks that facilitate the accomplishment of personal and professional objectives.

Consequently, the type of values prized by a company and the executive's adherence—or nonadherence—to these values can often explain how an executive can be assessed in terms of potential differently in different organizations. This divided representation among directors is omnipresent in management literature: "Management potential should be defined in terms of appropriate behavior, not in terms of personality traits. Candidates should be assessed on the basis of how they are likely to manage a situation in the future" (Badawy 1983).

CORE PRINCIPLES FOR THE MANAGEMENT OF EXECUTIVES

We share with other authors (Potts and Sykes 1993) the conviction that there are generally four core conditions central to the successful integration of a system for managing the fast track within company strategy: (1) a clear strategy communicated to the lower levels, (2) an underlying company culture, (3) the perception that managing executives is a strategic priority, and (4) the credibility of the human resources approach in general. We draw attention to several points in the discussion that follows.

Recruitment

In the case of experienced executives over age thirty, recruiting a senior manager for his or her potential can be a specific objective in the case of certain highly specialized professionals; alternatively, the company may not have been able to constitute a sufficient internal pool of potential. Potential is easier to detect within this group, and previous successful experiences are a good indication of behavior. Recruiting a higher-level executive from outside often indicates the aim to acquire proven managerial potential or to increase the choice of candidates for renewing the team of directors.

Performance Assessment

It is important to remember here that potential cannot be deduced merely on the basis of a yearly assessment. Yearly results do, however, provide several indicators for evaluating how the executive's potential has been inhibited or displayed. When fixing objectives for the year to come, the human resources team should confer on executives missions that are challenging and allow them to confirm their potential.

Remuneration

Should fast-track executives be remunerated differently? In other words, should potential be rewarded in anticipation of expected achievements? The large majority of international companies we interviewed argued against this policy, generally giving the following reasons. First, such executives receive, de facto, indirect nonfinancial advantages, if only through the variety and quality of posts they are offered (Aggarwal 1991). In addition, if they succeed, the average length of time they spend in a position is shorter, allowing more rapid attainment of higher remuneration.

Training and Career Development

The issue of training and career development has been the subject of many articles, and management specialists insist on the need to develop specific support systems (O'Neal and Thomas 1996). Developing the fast-track group is one of the first issues the management board considers in terms of maximizing shareholders' profits (Pearson 1989). It is also presented as one of general management's special missions that "the president must not delegate to human resource specialist, or to inferiors" (Kovach 1986, 41).

The reality of the career derailment of fast-track managers is insufficiently explored within the literature and within organizations. The reality is harsh: "The behaviors that lead to success in the first years are also those that lead to failure at the end of a career" (Kovach 1986, 41). Fast-track career derailment is almost a taboo issue (Powell and Butterfield 1994); our interviews with the directors of "failed" executives and with the executives themselves point to the need to support these managers "condemned to succeed"—who are often feared—when they fail because they may transmit their failure or ill luck to those around them.

INDIVIDUAL CHARACTERISTICS OF THE FAST-TRACK MANAGER

Personal Aspects of the Fast-Track Manager

Are there generic skills, common to several companies, that allow us to characterize a fast-track manager? Experts agree on a two-part answer: on the one hand, certain skills common to all companies have been identified, but another, more specific group of skills should not be ignored because they reinforce the first kind. Thus, with Dulewicz (1989), we suggest that at a comparable executive level, two-thirds[2] of the sought-after skills are generic, whereas the re-

Table 17.2
Generic Skills Required of a Fast-Track Executive

A) INTELLECTUAL:
  • Decision making
  • Capacity for analysis and synthesis (helicopter view)
  • Capacity for organization and anticipation

B) INTERPERSONAL:
  • Human relations
  • Leadership
  • Self-organization
  • Delegation
  • Written and verbal communication
  • Mobilization of new information technology

C) ADAPTATION:
  • Flexible behavior
  • Resistance to stress
  • Originality
  • Visionary and pragmatic use of new information and communication technologies

D) ATTAINMENT OF RESULTS:
  • Energy
  • Initiative and innovation
  • Control
  • Global potential

---

mainder are specific to a given company. It is not reasonable to contend that there exist as many different definitions and criteria for managerial potential as there exist companies (the "all-specific" approach is illusory and if correct implies the rapid demise of management training). In parallel, specialists agree that the proportion of generic skills increases with the level of managerial responsibilities. The higher one rises in the hierarchy, the more transferability of skills and experience can go into action. We illustrate our point with Table 17.2, which sets out the characteristic qualities of the fast-track manager.

The generic skills (Lévy-Leboyer 1996) required of higher and managerial executives such as those Thornton and Byham (1982) studied are communication (oral, written), analysis and attention to problems (intra- and interorganization), scheduling and organization, delegation, control, development of inferiors, sensitivity, authority, tenacity, negotiation, analytical mind, judgment, creativity, risk taking, decision-making capacity, energy, diverse centers of interest, initiative, resistance to stress, adaptability, independence, and motivation.

In terms of personality, studies confirm that their locus of control[3] correlates with their need for achievement: "Those with an internal locus of control seem to have a greater need for success than those with an external locus of control" (Hellriegel, Slocum, and Woodman 1983, 69). In the 1970s, McClelland developed a theory of motivation on the basis of attaining objectives and defined the profile of the high achiever. His empirical work uncovered three major characteristics common to such exceptional executives:

- They prefer fixing their own objectives rather than having them fixed by someone else; they want to be as close as possible to the success of the project, accepting the risks with the rewards.
- They avoid extremes of difficulty, rejecting objectives perceived as too simple, as well as missions that they consider impossible in relation to their present skills and capacity; objectives are seen as challenges.
- They prefer objectives with frequent opportunities for feedback; given the high stakes involved, they need to understand their progress and be able to correct their maneuvers in midroute.

A METHODOLOGICAL GUIDE FOR DEVELOPING A SYSTEM FOR MANAGING FAST-TRACK EXECUTIVES

As we have seen, developing a policy for managing executive potential cannot be reduced to the choice of such or such tool "that has proved itself" in some well-known international company or other. If no such predetermined system exists, a made-to-measure system for managing such potential can nevertheless be constructed by considering the responses of the general direction to a certain number of questions raised throughout this chapter. We summarize these questions in Table 17.3.

THE FAST-TRACK DYNAMIC IN MAJOR EUROPEAN COMPANIES

We analyzed practices in major European companies to consider the career and potential management dynamic utilizing two data sources:

- Quantitative data from the Cranet[4] network, on which we collaborated (a postal survey of over seven thousand companies with more than two hundred employees)
- Qualitative data from research on human resources management themes in major European companies (Point 2001)

QUANTITATIVE APPROACH TO FAST-TRACK MANAGEMENT IN COMPANIES

Table 17.4 highlights the main practices of European companies in terms of management of the fast-track and careers. The information it presents leads to several observations:

1. Roughly a third of European companies claim to have a system for managing fast-track potential; France, followed by Sweden and Norway, is the country where com-

Table 17.3
Guide for Developing Policy

QUESTIONS TO BE ASKED WHEN DEVELOPING A POLICY FOR MANAGING FAST-TRACK EXECUTIVES: METHODOLOGICAL GUIDE

STRATEGIES, STRUCTURES, CULTURES
- What are the main company characteristics (size, shareholders, sector of activity)?
- What is the company's strategic orientation?
- What is the expected evolution of the immediate periphery of the organization (fusion, acquisitions, cession, company takeover, networking with other companies)?
- What catchment area exists for fast-track executives?
- What are the characteristics of the organizational structure (functional, divisional)?
- Does the company operate within an international environment? What are the stages of its internationalization (number of branches)?
- What are the major traits of company culture?
- Is respect for company culture more dominant than respect for national cultures?

HUMAN RESOURCE MANAGEMENT PHILOSOPHY AND PRINCIPLES
- What is the basis of management of executives (instrumental model, management of contradictions where the individual is the key actor in his own success)?
- What are the roles of key factors for detection and development? What role is reserved for directors and superiors (coaching, mentoring)?
- To what degree are executives' personal projects respected?
- To what degree should tools be formalized? To what degree should variety in managerial procedures in different countries be respected?

PHILOSOPHY AND PRINCIPLES BEHIND MANAGING THE FAST TRACK
- What are the target populations (only directors, lower executive levels)?
- What objectives are at stake in the development of a policy for managing the fast track?
- How is potential defined? Do all agree? Why?
- What is the relevant piloting level for detection and development (specialized headquarters department, local human resource manager, branch director, division)?
- On what information system should management of executives rely?
- How do the tools, management processes, and other elements of fast-track management combine (remuneration, evaluation of performance)?
- Is there (and should there be) a career committee?
- To what degree should the system be transparent and communication open? What about secret lists?
- What systems are planned for audits and adjustments over time?

panies are the most concerned about the issue; Germany, where the concept of an elite is controversial, is much less preoccupied by it.

2. Human resources management policies are generally written in Nordic and Anglo-Saxon countries, compared to Latin countries, where they are not committed to paper.

3. The planning horizon for human resource policy has gradually decreased. For around 40 percent of companies, it is generally less than one year. For 20 percent the horizon continues to be over two years. Planning tends to be shorter-term in Italy and in Latin countries generally. Depending on the reader's cultural origins, this can be interpreted either as an indication of increased flexibility or as the sign of bad provisional planning.

4. Recruitment of top management has dual characteristics in Europe: whereas for half of the companies, top management mainly comes from within (less than 30 percent of representatives recruited externally), there is also a move toward wide-scale external recruitment for top management. There are two opposing currents: in Switzerland and Germany, directors are generally recruited internally, whereas in Denmark and Norway, there is greater permeability with the outside and more top managers are recruited externally. France is untypical with an almost bimodal distribution: companies where a career is pursued internally and companies where executives often change employers are both greater than the European norm.

5. In the majority of European countries, investment in training has tended to increase (60 percent claim to have made great efforts over the past three years). Information about the total spent on training is generally difficult to use, given fluctuations in legal requirements in the different countries. Whereas French countries are required to record all training expenses, in other countries training expenses are withdrawn directly from the profit centers and the human resources department is not necessarily informed.

6. In terms of career management, a yearly assessment is by far the most frequently used tool. With the exception of Denmark, 75 percent of companies regularly use this method in a structured way.

7. Other career management tools are less frequently used and reveal strongly marked national traditions:
   —Career plans are used on average in only 25 percent of companies, and especially in France (7 percent)
   —Career interviews are used very differently over Europe. Very little used in both Sweden and France (6 percent), the tool is much more frequently used in Britain (65 percent) and Denmark (66 percent).
   —Succession plans are well perceived by directors in Anglo-Saxon or Germanic countries but used less systematically in Latin countries.
   —Assessment centers (around 10 percent use) are most frequent in Britain (22 percent). In other countries, they are unknown or fail to inspire confidence. Despite the numerous advantages they present in terms of polyvalence and familiarization with different work contexts, planned post rotation for executives is rarely used in over 20 percent of cases: rotation occurs but is more a result of short-term opportunities.
   —Except in the Netherlands (29 percent) and Sweden (24 percent), missions for developing executives abroad are as yet little used by European firms; some experts consider that the economic and travel crisis that accompanied the Gulf War put an end to the process, which started up again in the 1990s.

Table 17.4
Cross-Cultural Fast-Track Comparisons

	PERCENTAGE									
	DK	N	S	UK	F	Sp	I	G	NL	Sw
Systems for managing high potential are nonexistent	28	38	41	29	**44**	39	28	**21**	24	33
Systems for managing high potential exist	72	62	59	71	**56**	61	72	**79**	76	67
The human resource director is a member of the board of directors	53	67	**87**	47	83	80	**18**	19	44	58
The human resource director is not a member of the board	47	33	**13**	53	17	20	**82**	81	56	42
The human resource policy is committed to paper	61	**74**	68	45	29	40	33	**20**	54	58
The human resource policy is not committed to paper	22	**16**	23	27	**46**	40	40	43	30	32
There is no human resource policy	14	**6**	10	22	17	15	11	**32**	12	9
The human resource planning horizon policy is less than 1 year	**22**	36	44	45	47	52	**64**	39	35	41
The human resource planning horizon is between 1 and 2 years	**35**	29	31	29	30	33	**23**	**23**	**35**	33
The human resource planning horizon is over 2 years	**21**	**21**	20	20	16	9	**8**	20	16	20
Human resource planning is nonexistent	**13**	11	**3**	6	5	6	5	5	11	4
Directors' posts are generally filled internally	67	48	46	**78**	58	58	64	**39**	68	66
Directors' posts are generally filled externally	33	52	54	**22**	42	42	36	**61**	32	34
Vacancies for directors' posts are published externally	**85**	83	82	81	**85**	39	**32**	79	70	82
Vacancies for directors' posts are not published externally	**15**	17	18	19	**15**	61	**68**	21	30	18
Less than 30% of directors are recruited externally	**35**	39	56	59	43	55	54	63	40	**66**
Between 30% and 60% of directors are recruited externally	23	25	22	25	25	18	18	**15**	**30**	26
More than 60% of directors are recruited externally	**40**	34	16	13	28	16	22	15	31	**5**
Less than 1% of the payroll is put aside for training	34	45	28	31	**3**	**50**	**50**	35	33	35
Between 1% and 2% of the payroll is put aside for training	**32**	**18**	29	31	22	26	26	**32**	29

256

	DK	N	S	UK	F	Sp	I	G	NL	Sw
Between 2% and 4% of the payroll is put aside for training	20	17	19	21	**43**	**14**	15	24	20	26
More than 4% of the payroll is put aside for training	13	19	25	18	**32**	10	**9**	16	16	11
Executive training programs have declined over the past 3 years	**51**	70	66	64	61	62	61	63	**74**	
Executive training programs have increased over the past 3 years	**49**	30	34	36	39	38	39	37	**26**	
Use of career plans	13	12	22	27	**7**	28	**34**	12	24	20
Career plans not used	87	88	78	73	**93**	72	**66**	88	76	80
Use of assessment interviews for career management	**29**	63	**90**	84	56	49	76	58	87	84
Limited use of assessment interviews for career management	**71**	37	**10**	16	44	51	24	42	13	16
Use of career development interviews	**66**	11	**1**	55	6	32	34	40	37	65
Limited use of career development interviews	**34**	89	**99**	45	34	68	66	60	63	35
Use of assessment centers	4	**3**	11	**22**	5	11	10	9	10	13
Limited use of assessment centers	96	**97**	89	**78**	95	89	90	91	90	87
Succession planned	**11**	41	42	43	17	27	39	48	17	**50**
Succession not planned	**89**	59	58	57	83	73	61	52	83	**50**
Planned post rotation for executives' development	23	28	24	19	**8**	21	**32**	12	22	13
No planned post rotation for executives' development	77	71	76	81	**92**	79	**68**	88	78	87
Use of international missions for executive development	12	9	24	19	14	**1**	26	9	**29**	18
Absence of international missions for executive development	88	91	76	81	86	**99**	**74**	91	80	82

Note: DK = Denmark, N = Norway, S = Sweden, UK = United Kingdom, F = France, Sp = Spain, I = Italy, G = Germany, NL = Netherlands, Sw = Switzerland.

Boldface numbers indicate the maximum and minimum figure for each line.

QUALITATIVE APPROACH TO ANNUAL REPORTS IN MAJOR EUROPEAN COMPANIES

Point's research (2001) was based on eighty-six annual reports[5] corresponding to French, German, or British firms. All belonged to the industrial sector and were among the leaders within their sector. In the sample 10 percent of companies directly addressed the issue of fast-track executives through detection and development systems set up for their "top-flight executives." Within the annual reports, German companies address the issue most frequently, and French and German firms insist on the international vocation of fast-track managers.

French Companies

According to Point (2001), Bull and Danone closely associate the idea of potential with the international. Bull's[6] "promising managers" and Danone's "young promising executives" are encouraged to deepen their experience internationally and to be highly mobile. Bull developed its itinerant program (in several European capitals) in 1996; sixty participants from all over the world are involved with the aim of developing a more "customer-centric" approach.

British Companies

Less expansive on the subject, British companies mainly discuss management tools. The BOC group mentions "systematic use of succession plans for senior management positions" and "necessary measures for regularly nurturing the organization of fast-track executives." The BTR group talks of the success of its Developing Executive Potential (DEP) program as a "system for developing young executives with potential." Pilkington has chosen the "Advanced Management Workshop" to help those already occupying senior management positions.

German Companies

Of the countries considered in the study, Germany most commonly has a system in its companies that specifies company philosophy and practices. Heidelberg presents its strategy for managing executive potential as being intimately linked with the strategic planning of "individual tailor-made development programs." The investment goes as far as to organize twelve-month programs for young executives from subsidiaries or from the German structure. At Krupp, the executive board boasts of "directly managing the careers of senior managers and young executives with well-over average potential." Metallgesellschaft has developed a Manager Development Committee, as well as an International Managers' Network, which regularly meets the Board of Directors. VEBA is proud of the way it "analyzes executive potential and redeploys them strategically"; Volkswagen has invested heavily in its Junior Management Program with the aim of identifying potential linked to technical, social, and economic aspects.

CONCLUSION

From a practical point of view, we happily adopt an idea from Potts and Sykes (1993) that was mentioned by several international human resource directors:

> The essential thing is first of all to create a culture within which individuals can clearly and realistically perceive their strengths and limitations in management, benefiting all the while from recognition of the added-value they bring to the organization, and without being led to feel they have failed if they decide not to compete for the most senior positions. (Potts and Sykes 1993, 144)

The fast-track issue can be summed up in two aspects: detection and development. If the first continues to be marked by national culture (even if that is gradually fading), one notes that development processes are largely the same throughout the major companies.

Old World Europe is beginning to adopt international management, and traditional career management systems are imploding. Generally, one distinguishes three types of organization:

- The public sector or the parapublic sector, which seems unaffected by change. In countries like France, the careers of top civil servants are still attached to concepts dating from the nineteenth century, only partially reviewed after the Second World War: civil servant status for life, limited allowance for individual performance, importance placed on length of career within the company. In some cases, one wonders about the capacity of the state to attract talent.
- International companies belonging to the "new economy and services" whose practices differ little from those of other international companies and for which the market regulates practice.
- The most affected are those from traditional sectors; they hesitate about an organized long-term career system and reject the idea of "mercenary managers" except for a very small percentage of experts. They see some of their competitors operating differently and are concerned with the changes they would have to apply to change models.

In all cases, public and commercial organizations have needed to structure themselves and find themselves a management elite. This beginning of the twenty-first century sees us at the threshold of a new paradigm, which overthrows the traditional foundations of power (social reproduction, in-house managers, legitimacy by the number of subordinates, national influence networks).

NOTES

1. In the sense of Iles's (1997) resource-based view.
2. This is of course a global figure, not a precise dosage to be achieved at all costs.
3. We invite the reader to whom this concept is unfamiliar to consider the issue more closely. An individual with an external locus of control will tend to impute problems to others, whereas a person with an inner locus of control is more likely to feel guilt.
4. Cranfield School of Management/EM Lyon and the Association Nationale des Directeurs et cadres de la Fonetion Personnel (ANDCP).
5. For the years 1997 or 1998.
6. Cf. the Bull Executive Advanced Management (BEAM) Programme.

REFERENCES

Aggarwal, S. 1991. Rewarding top managers for company's success. *Journal of General Management* (1):80–89.

Badawy, M. 1983. Managing career transitions. *Research Management* (July–August): 28–31.

Bailyn, L., J. Fletcher, and D. Kolb. (1997). Unexpected connections: Considering employees' personal lives can revitalize your business. *Sloan Management Review* (Summer): 11–19.

Clark, F. 1992. *Total career management*. Maidenhead: McGraw-Hill.

Dulewicz, V. 1989. Assessment centres as the route to competence. *Personnel Management* (November): 56–59.

Hellriegel, D., J. Slocum, and R. Woodman. 1983. *Organizational behavior*, 3d ed. New York: West Publishing.

Iles, P. 1997. Sustainable high-potential career development: A resource-based view. *Career Development International* 2(7): 347–353.

Kovach, B. 1986. The derailment of fast track managers. *Organizational Dynamics* 15(2): 41–48.

Lévy-Leboyer, C. 1996. *La gestion des compétences*. Paris, Editions d'organisation.

Michel, J., and D. Hambrick. (1992). Diversification posture and top management team characteristics. *Academy of Management Journal* 35(1):9–37.

Moorby, E. 1994. In A. Mumford, ed., *Handbook of Management Development*, 4th ed. Aldershot: Gower.

O'Neal, D., and H. Thomas. 1996. Developing the strategic board. *Long Range Planning* 29(3):314–327.

Pearson, A. 1989. Six basics for general managers. *Harvard Business Review*. IL: 67(4): 94–101.

Point, S. 2001. Annual company reports in Europe and the HR Dimension. Ph.D. diss. in Management. Université Lyon III, Lyon, France.

Potts, T., and A. Sykes. 1993. *Executive talent—How to identify the best*. Homewood, IL: Business One Irwin.

Powell, G., and D. Butterfield. 1994. Investigating the glass ceiling phenomenon: An empirical study of actual promotions to top management. *Academy of Management Journal* 37(1):68–86.

Thornton, G., and W. Byham. 1982. *Assessment center and management performance*. New York: Academic Press.

Perspectives from a Clinical Psychologist

Sylvie Roussillon

More often than not, psychological analysts investigate people's qualities, characteristics, aptitudes, capacities, and personalities. Their various topologies allow us to identify and categorize these elements and often to understand and even anticipate behavior. This scientific and experimental process attempts to differentiate behavior and attitudes while suggesting their relevant variations and validating their statistically significant deviations.

A clinical approach (that is, one based on observing and understanding an individual in a given situation) suggests concepts that describe and explain individuals' psychological mechanisms for interacting with the world. Therefore, the methods of clinical observation one chooses are vital to the outcome of the research. These choices should be made carefully—whether between independent introspection and professionally guided introspection (e.g., personal development coaching); between simple observation and observation with the use of technical tools, such as video recordings and experiments calculated to reveal a particular psychic or mental activity; or among the diverse methods of theorizing on therapeutic and educational operations. The processes are many, and the fact that their results often seem to contradict suggests the possibility of using the conclusions deduced in other fields besides management.

Since the science of management is also one of action, and since the theory of human resource management concerns action "on," "with," and "by" people (and sometimes "for" people), it is necessary to understand how individuals function. This understanding is even more vital in the training of future managers who will need to act strategically with real people, not with statistically interchangeable actors. In a broader context, how can we contribute to the development of an executive whom the firm sees as promising and potentially useful? And on an even more general scale, how can we ensure the skill development of the entire staff?

Without careful recruitment of "promising" individuals, one must question the efficacy of aiming explicitly to develop employees and prepare them for future leadership responsibilities. The issue then concerns the influence of the environment on individual behavior and learning mechanisms (particularly social skills), and the comparison of these phenomena with past experiences and real-world situations.

Here we use this way of understanding the interactions between one's psychological mechanisms and the external environment (people, events, actions, etc.) to suggest ideas that will help directors to observe and develop employees more effectively. Indeed, psychology is not restricted to the simple analysis of one's mental workings. Instead, in this chapter it seems essential to concentrate on the relations and influential shaping forces that individuals, groups, and institutions have in common.

In identifying, preparing, and managing highly promising executives, three important questions surface. These issues are pertinent to the manager and psychologist alike. And they are relevant regardless of which skills are being developed—managerial or professional, specialized, or general.

Innate versus acquired potential: what is the specific nature of the potential we seek to recognize? What exactly is the unlearned, innate potential that distinguishes some individuals? Are some people "born leaders," destined to lead in every situation and circumstance, or would a process of learning and experience allow each of us to become a leader? Is good leadership a changeless skill, or does the best method of leadership vary according to situation and context? Which leader is the right one for a given situation?

The nature of environmental influence: what does it comprise, and what are its limits? How do training and experience influence identity in both adulthood and childhood? How can we describe the process at work? How can we shape these processes to work efficiently for a firm with unique characteristics and a specific plan for the future?

The ever-present gap between workers' conscious desires and their real experiences: what is the possibility of controlling this process? How can we manage the discrepancy between a voluntary strategy and its involuntary effects, the former accompanied by choices and conscious action, the latter potentially adverse and subconscious?

First, we examine the essential elements of "high potential" in light of our contact with human resource managers and directors. Then we investigate certain authors' claims concerning the subconscious motivation of men and women in power. These motivations, when distinguished from the traditional list of recommended qualities and skills, give evidence for the command that subconscious desires have over individuals.

Second, we investigate organizational dynamics. Although this is not exactly "the organizational unconscious," it must be admitted that the existence and effects of organizational dynamics are not entirely the result of conscious and deliberate effort. After our study of organizational dynamics, we recall certain classic psychological mechanisms that profoundly influence high-potential executives.

Finally, we reflect on the development of professional identity and on the main mechanisms advancing this process. We also study the different forms of organizational training calculated to expedite the executive's professional development.

THE CONCEPT OF THE HIGH-POTENTIAL EXECUTIVE

In ancient history the Roman republic organized the *Cursus Honorum*, an ordered progression of magistrates who selected and trained future leaders of the state. Timeless indeed is the preoccupation with identifying and preparing leaders! The ancients had recognized the necessity to define the qualities expected of leaders, the stages in leadership development, and the rules for competing for power.

But what is "potential," and how is it best evaluated?

Over the last few years, during the contemporary "development of the business paradigm," France has experienced a profound change in companies' expectations regarding both managers and the difficulty of anticipating managerial problems and success. In such an uncertain environment, how is it possible to devise a process guaranteeing the development of high-potential executives? Is there a specific set of preferred psychological characteristics that could be recognized in managers and instill in new trainees?

What Is Potential?

It is odd that the notion of high potential is rarely contrasted with the notion of low potential; instead, high potential is distinguished from average potential, a comparison that excludes a whole facet of the issue. Likewise, the nature of potential is never explicitly specified: potential for what? potential to do what? These omissions make one wonder what elements are implicit in the notion of high potential. I offer five of these elements for examination.

First, the notion of potential implies a comparison between theoretically similar individuals. This comparison set in motion a selective process based on a company's specific criteria and modality. But this selection does not reflect the ability to take on a job (as does the recruiting selection); nor does it consider personal qualities and skills (as do evaluation and most promotion processes). Rather, it directly judges individuals by a framework of subtle but indispensable comparisons. Indeed, the potential most discussed (albeit implicitly) is the potential for management, or the *potential for progress* in the firm toward positions of responsibility. At a social gathering, an executive from a leading French bank offered this very precise definition: "For us, potential is the capacity of an individual to move forward two steps according to the Hay principle, in three years."

Such a discerning selection cannot be achieved simply by examining an applicant's credentials. The selection is made by observing and inferring qualities and capacities that, though presently untested, will be demonstrated in real-life situations. The tools and methods used in the selection process may be the following:

1. "Objective" methods: tests, questionnaires, simulations, training or skill assessment centers

2. Direct observation: evaluation of career interviews

3. Unobtrusive measures noting the prominence of applicants' roles in career committees, replacement organization charts, and other executive reviews in the course of which certain names recur

Second, all these methods involve the comparison of concrete observation, and in doing so, they are thought to reveal personal attributes that characterize potential. But the various levels of potential will be fully recognized only later, when applicants encounter external conditions that spotlight this *natural ability*. It should be noted that the choices made in these selection situations cannot be validated scientifically. From a practical point of view, the firm must have access to the right managers at the right time, even if others who might have achieved the same results are rejected.

Third, this potential concerns the very *essence of the person*; an individual has either great potential or little potential. Plus, high potential cannot be learned or acquired—otherwise, effective training and development would be enough to endow an individual with potential. High potential must be innate in an individual; it is considered to have been present in junior executives since adolescence or childhood. It allows them to assume the responsibilities of management better than others would. But this innate distinctive talent needs to be unearthed before it can be developed.

Fourth, in order to be recognized, potential must be *observable and quantifiable* on a scale that differentiates and classifies individuals. The indispensable quality of high potential must be specifically identified so that an aptitude for responsibility may be developed. In this sense, a managerial role can be learned—but only if the individual already has the necessary potential. Perhaps this potential is essentially the ability to learn, particularly by experience. But natural, innate aptitudes, including potential, would characterize a high potential who is not necessarily someone with significant acquired ability.

Finally, managerial qualities and skills, both acquired and innate, are *revealed* only through real-life situations. They are of a different nature than the qualities junior executives exhibit in certain situations. Behavior during the first part of one's career, therefore, is not sufficient to show whether one will be able to

Table 18.1
Assessing Competencies

CONCEPT HIDDEN/INFERRED	BEHAVIORAL COMPETENCIES	HOW TO OBSERVE
Potential Capacity Aptitude Factors Personality	General knowledge/skills Cross-boundary expertise Transfer across areas Social Specific tendencies Technical	Behavior Demonstrated expertise Demonstrated performance Results Personality traits Character

assume higher responsibilities successfully, this initial experience is often considered insufficient in itself, but nonetheless indispensable. Precise, organized observation of various people and situations indicates the necessity to define required potential by distinguishing the qualities expected of future leaders from those exhibited by a manager with more modest responsibilities.

Potential, Competence, Capacity, Aptitudes—Similar Notions

In psychology, the notion of competence is similar to that of potential in that it is different from actual performance: the competence of a baby (Brazelton and Als 1981) is its current capacity to adapt its behavior to fill its needs, particularly through interaction with its mother. Linguistic competence is defined as the capacity to understand and produce correct statements. Performance (Chomsky 1971), on the other hand, is the utilization of this competence.

The terms *aptitude* and *capacity* have long been used as having a similar meaning in psychology, even if *competence* is more common today. For M. Reuchlin (1991), aptitude is "a dimension according to which studied individuals are distinguished according to their behavior." This very general definition refers mainly to "cognitive characteristics responsible for the acquisition and processing of information" (Aubert et al. 1993, 22). The inference of characteristics that are probably already present can explain behavior observed in natural or experimental situations, but the notion of aptitude refers rather to the mental and cognitive mechanisms considered invariably to underlie capacities and behavior. Only if the corresponding aptitudes are present is it possible for a suggested behavior pattern to be acquired and developed.

Let us briefly consider these concepts across three levels that, though fundamentally distinct, are interrelated. Table 18.1 helps to understand how they are used psychologically and organizationally. High-level performance, as well as successful behavior in either natural or experimental situations, are considered an indicator that the individual exhibiting them has the necessary competence. Competence has a complex makeup that is not just manifested in an action—

which is finalized and temporary in consequence, but innate to a person (Aubert et al. 1993). This fact allows us to draw a sketch of competence based on its effects. High potential therefore

1. leads to *behavior* that exhibits leadership qualities
2. leads to team leader *ability* (on a more general level)
3. attracts communicational and organizational *capacities*
4. considers the sign of managerial *potential*

Individuals' potential, whether general or specific (for a certain project, job, field, etc.), can therefore be inferred from the aspects of their behavior and from signs of possessing capacities and competencies. A series of relationships logically follows:

X (behavior) is the sign of Y (potential), or

Y (potential) implies observation of X (behavior)

For example, brilliant results are the sign of great potential, or someone with real potential will obtain brilliant results.

More precisely, fast, outstanding results can be considered signs of a greater capacity for vision, influence, initiative, and other characteristics. These qualities themselves imply potential for self-confidence and composure under pressure, which are considered perhaps the most indispensable and distinctive characteristics of a manager!

Thus a whole network of inferences and graded scales is set up and implemented in many real-world business situations. In the firm, this collective and often implicit structure is developed from previous experience—that is, from the cause-and-effect relationships observed in previous monitored experiments. Obviously these cause-and-effect models depend on a shared culture within the firm or preconceptions about management on the firm's division of power and on its envisioned future. Ultimately they contribute to the unity of the human group that constitutes and expresses the firm.

This culturally and ideologically charged measurement system reveals significant employee differences and even more so between people of diverse backgrounds (nationality, profession, company, etc.). It may be observed that these differences are positive—that they give rise to a variety of skills for effective management (as other chapters amply demonstrate country by country). Even more often, however, these differences are directly related to the inferred links among potential, competence, and behavior.

Potential for Which Skills?

As jobs grow more complex, it becomes more difficult to specify the aptitudes and personality traits necessary for them. So we define these characteristics as *skills*. Skills concern "the integrated use of aptitudes and personality traits, and also acquired knowledge, in order to complete a complex mission." (Lévy-Leboyer 1996, 26).

If expected managerial skills are explained in detail at the time a new manager arrives, the new employees' operational definition of potential will be clearer and the development of personal potential will be facilitated. However, experience shows that it is difficult to refer to management as clear-cut "profession"; its skill requirements vary with the firm, market, social group, and circumstance.

Numerous businesses' experiences during the 1980s show that predictions of companies' future needs are inaccurate. Therefore, managers need to be competent in unanticipated situations. The evolution of management and technology, the flat corporate structures obtained by removing whole levels of management, and project management are all factors in this unpredictability, as is the international and cross-functional effort needed to confront intense competition and market globalization.

Many firms found that newly installed high-potential managers were unprepared for their responsibilities—despite having received high-quality generic training for effectiveness within hierarchical organizations. The new employees lacked autonomy, global vision, creativity, contact with the clients, capacity for risk taking, understanding of contradictory interactions within systems, communication and delegation skills, and ability to integrate their own leadership with new technology. These numerous complaints partly explain the current trend to establish in-house "business schools" and other managerial training programs. The emphasis of these new programs is on collective apprenticeship in new methods of management and leadership.

Moreover, these training strategies are considered to be flexible and subject to innovation; the human resource managers we interviewed admitted their inability to predict the characteristics of effective future managers. This leads us to question all fixed criteria for evaluating potential.

Certain well-known authors, through observation and analysis of real management experience, have attempted to define potential. They have identified some of its aspects, including the potential to adapt to different situations, learning potential, and innate potential in the form of talents and personal characteristics. Such attempts have too often resulted in impressive lists of qualities that do more to prescribe an image of the perfect manager than to identify executives with potential. Furthermore, it should be noted that this version of potential has more to do with an individual's personality than with technical knowledge and managerial skill.

Increasingly, firms are seeking competitive advantages and sources of productivity through revising their organization and management styles. Such organizational development encourages small, autonomous, responsible, appropriately skilled units. These units are expected to collaborate with parties both inside and outside the firm, drawing together specialists from various disciplines to work on a common goal. Needless to say, these units should not be managed in the style reserved for bureaucratic monoliths.

Skills that are linked to individual personality are much more important in an evolving firm than in a traditional organization. They require personal stability, self-knowledge, recognition of personal limits, and capacity to complete an individual project. Employees are questioned on their ability to cope with stress, contradictions, and paradoxical situations—all of which are generated by an evolving management structure.

Individuals' level of potential is too often considered to be one-dimensional. Rather, we should identify subcategories of potential that could contribute to success in certain fields. For instance, a particular type of potential is essential to success as a top-level athlete, and another type is necessary for success as a concert pianist. Potential may also be judged according to the level of position one may attain. We might ask, "Do you have the potential of a department manager or that of a director?" and "Are you just a good player, or are you a future world champion?"

If effort is necessary to realize potential, then how much effort is required for potential at high levels? It varies according to external factors and individual values. For example, as current statistics affirm, it is more difficult for a woman to attain a top executive or managerial position than it is a man of comparable potential.

Therefore, in order to evaluate and predict progress, potential should be analyzed according to three complementary factors:

1. The level of potential: how far will it take those who possess it?
2. The nature of potential: potential for what?
3. The cost of its realization: how much effort is required to develop this potential?

The Unintended Consequences of an Obligation for Excellence

The individual and collective excellence prescribed by so many company charters puts more pressure on a high-potential executive than on any other manager. The high-potential executive is permanently confronted with very high and changing standards, which are imposed by constant observation, evaluation, and high expectations and which demand displays of speed, accuracy, and skill. Furthermore, individuals with an unusually strong desire for recognition by the firm are especially sensitive to its injunctions and expectations.

The excellence in question is of an "exterior" nature: it consists of the customary compliance with the company's objectives, values (ideology, beliefs, and mode of management), and strategic choices. This definition of excellence has been greatly influenced by the interpretations proposed since Peters and Watermann (1983) and by a model based on sports competition. For Phillippe Perrenoud (1997), "Seeking excellence means going beyond our best, approaching perfection, conquering ourselves in the manner of the mountaineer who tries the highest peak, the athlete who tries to beat his personal best record, or the researcher or artist who wants to come closer to what he believes is truth or beauty."

This definition of excellence leads to continual competition with ourselves and others. Individuals are mobilized on a physical, sentimental, and cognitive level in their ongoing pursuit of superiority and improvement.

Organizations that propose such an ideology of excellence do so hoping to profit from the universal quest for self-realization. A firm's best high-potential executives, who are destined to work under the pressure of continual evaluation, are particularly affected by organized and programmed excellence. When upheld, this prescribed excellence has proved beneficial to both the firm and its employees. Employees build self-confidence, find pleasure and fulfillment, and construct good-quality human relationships—experiences that instill both a greater sense of firm loyalty and a renewed determination to strive for excellence. "It is the mobilization of relationships and loyalty for the company which produces the energy needed to compete more efficiently. The entire libido of the subject is solicited. This desire is channeled into productive objectives" (Aubert and Gaulejac 1991, 91).

This general compulsion to improve everything perpetually energizes the firm, leading individuals to adopt the firm's values and share its successes. In doing so, individuals see their achievements acknowledged by others and satisfy their desire for love and recognition. Afterward, individuals feel pressure to maintain this image of excellence, a pressure that can lead them to accept the price of being a high-potential (HIPO) employee. As other authors have remarked, these employees give up other interests, accept mobility and competition, and increase their work load (Derr 1987, 1988).

The firm reinforces the new link of loyalty by offering a host of incentives: salary raises, privileges, promises and promotion, financial security, feeling of power, and importance. Workers give themselves up for the firm, incorporating its objectives in their own ideals. They identify with the firm itself, live up to its expectations, and reflect its image.

It is conceivable that the efficacy of this system is even greater if the personalities involved are rather narcissistic—that is, if they recognize only vague boundaries between the self and the outside world (here, the organization and its demands). Such personalities have a continual need for personal reassurance, for identification with an ideal, and for a positive self-image. They then run the risk of pursuing, to the detriment of their real personality, an image that matches what the firm proposes. And the risk is all the greater when the firm's proposed image will likely change.

The fragility of the psychological condition becomes evident when employees can no longer follow this course to excellence, either because they have lost the constant support of or they can no longer meet the demands of the firm, or, as is often the case, they no longer possess the health and stamina to keep up the pace. This condition is observed particularly when changes in the firm's environment lead to a revision of managerial priorities and criteria for evaluating managers.

When multiple buyouts or changes in business strategy put the accepted characteristics of excellence in question, some executives, especially those hitherto considered as "high potential," find themselves faced with a distressing incongruity between the "real self" and the "ideal self." These executives find that they have been pursuing this ideal with neither objectivity nor real autonomy. Idealized self-perception that clashes with reality compounds a psychological weakness that can lead to the collapse of self-confidence. Freudenberger (1987) describes this "internal burnout": it destroys from the inside, leaving the victims without energy and zest for life. The victims of internal burnout then have severed all connections with their surroundings in a costly and alienating pursuit of imposed excellence.

The notion of excellence, when inculcated during a firm's selection and development of high-potential executives, exacerbates the narcissistic disparity between unfeigned personal values and idealized values proposed by external forces. J. F. Chanlat (1990) insists on the risk of fooling oneself and suggests developing personal values and attributes as an alternative to cultivating an ideal, conformed image. But what is the cost in company progress of allowing individuals to develop their own potential independently?

Managers' Psychological Characteristics

Leaving temporarily the subject of managerial evaluation, it may be pertinent to ask whether the evaluation of potential managers' psychological characteristics selects individuals with narcissistic tendencies, a strong need for reassurance, and inability to find a healthy degree of independence from the organization. Many firms, as they search for employees who fit a precise definition of excellence, present evidence that suggest this is so. It would be regrettable if the methods of evaluating high-potential executives favored only those individuals whose narcissistic fragility impeded their ability to evolve, innovate, and maintain independence.

If, as the chairman of the Boston Consulting Group claims, "what really separates productive firms from the others is the role played by their managers" (Hour and Carter 1995), it is essential both to understand the process used to select these managers and to identify the characteristics that make them so effective.

It has already been established that managers are influenced by a strong desire for power. Why do certain people desire positions of power more than others? Why are some prepared to invest so much energy in acquiring a managerial position? After all, such a position is accompanied by added responsibilities: an enormous work load, difficult decision making, personal sacrifice, and heated negotiation for the good of the firm, to name only a few issues. Surely, some would say, the greatest pleasures of life are freedom, interesting but nonexhausting work, and personal and professional investment that do not overwhelm one's values and talents. But all this is a far cry from the life-style of managerial responsibility.

The sources and systems of power are numerous, but they include few women in public administration and business. Women account for less than 10 percent of all high-potential executives (Bournois and Roussillon 1992) and less than 5 percent of top executives, board members, and directors in large French firms!

M. Berger's rather frighteningly titled work *The Hidden Madness of Men in Power* (1993) investigates the subconscious, psychological desire to exercise power over people and things. He aims for psychoanalytical understanding of political leaders when he says that "the despot is a madman who manages to share his vision of madness with others." The desire for power, says Berger, is the symptom of a narcissistic disease that leads one to abandon all other interests. He recognizes two characteristics of this behavior: "significant narcissistic fragility and excessive influence (on others)" (54). Such psychological fragility, or the often subconscious ultimatum, Be the best or be nothing, leads to hyperactivity and a constant need for reassurance. Questioning is extremely difficult in these circumstances and studying it is sensitive.

Hunger for power also has roots in childhood experiences. Children's lack of power over their environment can cause them as adults to desire influence over the people around them, thus perpetuating a problem-causing cycle. Finally, hoping to avoid future loneliness and powerlessness, these individuals commonly see to it that their subordinates rely upon them as much as possible.

Consequently, many people in power become perfectionists and acquire a mind-set that precludes admitting mistakes and accepting criticism; they generally avoid these unpleasant and humbling experiences by carefully manipulating facts and coworkers. This behavior certainly reinforces the common assumption that people in power are "killers."

Though reducing managerial qualities to a single subconscious dynamic can enable us to understand the way some organization and individuals work, they nonetheless should not be oversimplified. M. Kets de Vries and D. Miller (1985) have studied the extent to which the effect of power on managers' personalities impact the firm. For managers and companies alike, power acquisition can raise unsuspected problems—particularly narcissism.

The managerial characteristics recommended by experimentation are far from what narcissistic managers themselves believe to be important. Such managers seem ignorant even of qualities that are well established in the business community: self-questioning, cooperation, information sharing, development of collaboration skills, delegation (which implies power sharing), and negotiation (which can only exist if the other party's power is acknowledged).

F. Bournois (1996) reminds us of the importance that authors assign to managers' determination for power. This power enables them to control others and to impose their point of view on the rest of the firm.

So, there is a considerable discrepancy between tried-and-true managerial qualities and qualities that managers believe to be necessary (Bournois, Rome-laer, deMontmorillon 1996). Firms' administrations should therefore work to keep this discrepancy at a minimum.

Austin (1991) suggests that "to say is to do," referring to communication that itself effects an immediate change: "I baptize you," "I pronounce you man and wife," "I name you director," and so forth. By the same token, we could also assert that "to do is to say," since all actions and choices (such as salaries, transfers, or promotions) communicate what the firm and its managers see as valid. Thus, the firm communicates very effectively through its actions, reveal-ing information about subjects such as managerial expectations and company priorities.

These "hidden messages"—that is, communication not by words but by ac-tion—lead us to doubt that employees' real practices correlate with what their companies espouse. When a company's recently made promotions are analyzed on the basis of established criteria, the dichotomy between progressive vision (theory) and conservative, unchanging reality (practice) is often astonishing! But if we observe these acts and choices objectively, we find that it is often possible to discover patterns that constitute a measurable system.

Defending Poor Decisions

The fact that high-potential executive positions are fairly stable (with gener-ally less than 5 percent turnover per year [Beauvoise and Joule 1987; Beauvoise 1994]) suggests that people who choose the HIPOs tend to defend their initial criteria for future leader competencies (choices not influenced by force, threat, or promise of reward), even when new information prompts reconsideration. Such information, in these cases, is reinterpreted to suit the logic of the first choice.[1] Many manipulative techniques in business rest on these mechanisms, which ultimately constrain us to make choices we wrongly believe to be unaf-fected by external forces, rather than being part of a mesh that supports our original choice, even when it is more costly and less appropriate than we had at first thought.

Thus it is possible for high-potential executives' lack of results to be eclipsed by the positive results they obtain. The few positive results, in this situation, serve to confirm the executive's original decision. As for those considered to be of lesser potential, it is unlikely that they would possess the status and de-termination to follow through with poor decisions. Their positive results, if any existed, would not be sufficient to arouse the firm's forgiveness for the original lack of judgment. So, the relative permanence of high-potential executives is no longer a sign just that they are carefully selected, but also that those who selected them are determined to follow through with their decisions.

This idea is supported by the theory of cognitive dissonance (Festinger 1957). Experiments have shown that when acting against our beliefs and values, we find it easier to conform our opinions to our behavior than vice versa (for instance, it is easier to alter one's belief that smoking damages health than it is to quit smoking). In the same way, subjects who notice that evidence clashes with their beliefs generally prefer to modify the meaning of the facts in order to integrate them into their beliefs. The situation arises that directors and groups (career development offices), after erroneously designating a high-potential manager, alter performance evaluation criteria so as to confirm the choice and retain the manager on their list of chosen individuals—all in order to avoid degrading their own judgment!

So despite the apparent confidentiality of a firm's HIPO list and the desire to update it and redefine the criteria it uses regularly, as long as general company orientation and people in power remain stable, high-potential characteristics will be relatively unchanged. The group will remain the same. Those initially rejected will not have a chance to get on the list regardless of their performance or "late bloomer" potential.

Increasingly, high-potential firm managers are selected by groups (career development committees) of people accustomed to working with each other. In addition, a double effect is sparked by the rise of in-house schools, business universities, and prestigious training programs, which group high-potential executives into cohorts and networks. The aims of these programs are to establish networks, influence company culture, and introduce trainees to the culture and know-how of their trade.

Although training programs undoubtedly facilitate much sought-after transversality (cross-boundary spanning) and communication, they also help promote uniform values and behavior among high-potential managers, who feel pressured to conform to the company's wishes. Such movement toward homogenization of behavior and values neglects performance criteria and selection measures at each stage in favor of HIPO group names and values (conformity). This social cloning tends to produce less-diverse, less-adaptable individuals.

Since identifying high-potential executives requires such a significant investment, it would be profitable to analyze problem-causing psychosocial mechanisms as they relate to classic procedures for detecting and developing high-potential executives, but we could just as well have examined them in light of any other system that prepares managers.

The next section of the chapter further elaborates the psychological problems that develop in future leaders and attempts to deal with characteristic elements in constructing a professional identity, and with the psychological mechanisms necessary for developing potential.

THE CONSTRUCTION OF IDENTITY

Development of Personality and Adult Identity

Individuals constantly discover and build their identity throughout life by continually reexamining their history, external events, and internal developments. The professional and personal identity of a forty-five-year-old manager are not those of the junior executive she once was. The life cycle suggested by M. Kets de Vries (1985) describes the evolution of work-related needs, demands, and sources of satisfaction. The period from twenty-five to thirty years old is characterized by the shock of reality; between thirty and forty, by socialization and growth; between forty and fifty, by midlife crisis; and from fifty on, by acceptance and eventual retirement. But this proposed life cycle, however plausible, does not consider that work responsibilities change constantly.

Construction of a strong, coherent, and adaptable personal identity becomes more important as responsibilities grow and generate stress, and as a changing environment requires ceaseless adaptation to new subjects and new people.[2] Only a strong personal identity can effect coherent, flexible action while remaining free of pathological behavior patterns, such as the aforementioned personality disorders.

The feeling of identity rests on five elements:

1. Internal unity: The need for internal unity can lead individuals to avoid harboring certain incompatible behavior traits or at least to justify them by citing previously declared values. Individuals with true internal unity never shift their underlying values to fit the present situation, whatever the place or moment. Fortunately, unity can be increased and internal conflict abated through analysis of the past and planning for the future.

2. Uniqueness: Individuality is the second element of identity. Desire for it could lead more fragile personalities to a conscious attempt to stand out from the crowd. Recognizing one's unique qualities naturally involves recognizing one's limits and accepting others' diversity. A sense of uniqueness is essential in all cooperative actions, which by definition are based on self-perception and on admission of one's own failings.

3. Similarity: Identity also links us with others as we develop mutual understanding and a real feeling of belonging to a group or community. A knowledge of one's similarity to others contributes to effective communication.

4. Continuity in time: A stable sense of identity is continuous over time—despite crises, break-ups, and new developments.

5. Ability to act: Finally, identity is defined by one's perceived ability to act, determined by previous accomplishments. The results that individuals manage to obtain are fundamental to self-image and self-esteem. This feeling is very different from childish omnipotence, which is always susceptible to failure.

So, a rapid succession of tasks does not lead to an accurate evaluation of results. The obligation to act under the pressure of conflicting personal values and frequent team breakups hinders managers in their quest for self-knowledge. And self-knowledge, since it leads to a feeling of personal identity, is essential for developing self-confidence and efficiency.

Sociologists investigating the workplace describe types of collective identity.

Collective identity, which is essentially determined by professional or working situations that require interdependence, characterizes groups recognizable by members and outsiders alike. A group of directors, chief executives, or potential executives is artificial and sometimes purely administrative; however, with uniform treatment, similar training programs, and collective projects, the group can develop its own culture, values, and means of communication.

The collective identity can contribute to external signs of identity such as profession and salary, which in turn help to determine individual identity. The way executives (particularly future managers) and their careers are managed (i.e., through behavioral expectations and control of the way executives gain experience) can encourage the forming of relatively homogeneous professional groups.

A uniform professional identity is shaped by elements of the executive environment. These include common experiences and projects, interpersonal ties, fulfilled expectations and roles, and distinction from the crowd.

In addition, executives' desire to belong to a certain group (i.e., a group of directors) prods them to acquire the behavior and characteristics of that group. The more attractive the group, the greater the pressure to conform to it. Individuals tend to model themselves after these groups' values, and in the end, their self-esteem is greatly influenced by the corresponding standards for prestige.

At this point, it is pertinent to examine the psychological mechanisms that contribute to the five elements of identity. We must also investigate the roles of authority figures (bosses and managers) and of the environment in developing self-image, self-confidence, and self-esteem—all of which are fundamental ingredients in identity.

Building Self-Confidence and Self-Esteem

Self-confidence develops throughout life (but particularly during childhood), usually through emotional experiences and through the influence of environment. The two elements of experience—environment and relations—serve both to classify each episode objectively and to measure its significance from the subject's point of view.

Affection from parents (especially mothers) helps small children discover their worth, the interest others have in them, and their very existence. This parental love is the root of the self-respect that engenders self-confidence, a sense of existence, and enthusiasm for life. Essentially, then, children depend on their environment and on their relationships with others. Furthermore, recent studies have shown that children sense this dependence: even infants actively solicit interaction with their entourage.

In conclusion, self-confidence is built on external opinions and on the self-image they help to create. But self-confidence is also bolstered by experimenting with one's capacity for creation and for influencing the outside world. Such capacity guarantees autonomy and self-reliance.

The enduring importance of others' regard and of one's own capacity to affect the environment is highly apparent in adult society—which includes the world of managerial development.

Taking Advantage of Others' Positive Opinions

When adults are questioned about the most influential people in their life, it is observed that others' opinions truly do build self-confidence. Subjects are affected by a number of factors, including the trust put in them, the importance placed on their opinions, and their overall feeling of worth. This confidence is manifested in both words and actions, particularly during demanding, educational situations. Therefore, the confidence a manager displays—perhaps despite inexperience and previous negative results—can be a fundamental element of progress.

It is a recognized fact that the first "boss" young manual laborers, technicians and executives work under influences the course of their career (Bandura 1970; Bernard 1992). Self-confidence and identity are constructed during this initial career phase, when young workers are particularly malleable.

Psychosociological experimentation on children and on commercial teams has demonstrated that this first authoritative opinion deeply affects workers' behavior and results. This phenomenon, dubbed the *Pygmalion effect* after the mythical sculptor, works on the same mechanisms of relational dependence that permit children to build self-confidence.

It is observed that many adults never move beyond this stage; they are confident, efficient, and satisfied only when others provide outside reinforcement. Thus being designated high-potential becomes for many a needed vote of confidence. Through it, many young executives feel confirmed in their ability to progress professionally and work closely with their respected bosses.

In such cases, the confidence shown by other individuals—even subordinates—can play a vital supporting role in protecting one's self-esteem and confidence. In this way, confidence begets self-confidence in a perpetual cycle of positive interactions. However, this interaction is also a source of vulnerability since the people involved are bound by pacts of conventions that are implicit in the relationship and not easily changed. This situation can both impede effective decision making and cause problems during changes that would offset the balance of these relations. It is only by seizing the reins of confidence that adults can take control of their surroundings and ultimately reinforce their autonomy.

So confidence is constructed through a process of finding and creating in which adults, like children, first decide what they need from their environment then find it. But adults differ from children in that they know how to manipulate their environment in order to bring about desired conditions. From childhood to adulthood, the techniques for developing this autonomy are acquired progressively.

Let us now illustrate the roles played by aggression and failure, both for the child within a group and for the confident, independent adult.

Aggression and Failure as Tests

Only periods of tension and conflict can prove that members of a group truly have common goals and values and are certain of their individual worth (Moscovici and Doise 1992). It is for this reason that groups based on an illusory absence of conflict and tension can never be efficient and many even engage in "group think" (Anzieu and Martin 1973).

People under this illusion believe their group to be the best, and its members all friendly and united. In reality, the group is based on the shared unconscious fear of destructive conflict followed by a breakup. This information in fantasy stamps our tension and divergence, which are seen as part of traitorous attempts to split the group.

In professional life, confidence-demonstrating conflict is often replaced by imminent failure. In other words, it is only when faced with failure that subjects can be sure of the real confidence bosses have in them.

Indeed, confidence is all too often believed to be something earned by positive acts and results. A manager's successful action certainly contributes to the confidence of all parties involved, particularly when it prompts the evaluator to adopt its underlying values. Still, though, a confidence-building action does not test the extent of this confidence.

Everyone knows that "you can't win 'em all." Despite firms' productivity, optimal conditions are sometimes never reached. For instance, if the workers one supervises live with constant internal tension and insecurity, believing they are worth only as much as their last success, a real relationship of personal trust with them is impossible, as is the development of their autonomy.

Surprisingly, divergence, confrontation, aggression, and failure do not always destroy confidence; rather they can serve as gateways to efficient revelation and experimentation. New people (directors, managers, human resource specialists, etc.) and new situations that high-potential executives encounter all contribute to the construction of personal identity and self-knowledge.

In this way, executives can judge to what extent employees should be confident, complementing the confidence that authority figures have in them. In addition to having value in educational processes, experience with failure is fundamental to self-confidence and intelligent risk taking—particularly when trusting other members of a delegation or when dealing with truly autonomous groups.

This construction of personal identity through experiences and encounters helps develop the generic and supplementary skills that managers depend upon when faced with the specifics of different types of power. Such abilities would include managing stress, time, emotions, and limits; setting personal values; making decisions and developing projects alone or in a team. In addition, while constructing a strong personal identity, one would develop interpersonal skills and ability to cooperate. One would learn the skills of conflict management, delegation, power, communication, and negotiation. One would become adept at handling situations that are mentally demanding, complex, uncertain, diverse, limiting, or stimulating.

The Social Learning Techniques

Social learning involves developing supplementary skills used for action and reacting in an ever-changing environment—either alone or with other people. We have already seen that such skills are essential to directors' personal development.

Just as varied formative situations contribute to the construction of self-image, high-potential executives shape their identity by interacting with those around them. We may consider these points concerning the mechanisms at play in this process:

Confronting varied and progressively weightier responsibilities encourages learning through trial and error. Feeling the pressure caused by diverse experience, executives put themselves to the test to invent new courses of action. This learning through action is indispensable but perhaps should not be practiced universally, since it is relatively costly in terms of time and risks.

One of the most frequently and spontaneously used tools for social learning is the positive and negative reinforcement of behavior. People and organizations alike use this system of rewards and sanctions to guide subjects toward a predetermined set of conditioned reflexes.

Company turnover gives executives the opportunity to learn from observing the practices of different bosses. This vicarious learning—education based on observing the results of others' actions—allows faster, risk-free learning. Executives can study other managers' actions, comparing them to their own values, spontaneous practices, project, and identity. In this process they recognize their personal identity.

Individuals' identification with reference groups is also a factor in "vicarious learning." Through these reference groups, subjects are socialized to copy thoughts and actions desired by their firm. Familiarity with job expectations facilitates the development of productive attitudes and enables new managers to practice their skills in real-world situations.

Retrospective analysis is a learning method applicable to many fields, such as coaching and mentoring by either close associates inside the firm or external professionals paid as counselors. This technique, a reexamination of experiences long past, often allows enough objectivity and emotional distance to increase subjects' self-knowledge. Establishing models for job-related expertise is one form of this *metacognition* whose impact on learning is examined later.

The Model for Personal Excellence of Managers in Training

It should be emphasized that *personal excellence* characterizes individuals who act successfully, and *external excellence* proposes a firm's objectives, values, and results; these are two distinct ideas. They must be differentiated to prevent confusion of the procedures that build personality with those that tear it down.

Currently, management research tends to analyze the characteristics and expertise that managers develop for making strategic decisions, understanding the environment, learning, leading teams, and creating projects. Cognitive psychology, which studies the processing of information, attempts to formalize this individual expertise in order to make certain generalizations (Vogler 1996). Research into the characteristics of personal excellence aims, then, to hone individuals' specific abilities in keeping with firms' evolving expectations, with the defining skills of strategic value, and with the importance placed on individuals with these skills.

Personal excellence stems from a psychological process that integrates conscious and unconscious skills and draws on values that often subconsciously influence behavior. Excellence is a product of self-discovering experiences lived since childhood. These are experiences that promote unity and internal coherence; they allow good-quality relations, efficient actions, and personal satisfaction. In such circumstances, though, subjects are apparently unaware both of their own behavior and of these skills.

Our next task after living such memorable and unique experiences is to recognize them as such—at first without actually identifying their distinctive components. In the end, knowing precisely how we act is not a product of education: rather, it is a process of metacognition that facilitates generalization and learning. It allows us to understand the way we learn.

Subsequent actions modeled after these moments of excellence allow personal development as well as the reinforcement of identity and self-confidence. Benefits such as these are obtained by evaluating and improving one's originality, unity, and continuity over time, always from the reference point provided by one's best performances. This kind of examination of individuals or team excellence in a variety of new contexts and environments can illuminate the fundamental characteristics and conditions of high performance. As a result, excellence is promoted in all situations.

Consciously adapting expertise and performance to fit these new situations can be a simple and efficient process, for groups as for individuals. After all, the basic values and knowledge needed for success in a new situation are already present; they need simply to be set in motion. Consequently, adapting performance to new situations no longer involves copying outside models or implementing traditional, generic, prescriptive strategies. Instead the emphasis is on individuals' learning how they act when at their best and discovering which conditions help them naturally to access that mastery.

In many cases, changes in conditions make us forget techniques we use naturally and unconsciously in other circumstances. For instance, one manager, an adept conversationalist and listener in situations outside the workplace, loses the simple art of listening when faced with a difficult decision. He feels trapped inside his authority until it dawns on him that he has always possessed the skill of listening. He has simply to recognize his skill as a nonauthoritative listener and model his decision-making actions after it, thereby transferring social proficiency to a new context.

The process also identifies certain aspects of one's role, person and situation that hinder the transfer of previously developed expertise. This theory does not close with established theory; rather it anticipates the negative effects of change when one does not know how to reactivate old skills. Using old skills in a new context leads to reflection on two points:

1. Intuitive awareness and analysis of the hindrances to performance adaptation
2. Identification of the best conditions for accessing old aptitudes and subsequent generation of those conditions

Such observation of individuals and their experiences does not aim to discover what managers are or how they normally work (Mintzberg 1973). Rather, its goal is to use strict working procedures and specific tools of observation to give managers an idea of the complexity of their psychological processes.

There are three main concerns in this kind of research: (1) finding the connection between one's perception of an action and the action itself; (2) identifying the methods for recognizing and integrating expertise; and (3) identifying the conditions necessary for the transmission and possibility of development of managerial skills.

We are no longer looking for efficient behavior, since it can be learned. Instead we are seeking to create a model of expertise that takes diverse personal leadership styles into account.

The quest for personal excellence can help individuals recognize and act in accordance with their fundamental characteristics and needs, and it can also help them understand their limits as well as their capabilities. Not only is this process indispensable to individuals attempting to convert their imaginary omnipotence into a sufficient control of reality; it also allows them to identify complementary skills in themselves and other team members. In addition, it helps define individuals' volition, values, and beliefs—factors that often subconsciously incite action.

In the interest of firmwide versatility, personal stability, behavioral development, managerial skills, identity, and style, it is essential to suggest a method of personal development that does not cramp individual characteristics. According to Bateson (1973), four levels of training can be carried out, either in groups or in personal coaching:

Level 1—Building skills tailored to a given environment: knowing when to make decisions and when to stand back, knowing how to put a project together, and so on.

Level 2—Establishing *how* you know what to do: defining series of thoughts, acts, and feeling; identifying what values come into play in decision making, allowing autonomy, putting together a project, and so on.

Level 3—Learning how to prioritize: simplifying the plan of action in order to develop it or transfer it to other contexts; knowing how to observe, how to question, how to reformulate and identify stages of development, and so on.

Level 4—Knowing how to use prioritization: analyzing and developing all plans of action, both for oneself and others, prioritization is the key to self-knowledge and change; it is general in method and structure but entirely specific in content and usage.

The Organization's Role in Developing Identity

The term *organization* unites the following ideas:

- *Role sharing within a hierarchy*: for collaboration or for distribution and coordination of power, responsibilities, projects, information access, status, and relations.
- *Rules of formal and informal management*: concerning people, information, and means of control and reward. These rules govern information systems, management control, reporting, and the whole system of human resource management (evaluation, promotion, remuneration, training, qualifications, career development, etc.)
- *Social machinery*: often referred to as *company culture*. Managers often try to observe, understand, and influence it in order to facilitate collective productivity. Common situations contribute to create social groups and "company culture."

The influence of these three factors is probably felt more by high-potential executives than by other workers. This fact makes it important that executives know the managerial rules and understand their role in shaping company psychological characteristics. This way, high-potential executives will be able to support future managers as they develop their own professional identities. By helping to select and prepare employees with a variety of profiles and skills, these executives provide their companies with the diversity essential to face uncertainties of company evolution and stagnant attitudes and behavior successfully.

Organizations intervene in individuals' development on two levels. First, firms constitute symbolic and imaginary cultural systems (Enriquez 1992) that require the following:

- Conforming to a set of values, norms, images, and behavior
- Participating in common, unifying myths (history, initiation procedures, and heroes)
- Casting away fear and carrying projects to fruition

Accepting these common values and ideas, which eventually bring about the behavior expected by the company, has a profound influence on individuals. Since all workers, especially high-potential executives and future managers, are so involved in their company through investments and promises, it has the authority to speak directly to their most intimate motivations and fears.

However, the firm affects each staff member in a more sweeping way than with the aforementioned interpersonal appreciation given by authority figures. Through the words, decisions, and actions of respected people, individuals are faced with a multitude of self-images that, though they may lead to anguish and fear, contribute to constructing identity (Sainsaulieu 1977).

The impact of the firm as a place of investment, of identity, and of behavioral and regulatory norms appears so fundamental that certain sociologists (Sainsaulieu and Segrestin 1986) believe it tends to become a place of "new social adjustment" (335).

The organization is a framework that supports psychological workings, not only by mobilizing an ideal self or by reflecting self-image, but also by constituting a system of collective feedback (Kaës et al. 1979) that makes sense of one's personal experiences. Every company suggests particular ways of dealing with conflict, understanding the environment, managing stress, reacting to change, confronting aggression, seizing opportunities, and so forth.

Through work groups, corporate culture, and the study of recommended procedures, individuals learn to act acceptably and effectively in a variety of situations. In this way they avoid insecurity, difficulties, and uncertainties related to new and troubling situations, reducing the risk of stress and crisis.

Company procedures impose certain ideas on the individual. They dictate which situations are more significant than others, and they prescribe lines of action to be carried out. Firms thus attempt to transmit the experience and expertise that constitute key skills. With exposure to a variety of situations, high-potential executives in all professions can acquire competency for their own positions and can then learn how to implement those skills effectively for other assignments.

We have identified four major influences on the personal and professional development of all employees, especially future managers:

1. *The organizational structure* with all its values and guidelines.
2. *The rules of management*, particularly those that relate to human resource management, help form the rules of competition and collaboration, and deal with future expectations.
3. *Reference groups* that impose behavioral norms and offer advice for handling various situations.
4. *The superiors* who, in collaborating with employees, help them build self-image and confidence, thus preparing them to act boldly.

The analysis is not limited to the organization's impact on the development of high-potential executives and future managers: it can also include the more general objective of developing potential within the firm as a whole.

Indeed, by implementing the same process that firms use to develop high-potential executives, complex global companies can promote good managerial skills, efficiency, company spirit, autonomy, risk taking, teamwork, and adaptability. This process includes the following:

- *Augmenting employees' real self-knowledge* through the experiences that are provided by personal and professional projections based on personal values and talents
- *Developing true personal stability* in a changing and complex environment—remaining productive, motivating networks, and assuming functions of power and influence
- *Using interpersonal and cognitive skills* that enhance the effectiveness of one's technical and specific skills

SUMMARY

This agenda requires the invention of strategies for developing individuals and their skills, strategies that fit each employees' profiles and projects. But in the end, individual and corporate skills (Amadieur and Cadin 1995) will become the source of the firm's competitiveness. As we have seen, the development of high-potential executives and future managers is a field of study that invites experimentation.

NOTES

1. This experimental work follows Milgrams (1990) on external conditions that, without revealing themselves to the subjects, generate submission to a recognized authority.

2. J. L. Delpeuch and A. Lauvergeon (1988) claim that the average manager interacts with twenty people a day and perhaps deals with numerous subjects in a matter of minutes.

REFERENCES

Adler, L. 1993. *Les femmes politiques*. Paris: Seuil.
Aktouf, O. 1989. *Le management entre tradition et renouvellement*. Quebec City: G. Morin.
Amado, G., and A. Guittet. 1975. *La dynamique de communication dans les groupes*. Paris: A. Colin
Amadieu, J. F., and L. Cadin. 1995. Compétences et organisation qualifiante. *Economica* 1:36.
Anzieu, D. 1976. L'illusion groupale. *Nouvelle Revue de Psychanalyse* 4: 73–93.
Anzieu, D. 1984. *Le groupe et l'inconscient*. Paris: Dunod.
Anzieu, D. 1985. *Le moi-peau*. Paris: Dunod.

Anzieu, D., and J. Y. Martin. 1973. *La dynamique des groupes restreints*. Paris: Presse Universitaire de France.

Aubert, A., P. Gilbert, and F. Pigère. 1993. *Savoir et pouvoir, les compétences en questions*. Paris: Presse Universitaire Française Gestion.

Aubert, N., and J. V. Gaule. 1991. *Le coût de l'excellence*. Paris: Seuil.

Austin, G. 1991. *Quand dire c'est faire*. Paris: Seuil.

Bandler, R. 1990. *Un cerveau pour changer*. Paris: Interedition.

Bandura, A. 1970. *L'apprentissage social*. Paris: Editions Mardaga.

Bateson, G. 1973. *Vers une écologie de l'esprit*, vols. 1, 2. Paris: Seuil, 1995.

Bauer, M. 1993. *Les patrons de PME: Entre le pouvoir, l'entreprise et la famille*. Paris: Interedition.

Bauer, M., and B. Bertin Mourot. 1987. *Les 200: Comment devient-on un grand patron?* Paris: Seuil.

Beauvois, J. L., and R. V. Joule. 1987. *Petit traité de manipulation à l'usage des honnètes gens*. Grenoble: Presses universitaires de Grenoble.

Beauvois, J. L. 1994. *Traité de la servitude liberale*. Paris: Dunod.

Berger, M. 1993. *La folie cachée des hommes de pouvoir*. Paris: Albin Michel.

Bernard, A. 1992. *Le développement des jeunes cadres*. Paris: Liaisons.

Boltanski, L. 1982. *Les cadres: la formation d'un groupe social*. Paris: Editions de Minuit.

Bourdieu, P. 1979. *La distinction, critique sociale du jugement*. Paris: Editions de Minuit.

Bourdieu, P., and J. C. Passeron. 1966. *Les Héritiers: les étudiants et la culture*. Paris: Editions de Minuit.

Bournois, F. 1991. *La gestion des cadres en Europe*. Paris: Eyrolles.

Bournois, F. 1996. Portrait comparés de managers Europeéns. *Revue Française de Gestion* 111:115–132.

Bournois, F., and P. Metcalfe. 1991. Human resource management of executives in Europe: Structures, policies and techniques. In C. Brewster and S. Tyson (eds.), *International comparisons in human resource management*. London: Pitman.

Bournois, F., P. Romelaer, and B. de Montmorillon. 1996. La formation des cadres dirigeants et des futurs cadres dirigeants. Paris: FNEGE.

Brazelton, T. B., and H. Als. 1981. Quatre stades précoces au cours du développement de la relation mère-nourrisson. *Psychiatrie de l'enfant* 24:39–418.

Brunstein, I. 1996. Pour une sociologie de l'activité solidaire. In S. Roussillon and F. Bournois, *Les Enjeux de l'Emploi*. Lyon: Collection CNRS, 177–201.

Caralli, M. 1985. *Les cavaliers de Marianne*. Paris: Hachette.

Carroll, L. 1984. *Alice au pays des merveilles*. Paris: Hachette.

Chanlat, J. F. 1990. *L'individu dans l'organisation—les dimensions oubliées*. Quebec City: Edition Eska.

Chomsky, N. 1971. *Aspects de la théorie syntaxique*. Paris: Seuil.

Codol, J. P. 1989. Vingt ans de cognition sociale. *Bulletin de psychologie* tome 42 (390): 472–491.

Dalton, G., P. Thompson, and R. Price. 1977. The four stages of professional careers—a new look at performance by professionals. *Organizational Dynamics* Summer: 19–42.

Damasio, A. R. 1995. *L'erreur de Descartes*. Paris: O. Jacob.

Dejours, Ch., and E. Abdoucheli. 1991. Itinéraire théorique et psychopathologique du travail in *Travail et santé mentale*. Paris: ANACT.

Delpeuch, J. L., and A. Lauvergeon. 1988. *Sur les traces des dirigeants*. Paris: Calman-Levy.

Derr, C. B., C. Jones, and E. L. Toomey. 1988. Managing high-potential employees: Current practices in thirty-three U.S. corporations. *Human Resource Management* 27(3):273–290.

Doise, W., and S. Moscovici. 1992. *Consensus et dissensus: Une théorie générale des decisions collectives*. Paris: Presse Universitaire Française.

Dortier, J. F. 1993. Les dimensions cachées des organisations. *Sciences Humaines* no. 30 (July): 22–27.

Dubar, Cl. 1991. *La socialisation*. Paris: A. Colin.

Enriquez, E. 1992. *L'organisation en analyse*. Paris: Presse Universitaire Française.

Ernoult, V., J. P. Gruere, and F. Pezeu. 1984. *Le bilan comportemental dans l'entreprise*. Paris: Presse Universitaire Française.

Festinger, L. 1957. *A theory of cognitive dissonance*. New York: Peterson.

Festinger, L. 1971. Sur la pression de conformité des groupes de reference. Paris: Seuil.

Festinger, L. and E. Aroson. 1978. Eveil et réduction de la dissonance dans les contextes sociaux. In A. Levy, *Psychologie sociale, textes fondamentaux anglais et americains*. Vol. 1. Paris: Dunod.

Freud, S. 1913. *Totem et tabous*. Paris: Payot.

Freudenberger, H. 1987. *L'épuisement professionnel, la brulure interne*. Quebec City: Gaetan Morin.

Fridberg, E. 1987. *L'analyse sociologique des organisations rééd*. Paris: L'Harmattan.

Gentil, B., 1988. La gestion des ressources potentielles en cadres de haut niveau. *L'enjeu humain de l'entreprise*. Paris: CEPP, 403–406.

Gentil, B. 1991. La question du potentiel au sein de la gestion des cadres. Working paper, Entreprise et Personnel.

Goguelin, P. 1989. *Le management psychologique des organisations*. Paris: Editions ESF.

Hall, E. T. 1979. *Au delà de la culture*. Paris: Seuil.

Handy, C., C. Gordon, I. Gow, and C. Randlesome. 1988. *Making managers*. London: Pitman.

Hour, T., and J. Carter. 1995. Getting it done: New roles for senior executives. *Harvard Business Review* (November–December):48–60.

Ibarra, H. 1993. Network centrality: Power and innovation involvement. *Academy of Management Journal* 36: 471–501.

Iribarne, Ph. 1989. *La Logique de l'honneur: Gestion des entreprises et traditions nationales*. Paris: Seuil.

Jacoud, R., and M. Metsch, 1991. *Diriger autrement*. Paris: Editions d'organisation.

Jaques, E. 1965. Des systèmes sociaux comme défenses contre l'anxiété. In A. Levy, *Textes fondamentaux de psychologie sociale*. Paris: Dunod.

Jennings, R., C. Cox, and C. Cooper. 1994. *Business elites—The psychology of entrepreneurs and intrapreneurs*. London: Routledge.

Jodelet, D. 1989. *Les représentations sociales*. Paris: Presse Universitaire Française.

Kaës, R. 1994. *La parole et le lien: processus associatifs dans les groupes*. Paris: Dunod.

Kaës, R., and A. Missenard. 1979. *Crises ruptures et dépassement*. Paris: Dunod.

Kets de Vries, M. 1986. *The irrational executive*. Madison: University of Wisconsin Press.

Kets de Vries, M., and D. Miller. 1985. *L'entreprise névrosée*. Paris: McGraw-Hill.

Koenig, G. 1993. Production de connaissances et constitution des pratiques organisa-
    tionnelles. *Revue Française de Gestion*, no. 9: 4–17.
Landier, H. 1991. *Vers l'entreprise intelligente*. Paris: Calman-Levy, 269.
Leleu, P. 1995. *Le développement du potentiel des managers*. Paris: Harmatan.
Lévy-Leboyer, Cl. 1996. *La gestion des compétences*. Paris: Editions d'organisation.
Livian, Y.-F., F. Dany, and P. Sarnin, 1992. Gestion des carrieres des cadres vue par les
    cadres en France. Paris: Proceedings of the Association de Gestion des Resources
    Humaines (AGRH) November.
Lorenz, K. 1990. *Evolution et modification du comportement: L'inne et l'acquis*, trans.
    L. Jospin. Paris: Payot.
Louart, 1994. La Gestion des ressources humaines à l'heure des segmentations et des
    particularismes. *Revue Française de Gestion* 89: 79–94.
Milgram, St. 1990. *Soumission à l'autorité*. Paris: Calmann Levy.
Mintzberg, H. 1973. *The nature of managerial work*. New York: Harper & Row.
Mintzberg, H. 1996. Une journée avec un dirigeant. *Revue Française de Gestion* 111:
    213–224.
Morgan, G. 1989. *Images de l'organisation*. Quebec City: Presse de l'université de Laval
    ESKA.
Moscovici, S. 1984. *Psychologie sociale*. Paris: Presse Universitaire Française.
Moscovici, S., and W. Doise. 1992. *Dissensions et consensus*. Paris: Presse Universitaire
    Française.
Nuttin, J. 1985. *Théorie de la motivation humaine*. Paris: Presse Universitaire Française.
Pages, M. 1984. *la vie affective des groupes*. Paris: Dunod.
Paris, H. 1994. *Mobiliser les potentiels personnels*. Paris: Editions d'organisation.
Perrenoud, Ph. 1997. *Construire des compétences*. Paris: Boeck.
Peters, T., and R. Waterman. 1983. *Le prix de l'excellence*. Paris: Inter Editions.
Pralahad, C. K., and G. Hamel. 1995. *La conquête du futur*. Paris: Inter Editions.
Reuchlin, M. 1991. *Grand dictionnaire de la psychologie*. Paris: Larousse.
Rosenbaum, J. 1979. Tournament mobility: Career patterns in a corporation. *Administra-
    tive Sciences Quarterly* 24: 220–241.
Roussillon, S. 1988. Les processus de groupe. *Management des ressources humaines*.
    Paris: Eyrolles.
Roussillon, S. 1991. Developper les competences de ses collaborateurs. *Revue Personnel*
    12: 321–333.
Roussillon, S. 1995. La confiance en soi comme résultat et condition de la confiance en
    l'autre. *Confiance, entreprise et société*. Quebec City: Editions ESKA.
Roussillon, S., and L. Lafoy, 1995. Vous avez dit compétences? *Revue personnel* 363:
    11–13.
Sahuc, L. 1985. *Comment identifier les futurs managers?* Paris: Editions INSEP.
Sainsaulieu, R. 1988. *L'identité au travail et les effets ultursels de l'organisation*. Paris:
    Presses de la fondation nationale des sciences politiques.
Sainsaulieu, R. 1990. *L'entreprise une affaire de société*. Paris: Presses de la FNEGE.
Sainsaulieu, R., and D. Segrestin, 1986. Vers une théorie sociologique de l'entreprise.
    Sociologie du travail no. 3 (86): 335–352.
Scheid, J. C. 1990. *Les grands auteurs en organisation*. Paris: Dunod.
Sterling, J., and J. L. Livingston. 1989. Pygmalion et le management. *Harvard Business
    Review* 53: 59–69.
Suleiman, E. and Mendras. 1995. *Le recrutement des élites en Europe*. Paris: Découverte.

Tabatoni, P., and P. Jarniou. 1975. *L'entreprise comme système politique*. Paris: Dunod.

Tapernoux, F. 1984. *Les centres d'evaluation*. Lausanne: Payot.

Tarondeau, J. C., A. Jolibert, and J. M. Choffray. 1994. Le management à l'aube du XXI siècle. *Revue Française de Gestion* 100: 9–21.

Turnage., J., and P. Muchinsky. 1984. A comparison of the predictive validity of assessment center evaluations versus traditional measures of forecasting supervisory job performance: Interpretative implications of criterion distortion for the assessment paradigm. *Journal of Applied Psychology* 69: 595–602.

Vermot-Gaud, C. 1990. *Detecter et gerer les potentiels humains dans l'entreprise*. Paris: Liaisons.

Villette, M. 1996. *Le manager jetable: Récits du management réel*. Paris: Découverte.

Vogler, E. 1996. *Management stratégique et psychologie cognitive*. Vols. 1 and 2. *Cahiers dans recherche du Groupe ESC Lyon*, nos. 9510 and 9605.

Watzlawick, P. 1978. *La réalité de la réalité: Confusion, désinformation, communication*. Paris: Seuil.

Watzlawick, P., J. Weakland, and R. Fisch. 1975. *Changements, paradoxes et psychothérapie*. Paris: Seuil.

Winnicott, D. W. 1971. *Jeu et réalite*. Paris: Gallimard.

Conclusion

C. Brooklyn Derr, Sylvie Roussillon, and Frank Bournois

The introduction to this book presents the Diversity-Collaboration, or DC, Model. We return to it here as an organizing concept to the information and examples presented in the chapters that the body of this book comprises. Those chapters present various ways that diverse businesses and organizations in different countries perceive leaders and select and develop future leaders, with some apparent similarities and some differences. Two critical questions emerge from an examination of this information, and we hope to address them in this concluding chapter:

- When is it important to accept and encourage cultural diversity, and when should companies push toward more global homogenization or cross-national collaboration?
- How do companies honor the requirements for heterogeneity or cultural diversity, while also enhancing required collaboration?

FORCES FOR DIVERSITY AND COLLABORATION

Forces for Diversity

Table C.1 serves as an overview of the information gathered from companies internationally and presented in this book. As discussed, the very idea of a leader may be culturally embedded and, therefore, dependent on national culture. For example, in the United States, the leader is often a CEO "free agent star" who, like a sports star, works under contract, delivering short-term but impressive results and then spinning off to the next highest bidder. Roussillon's chapter on

Table C.1
Cross-National Leadership Differences

		U.S.	Latin America	France
Leadership Definition	What is the cultural leadership prototype?	**Free Agent Star.** A winner, who gets short-term results; money as indicator of worth	**General.** Strong man in charge, keeps order, promotes change, controls	**Genius.** Smartest one, best exam scores, member of intellectual elite, graduate of the best school
Importance of an Elite	Is the idea of an elite culturally encouraged?	No	Yes	Yes
Selection Differences	Does the use of psychological tests and HR experts dominate?	Yes	No	Yes/No
	Does social/political selection (networks) dominate?	Somewhat important	Key	Key
	How important is a prestigious educational background (best schools)?	Important	Somewhat important	Key
	How important is a certain educational degree?	Key (MBA)	Important	Important
Advancement Differences	Competency profiles	Key	Yes	Yes
	Age	No	No	No
	Measured performance	Yes	Yes	Yes
	Informal recommendation	Yes	Key	Key
Diversity Differences	How extensive are the presence and promotion of ethnic minorities?	Significant	Growing (depending on country)	Significant
	Presence and role of professional women	Yes	No (except Argentina)	Yes (Magreb, Africa)
	Globalizing management	Growing	Growing	Growing

access to leadership in France (Chapter 4) describes a national elite, the members of which are destined to reach the top by virtue of their national examination scores in competition with peers, the school they attend, and their roles in national networks. We have called this the "Examinations" model. In Germany, a leader must demonstrate extraordinary skill and be a kind of broad-minded "master" craftsman in his or her area of expertise. In Japan, a leader is competent, loyal, wise, male, respected, and a product of the group—a kind of "senior statesman." Different countries and cultures produce different concepts and definitions of leaders.

Another key cultural difference in the perception of leaders is the acceptance

Table C.1 (*cont.*)

U.K.	Germany	Italy	Holland	Poland
Diplomat. Big thinker, well-educated, well-traveled, good social skills	Master. Most respected by peers, expert in field, has in-depth knowledge	Godfather. Holds together conflicting factions, punishes and favors, paternalistic	Marathon Winner. Outworks the rest, runs hard, trains well, endures, at head of pack	Baron. Protects castle and fiefdom, exercises power for self and close associates
Yes (historically) No (currently)	No	Yes	No	Yes
Yes	Yes	No	Yes	(Interview)
Important	Somewhat important	Key	Somewhat important	Important
Important	Not important	Somewhat important	Not important	Somewhat important
Important	Key	Important	Important	Somewhat important
Key	No	Yes	Key	No
No	No	No	No	No
Yes	Key (diplomas and apprenticeship)	No	Yes	No
Yes	Yes	Key	Yes	Key (interview)
Significant	Not significant	Not significant	Growing	Significant
Yes	No	No	Yes	No
Yes	Growing	Growing	Yes	Growing

of a carefully selected elite group as the source of leadership potential (e.g., in France, Japan, Latin America, China) versus the leader as a self-made person who outperforms others and rises to the top (e.g., in the United States, Scandinavia, Israel, Holland, Germany). Table C.1 indicates which countries do and do not commonly accept the concept of an elite. If one has been groomed for leadership from an early age, leadership selection, advancement, and development systems may be quite different—emphasizing a measurement of potential at an early stage and focusing later on grooming political and networking skills, rather than strictly on job performance.

Table C.1 *(cont.)*

Japan	China	Vietnam	Israel	Africa
Senior States-man; Older, wiser, from the group; survivor, consensus builder	**Warlord.** Local power; uses *quanxi* (favors) for loyal supporters; rich	**Communist Party Boss.** Wears numerous hats; favors to family and friends; ideological	**Field Commander.** Smart, energetic, creative, tactical, self-made	**Tribal Chief.** Older, wiser, consultative; orchestrates various networks, builds factions
Yes	Yes	Yes	No	Yes
No	No	No	Yes	No
Key	Key	Key	Important (army)	Key
Key	Somewhat important	Not important	Important	Not important
Somewhat important	Important	Important	Key	Not important
No	No	No	Key	No
Yes	Yes	Yes	No	No
No	No	No	Yes	No
Key	Key	Key	Yes	Key
Insignificant	Growing	Growing	Significant	Not significant
No	No	No	Yes	No
No	Growing	No	Yes	No

Selection Differences

In nations such as Germany and the United Kingdom, human resource professionals are considered experts and are generally trusted in their companies to help select future leaders from the labor market and from within the company's high-potential pool. In the United States, the United Kingdom, Holland, and Israel, leaders are likely to be selected by a variety of systematic methods: psychological tests, assessment centers, interviews, a careful reading of curriculum vitaes (CVs), checking of references—and especially, measured performance reviews and boss/colleague recommendations. Usually informal recommendations of the leadership elite are not valued or sought openly. In the United States, where leadership mobility is prevalent, recruitment is ongoing and systematic and includes the Internet more and more. For example, it was predicted that by 2003, American employers would spend $1.7 billion for online recruiting (Useem 1999).

In countries such as France and Japan, on the other hand, the most important selection criterion is the place where one was educated. In Germany, it is one's degree (e.g., Ph.D. in a science). In China, Vietnam, Africa, Italy, and Latin America, it is one's social, family, and ethnic contacts. The social networks and referents from elite educational institutions are also critical in France and Japan.

Advancement Differences

Some countries, such as the United States and the United Kingdom, are more market-oriented and prone to using various measurement devices and selection tools to recruit more senior leaders from the marketplace. Therefore, a variety of approaches are valued, such as competency profiles, measured performance, CVs, formal recommendations, skill sets, interviews, and reference checking. This is necessary because it is estimated to cost 150 percent of a former employee's salary to select a replacement (Cook 1999, p 43; Bravo 1995, 95). Recruitment and retention of valuable employees in a market-oriented economy are costly but important. This is also true for most global companies where talent is scarce.

However, some countries (e.g., France, Israel, Italy, and Latin America)—having selected their leadership elite early on—rely more on the informal recommendation of the elite group and are not so likely to measure and assess senior candidates carefully. Other countries, such as Japan, China, Vietnam, Africa, and Poland, promote mostly from within the organization on the basis of informal recommendations of the leadership group. Other countries, such as Germany, promote from within on the basis of constant training, retraining, and certifying.

Embracing Diversity

The United States and Israel are diverse because of long-standing immigration policies; even though Canada and Australia are now the immigration leaders. However, the United Kingdom, Holland, and France have also permitted a lot of immigration from their former colonies since World War II, and Germany has become one of the most popular European countries to which people currently immigrate (Caramel 2000, I). In some of the countries, such as the United States, governmental policies and equal opportunity laws that require more minorities and women in educational preparation programs and leadership positions have enhanced diverse leadership and promoting women into meaningful managerial and professional positions is an indicator of required diversity. Sixty percent of U.S. women work for pay outside the home (*101 Facts* 2000, 1) compared to only 35 percent in Italy but 80 percent in Sweden (Boujnah 2000, 14). Thirty-one percent of all American working women are managers and professionals (*101 Facts* 2000, 1). In a 1995 United Nations survey of those countries that are most open to gender equality at work (Boujnah 2000, 14), the first

four were the Scandinavian countries, followed by Canada (fifth), the United
Kingdom (nineteenth), and France (thirty-first).

On equal pay for equal work, the average American woman earns 73 cents
for every $1 made by a man (*101 Facts* 2001, 1), whereas the average French-
woman does better and makes 76 French francs (FF) for every 100 FF earned
by a man, British women earn 73 FF, and Dutch women 71 FF. Since 1983,
France has had important laws governing pay equality among the sexes; Germany, on the other hand, is considered one of the least gender-equal countries
in Europe (Boujnah 2000, 15).

Diverse Personalities

As Roussillon's Chapter 18 indicates, it is possible to distinguish personality
differences in leaders across national cultures. Indeed, anyone who has ever
taught in a multicultural classroom is aware that although culture, gender, and
ideology are all important, distinct personality differences cut across these cultural cleavages. The importance of using translated but similar selection instruments across cultures (such as the Myers-Briggs Type Indicator, the Predictive
Index, the Career Success Map Questionnaire) attests to the idea that diverse
personality groupings exist in every nation.

Derr's earlier work on the career success orientations of talent and leaders
(Derr 1986; Derr and Laurent 1989) points to the need to recognize and manage
the cognitive and stylistic diversity of leaders. This means developing leadership
systems that push out the opportunity structure and offer more choices for different kinds of individual leaders.

Table C.1 delineates these various forces for diversity in the countries studied
in this volume. Some of these schemas are based on the editors' collective
perceptions as well as the individual chapters. A similar table exists in Bournois
and Roussillon's (1998) earlier edition.

Forces for Collaboration

At a societal level, forces pushing in the direction of developing a common
ground and a global infrastructure for enhancing collaboration include common
trade practices (e.g., General Agreement on Tarriffs and Trade [GATT], European Union, North American Free Trade Agreement [NAFTA]), comparable
reporting and accounting systems required by the financial markets, comparable
preleadership educational curricula (e.g., the M.B.A. degree), use of English as
the world business language, similar technologies (e.g., Microsoft Word and
Windows), and greater international exposure through global travel. But the
following are forces that directly impact leadership selection and development.

A Common Need for Different Kinds of Leaders

A movement away from large command-and-control hierarchies and toward
smaller, faster, more decentralized, more technology-based companies as we

shift to the information economy (see Chapter 16) means the worldwide definition of a leader is broadening. Despite cultural diversity and dependence on
local situations (e.g., some state-owned enterprises in China and Vietnam, organizations in Africa, government agencies in France and Italy, a small shop in
Germany), the following generalizations can be made:

• There is less need for hierarchical-type managers than before 1990.
• There is a greater need for team leaders, technical gurus, product champions, customer
  managers, entrepreneurs, and functional specialists.
• Information technology has made work more flexible, and fewer people keep regular
  hours at an office—even though they may work harder and be more productive and
  leaders must still achieve unity of effort.
• Leaders are responsible for orchestrating the efforts of a larger group and a more
  diverse work force than before 1990.

Common Competencies

Some common leadership competencies are emerging as important factors
across national boundaries. Abilities such as writing/speaking English, possessing technical competency with computers and other information technology,
being able to work effectively in cross-boundary teams (cross-function, cross-
gender, cross-culture, cross-company, cross-generation), being flexible, learning
to learn new things, embracing change quickly, and knowing how to serve and
add value to customers are increasing in importance and necessity for leaders
in all situations.

The Talent Wars

The new demographics underscored by Hesterly and Derr in Chapter 16 mean
that the hunt is on in certain industries for similar worldwide talent. These
engineers, scientists, software developers, marketers, and managers will work in
similar settings for similar companies (e.g., Philips, Alcatel, GE), and under
similar conditions in many parts of the globe. The high-technology park in
Podong near Shanghai is not very different from the one on Route 128 near
Boston; nor is Bangalore, India, so different from Cambridge, England. To win
over this scarce talent, companies will develop similar compensation packages,
facilities, opportunity structures, and management styles. If not, the talent will
simply go next door, where there are more opportunities and a better match.

Common Gender Issues

As more women become part of the leadership pool, certain commonalties
(e.g., equal pay for equal work, equal opportunity to achieve leadership positions, the importance of relationships, demand more family-friendly policies) are
likely to emerge. As Hofstede (1991) points out (see Chapter 2), some cultures
are more typically masculine (e.g., Japan) and others more feminine (e.g., Denmark). Although this difference might be a force for diversity, it might also be

a force for collaboration. To work in one gender mode or the other, to feel free to express one's male or female side, may help people inside organizations find common ground. The worldwide acceptance of homosexuals in the workplace, despite controversy about such acceptance, pushes for a less homophobic workplace culture and opens up a more gender-compatible workplace environment.

THE NEED FOR INTEGRATION

Integration Theory

Classical organizational behavior theory is often still relevant to modern problems. On the basis of the work of Burns and Stalker (1961), Woodward (1965), and Paul R. Lawrence and Jay W. Lorsch (1967), we can create an organizational theory that is relevant to the questions examined here: when to encourage the cultural diversity of leaders and when to focus on collaboration, and how to develop future leaders who both appreciate and utilize diversity while also fostering enough unity of effort/collaboration to get the job accomplished.

According to Lawrence and Lorsch, the requirements for diversity depend on the needs of the firm to function effectively in a particular setting. Therefore, as Bournois points out in Chapter 17, three different kinds of organizations are likely to exist in most industrialized economies: organizations in the public sector, large local organizations in transition, and multinational organizations or companies (MNCs). It is expected that MNCs will focus on managing their cultural diversity and requiring more worldwide collaboration. Public sector organizations will focus on unity of effort with some need to diversify, depending on equal opportunity laws and practices. Those enterprises in transition will have to discover the best mix of required diversity and the continuing need for collaboration.

Different cultures will require different cross-cultural emphases as well. In Chapter 15, Mutabazi bemoans the fact that Africa has not been invited into the world economic equation—so global diversity requirements are low. In China and Vietnam, ambivalence exists about how much diversity to allow versus how to maintain control, whereas in Israel and Holland, cultural diversity is the norm and it is necessary to manage it effectively.

The requirements for collaboration, according to Lawrence and Lorsch, depend on how much people need to cooperate and interact to be effective. A cross-cultural problem-solving team will have to manage whatever differences get in the way of their effective collaboration or they may not be effective. Add to this problem cross-functional, cross-gender, and cross-generational differences, and you have a situation that requires both high diversity and high collaboration.

Lawrence and Lorsch postulate that in some work situations (e.g., the public sector), the requirement for diversity may be low and collaboration high. In other situations that need a quick cross-boundary response, requirements for diverse opinions, perspectives, styles, knowledge, and skills are needed, as is a collaborative effort. In a third situation (e.g., in R&D or consulting accomplished by various parties contributing individually and another party integrating all the pieces at the end), high diversity requirements may coexist with low collaboration requirements.

For example, as Malone and Laubacker (1998) point out, a lot of important work in the information economy may be accomplished by "e-lancers," freelance specialists who work primarily at home on powerful computers as independent contractors. They "join together into fluid and temporary networks to produce and sell goods and services. When the job is done—after a day, a month, a year—the network dissolves, and its members become independent agents again, circulating through the economy, seeking the next assignments" (146). The role of the leader in such an instance of the e-commerce economy is to act as a broker of the various parties and an integrator of what they independently produce. This typifies acting under conditions of high required diversity, but low required collaboration.

High collaboration requirements usually mean a lot of face-to-face communication and are normally accompanied by rather strongly felt differences of opinion, therefore the presence of interpersonal, intergroup cross-cultural and cross-company conflict. The need for integration occurs when there exists at the same time—as it often does in global enterprises—the need for diversity and collaboration, according to Lawrence and Lorsch. In such situations, the organization must not overly minimize the presence of diversity conflict (because it is necessary to get the job done); it must rather focus instead on integration management. Integration management is accomplished by the following components:

- Successfully managing diversity-related conflict—rather than resolving or diminishing such needed conflict
- Using corporate culture as a "glue" to help hold together diverse parties
- Using various management systems to help integrate efforts such as common information and reporting systems, e-mail, team meetings, group training events, use of cross-cultural teams for development as well as task accomplishment
- Selecting and developing leaders who understand how both to encourage diversity for improved performance and require collaboration for a more integrative and synergistic effort

The DCI Model

According to integration theory, the DC Model described earlier becomes a diversity-collaboration-integration (DCI)—model (Figure C.1) when there exists a need for both high diversity and high integration.

What is important about selecting and developing future leadership for the new information economy, then, is that (1) the leaders themselves may be culturally diverse and need to be integrated and (2) the leaders need to understand cultural diversity better so that when it exists and a collaborative effort is also

Figure C.1
The DCI Model

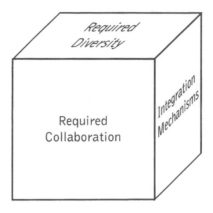

needed, future leaders will be able to use appropriate organizational mechanisms to integrate efforts.

Table C.2 summarizes more specific suggestions about when to use what method for effective cross-cultural leadership and how to manage diversity and collaboration.

FUTURE TRENDS

To summarize the preceding chapters, we believe that in the future managing diversity in all its forms, especially those arising from diverse national cultures, will be a critical issue. Depending on the kind of organization, more or less collaboration and managerial integration will be needed. Among future trends, as we see them, are the following:

The definition of leadership is broadening, and, although high-level managers will remain necessary, fewer of them will be required, and they will play different roles in the future: team leader, broker, information integrator, network facilitator, resource provider, bureaucratic interfacer. More technical gurus, product contracts, and network maintainers will emerge in key leadership roles.

New economy flat and supple leadership systems (see Derr, Briscoe, and Buckner, Chapter 1; Vloeberghs, Chapter 8), will exist in parallel—often in the same organization—with more traditional systems (see Roussillon and Bournois, Chapter 3; Petit and Scholz, Chapter 6). More on-the-job development of future leadership will take place via growth-oriented job rotation and less formal training will occur. Major educational events will be used to help articulate the company's vision, its culture, and its changing direction. So as to prepare future leadership rather than "clone" the status quo, helping future leaders be invested in important peer networks and providing external executive coaching will, in many companies, replace the past emphasis on managerial mentoring.

About half of all future leaders will be selected, developed, and trained from within, and an emphasis will be placed on their loyalty to the organization. About half will be selected into the enterprise from the labor market, and they will be viewed more as "temporary leaders" who are there to do a short-term assignment. Some leadership functions will be outsourced to consultants.

Leaders from the outside whose particular competencies are valuable at a particular moment in time may earn considerably more income than those being groomed from within. However, they will be less likely to receive costly training and development or have long-term job security than those recruited from within. Human resource directors will act more and more as internal and external headhunters as the search for talent needed to compete becomes more intense. At the same time, retention of leadership talent will be a critical issue in the early part of the twenty-first century, and so-called soft factors will become increasingly critical to hire and hold competitive talent from the labor market long enough to derive full benefit.

These soft factors are beyond compensation and include such elements as more flexible work (e.g., wired to the office computer, one can work productively at home one to two days a week), more consideration for work/life balance issues, more training and development, more appreciation expressed by leaders for a job well done, and more diverse opportunity structure to fit diverse personal needs. Leadership talent will be increasingly interested in meaningful international experiences—not necessarily disruptive expatriate moves of two to four years, but more "long" business trips, cross-national task force assignments, transfer abroad at a younger or older age more compatible with raising children, and meaningful executive experiences for talented women (see Derr and Oddou, 1993).

A NOTE ABOUT WRITING A CROSS-CULTURAL BOOK

This project began in 1994 and had as its focus at that time changes in high-potential management. A number of researchers convened at EM Lyon and eventually produced a book in French (Bournois and Roussillon 1998).

At first, we considered translating and reproducing the same book into English, but it became increasingly apparent that the field of leadership selection and development was changing so rapidly in the United States that the system of high-potential management per se was in question. Moreover, it became increasingly clear that research, thinking, logic, and what might be marketable to an American audience were basically different from those appropriate for a French one. Producing a book was a culturally embedded process.

In the French volume (Bournois and Roussillon 1998), lengthy and more esoteric theory about the nature of high-potential management covers the first 136 pages. The country chapters follow (pp. 137–296), there are four case studies, and then come 100 pages of models, tools, and methods. This is an excellent book that has since won the Menpower Prize in 1999, and it is read by French

Table C.2
Diversity Versus Collaboration

Situation	Diversity	Integrative Mechanisms	Collaboration
A. Public Sector (requires high collaboration, low diversity)	• More women in leadership, professional positions • More minorities • More diverse talent opportunities	• Hierarchy • Educational degrees and common training • Defined career paths • High-potential systems and profiles	• Information technology • Competency profiles • Training programs and educational curricula • Common recruitment, retention issues
B. Multi-National Corporation (requires high diversity and collaboration)	• Expatriation • Inpatriation • Cross-cultural teams • More international leaders • Broader definition of leader • Recruiting/retaining diverse global talent	• Common vision • Common corporate culture • Information and reporting systems • Corporate training • Use of cross-cultural teams • Recruitment from similar pools	• Similar degrees (MBA) • Similar competency profiles • Gender similarities • Similar recruitment of talent • Similar technology accounting/reporting requirements • Use of English

C. Quasi-National Global Organization (requires medium diversity and collaboration)	• Same as for public sector except: • Some international leaders recruited • Broader definition of leaders • Recruiting/retaining of very diverse talent • More diverse clients	• Cross-boundary teams • Role of leaders as integrators • Joining of cross-cultural alliances • Allowance for the co-existence of traditional and new economy recruitment, selection, reward and development systems	• Mixture of A and B above • Use of both English and host-country language • Struggle to allow for more diverse selection and advancement criteria
D. E-Commerce and Independent Contractor Networks (requires high diversity and low collaboration)	• Very multi-national and multi-cultural, without leaders • Knowledge and skills • Orientations and ideologies • Personalities • Age • Work setting, styles, behavior	• Legal contracts • Up-front negotiations and psychological contracting • Reward systems • Leader as broker and integrator • Clear guidelines and deadlines	• Common work specifications • Common selection systems via the Internet • Common modus operandi • Use of English • Use of common technologies • Common competency profile

301

academics and managers. However, we question whether North American, British, Australian, or other English-language readers would want to go so in-depth conceptually and philosophically.

After the decision to use some of the same country chapters (France, United Kingdom, Germany, Italy, Poland, Israel, and Africa), the translation from French to English was a costly, time-consuming, and cross-cultural endeavor. Using a professional translator, the chapters arrived in a language not appropriate to American readers and especially not to American academics, managers, and human resource professionals. These chapters had to be heavily edited again in the United States.

One of the most interesting cultural differences concerned the logical flow of the chapters. Some in French Cartesian logic had to be recast into Anglo-Saxon "loose thinking" with a problem or brief conceptual introduction, a case study or research, and a conclusion. In the French form, the reader may be treated to a broad, lengthy philosophical rationale before proceeding with a much shorter resolution of the problem. Theory and philosophy are often at least as important as problem resolution.

It would also be difficult in the United States to produce a cross-cultural volume that omitted at least one chapter about Mexico or Latin America and overrepresented Europe at the expense of Asia. So, additional country chapters were added: one on modern China, one on Japanese women leadership issues, one on Vietnam, one on Holland, and one on Latin America. Chapter 1 on the United States was extensively revised to reflect trends in the year 2002, and the theory chapter by Hesterly and Derr (Chapter 16) and Bournois (Chapter 17) were rewritten.

The production of this book has been its own interesting cross-cultural experience, one sometimes fraught with frustration but always worthwhile and challenging. It was important that the cross-country chapters were written by scholars from those countries.

REFERENCES

Boujnah, M. 2000. L'inegalite des femmes. *Air France Aero Magazine* June: 12–15.

Bournois, F., and S. Roussillon. 1998. *Prepare les dirigeants de demain*. Paris: Editions d'Organizations.

Bravo, E. 1995. *The job/family challenge: Not for women only*. New York: John Wiley.

Burns, T., and G. M. Stalker. 1961. *The management of innovation*. London: The Tavistock Institute.

Caramel, L. 2000. L'immigration, proclaim stimulant de la croissance. *Le Monde Economie* June 20: i–ii.

Cook, J. M. 1999. A change in corporate culture is a key to retaining working moms. *Salt Lake Tribune*, October 31, A43.

Derr, C. B. 1986. *Managing the new careerists*. San Francisco: Jossey-Bass Publishers.

Derr, C. B., and A. Laurent. 1989. The internal and external career: A theoretical and cross-cultural perspective. In M. Arthur, B. Laurence, and D. T. Hall, *Handbook of Career Theory*. New York: Cambridge University Press.

Derr, C. B., and G. Oddou. 1993. Internationalizing managers: Speeding up the process. *European Management Journal* 2(4): 435–442.

Hofstede, G. 1991. *Cultures and organizations: Software of the mind*. New York: McGraw-Hill.

Lawrence, P. R., and J. W. Lorsch. 1967. *Organization and environment: Managing differentiation of integration*. Boston: Harvard Business School Press.

Malone, T. W., and R. J. Laubacker. 1998. The dawn of the e-lance economy. *Harvard Business Review* September/October: 145–152.

101 Facts on the status of working women. 2000. Business and Professional Women/ USA, 2012 Massachusetts Avenue, NW, Washington, DC, 20036.

Woodward, J. 1965. *Industrial organizations: Theory and practice*. London: Oxford University Press.

Useem, J. 1999. For sale online: You. *Fortune*, July 5, 67–78.

Index

About the Contributors

JOSEPH C. BENTLEY has taught at Clark University, Holy Cross College, and the University of Utah. Dr. Bentley has been a visiting scholar at Yale University, at Stanford University, and at MIT. He has taught at universities throughout Mexico and Latin America, including Monterrey Tech (in Monterrey, Mexico City, State of Mexico, and Queretaro), University of Monterrey, University of Nuevo Leon, National University of Venezuela, National University of Panama, and universities and institutes in Colombia and Peru. Dr. Bentley has consulted for many Fortune 500 companies in the United States of America and for large Mexican and Latin American industrial groups. In the early 1970s Dr. Bentley was instrumental in introducing the principles of planned organizational change and the practice of organizational development (OD) in Mexico and other Spanish-speaking countries. More recently, he worked with AT&T (Consumer Products Division) and with Swiss Bank Corporation in New York on major cultural change programs.

FRANK BOURNOIS is a professor of management at the University of Paris Pantheon-Assas (Paris II). He previously taught at EM Lyon and at the University of Lyon III and is currently a visiting professor in the Cranfield School of Management United Kingdom and in several other European universities. He was assistant to the director of human resources at the Rhone Poulenc Company and is a member of the editorial board of three journals: *Journal of Human Resource Management, Journal of Managerial Psychology*, and *French Journal of Geoeconomics*. He has published widely on the subject of comparative European management, is the author of eight books, has contributed to twenty chapters, and has written over thirty articles in French and English on human resource management.

JON P. BRISCOE is an assistant professor of management at Northern Illinois University, where he teaches organizational behavior. He has been visiting assistant professor at the David Eccles School of Management, University of Utah, and research associate with the Executive Development Roundtable at Boston University. Research related to Dr. Briscoe's contributions in this book has evaluated approaches to competency-driven leadership selection and development and has focused upon developing the "global executive." His current research investigates the expression and suppression of personal values in the workplace, and how such value expression and suppression are shaping and being shaped by the new "protean" career.

KATHY BUCKNER is a vice president with BT Novations, a Provant company. She has led global implementations of employee and leadership development initiatives with Fortune 500 organizations in a variety of industries. She continues to research employee and leadership development issues, particularly with regard to competency-based HR processes and systems.

PATRIZIA CASTELLUCCI graduated in psychology from Padua University. She worked more than ten years as a psychologist and psychotherapist in Italy's Public Health Administration, where she dealt with the clinical and organizational aspects of personnel recruiting, training, and services organization. She has conducted qualitative market research in the automobile, pharmaceutical, printing, and consumer goods industries. She is currently teaching human resources management at the University of Castellanza (Varese, Italy).

CHANGJUN DAI is head of the department of management and director of international programs at the Glorious Sun School of Business, Donghua University (Shanghai, China), and was a visiting scholar in economics and management at Temple University and the University of Utah. He is a former faculty member in international business at Nankai University.

C. BROOKLYN DERR is Staheli Professor of International Business and Executive Director of the Global Business Center at the Marriott School of Management at Brigham Young University, and is affiliated with the Lyon Graduate School of Management (EM Lyon) in Lyon, France.

NOELEEN DOHERTY is a senior research fellow at the Human Resource Research Centre at Cranfield University. A member of the British Psychological Society, Occupational Division, she holds an M.S. in applied psychology. Since joining the Human Resource Research Centre in 1987, she has managed a wide variety of research and consulting projects. Her current interests include the auditing of human resource management strategies, policies, and practices and the investigation of HR strategies that support personal transition and organizational change.

WILLIAM S. HESTERLY is the Dumke scholar and a professor of management in the David Eccles School of Business, University of Utah, where he teaches strategic management, leadership, and organization theory and design. His research interests focus on efficient and effective organization design. Professor Hesterly has also studied emerging organizational forms as well as interfirm alliances and networks. Most recently, his research has been published in *Academy of Management Review, Organization Science, Strategic Management Journal, Journal of Corporate Finance, Journal of Management*, and *Journal of Economic Behavior and Organization*. In addition, he coauthored a chapter in the *Handbook of Organization Studies*, which was recognized by the Academy of Management as the outstanding book in the field of management for 1997.

NGUYEN NGOC HOANG was a well-known journalist and business consultant in Vietnam before immigrating to the United States in 1995. Now a freelance writer, he is presently working on two books that deal with the future of Vietnam's political and economic renovation in the light of Southeast Asia's current "revolutionary changes."

EVALDE MUTABAZI is currently a professor of sociology, intercultural management, and human resources management at EM Lyon (Lyon, France). Of French and Rwandan nationality, he currently teaches courses in social science and human resources management, the sociology of business, national cultures and managerial practices, and managing of change. Some of his recent publications include *La Diversite des cultures et des modeles au sein des entreprises africaines* (The diversity of cultures and models at the heart of African business) and *Les Dirigeants d'entreprises en afrique noire* (Business leaders in black Africa).

MICHEL PETIT, associate professor of German and human resource management at EM Lyon, is also a faculty member in the Department of Economics at the Université Lumière Lyon II. He has held fellowships at the universities of Frankfurt, Munich, and Bielefeld (Germany). He is the editor of *Management d'equipe—concepts et pratiques* (Team management: concepts and practices) and a member of the editorial board of *Management et conjoncture sociale* (Management and social climate). His current research interests are in intercultural management. He teaches organizational behavior, intercultural management, and economic and social aspects of modern Germany.

DANIEL ROUACH is a professor at ESCP-EAP (Paris) where he has been the dean of the M.B.A. program, professor of technology transfer management, associate professor in European business programs, and currently is the director of projects for the EAP International Executive Centre. He is the author of numerous textbooks, books, and articles.

SYLVIE ROUSSILLON is a professor of organizational behavior at EM Lyon, France. She currently teaches courses in personnel development and management, individuals and organizations, presentation techniques, and international human resources management; she consults with many large companies and is an executive coach. Her published books include *Preparer les dirigeants de demain: Une approche internationale de la gestion des cadres a haut potentiel* (Preparing tomorrow's leaders: An international approach to managing high-potential executives); and *Les Enjeux de l'emploi: Société, entreprises et individus* (The stakes of employment: society, businesses and individuals).

CHRISTIAN SCHOLZ is a professor of management and the director of the European Institute at the University of Saar. He is also an associate professor of human resource management at the University of Vienna. Having authored many books and articles, he currently focuses his research on strategic behavior in organizations, on international human resource management, and on virtual organizations.

CZESLAW J. SZMIDT, founder of the organization and management faculty at the University of Lodz (Poland), has managed human resources for several large Polish financial institutions and has been a visiting professor at the University of Cranfield (United Kingdom). His current research investigates the general strategy and evolution of human resource management, as well as the recruitment and selection of personnel.

MAMI TANIGUCHI, an associate professor of human resource management at the Graduate School of Social Sciences, University of Hiroshima, researches the characteristics of female managers in Japan. She is also interested in the integration of North American management practices into Japanese companies, as in the case of the Ford-Mazda alliance, and in the comparative study of organizations' management strategies, human resource policies, and employee well-being.

LUCIANO TRAQUANDI has worked in electronics design and in international marketing, organization, and management training. He is currently a professor in human resources management at the University of Castellanza (Varese, Italy) and is a visiting professor at the University of Lyon III and at the University of Paris—Panthéon Assas.

SHAUN TYSON is currently a professor of human resource management at Cranfield University (United Kingdom). Professor Tyson has published eighteen books and over one hundred articles on human resource management and has been HR director and consultant in a range of public- and private-sector organizations in the United Kingdom and overseas. His interests include the study of HR strategy and the evaluation of human resource management.

DANIEL F. J. VLOEBERGHS is a member of the economics faculty at the University of Antwerp, where he is the director of the M.B.A. program, and also a member of the social sciences faculty at the University of Leuven (Belgium). He currently teaches courses in management, organizational behavior, human resources management, and organizational development. He has recently published in the following international journals: *The International Journal of Human Resource Management, European Management Journal, Journal of Management Development*, and *Journal of Management Psychology*.

XUCHUAN YANG currently works for Globus, a private consulting company in Salt Lake City, Utah, as the associate director of its U.S.-China Center. He also teaches as an adjunct professor of political science at the University of Utah.

ZHI-GUANG ZHENG is a professor emeritus of management at the Education Research Institute, Nankai University (Tianjin, China). His principal research efforts and expertise lie in the general domain of human resources and in the specific field of management teams.